THE STEP-BY-STEP CHINESE COOKBOOK

THE STEP-BY-STEP
CHINESE
COOKBOOK

GEORGES SPUNT

illustrations by Halcyon Cowles

THOMAS Y. CROWELL COMPANY
New York   Established 1834

For the Engmanns—
Masha, Joe, Douglas and Michael

DESIGNED BY VISUALITY
MANUFACTURED IN THE UNITED STATES OF AMERICA

ISBN 0-690-77317-X
10 9 8 7 6 5 4 3 2 1

Library of Congress Cataloging in Publication Data

Spunt, Georges.
  The step-by-step Chinese cookbook.
  1. Cookery, Chinese. I. Title.
TX724.5.C5S68   641.5'951   72-83770

ACKNOWLEDGMENTS

Cookbook writers, like opera singers, tend to perpetuate the myth of having arrived full bloom, without help from anyone. In the twelve years since I began this book and through its five total reconceptions, I have to admit to owing nearly *everyone*. Some are colleagues with whom I have had the good fortune to work; others I studied for reference. Let me thank the following persons especially. My old cook Dah Su, for the rare privilege of early apprenticeship, underfoot as it was, most of the time. The great Henri Charpentier, from whom I learned the remarkable feat of shortcuts to gourmet cooking. Madame Simone Beck, whom I know only through correspondence, and who was kind enough to give me both praise and constructive advice on an earlier work.

And my thanks to the National Fisheries Institute and the Agricultural Extension at the University of California for providing me with essential research and statistical information. To the helpful food departments of the *San Francisco Chronicle* and the *San Francisco Examiner* for putting up with and diligently answering my phoned-in questions; Colonel George Chow of the Golden Pavilion Restaurant for his careful evaluation and flattering conclusions; my dear friend Evangeline Baker for her continued interest in my work, expressed so many times on her weekly radio show. To my chum Jacqueline Low, a long overdue thank-you for putting me in touch with everybody. To my niece Jacqueline Gensburger, for typing each of the five versions of this book. To Margaret Shedd, writer, friend and teacher. To Harvey Phillips, a fine editor who saw merit in this work in the first place. To Joanna Morris, a fearless and talented lady who took on the editing of this book, and who could only improve it. To Marian McNamara, my agent, and to F. Davidson, who, loathing Chinese cuisine, ate all the food tested in these recipes.

CONTENTS

FOREWORD

For years I had given considerable thought to the idea of producing a book based on the recipes of my own venerable Dah
Su, the graduate master chef who had worked for my family in
Shanghai for over forty years. I planned to present these recipes,
which I had culled from his notes, with excerpts of his superbly
individualistic English. What phrasing could have more charm
than "Boil beef to rags" or "Heat oil until it sings"? However,
in so doing, I would join the legion of writers dedicated to
sharing the mysteries, secrets and pleasures of Chinese dining
without offering any of the practical processes. What good is it
to instruct a reader to heat oil until it sings unless he knows in
what key the oil will sing?

   As a result, my cooking groups, both here and in China,
have always concentrated on the basics. They have learned
about ingredients: how and when they should be combined, the

ways in which they must be cut and, most important, what technique to use in cooking them. These are the steps that lead to competence in the preparation of any dish. It occurred to me that this system could be as effective in a cookbook as in the classroom. And thus this book—a step-by-step handbook on Chinese techniques.

Proficiency in any art requires an elementary knowledge of "how to." One must know each procedure before one can progress to the combination of techniques so often required in a single dish. I can hear some readers saying, "But I know how to stir-fry, braise, steam and what have you." Well and good—perhaps you do these things automatically, like driving and parking. But do you know why a recipe works brilliantly on one occasion and fails miserably the next (usually when you are depending on it most)? If you asked the average person to distinguish between the perfection of one Chinese dish and the mediocrity of another, you would most likely find that he would not be able to give you a clear reason for the difference, although he would certainly say that one tastes better. Analysis of the recipe would undoubtedly reveal that very much the same ingredients were used. What makes the difference ultimately is how they were put together.

A current tendency is to equate French and Chinese cuisine and to believe that what holds true for one must likewise hold true for the other. This is not the case. Certain similarities are undeniable—for example, that in common with his French counterpart, the Chinese chef wastes nothing (it is said in China that a master chef can utilize everything between the snout and tail of a pig except the squeal). Still, there remain significant and unalterable differences between the two approaches to cooking. France's reputation for *haute cuisine* dates only from the sixteenth century, when Catherine de Medici, a plump teen-ager, arrived from Italy with her retinue of chefs. At that time China was already an old civilization. In one respect, I'm inclined to agree on the notion of similarity—most of the cooking techniques we use in the Western world undoubtedly originated in China. But that is the extent of the relationship.

In the Middle Ages, the French began to chronicle and standardize their procedures and recipes. Cooking became for them a separate art. A French chef will not deviate from an established classic unless it is for the express purpose of creating a specific new recipe, hopefully another classic.

On the other hand, cooking began for the Chinese as a regional art interwoven with many other arts. So it is that in so many ancient Chinese literary works a recipe will suddenly crop up or a banquet will be described in infinite detail. Cookbooks *per se* were virtually unknown in China, and even if one were available, no self-respecting master chef would duplicate the dogma of another. And so it became the custom for a chef to take a recipe, usually learned while in apprenticeship to an older chef, and consider it a challenge to his ingenuity to progress from there. The inherent advantage to this type of freedom is the resulting wide assortment of dishes passed down through the ages, with each generation of chefs doctoring up the recipes of the last. One count numbers 100,000 different Chinese dishes.

The only glaring disadvantage of not having set recipes on which to fall back is the business of trying to impart what one has learned from one's own master chef without succumbing to further adornment. Thus, when I speak in this book in terms of a ''Classic'' recipe, I do not intend to imply that there are no variants, but merely that the recipe is a basic representation from which variations may be produced.

A word of caution: If you don't know exactly what is involved in the preparation of a dish, don't attempt any short-cuts or any substitutions other than those given as alternatives. To begin with, stay as close as possible to the recipe as it is written. And remember that when Confucius said, ''There should be a little ginger in everybody's food,'' he was not necessarily referring to the spice.

INTRODUCTION

Even with unlimited space it would be impossible to assemble every original Chinese recipe between the covers of one book. For practical reasons, I have therefore not included recipes with ingredients of such dubious appeal to American tastes as fish lips or sea slugs, both of which require seven days of pre-soaking. And because of the detailed nature of the instructions and recipes in this book, I have also been obliged to bypass many well-known Chinese dishes.

On the other hand, I have been mindful that once you have mastered the fundamentals of each technique, you might want to experiment with the most exotic of menus. So, along with the descriptions of the different methods of cooking and particularly in the chapter on varied techniques, I have included recipes for dishes that are not found in most Chinese restaurants. These are offered to the serious student who has become advanced enough to reproduce a delectable duck smoked in tea leaves or a succulent chicken baked in clay. Or, for the more casual reader, who may wish merely to discourse on its merits, Three in One Peking Fowl.

I have also tried to avoid the common habit of providing too many fully detailed recipes for what is essentially the same dish. For example, take a simple dish like sliced pork with asparagus. By merely restating the entire recipe and substituting snow peas or any other vegetable, one can come up with as many pork recipes as there are vegetables. To avoid this unnecessary multiplicity, a certain amount of cross-referencing becomes necessary. Wherever possible I have given the "Classic" recipe, followed by acceptable variations and substitutions.

HOW THE RECIPES ARE PRESENTED

Since learning how to master each technique is our purpose in this book, the recipes are grouped by method of preparation rather than by major ingredient. The latter arrangement is followed in most cookbooks, and is perfectly acceptable as long as technique is not stressed. My object, however, is to familiarize you thoroughly with each technique before moving on to the next. Under the heading Stir-Fry-Toss—Technique 1, for example, we begin with vegetable stir-fry-toss dishes and then proceed to meats, poultry and fish. You will find Diced Shrimp with Cucumbers in the same chapter with Dredged Sliced Beef and Curried Breast of Chicken with Walnuts and Green Peppers. Exceptions are appetizers and desserts, which appear in separate chapters for your convenience.

You can determine when you want to move to the next technique, whether it be after you have produced one stir-fry dish or ten. To plan a menu then becomes just a matter of learning the methods, being able to identify any dish by its method of preparation and selecting from each group.

In some instances you will discover recipes in which two techniques are combined. If, for example, a certain dish calls for both steaming and shallow-frying, you will find it listed under the technique that is predominant in its preparation. You will also find recipes that entail procedures not common enough to be classified as bona fide techniques. In these cases the recipes will appear in the chapter called Varied Techniques.

The time needed for actual cooking from start to finish is given under the heading "Cooking Time." Preparation time cannot be accounted for, since one person's speed in the kitchen differs from another's. Specific utensils such as skillets, woks, Dutch ovens and electric frypans are listed next under "Utensils." The "Ingredients" are presented in the order in which they should be prepared. To ensure that all ingredients are correctly prepared and ready to go, the next instruction is headed "Before Cooking." (To interrupt the cooking process while you begin to soak and drain a dry ingredient or peel and chop a fresh one can result in an overcooked mass of indistinguishable textures. This is the most common failing of beginners.) Next come the actual "Cooking Instructions," which are self-explanatory. A description of how the finished dish should look follows. Obviously, factors such as the varying moisture content of vegetables and meats and the density of packaged sauces, condiments and thickening agents make absolute predictability impossible. But a general guideline can establish whether or not you have achieved approximately the right consistencies. For example, in Egg Flower Soup, when the beaten eggs are poured into the stock, a tracery of egg-like flowers is formed. This is intentional and in keeping with the name of the recipe. Unadvised, a reader might assume that the curdled appearance of the egg had ruined the soup.

Finally, "Servings" or "Amounts." This, of course, depends on the number of dishes served and what size appetites are involved.

On the whole it may seem, when glancing at the recipes, that they are overwhelmingly complex and detailed. Remember, please, to let your own proficiency be your guide. The suggestions on utensils are there merely for your convenience. You will be able to determine very soon which instructions you must follow faithfully and which you can eliminate.

QUANTITIES

At an informal dinner the Chinese rarely serve less than four dishes. A safe rule of thumb when planning a Chinese dinner is to provide one dish per guest, as well as a soup and rice. However, an adaptable Chinese friend living in the United States waives this ceremony and, in keeping with her servantless circumstances, doubles or triples a recipe depending on how many she plans to serve. She presents just this one dish plus rice to her guests, much in the manner of a typical American entrée.

It is more difficult to discuss Chinese recipes in terms of amounts or servings than it is with American or European dishes, where a meal so often consists of one main dish. An accurate estimate of Chinese servings can only be determined by knowing what total quantity of dishes you plan to serve. Therefore, I have given the number of servings based on a single-course meal that includes rice, and servings based on being one of a full complement of dishes.

WEIGHTS AND MEASURES (pages 36–42): Here you will find estimated servings per pound. Planning a menu in conjunction with those amounts will tell you more accurately if the dishes you have in mind are enough for the number of people to be served. Then it is just a matter of either adding more dishes or doubling a recipe.

INCREASING AND DECREASING QUANTITIES: A note of caution on the business of halving, doubling or tripling the amounts specified in a recipe. Doing this can wreak havoc with a recipe. In the matter of seasonings, to double or triple salt, pepper and soy sauce can be disastrous, and halving these amounts can result in innocuous-tasting food. Here, common sense must be the guide. Taste the food as you cook and adjust seasonings until they seem right. This is what is meant in recipes that require you to "correct" the seasonings.

PLANNING AHEAD

PREPLANNING: Let us assume that you have mastered the basic techniques required to cook a Chinese meal. You are going to serve a soup, a stir-fry-toss dish, a steamed dish and a red-stewed casserole. Check each recipe for the time required to execute it correctly. Should you plan on starting your stir-fry dish before your soup or the red-stewed recipe? Since stir-frying takes a matter of minutes and most soups and red-stewed dishes involve long slow simmering, obviously not.

Make a list of all ingredients required under the heading of each recipe. Don't buy excessive amounts of ingredients you will use only sparingly. Experience will teach you that a small package of five-spice seasoning goes a long way but that a gallon can of peanut oil is more economical than a smaller size. Examine the list of Chinese ingredients given in this book. Note what things, once opened, should be stored in the refrigerator (such things as Hoisin sauce, fermented black beans and pickled greens). Note, too, what can be kept indefinitely without refrigeration (e.g., dried mushrooms, chestnuts, tiger lilies and wood ears). Many American supermarkets today carry Oriental food products, but, if possible, always shop in a Chinese grocery store. The foods listed under the heading Ingredients are given in Cantonese. Try to learn the phonetic pronunciation of these items. If you become acquainted with your Chinese grocer, butcher or poulterer, he'll probably perform many amazingly timesaving services for you—boning a bird while leaving its shape intact, for example, or simply choosing a choice cut of meat and perhaps doing the fine diagonal slicing necessary.

PREPARATION: Much of the success and most of the effort required in Chinese cooking lie in the preparation. The actual cooking is simply a matter of learning what procedure to follow. Having decided what dishes you are going to cook and in what order, assemble your ingredients and utensils. Be sure, too, that all ingredients are sliced or chopped as directed for the particular recipe. No one factor is more apparent in inferior Chinese cooking than haphazardly cut ingredients. From the standpoint of both aesthetics and practicality, the meat and vegetable components should be cut in similar sizes and shapes. When using chopsticks it is much easier to transport food cut in the same style and size than odd-shaped pieces. While French cuisine satisfies the eye largely by relying on garnishes, Oriental chefs fill this requirement by the design of the food itself.

You will find it useful to have handy all necessary utensils, such as skillets, small bowls, measuring cups and spoons, slotted spoons and sieves. Pyrex or aluminum pie plates, which can be warmed readily for transfer and temporary storage of the cooked food, should be within easy reach. If you are a beginner cook, be sure that you measure items such as oil, soy sauce, salt and sugar. It takes a bit of experience to gauge how much 2 tablespoons of oil is by pouring. With practice you will begin to know instinctively what amounts to use; then you can rely on your own judgment.

TABLE SETTING: It is a good idea, once you have assembled your materials, to set your table before you start the preparation and cooking. Stir-fried dishes must be served at once and you do not want to be scurrying around looking for dishes and bowls while the food is cooling in the kitchen. A round table and a lazy Susan are ideal for a Chinese meal but are not essential. For a simple dinner you will need for each person a bowl for rice, a smaller bowl for soup (if you are serving it), a plate, a teacup, a small saucer-like dish for condiments and a pair of chopsticks. The Chinese use porcelain spoons for their soup and are amused at the Western use of metal spoons, which are conductors of heat and tend to burn the lips. It is not necessary to purchase Chinese dinnerware, although when you become adept at this type of cooking you may wish to do so to further the Oriental mood of your meal. In the meantime, however, soup plates do nicely as serving dishes, and cereal bowls can be used for the rice and soup. Because of a chronic scarcity of fuel, Chinese food is never cut into pieces larger than bite-size. Chopsticks, therefore, are both practical and totally appropriate. Once their use is mastered, eating Chinese food with a fork is never entirely satisfactory. In the kitchen, chopsticks are invaluable for stirring, tossing and beating eggs. For further information see the illustration and instructions on page 12.

THE STEP-BY-STEP CHINESE COOKBOOK

THE FOODS OF CHINA

CLASSES

Chinese cuisine may be divided roughly into two classes: Mandarin food, which is the exotic fare served at banquets, and coolie food, which is the cooking of the vast majority. The term Mandarin derives from the system under the Chinese Empire whereby a public official of one of the nine grades was permitted to wear a button on his hat. Colloquially, Mandarin refers to anything of a higher order. For example, Mandarin is the name given to the dialect of the official classes.

A Mandarin banquet, in the days of the Empire, was usually given by Chinese political officials, bankers and business magnates. At these affairs, hundreds of dishes were served at a number of round tables. The menu might very likely include dried bear paws from the North, stewed ducks' tongues, fish lips or fish tripe, carps' tongues, cockscombs pickled in wine lees, soup made from a turtle that had the marking of fourteen squares on its shell, a black-skinned fowl brewed into a broth that had allegedly potent aphrodisiac qualities, boiled mountain ant eggs from Southwest China, a species of dried beetle, and, of course, shark fin and bird's nest soup. Because of the difficulty in obtaining these last two foods, they have the same significance to the Chinese as caviar has to the Western gourmet.

When a foreigner in China gave a Chinese banquet, the food served, as a rule, was classified as "coolie" food. The word "coolie" is defined as a native unskilled laborer. In every part of the Orient there are castes within the castes; hence, there were ricksha coolies, wharf coolies, and even coolies who wheeled barrows of excrement along certain streets of the city.

It would be misleading, I think, not to state that coolie food corresponds to what we might call middle-class or family-style cooking rather than either to the humblest of cooking or to the extremes of Chinese *haute cuisine*. Even within this range there is such variety and exotic ingredients are so often used that to identify this food with the lower classes would be extremely misleading. Typical of the so-called coolie dishes are a large variety of soups, meat, fish or bean-filled pastries and salted greens, bean curd, noodles and always congee rice, a breakfast mainstay.

REGIONAL FOODS

NORTHERN: The Peking school of cooking is as ancient and as varied as that city's colorful history. Here is the blending of the Mongol and the Manchu, the barbarian and the sybarite. Wine, garlic and scallions are used liberally, and many of the recipes are reminiscent of French cuisine. Northern food, in contrast to Southern (Cantonese), tends toward lightness rather than richness. Not many stir-fried dishes are encountered in Peking cuisine. Although there is less variety to Northern cooking, it is infinitely more elegant than Southern. The Northerners depend far less on rice than does the rest of the country. Noodles, rolls, pancakes and meat-filled turnovers originated here and spread in popularity from province to province.

In the Northeastern section, the foods of Shantung and Honan are similar to those of Peking—but they have refinements of their own. Honan, on the Yellow River, is particularly noted for its sweet-and-sour specialties. The natives of Shantung are great eaters of raw scallions, which they believe have health-giving and body-building properties. Chefoo, in Shantung province, is famous for its grapes and its peaches, which turn purple when stewed, as well as for a certain crisply juicy pear, which I have never seen elsewhere, called the water pear.

The interior Northwestern region does not contribute much to the aggrandizement of Chinese cuisine. Removed as it is from the coast, fresh fish is unavailable in this area. Agriculturally, the people are quite poor; and they are not particularly imaginative when it comes to seasoning, since vinegar is most widely used. Whatever recipes may have originated in Kangsu and neighboring areas have not been widely adopted—with the exception perhaps of hot-pot cooking.

SOUTHERN AND SOUTHEASTERN: Canton, the capital of the Kwantung province, can boast of having provided China with some of its most exotic culinary innovations. Rich and colorful, Cantonese cooking does not rely on soy sauce for seasoning; the use of tomatoes and snow peas in cooking is characteristically Cantonese.

The Cantonese have always been a seafaring people and much of the extensive cuisine of Canton reflects its contact with the outside world. From Kwantung province comes a wonderful array of fruits, mainly tangerines (called Mandarins), pomelos (a slightly acrid type of grapefruit, always peeled and eaten in sections), loquats (called beebos) and sugar cane.

The Southeast, with its long coast and rich agricultural land, has yielded the greatest range of cuisine. Here is an abundance of freshwater fish, excellent crops and livestock. Fukien food has a delicacy rivaling that of Peking. Farther east, the cities of Shanghai, Nanking and Yangchow, in Kiangsu province, have also contributed their own Classic dishes.

Shanghai cooking is something of a mixture of styles, relying largely on ample use of soy sauce. Shanghai Chinese are fond of red-stewed dishes (simmered in soy sauce), but at the same time they are equally capable of extremely subtle dishes, such as Shanghai-style shrimp. Shanghai, and Ningpo in neighboring Chekiang province, are famous for their pickled and preserved foods. Pickled and salted greens are commonly cooked with meat. Ningpo is also noted for its preserved winter melon, a pungent odoriferous product which I suspect would be quite repellent to most Western tastes. Except for the very lowest classes, the majority of people in Kiangsu province eat little garlic. Much sugar is used, especially in very salty dishes, but the final result is not one of sweetness. Rather it is one of judicious balance—what the Chinese call cooking and blending of flavors. Changchow and Wusih are best known for their inclination to use sugar. People in this region use considerably less cornstarch than do the Cantonese.

The Southeast and central Easterners are fond of noodles, pastries and dumplings of Northern origin. *Pao tsu, chiao tsu* and little flattened pancakes with scallions or sesame seeds were sold by vendors on most street corners in my day. A favorite in this area is a type of cruller, encased in either a ball of steamed firm rice, *tsu veh yusakwei,* or sandwiched between a tortilla-like pancake, *dah ping yusakwei.*

SOUTHWESTERN: The climate in this relatively fertile part of the country is hot in summer and the natives of Szechuan province are disposed toward heavily spiced food. In the 17th century, there was a great migration from the North to the Southwest. Consequently much of the Szechuanese cooking of the higher classes reflects Northern influence. However, the characteristic diet of the natives of Kunming, Fengkieh and Chungking includes a liberal lacing of pepper.

Many recipes of regional origin were adapted, with either major or minor modifications, throughout the country. Therefore, only those recipes that are significantly recognized as from a certain region are so indicated. Bearing in mind the regional cooking characteristics, it is a simple enough matter to adapt many "Classic" recipes to the styles of Canton, Shanghai, Peking or Szechuan. These are indicated in the recipe sections under the heading of Regional Variations.

CHINESE TEA

Although tea was known in China in the first and second centuries A.D., it is only from a third-century account that we have any indication that it was appreciated as a beverage. According to this ancient source, tea came into use as a delicacy rivaling wine in the Wu district (which is known as Shanghai today). However, it was not until the eighth century, when Lu Yu wrote his classic *Chaching*, that the details of tea's growth, its locations and the manner of its preparation became more or less nationally known and accepted. At this time, during the T'ang dynasty, the method of preparing tea for sale or barter was to press the ground dried leaves into bricks. Pieces of the brick were broken off as needed and boiled with water. The only part of China where this method is still used is Mongolia—brick tea is not known for its quality. During the Sung dynasty (A.D. 960 to A.D. 1280), a method of preparing tea as a drink by whisking powdered tea with hot water had evolved. The Japanese still prepare some tea in this manner. In 1475, during the Ming dynasty, Chen Chien abridged Lu Yu's original classic but added a number of his own observations. It was during this period that the method of steeping tea, which has remained popular to this day, began. Then, as now, tea purists frowned upon the addition of flower petals to the leaves.

Incidentally, the Northern Mandarin name for tea is *cha,* and the Russians, whose tea came from Northwest China, pronounce it *chai.* The English and French, whose tea first came via the Dutch traders from Amoy, on the Southeastern coast, call it tea or *thé,* because the Amoy dialect word for the fragrant leaf is *tay.*

There is at least as wide a range of teas as there is of wines, and the Chinese connoisseur of tea vies with the European wine expert in his ability to judge flavor and bouquet. As with wine, the quality of a tea is established by evaluating the grade of the leaf, how it is processed and where it is grown. It is no exaggeration to say that rare teas are literally worth their weight in gold.

The two main types of tea sold are the green (*chang*) and the red (*hoong*). Most of what we in the Western world know as black tea is called red by the Chinese because black has unhappy connotations. Many of the finest grades of tea, both green and red, come from Kwangtung province in the South. Among them are the green Water Nymph, Silver Needles and Dragon's Beard teas. The red or red-black teas include the Black Dragon and Clear Distance tea.

Formosa has contributed the famous semi-fermented *oolong* tea, grown on mountains, as well as the fully fermented *keemun* tea, much favored by the last Chinese dynasty.

Fukien produces the black Iron Goddess of Mercy tea, whereas Yunnan has contributed a classic black tea called the *p'u-erh*.

On a train trip to historic Hangchow, the capital of Chekiang province, I tasted China's finest green tea. In my compartment, seated opposite me, was a very stout Chinese gentleman in blue silk. On his forefinger he wore a wedding band of the most perfect Imperial jade that I had ever seen. I could not help expressing my admiration for it. "I will show you a gem of even greater quality," the Mandarin said. From an inner pocket he withdrew a square of folded paper, which he opened, revealing the dried leaves of a green tea. Summoning the boy in charge of our coach, he asked him to fetch water. I noticed with some amusement that he was very specific about the water, insisting that it be boiled until it billowed, but no more, lest, as he said gravely, it become too old. He emptied some of the leaves into a glass for me and the rest into another glass for himself. The water was poured, each glass covered with its special lid, and the leaves began to settle. Thus, I tasted my first Dragon Well tea.

The actual preparation of tea, while simple enough, is considered very important. The Chinese consider spring water the most suitable for the steeping of the leaves. The Dowager Empress, however, was such a purist that she had her ladies-in-waiting collect early-morning dew in marble vessels. Tea is best brewed in an earthenware pot, since metal tends to affect the color and flavor. The best ratio of tea leaves to water is 1 teaspoon of tea to 1 cup of water. More water may be added to the leaves after the first cup has been drunk, as it is thought that the second infusion of tea is often superior to the first.

Serving tea during the meal is a Western compromise. Traditionally, the Chinese serve tea after meals and at all times during the day. Tea, particularly with Chinese meals, should be drunk plain, the addition of sugar, milk or lemon being considered adulterants to the true flavor.

WINES

The main beverage in China is tea. Chinese wines are served at formal dinners or banquets. At these affairs there is much toasting and wagering among the men.

Wine, as it has been known in China for centuries, means *shaoshing,* or rice wine, the better grades of which are served warm in tiny cups. Generally, when a recipe calls for wine and has been adapted for Western usage, pale dry sherry is substituted for rice wine. The principal use of wine in Chinese cooking is to neutralize odors and to blend flavors.

Kaoliang, manufactured in the North from a sorghum type of grain by the same name, and *ng gar pei,* made of fruit peel and herbs, while loosely called wines by the Chinese, are, in effect, liquors. Lesser-known Chinese wines are the rose-petal, pear and celery wines. In many of the recipes, particularly those of Northern origin, liquor is called for rather than wine. A good substitute here is either vodka or gin.

Since many Americans and most Europeans enjoy wine with their meals, I am listing some that are compatible with Chinese food. These suggestions are made solely for your convenience; in no way are they meant to set an authentic drinking pattern for traditional Chinese eating. Hard liquor, if served at all, should only accompany Chinese appetizers.

For Chinese food, regardless of whether the dish is meat, fish or fowl, you had best keep strictly to white wines. Any of the white Burgundy family—Chablis, Pouilly Fuissé, Montrachet or Pinot Chardonnay—are excellent. The dry Loire wines—Muscadet, Vouvray or Pouilly Fumé—are quite acceptable. Next in choice would come the Moselles—Ockfener Bockstein or Piesporter Goldtroepchen Spatlese—and finally any of the good domestic equivalents.

EQUIPMENT
AND UTENSILS

ㄹㄹㄹㄹㄹㄹㄹㄹㄹㄹㄹㄹ

In the Equipment Section of almost every Chinese cookbook, the writer assures the reader that special equipment is not necessary and then goes on to list certain almost "indispensable" Chinese utensils. Let me differ to the extent of saying outright that there are several basically Chinese utensils which, while not expensive, will greatly facilitate your preparation of Chinese food. This is not to suggest, however, that you should consider costly smoke ovens, ranges with running water outlets or special presses. The average Chinese household in the best of times was not so equipped and, generally, the Chinese chef makes do with fewer conveniences than his Western counterpart. In the following pages I will discuss what I consider essential cooking equipment, both Chinese and Western, as it applies to Chinese cuisine.

STOVES

Since the majority of Chinese cooking requires high heat for a minimal cooking time, gas ranges are ideal. The Chinese process of steaming takes the place of Western baking and with a few exceptions, such as barbecuing, the oven as we know it is not used. Ranges with simmer controls are most useful for slow cooking techniques, like Red-Stewing or Clear-Simmering. For the Stir-Fry-Toss Method, which is the most popular of Chinese techniques, the gas stove ranks first. (Intensity of heat is the key to a successful finished product in this technique.) The flame is controllable, so that the required intensity can be achieved and the burners, when turned off, cool rapidly and do not continue the cooking process. The more modern electric stoves are able to achieve high heat but do not retain the heat as long as the older type. Therefore, although they are not as satisfactory as gas stoves, they can be used with good results. The commerical gas burner, used in restaurants, has an intensity of heat roughly triple that of the home gas burner. This intensity of heat is what accounts for a restaurant's ability to turn out vegetables that are crisp yet cooked through. Regrettably, a good many Chinese cookbooks specify cooking times that have been based on the operation of these commercial stoves. Perhaps this is why you have found yourself with almost-raw vegetables instead of crisply done peas. Although I have taken the desired crispness into consideration, I have increased the cooking time in the Stir-Fry-Toss recipes in this book. Still, I urge that the reader observe the heat variation factors of his own stove. Each type of stove performs with different intensity. When you are called upon to stir-fry for 2 minutes, remove the pan from the stove and taste-test a portion of the vegetable that is being cooked. If it is too raw, cook for another minute and test again.

This may seem like a lot of unnecessary bother, but you will really only have to do this once or twice before you realize how your stove works. From then on it will simply be a matter of increasing or decreasing the frying time by a minute or two.

POTS, WOKS AND CASSEROLES

Cast-iron skillets are excellent for Chinese cooking. The enameled Belgian or French ware serve perfectly because iron is a rapid and even conductor of heat and enamel is easy to clean and will not discolor food. Copper utensils distribute heat evenly enough, but they do not conduct heat rapidly, nor with the intensity of iron. For slow-simmering dishes, where high heat is not needed and, consequently, the danger of a tin lining melting is eliminated, lined copper casseroles work very well. For Braised, Red-Stewed and Clear-Simmered recipes that do not demand intensely high heat initially, electric appliances, both skillets and deep-fryers, are ex-

Wok with and without
Lid and Ring

cellent. They also leave the stove free for Stir-Fry-Toss dishes. Pyroceram (Corning Ware) and Pyrex casseroles may be used in this type of cooking as well. Pyroceram utensils have the advantage of being impervious to temperature changes. They can also be used as serving bowls and brought from the kitchen to the table. The 1-quart saucemaker with measurements on the inside and the 3-cup pitcher with lid can be used for mixing sauces, marinades, stock and an infinite variety of other tasks.

King of all Chinese cooking utensils is the wok. This is a basin-shaped pot with handles and is made of iron, copper, aluminum or stainless steel. The traditional woks are made of iron, and while they require somewhat more care than those made of stainless steel, I prefer them because of their ability to conduct heat evenly. The advantage of using a wok rather than an ordinary skillet or deep-frying pan is that the flared sides of the wok permit rapid tossing of many ingredients and the use of a minimum of oil. The wok is placed upon a perforated ring resembling a crown. This ring was developed to allow the wok to be set on the stove. If you have a gas stove, place the wok ring right-side-up on the stove; if you have an electric stove, turn the ring bottom-side-up, set the wok on it and proceed with your cooking. The wok comes with a high-lidded cover, usually made of aluminum. The total cost of a 12-inch wok, cover and ring is approximately the price of a good skillet. With a wok, however, you can do more things—deep-fry, stir-fry-toss, braise, steam, pot-cook, boil, clear-simmer or red-stew. And these are eight of the most common techniques of Chinese cooking. As for barbecuing, you could if you wished line a wok with coals and put a rack over them. However, make sure that you have two of these versatile utensils before you use one for barbecuing, because the one used for that purpose might no longer be suitable for the other methods of Chinese cooking.

Woks range in size from 12 to 24 inches and are available in most Chinese hardware stores (see page 376). Your wok should be washed out after each dish has been cooked to get rid of any of the previous flavors. Before putting away your wok, wash it out in soapy hot water, rinse it clean and set it on the stove over low heat until the wok is absolutely dry. Otherwise, if it is iron, it will rust.

CHINESE STEAMERS

See Steaming—Technique 5 (page 203) for a full description of bamboo and aluminum steamers and steaming equipment improvised from Western cooking equipment.

KNIVES

What the Chinese know as a vegetable cutting knife is a most useful utensil. Actually this is a cleaver that can also serve as a meat chopper. The traditional Chinese cutting knife is made of iron and is rectangular in shape. This knife is available in several sizes and is now being manufactured in stainless and in carbon steel. The most popular has a 3x7½-inch blade and a 4-inch wooden or bamboo handle. I prefer the iron because the steel knives are generally too flexible and are difficult to sharpen. The cutting edge of the cutting knife should always be kept razor-sharp. It can be used for cutting, chopping, slicing and mincing. It is heavy enough to chop through bones and sharp enough to scale fish. The blunt edge of the knife is useful for crushing garlic or ginger or for pounding and mincing. The width of the blade, functioning as a spatula, may be used to transfer chopped food to the pan. For paring, slicing and paper-thin cutting, hollow-ground knives are excellent.

INCIDENTAL UTENSILS

CHOPPING BOARD: The Chinese chef uses the smoothened bole of a tree about 15 inches in diameter and 8 to 10 inches high as a chopping board (*jum baahn*). However, for most Chinese cooking, an ordinary pastry board, 22x28 inches, or a thicker chopping board serves very well.

LADLES, SPOONS AND SPATULAS: Many utensils used in Western kitchens serve perfectly well for Chinese cooking. There are brass mesh and wire ladles (available in Chinese hardware stores) that are excellent for lifting deep-fried foods or for serving the solid portions of "pot-style" meals. However, a slotted spoon works almost as well. Chinese spatulas as a rule come without slots and are used for turning foods. A Western spatula with slots is even more satisfactory than the Chinese one. A deep ladle is necessary for serving soups and sauces. In stir-frying, a pair of wooden chopsticks are useful for keeping the ingredients tossed. If you have a long pair of tongs, such as those used for barbecuing, you will find them invaluable for tossing the ingredients at relatively long range from the heat.

CLEANING WHISK: A useful adjunct to your wok, or any skillet for that matter, is a Chinese whisk. This is about 10 inches long and consists of thin strips of bamboo tied at the top, much in the manner of a whisk broom. The whisk keeps your hands out of the hot water when you are cleaning your utensils and helps to re-move particles of food that have stuck to the pan.

USEFUL WESTERN UTENSILS: The following ordinary kitchen utensils can be partic-ularly useful in Chinese cooking. Good-sized soup kettles or pots with covers are necessary for simmered or stewed recipes involving large cuts of meat or whole fowl. Double boilers in several sizes are used for these methods as well. Foil roast-ing pans (9x12x3 inches) have many uses. Heavier and larger pans are needed for steaming and frying whole fish. Standard soup or pie plates are convenient for re-serving ingredients to be cooked. The small bowls for seasonings mentioned in the recipes can be 6-ounce Pyrex custard cups. Use 10-ounce custard cups for larger amounts of stock or seasonings.

Have available a manual can opener for the square-cornered cans of Chinese sauces, at least one colander and several wire strainers, ranging from 4 to 12 inches in diameter. Cake racks are handy for both steaming and barbecuing. Not in the category of utensils but almost essential, nevertheless, are long asbestos gloves for handling hot utensils and lined rubber gloves for handling steamed foods or spiny and sharp ingredients such as shellfish.

Utensils
1. Ladle.
2. Chinese spatula.
3. Wire mesh ladle.
4. Chinese whisk.
5. Brass mesh ladle.
6. Pyroceram 3-cup pitcher.
7. Pyroceram saucemaker.

CHOPSTICKS AND HOW TO USE THEM

To use chopsticks correctly, remember that there is an upper and a lower chopstick. The lower chopstick is always stationary. Chopsticks are held with the square ends up and the rounded or tapered ends down. Follow these simple steps:

1. Pick up a chopstick as you would a pen or pencil and let an equal amount of the chopstick protrude on each side of the hand. Now instead of holding the chopstick with your thumb and index finger, the way you would hold a pencil, hold it with the tips of the fourth and the little finger and let the upper part of the chopstick rest comfortably in the base of the thumb and the index finger. This is the stationary chopstick.

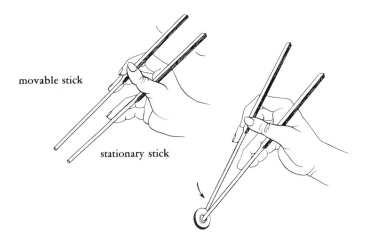

movable stick

stationary stick

How to Use Chopsticks

2. With your other hand pick up the second chopstick. Place this chopstick directly above and parallel to the stationary chopstick. Grasp the upper stick with the thumb, index and middle finger as you would a pencil. Use the thumb to brace the stationary chopstick securely against the tip of the fourth finger. There should be about an inch of space between the sticks. Press the upper chopstick down with the index and third finger. It will meet with the stationary stick to pick up the food. Chopsticks must be evenly aligned or they will not work efficiently. Make sure that the tips are even by tapping them gently on the table.

INGREDIENTS USED
IN CHINESE COOKING

CHINESE INGREDIENTS

All the ingredients listed here are available in Chinese groceries, and a good many may be found in larger supermarkets. If you are not within close range of a Chinese market, consult the list of Chinese grocers who will mail supplies (this is given at the end of the book). Use good judgment when it comes to substituting. American broccoli can be used in place of Chinese broccoli and the same is true for cabbage, eggplant, turnips and squash.

ABALONE (*bow yu*): Sold in cans, this shellfish is used in a number of Chinese dishes. The canned baby abalone, cut in slices and served on picks, is excellent as an appetizer. There is a dried abalone, too, which must be soaked several days before using. The canned variety from Mexico is more convenient and excellent in quality. Never cook abalone for more than a minute or two as it tends to toughen.

BALSAM PEAR: See Bitter Melon.

BAMBOO SHOOTS (*jook suen*): Available both fresh and canned. If using the canned variety, make sure they are unsalted. They may be stored by pouring off the liquid, replacing it with fresh water and keeping shoots covered in the refrigerator. If not used within a couple of days, change the water. The canned variety from Taiwan or Japan retain the necessary crispness and are more practical to use than the fresh, which may be found at Chinese grocery stores and are sold in tubs. These must be pared and parboiled before using. Dried bamboo-shoot membranes (*sun ha*) must be soaked for at least a couple of hours before using. These turn from dark reddish brown to ivory after soaking. They are best used in slow-cooked dishes. Pickled bamboo shoots (*seen sun yee*) come in 1-pound cans—they are packed in brine and are best used for steamed or marinated salad-type recipes.

BEAN CURD OR CAKE (*dow foo*): Usually sold in 3-inch squares that resemble cream cheese. Keep covered in water in closed containers until ready to use. They are cooked most often as a vegetable. Handle them carefully when cooking, as they break easily. Bean curd is often deep-fried and sold in the form of airy golden-brown balls. When sold in jars, this curd is fermented in wine and is used as a type of cheese or condiment (*foo yu*). It can also be made of red beans, wine and salt (*naam yu*). When used as a sauce (for vegetable dishes primarily), *foo yu* and *naam yu* must be mashed with their own liquids until smooth.

BEAN CURD, DRIED (*tiem jook*): Sediment of soybean milk dried into glazed-looking, stiff boards. They are usually broken off in pieces and soaked before cooking.

BEAN SPROUTS (*dow ngaah*): Not to be confused with pea sprouts. These have a larger golden-yellow flower, a stronger flavor and take longer to cook. While washing the sprout, remove its hood. Canned bean sprouts must be well soaked in cold water before using.

BEAN THREADS (*fun see*): Glasslike threads which, when soaked in hot water, become clear vermicelli. Bean threads should not be soaked too long, as they tend to become rubbery on standing. They are also known as cellophane noodles. Buy bean threads in ¼-pound packages. They expand greatly on soaking.

BIRD'S NEST: See Swallow's Nest.

BITTER MELON OR BALSAM PEAR (*foo quah*): This fruit has a bright green wrinkled surface. The spongy pulp and pumpkin-like seeds must be removed before cooking. The cool but distinctly bitter taste has to be acquired. I do not recommend it for beginners in Chinese cuisine.

BLACK BEANS, DRIED (*woo dow*): Available in bags, they are unfermented and hard and are used in soups and slow-simmered dishes.

BLACK BEANS, SALTED (*dow see*): Sold with or without garlic in polyethylene bags, these are fermented soft black beans. They should not be confused with the hard black beans above, available in similar bags. They add a distinct flavor to seafood and pork and will keep indefinitely, stored in the refrigerator in a tightly-closed jar. These should be used in recipes calling for soft black beans. They must always be rinsed to remove excess salt.

BUTTON MUSHROOMS (*maw gwooh*): The canned variety are excellent.

CHINESE CABBAGE or CELERY CABBAGE (*sui choy*): This vegetable is frequently found in supermarkets. It is sold in Japanese markets as *nappa*. It is long and white, tinged with pale green.

CHINESE CHARD (*baak choy*): A leafy green vegetable with white stems and often tiny yellow flowers. It is sold either by the whole cluster or by the heart, including the most tender stems.

CHINESE CHESTNUTS (*lut gwoh*): These are bought dry in packages. They should be rinsed and soaked in warm water for at least an hour and then cooked in the same water for an hour or until tender. In spite of a slightly smoky taste, they substitute very well for fresh chestnuts.

CHINESE EGGPLANT (*kair*): These are either purple or white (*bok kair*) and are shaped like cucumbers. They are finer-grained than large eggplants and more convenient to use. Sometimes sold as Japanese eggplant.

CHINESE PARSLEY or CORIANDER LEAVES (*yuen sai*): Lacy-leafed, with a distinctive flavor. Use sparingly at first.

CHINESE PEAS, SNOW PEAS, MANGE TOUT (*haw laahn dow*): These many-named peas are cooked, pod and all, after snipping the ends and removing the thread along the length of the pea.

CHINESE SAUSAGE (*lop cheong*): A native pork sausage available, like Italian sausages, in bunches. They may also be bought individually. These should be steamed on rice or parboiled, sliced and used as an ingredient in fried rice or with meat and vegetables.

CHINESE TURNIPS (*law bok*): Large and cream-colored, this vegetable is used in many techniques of Chinese cooking. Grated raw, it adds zest to salads and sauces.

CLOUD EARS (*wun yee*): An edible fungus which on soaking swells to a soft brown gelatinous shape like a tiny ear. Make sure that these are carefully washed before and after soaking, as they sometimes retain grit.

CORIANDER LEAVES: See Chinese Parsley.

DRAGON'S TEETH: See Swallow's Nest.

GINGER ROOT (*san geung*): Available at all Chinese groceries and at many supermarkets. It has a gnarled root shape and is covered with a light brown skin, something like a potato jacket. The inside is pale yellow, with a fibrous texture and sharp lemony fragrance. Ginger root must be peeled before using, then sliced or finely chopped. Ginger juice, called for in some of these recipes, is made by cutting small slivers of the root and putting them in a garlic press to extract the liquid. Ginger root keeps best refrigerated, but do not freeze it because it tends to become soggy. It is not interchangeable with powdered ginger.

GINGKO NUT (*bok gor*): These have a hard shell and creamy-colored meat and are used in soups and braised dishes. Use the shelled type available in 6⅓-ounce cans.

GLUTINOUS RICE (*nor may*): This is a special round rice unlike the type used in everyday cooking. Glutinous rice, uncooked, is creamy white and resembles seed pearls. When cooked, it becomes sticky and translucent. It is used in festival dishes and desserts. Sold by the pound.

HAIRY MELON (*jeet quar*): A fuzz-covered oval-shaped vegetable of the marrow species. Inside it has a texture much like that of zucchini. Used a great deal in soups.

HUNDRED-YEAR EGGS (*pay don*): These are eggs preserved in lime and ashes for a hundred days. They are sometimes called thousand-year eggs. The coverings of lime and ash are removed, and the eggs are washed and peeled. They are then quartered and served with soy sauce. In the process of aging, the whites become amber-colored and translucent, while the yolks turn green.

LOTUS ROOT or STEM (*lien gow*): The underwater stem of the water lily. Used in stir-fry and red-stewed dishes or soups. Sold by the ounce. This root resembles a pinkish-brown hose that has been cinched every foot or so. Crosswise slices reveal an interior of holes and fiber.

LOTUS SEEDS (*lien gee*): These are available dried, canned or sugared. Use the dried and canned variety for ceremonial dishes, soups and braised recipes. The sugared seeds are eaten as a confection.

MANGE TOUT: See Chinese Peas.

MUSHROOMS, DRIED (*doong gwooh*): Blackish-brown mushrooms that expand when soaked. They should be rinsed and then soaked in warm water until soft and fleshy. Baby dried mushrooms (*doong gwooh jai*) can be used whole. Most of the dried mushrooms on the market are imported from Japan. Grass or straw mushrooms (*cho gwooh*) are similar to Italian dried mushrooms but are thinner and crisper. When soaked, they resemble miniature umbrellas. Use in the same way as you would ordinary dried mushrooms.

MUSTARD GREENS, SALTED (*haam choy*): This is one of several types of preserved greens, and it is extremely popular, particularly in Shanghai and Ningpo. *Haam choy* is usually salted or pickled mustard cabbage. It is brownish-green in color and has limp, olive-green leaves. It is found at Chinese groceries either in tubs or in cans. *Haam choy* must always be well rinsed before using. When using this type of salted cabbage, other salty agents must be reduced in quantity. There is also a dried salted mustard green that must be soaked before using. Pickled *haam choy* is usually found in cans and should not be rinsed. Red in Snow is another variety of preserved greens. The canned type, packed in oil, should not be soaked.

NUTS: Almonds, cashews and walnuts. Buy these blanched in Chinese groceries. If blanched nuts are unavailable, blanch them before using. To blanch shelled nuts, pour boiling water over them, let them simmer for 2 or 3 minutes and slip the skins off. Place nuts in a sieve and rinse them with cold water. Drain them on absorbent paper and be sure that they are thoroughly dry before frying.

OILS (*yow*): Each technique section discusses the appropriate fat to use for that type of cooking. Generally, peanut oil is best, then corn oil, cottonseed oil and lard. Butter is not suitable because of its flavor and low smoking point. Sesame oil (*gee ma yow*) is a wonderfully fragrant oil sold in 6-ounce bottles, but it is used mainly for flavoring rather than cooking because of its price and its tendency to burn. A few drops are sufficient to enhance the flavors of most dishes. For pastry-making, the Chinese use *joh yow,* a type of strained pork suet.

OLIVES, DRIED (*lom gok*): These are cured sections of black olives and are highly pungent. They are sold in packages of varying sizes and are used mostly for steamed dishes.

ONIONS (*choong*): Chinese, particularly Northerners, are fond of onions and use a wide variety, from the round kind to scallions and leeks.

PEA SPROUTS (*ngaah choy*): Often mistakenly called bean sprouts, these are more delicate, having tiny shoots with snow-white stems. Remove the pale green hoods and husks and use them while they are very fresh.

RED DATES, DRIED (*hoong jo*): Wrinkled, shiny red jujubes with a wide variety of uses. As a sweetening agent in desserts, they are used like ordinary dates. They are often combined with fish or poultry in steamed dishes or turn up in soups for flavor and sweetness. They must be pitted and soaked before using.

RED IN SNOW: See Mustard Greens, Salted.

RICE STICKS (*mei fun*): These are noodles made of rice and wound like threads. Sold in packages, they resemble bean thread noodles. They are usually deep-fried and used as a garnish, but they may also be treated as ordinary noodles.

SCALLOPS, DRIED (*gong yue chee*): Purchased by the ounce. These come in gold-colored disks and must be soaked for at least an hour before using. They turn a creamy ivory after cooking. Used in soups and as a flavoring for congee rice.

SHARK FINS (*yu chee*): These are imported treated as well as untreated and sun-dried. Sold in Chinese markets. Try to buy the treated variety rather than the whole fin, because the preparation is much simpler. Treated shark fins come in $\frac{1}{2}$-pound packages and look like coils of fine, glazed hair. They expand on soaking. After precooking, shark fins become gelatinous.

SHRIMPS, DRIED (*har me*): Buy in ounce weights. Rinse in cold water and soak for 20 to 30 minutes. These are tiny and flavorful, used mostly to enliven bland foods such as congee rice, bean threads or vegetables.

SNOW FUNGUS (*sut yee*): A white fungus that becomes soft and gelatinous when soaked. It is used in soups and festival dishes and is by far the most expensive of

Chinese delicacies, costing approximately $60.00 per pound. Because of its expanding properties, a little goes a long way. Snow fungus is tasteless and used mainly because of its extremely delicate texture.

SNOW PEAS: See Chinese Peas.

SWALLOW'S NEST or BIRD'S NEST (*yien waw*): Sold as dried, golden cuplike nests. Used in bird's nest soup. Dragon's teeth (*loong ngaah*) are bird's nest in the shape of dried chips and are sold usually in boxes of 4 to 6 ounces. Like shark fins, bird's nest expand on soaking.

TANGERINE PEEL (*gaw pay*): Skins of Mandarin oranges (tangerines) are sun-dried and aged to a deep russet color. They are soaked and then used to accentuate the flavors of duck dishes. This peel has varying grades: the older it is, the more expensive. You can make your own peel by cutting the skin off tangerines and drying them in a heatless oven for several days. Then store the peel in tightly closed jars. These can, and in fact should, be kept as long as possible; the older the peel, the more pronounced the flavor.

TARO ROOT (*woo tow*): Somewhat like a potato in texture, it is used in soups and braised recipes as well as in some ceremonial dishes.

TEA MELON (*cha gwah*): A golden, crunchy sweet-and-sour pickle, shaped like a small Italian pepper. Sold in bottles and cans, it is used mainly to add zest to congee rice or steamed fish or meat.

TIGER LILIES or LILY FLOWERS, DRIED (*gum jum*): Called "golden needles" by the Chinese. These are actually lilies dried a golden brown, which, when snipped and soaked, add a subtle flavor to fish, poultry or vegetables.

TURNIPS, SALTED (*chung choy*): This is actually a native vegetable but is similar to our turnips. It comes in little individual bundles of amber-brown stalks tied with dark green leaves. The bundles are sold in 1-pound packages. *Chung choy* is extremely salty and must be soaked at least an hour before using.

TURNIPS, SPICED (*jar choy*): Spiced preserved turnip greens or mustard greens. These should not be soaked, but they must be used sparingly in stir-fried or steamed dishes. Sold in jars.

VINEGAR (*cho*): The Chinese use rice vinegar, which comes in several varieties. For light-colored or sweet-and-sour dishes, use pale rice vinegar. For dipping sauces, try the dark rice vinegar. If you are unable to find them, use cider vinegar for the light or malt vinegar for the dark.

VIRGINIA HAM (*gum wah tooey*): Use wherever ham is called for in a recipe. The smoky flavor is closest to the famous golden coin hams of China. This type may be purchased by the slice, the pound or the whole leg. In these recipes, Virginia and Smithfield ham are interchangeable with Westphalian ham and prosciutto, but not with boiled ham.

WATER CHESTNUTS (*maah tuy*): The canned variety is the easiest to use. These chestnuts may be stored by pouring off the liquid, replacing it with fresh water and keeping the container covered in the refrigerator. If chestnuts are not used within a couple of days, change the water.

WINTER MELON (*doong gwah*): A large melon with frosted, greenish skin. It is purchased in wedges and by the pound and, in spite of its name, is sold throughout the year.

WOOD EARS (*mook yee*): These are larger and coarser than cloud ears. They, too, are a dried fungus that must be soaked before using. Be sure to rinse thoroughly and break off any bits of bark that may adhere to the wood ears after they are soaked.

SPICES AND SEASONINGS USED IN CHINESE COOKING

BLACK PEPPER: Coarsely ground and used chiefly for seasoning bland foods or for a peppery flavor when the color of the dish is not important.

CHINESE CINNAMON (*yook gwuy*): A thick bark of somewhat less delicate flavor than ordinary cinnamon.

CHINESE STAR ANISE (*baat gok*): A dried 8-pointed star-shaped spice of dark brown color. Much used in dishes with soy sauce.

CLOVES (*ding heung*): Dried brown spikes which impart a distinct and pungent flavor.

CORNSTARCH: Used to seal in flavor and tenderize chicken, fish and meats, to provide crisp coatings for deep-fried foods, and to thicken sauces. Cornstarch is an essential in Chinese cooking. Primarily a unifying ingredient, cornstarch should not be used indiscriminately. Gluey sauces, in which cornstarch has been appointed the cure-all, are sure signs of inexperienced Chinese cooking. In China, water chestnut and lotus root flour are used instead of cornstarch.

FENNEL (*wooi heung*): Pale green seeds that give off a highly aromatic fragrance.

FIVE SPICES (*heung new fun*): A combination of five spices (anise, cloves, fennel, star anise and cinnamon) sold already ground in packages. This is used in many Chinese dishes. These spices are, of course, sold individually so you can if you wish mix and grind them yourself.

MONOSODIUM GLUTAMATE (*mee jing*): A neutral salt of glutamic acid, monosodium glutamate was originally derived from wheat protein and more recently from beets and corn. For centuries it was judiciously used by Chinese chefs to enhance natural flavors. The question of whether or not to use MSG is a moot one. My family's chef in Shanghai, Dah Su, kept a bottle of "taste powder" in the kitchen, but he was artfully selective in its use. The tendency today has become to sprinkle MSG indiscriminately into all dishes, resulting in an overwhelming similarity of flavors. This crutch approach, plus the fact that certain ingredients required in Chinese cooking—soy sauce and canned stock primarily—already contain amounts of MSG, make me disinclined to use it. My advice, therefore, is to select the freshest foodstuffs and allow the natural taste of the ingredients to predominate.

RED PEPPER FLAKES, DRIED: Used in place of whole chili peppers for intense hotness, mostly in Szechuanese cooking.

SALT: Unless otherwise stated, table salt should be used in the recipes in this book. Salt and soy sauce are not interchangeable, although recipes heavy in soy sauce will require a minimum of salt. Where foods are presalted or preserved in salt, no additional salt and a minimum of soy sauce should be added.

SUGAR: Acts as a negative balancing factor when salt and soy sauce are the positive ones. Sugar is used in varying amounts in Chinese cooking. In the East, where Red-Stewing is a specialty, sugar plays a major part in the cooking. In recipes where no soy sauce or other darkening agent is called for, use white sugar to preserve the pale color of the dish. In Braised or Red-Stewed recipes or wherever a light color is not important, use brown sugar. The Chinese prefer rock sugar for Slow-Simmered dishes, claiming that it imparts a glaze. Some recipes may call for honey or syrup, but they are usually used to glaze duck.

SZECHUAN PEPPER (*faah jui*): A reddish peppercorn with a tiny black seed. Mildly hot, with a spicy fragrance reminiscent of coriander seeds. Sold whole or ground, in packages.

WHITE PEPPER: Used for more delicate pepper flavor and when the light color of a dish must be retained.

CHINESE CONDIMENT SAUCES

BROWN BEAN SAUCE (*mien see jeung*): A pungent, salty mass of beans and sauce, dark brown in color. Use sparingly in cooking or as a savory dipping sauce. Sold in cans.

HOISIN SAUCE (*hoy sien jeung*): Although dark red in color, this sauce is made from yellow beans; it has a wide variety of uses. It is perfect with duck and may be used in the cooking of chickens and prawns to impart a delicate flavor. Combined with soy sauce, it makes an excellent barbecue sauce for spareribs. Served in small dishes, it makes an excellent dip for poultry or pork dishes. It is very inexpensive and will keep for months in tightly closed jars stored in the refrigerator. Sold in 1-pound cans.

OYSTER SAUCE (*ho yow*): Sold in bottles, this is a velvety golden-brown liquid which, when used in cooking, has the happy faculty of "marrying" with other flavors. Served alone as a dip, it has no predominant fish taste but adds a subtle flavor to vegetable, egg, meat, chicken or fish dishes.

PLUM SAUCE (*duk jeung*): This has the consistency and quality of chutney. It is used as a dipping sauce for roast duck, pork and fried pastry. Sold in cans.

SHRIMP PASTE (*hom hah*): This concentrated sauce has a salty, shrimplike flavor and is used a great deal in Fukien cooking. As with many Chinese condiments, the taste for shrimp paste is an acquired one; therefore the paste should be used sparingly on bland and steamed foods. Sold in bottles.

SOY SAUCE (*jeung yow*): This has been the food unifier and general flavoring ingredient in Chinese cooking since before the birth of Christ. The sauce originally involved boiling soybeans, straining the liquid and exposing it to the sun for several days until a "crust" was formed. Next came a process of skimming the crust and leaving the mixture exposed to the sun; this continued until there were no more surface layers to be skimmed. Advanced methods of producing soy sauce were arrived at through a technique of fermentation using soybeans, salt, broiled wheat and yeast mold.

The best Oriental soy sauces are still made by the method of natural fermentation, as opposed to chemical productions. In the natural fermentation process, it is not unusual for the mash of beans and wheat to be stored in vats of reinforced concrete and to be stirred by compressed air for 1 to 1½ years. It is then filtered, pasteurized and bottled.

There are many grades and qualities of soy sauce on the market, with few, if any, exacting standards. Here are some things to consider when you purchase soy sauce: Avoid the dark dense type called *chu yow*, which has more color than flavor; *shang cho* is lighter in color and is fine for delicate flavoring; *chan yow* is best suited for all-around Chinese cooking and is manufactured by several companies in this country. As a rule, I do not like to recommend brand names, but I feel that the correct choice of soy sauce can largely determine the success or failure of a Chinese dish. Try to find the Yellow Label soy sauce put out by the Amoy Canning Corporation in Hong Kong. Some Chinese cooks advocate the use of Japanese *shoyu*, particularly as a dipping sauce. While the most popular brand of *shoyu* is of high quality, it is too sweet for most Chinese dishes. For a light or dipping soy, look for Silver Label soy sauce, also produced by the Amoy Canning Corporation.

MEAT IN PROPORTION TO VEGETABLES

Because of a national scarcity of meat as well as purely economic factors, Chinese recipes depend on vegetables. This tendency toward small portions of meat in their dishes has been perpetuated by the Chinese, mostly by the poorer classes, who came overseas and established the first chop suey restaurants in the United States.

Even today the habit persists, and in many restaurants you will find that a dish such as pepper steak will be full of green peppers and contain very little beef— sometimes even less than the usual one-to-three ratio. While this meat-versus-vegetables ratio was indeed common to mass Chinese cooking, it did not apply to the Chinese epicure, who could afford higher proportions of meat, poultry or fish in his meals. For this reason and because Americans relish a good deal more meat, I have considerably increased amounts in these recipes. However, the choice is yours. If, in a recipe such as Dredged Pork with Fresh Vegetables, 1 pound of pork seems excessive in relation to 2 cups of vegetables, decrease the pork to ¾ or ½ pound and increase the vegetables accordingly.

MEAT IN CHINESE COOKING

In the sections devoted to each technique I will explain in detail what cuts of meat, poultry or fish are to be used for that method of cooking.

In Chinese cooking, pork is the most popular of all meats. It is to the Chinese what turkey and goose are in the Western holiday traditions. A roasted whole pig, its skin crackling and burnished like lacquer, is the featured part of a Chinese wedding celebration or New Year's feast.

Beef is less acceptable to the Chinese for a number of reasons. In China, the water buffalo is necessary to the agricultural economy of the country. Confucian analects deplore the slaying of cattle, and Buddhism, introduced after Confucianism, strengthened the sacred position of cattle. Nonetheless, a certain amount of beef was raised in China, the best of which came from Tsingtao in Shantung province. Calf and veal were available, too, but primarily for consumption by foreigners.

In North China, Moslem sects, whose religious laws caused them to abstain from pork, popularized the taste for lamb and mutton, but it is still not much favored in the South.

Because pork is tender regardless of cut, it is ideally suited to the various methods of Chinese cooking. A shoulder, Boston butt or pork loin lends itself equally well to finely sliced, rapidly cooked dishes as well as to braised, simmered or stewed ones. The exception here is belly pork, or, as the Chinese call it, five-flower pork, which requires long, slow cooking to break up the tendons.

Beef, with its coarser grain, is not as versatile as pork. In Chinese cooking terminology, the term for roasting, broiling, pan-broiling, pan-frying and deep-frying is dry-heat cooking. For pan- or stir-frying, as it is done in the Chinese manner, very tender cuts of beef must be used. The most suitable meats for this method are flank steaks, sirloin steaks and filet mignon. For thicker slices or diced meat, top round is suitable. The cuts just named are less desirable for what we term moist cooking, that is, braising, simmering or stewing, since they tend to dry out and toughen after long cooking. For moist-heat cooking, the most satisfactory cuts of beef are those which are less tender—beef shin or shank, plate beef and chuck roasts. The combination of moisture, heat and long, slow cooking periods causes the meat to become tender as gelatin is gradually formed from fibrous tissue and toughening of the protein is kept to a minimum.

Shoulder and leg of lamb are equally well suited to most methods of Chinese cooking. Riblets and neck slices are used in soups as well as in slow-cooked dishes.

A considerable amount of minced or, as we know it, ground meat is used by the Chinese. To insure the tenderness of your meat balls or patties, always purchase meat that has a relatively high amount of fat (about 25 percent). This is one time, when faced with the choice of ground sirloin, chuck or ordinary ground beef, you would choose the least expensive article with the comforting knowledge that you were buying what is best suited to your purpose. The kidneys, liver, heart, brains and gizzard of all animals are looked upon by the Chinese as great delicacies and are cooked in many ways.

Depending on what technique of cooking you are planning, it is well to bear in mind these simple facts: The portion of the animal's body which has had little exercise, the rib and loin area for example, is bound to be more tender than the parts of the animal like the shoulder and rump, which have been involved in extensive activity. In buying meats of any kind, always buy the highest grade—prime or choice. The additional money pays for the increased tenderness of the meat.

POULTRY IN CHINESE COOKING

Second to pork, poultry is the most popular food for the Chinese. It also plays an important symbolic role. The cock represents Yang, the male, positive and aggressive. Ducks symbolize happiness and fidelity. And pigeons, while not noted for their brightness, epitomize filial concern and longevity. As a banquet feature, duck is the favorite Chinese poultry, but chicken, squab, goose and pheasant are also eaten in quantity. The Long Island ducklings seen today in most supermarkets are descendants to those first brought to this country in 1873 from the Imperial aviaries in Peking. (Pheasant, not widely used in this country, is fairly common in China.)

When selecting a broiler, look for smooth thin skin, tender muscles with thin connective tissue and small amounts of fat over the back. The breastbone should be flexible and tipped. Use as indicated in recipes where quick cooking is required (Stir-Fry-Toss).

The general appearance of a fryer is similar to that of a broiler except that age contributes to its larger size and greater meatiness. There is usually a layering of fat under the skin. A fryer is more readily cut into serving pieces and can be used successfully in short-term braising, steaming, shallow- or deep-frying. When chicken breasts are called for, use fryer breasts (¾ to 1 pound unboned).

Roasters are usually tender, meaty and large enough to be either roasted or barbecued whole. There is considerable layering of fat under the skin and the breastbone is still tipped and flexible. Older roasters are best used in recipes that entail longer braising and steaming.

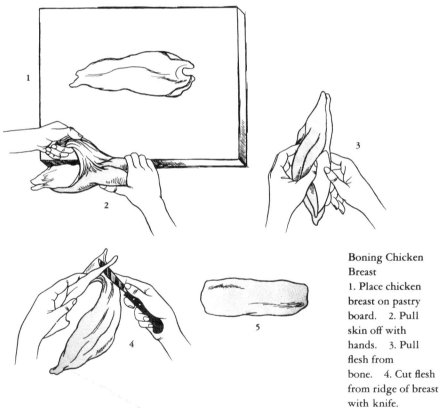

Boning Chicken Breast
1. Place chicken breast on pastry board.   2. Pull skin off with hands.   3. Pull flesh from bone.   4. Cut flesh from ridge of breast with knife.
5. Boned breast filet.

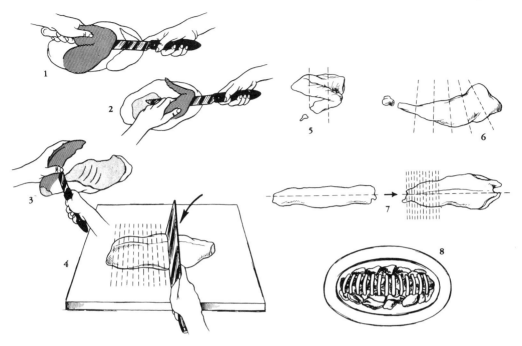

Cutting Poultry Chinese Style
1. Cut off legs in one piece.   2. Cut off wings.   3. Scrape off breast.   4. Chop back into 1-inch slices.   5. Cut wings into 3 pieces each, discarding wing tips.   6. Cut legs into 6 pieces each, discarding knobs of drumsticks.   7. Split breast through its thickness and slice crosswise into ½-inch strips.   8. Arrange on serving platter.

Hens have a coarser skin and well-developed muscles with thick connective tissue. They have a high proportion of fat. The breast meat is less delicate than that of the poultry already discussed, and the breastbone is rigid. Hens are mainly used in Clear-Simmering (soups) and Red-Stewing.

For most of the duck recipes, frozen Long Island ducklings can be used very nicely. These range from 4 to 7 pounds. Peking Duck requires a larger bird whose neck is intact. (Certain essential precooking procedures will be discussed fully in the recipe for its preparation.) To test freshly killed duck for tenderness, pinch the bird's windpipe; if it is resilient, the duck will be young and tender. A windpipe that cracks or tends to stiffness indicates an older bird.

In China, poultry is always purchased live and killed at home. Since this is rarely possible in the United States, always make sure that the skin of the bird is smooth and not sticky and that the flesh is bright in color and springy to the touch. Frozen chicken parts should be examined for evenness of color. Avoid pieces encrusted with dark, bloody ice.

FISH IN CHINESE COOKING

In Chinese, the word for fish is *yu* and it is pronounced the same way as the character for bounteousness. The high rate of reproduction among fish has made them the symbol for regeneration. Because it has no natural confinement, except within its watery realm, and because of its speed, the fish is also looked upon by the Chinese as the symbol of freedom. At Buddhist funeral banquets the serving of fish signifies the departed's freedom from earthly restraints. On the practical level, China's extensive coastlines, rivers, lakes and networks of canals offer an enormous variety of fresh- and saltwater fish, many of which are unheard-of in other countries. The business of buying and cooking fish is treated seriously in China and no housewife with any pride would dream of buying anything but a live fish. These were purchased in leakproof, water-filled baskets, brought home and kept alive in tubs until just before cooking. In the United States, the buying of live fish is difficult as well as inconvenient. Refrigerated transportation and strict regulations insure fresh merchandise. Nevertheless, always buy top-quality fish.

The Chinese favor cooking fish that is not dressed: they prefer to cook whole fish drawn (entrails removed) but with the head and tail intact. Fish cooked in this manner is infinitely tender and juicy. While fish is a highly esteemed food, the Chinese abhor fishy smells. Ginger root, garlic, scallions and frequently wine are used to conceal such smells. Among the fish most popular with the Chinese are carp, bass, bream, Mandarin fish (a type of perch), shad, snapper, sole and turbot. Shellfish, such as clams, crab, crawfish, prawns, lobsters and shrimp are also abundant in China. Freshwater crabs, with their soft shells, are considered a great delicacy.

When buying fresh fish look for the following qualities. The skin must not be sticky or dry but smooth to the touch and moist. The flesh should be firm and springy. Tug at the scales; if they are loose, the fish is not fresh. The eyes must be bright and clear, full and not sunken. The gills should be a coral pink. While fish will have a characteristic smell, the odor should not be one of decay. Generally, fresh fish should have a "still alive" look, as though it would swim at once if put back in water.

Fish is extremely perishable. Refrigerate or wrap and freeze at once. Use refrigerated fish within 24 hours. Allow frozen fish to thaw in the refrigerator before using. Never refreeze thawed fish.

Whenever possible, crabs, lobsters, clams and oysters should be bought live. Oysters and clams must be tightly closed; gaping shells are an indication that the creatures are dead. Already-shucked shellfish should always be kept on ice. Prawns and shrimp should have a blue rather than a pinkish-brown cast. If you are purchasing a cooked lobster, pull back the lobster's tail; if it springs back into a curl, it was cooked alive.

When preparing prawns and shrimp for cooking, remove the feelers, shell and tail unless otherwise stated in the recipe. With the point of a small sharp knife, make a slash down the center of the shrimp's or prawn's back. The threadlike black vein should come away with the tip of the knife. Gently scrape out any stubborn threads. Rinse the shellfish in cold water. Drain well before cooking.

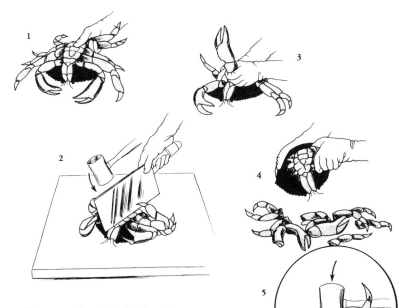

How to Prepare a Live Crab for Cooking
1. Grasp one or two of the crab's rear legs from either side. Make sure that you are holding on to them firmly and wear lined gloves during this operation. Place crab with its back down on the cutting board.   2. Place Chinese cutting knife in center of crab. With a mallet hit back of knife quickly and hard to kill crab instantly.   3. Grasp front claws and twist them off where they join the body. Twist off legs. Scrub, rinse and drain.
4. Pry off top shell. Remove gills and spongy matter. Wash and drain.   5. Hold legs and claws by their tips. Crack them, using the mallet.
6. Again using the mallet and the Chinese cutting knife, cut the body in half. Then cut each half into 2 pieces.

THE TECHNIQUES OF CUTTING

Of primary importance is the understanding and practice of cutting as applied to each method of cooking. Cutting in the Chinese manner is not merely a matter of reducing in size. Apart from the pleasing uniformity created when all ingredients are of a similar shape, there is also the matter of required cooking time. This is easier to establish if all the ingredients are of similar dimensions.

HOW TO USE A CHINESE CUTTING KNIFE

With the cutting board directly in front of you, grip the cutting knife in whichever hand you cut with. Hold it so that your thumb and forefinger rest on opposite sides of the blade. Cut so that the blade falls across the board at a 45-degree angle. With the other hand, grasp the food to be cut in a clenching gesture, allowing the

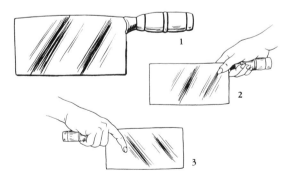

How to Use a Chinese
Cutting Knife
1. Chinese cutting knife.
2. Grip handle with thumb
on blade.   3. Extend index
finger on other side of blade.

knuckle of the forefinger to just touch the blade. Press the blade in a down-thrust, first pushing the object to be cut against the blade. Do not use a seesaw motion. The blade's sharpness and heaviness means that very little exertion is required from the person cutting. The degree of fineness of your chopped ingredient depends on how much you repeat this operation. You will find that with a little practice it is quite simple to master this method of chopping.

DIAGONAL CUTTING: To many, cutting on the diagonal constitutes no problem, but for others it does present an obstacle. So, let's begin with how to cut diagonally and then progress to what should or should not be cut in this manner. This method of cutting simply means that the meat is cut across the grain at a slant. (Vegetables are also cut in this manner.) Let's assume we are going to cut a piece

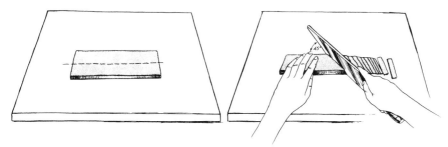

Diagonal Cutting
Divide the meat into 2 long strips. Holding the Chinese cutting knife at a 45-degree angle to the surface of the meat, slice diagonally across the grain of the meat at a 45-degree angle.

of flank steak into diagonal slices. Flank steaks, in general, run from $1\frac{1}{2}$ to $2\frac{1}{2}$ pounds. For easier slicing, divide the meat into 2 strips by cutting it in half lengthwise. You will have approximately $\frac{3}{4}$ to $1\frac{1}{4}$ pounds in each strip, the average amount you will require for most of the Stir-Fry-Toss recipes. Lay a strip of the steak horizontally in front of you on the cutting board. Slant your knife at a 45-degree angle. (In other words slant it as far as you can and still be able to cut comfortably.) Begin from the right end and cut with a shearing, scraping motion to the right. The meat will fall away in diagonal slices. Continue until you come to the end of the strip. Average diagonal slices should be from 1 to $1\frac{1}{2}$ inches long, $\frac{1}{2}$ to $\frac{3}{4}$ inch wide and about $\frac{1}{8}$ inch thick. What should be cut diagonally? All meats to be used in rapid, short-term cooking; tubular vegetables, such as asparagus, broccoli, carrots, celery, string beans or any cylindrical vegetable when thinness in each slice is desired.

STRIP CUTTING: This method of cutting is used whenever extra thinness is required. Begin by cutting meat or vegetables in diagonal slices. Then cut each slice again so that you have 2 or 3 strips.

SHRED CUTTING: This means literally to cut into shreds, as in julienne cutting. To achieve this, first cut the ingredient into average diagonal slices. Next, cut again into 2 strips; then cut each thin strip at an angle so that you have 2 tapered slivers.

STRAIGHT SLICING: As a rule, leafy vegetables such as spinach, watercress, parsley and dandelion greens are straight sliced, while bunchy vegetables like cabbage, chard and mustard greens can be either diagonally or straight sliced. To slice a bulky vegetable such as Chinese cabbage, split the cabbage in half lengthwise. Then, starting from the stalk end, either diagonal slice or straight slice. Slices should be from $\frac{1}{2}$ to $1\frac{1}{2}$ inches wide, depending on the requirements of the recipe.

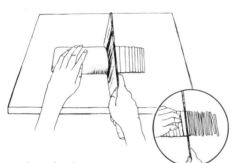

Strip Cutting
Cut meat in diagonal slices, then cut each slice into strips.

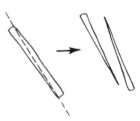

Shred Cutting
Cut ingredient in diagonal slices. Cut each slice into 2 strips. Cut each strip at an angle into tapered slivers.

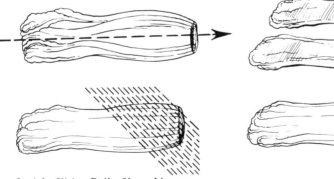

Straight Slicing Bulky Vegetables
Split Chinese cabbage in half. Place flat and slice diagonally starting at stalk. Place flat and straight slice starting at stalk.

To straight slice a leafy vegetable like spinach, trim and pare root ends but leave the roots intact. Cut each cluster crosswise into two or three sections. Treat watercress and parsley in the same manner. Chinese chard, which is both stalky and leafy, may be either straight or diagonally sliced. The same applies to Chinese mustard greens or mustard cabbage. Round objects are either cut into wedges or straight sliced from top to bottom. Scallops and water chestnuts, for instance, are straight sliced into thin rounds or coin shapes. Mushrooms are sliced straight up and down, with each slice resembling a T.

ROLLING KNIFE, OR OBLIQUE, CUTTING: This is applied to round or cylindrical vegetables. It is used most often in slow cooking techniques wherein the faceted vegetable can cook more rapidly and absorb flavors. For some reason there seems to be confusion about this cutting method. So let's approach it step by step. Place a carrot or turnip horizontally on your cutting board. Start at the root end of the vegetable and make a 30-degree diagonal slice. Now the ingredient must be rolled. So, roll the uncut portion of the carrot just one-quarter of a turn towards you; the cut surface should be facing upward. Make another 30-degree cut, slightly above and partly across the surface of the first cut. Then roll the remaining carrot one-quarter of a turn again and repeat the 30-degree cut. Do this until the whole carrot is cut into triangular wedges, each with two cut sides. Two things to remember: Roll one-quarter of a turn, and diagonally slice (at a 30-degree angle) just across the last cut.

CHUNK CUTTING: Applied when the meat or vegetable is bulky in shape or is intended for long slow simmering, as in Braised or Red-Stewed dishes. The meat is cut into 1½- to 2-inch chunks or wedges; the vegetables, depending on their shape, are cut into rolling knife pieces or chunks of the same dimensions.

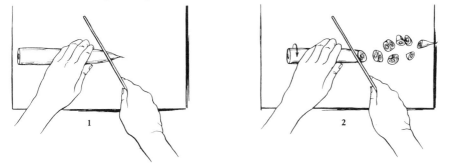

Rolling Knife, or Oblique, Cutting
1. Cut a diagonal slice from the vegetable.   2. Make a one-quarter turn of the vegetable toward you and make a diagonal slice slightly above and partly across the face of the first slice. Continue until vegetable is completely cut.

CHOPPING: A number of the recipes call for chopped ingredients. The degree of fineness in the chopping should be somewhere between coarsely chopped and minced. The pieces should be approximately the size and shape of confetti. To chop for this purpose, begin by straight slicing. Then bring the cleaver down and chop, using a down-thrust rather than a seesaw motion.

DICING: Cut ingredients into cubes, generally ½ inch square. If you are cubing a carrot, cut it lengthwise into 4-inch strips, then cut each strip crosswise into ½-inch cubes. This procedure applies to other cylindrical vegetables as well. The method of cubing meat depends on its thickness. If the piece of meat is a steak, it can be pounded into the desired thickness before dicing. In the event that the piece of meat to be used is too thick for pounding and you want to dice it into ½-inch cubes, lay the meat flat on the cutting board, pressing down on it with the fingers of one hand. Slice through the meat with the knife (held parallel to the board), splitting the meat evenly between the board and your fingers. If the meat being prepared is a thin piece like flank steak, the vegetables in the recipe should be

1 Chopping
2 Splitting Meat
3 Dicing
Split ingredient to be diced lengthwise into thin strips, then cut crosswise into cubes.
4 Mincing with Blunt Edge of Chinese Cutting Knife
This technique is used for very fine mincing and to mince garlic and ginger root.
5 Mincing with Two Chinese Cutting Knives

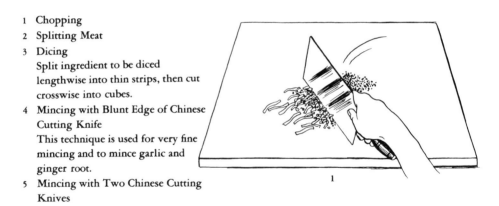

1

cubed accordingly. With pork, the meat most often used, it is just a matter of trimming the pork of its fat and splitting it down to size before dicing. The ½ inch given for dicing here is for average-size dicing and applies to all recipes that do not specify fine dicing. Fine dicing requires that each cube be from ¼ to ⅛ inch. Anything finer is minced.

MINCING: There are at least two schools of thought on the correct procedure here. Mincing is close to grinding, and some Chinese authorities feel that the meat grinder offers a workable solution. The orthodox method of mincing involves placing the object to be chopped on a solid cutting board and bearing down rhythmically with 2 Chinese cleavers. To be truthful, I have used both the grinder and the cleavers and have had good results with each. However, the determining factor is the recipe. The cleaver approach is fine for mincing prawns into a paste for Shrimp Balls; it works well on ham and for preparing the chicken breasts in Chicken Velvet. Because I believe that the more work you can get your butcher to do for you the better, I quite often have pork or beef ground for me on the medium blade and use it in recipes calling for minced meat, such as Yangchow Lion's Head. If you do decide to use the cleaver method, begin by pounding the ingredient to be minced with the blunt edge of the cleaver. When it comes to larger portions, first slice them into pieces, then, using a down-thrust rather than a seesaw motion, mince them to the degree of fineness necessary in your recipe. Finally, if you wish to mince the object almost to a pulp, use the blunt edge of your cleaver and pound. Be careful not to continue using the sharp edge of the blade, or you may arrive at what the Chinese call "chopping board flavor," which means that your ingredient has acquired particles of wood from the board itself.

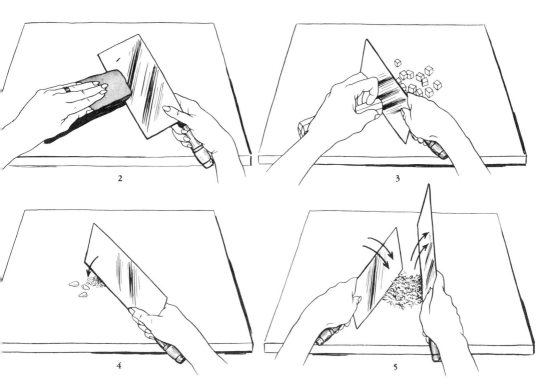

2

3

4

5

HOW MUCH TO BUY—
WEIGHTS AND
MEASURES

MEAT SERVINGS

1 pound boned sliced pork shoulder or loin......	2 to 3 servings
1 pound boned sliced pork shoulder or loin with 2 cups vegetables.........................	3 to 4 servings
2 pounds pork spareribs........................	2 servings
1 pound ground pork, beef or lamb............	2 to 4 servings
1 pound sliced flank steak, sirloin or filet of beef..	2 to 3 servings
1 pound sliced flank steak, sirloin or filet of beef with 2 cups vegetables......................	3 to 4 servings
1 pound boned sliced shoulder or leg of lamb....	2 to 3 servings
1 pound boned sliced shoulder or leg of lamb with 2 cups vegetables..........................	3 to 4 servings

MEAT MEASURES

1 pound raw ground pork, beef or lamb.........	2 cups
1 pound cooked ground pork, beef or lamb......	3 cups
1 pound pork, beef or lamb, cut in thin strips....	3 cups
1 pound pork, beef or lamb, cut in ½-inch dice..	2½ cups
1 pound Virginia ham, cut in ¼-inch dice.......	2 cups
1 pound thinly sliced bacon....................	30 slices
1 pound thickly sliced bacon...................	15 to 20 slices

MEAT WEIGHTS, BONED AND UNBONED

2½ pounds pork (fatty cut), with bone in.......	1½ pounds
2½ pounds beef (fatty cut), with bone in........	1½ pounds
2½ pounds lamb (fatty cut), with bone in.......	1½ pounds

POULTRY SERVINGS

1-pound squab..................	1 to 2 servings
1½- to 2½-pound broiling chicken.............	3 to 4 servings
2½- to 3½-pound frying chicken..............	3 to 4 servings
3- to 5-pound roasting chicken................	4 to 6 servings
4- to 6-pound fowl (hen over 1 year old)........	6 to 8 servings
4- to 6-pound duck..........................	3 to 5 servings

CHICKEN WEIGHTS, BONED AND UNBONED

3-pound fryer, boned and skinned..............	1¼ to 1½ pounds
¾-pound fryer breast, boned..................	½ pound
¾-pound fryer leg, boned.	½ pound

CHICKEN MEASURES

1½ pounds fryer breasts or thighs, boned and diced	2 cups
¾-pound fryer breast, boned and cut in thin strips	1 cup
1¼ to 1½ pound boned chicken meat, ground...	2½ cups
1 pound chicken livers........................	3 cups

CHICKEN PARTS PER POUND

1 chicken breast.............................	¾ to 1 pound
2 chicken legs.............................	¾ to 1 pound
6 chicken thighs............................	1 pound
6 to 8 chicken wings........................	1 pound
6 to 9 chicken drumsticks....................	1 pound

FISH SERVINGS

1 pound whole fish..........................	1 to 1½ servings
1 pound drawn fish (entrails and scales removed)..	1 to 2 servings
1 pound dressed fish (entrails, head and tail removed)............................	3 servings
1 pound fish steaks or filets...................	3 servings
1 pound unshelled crab......................	2 servings
1 pound cooked shelled crab meat.............	3 servings
1 pound unshelled shrimp....................	3 servings
1 pound cooked shelled shrimp...............	4 servings
1½ pound unshelled lobster..................	2 servings
1 pound cooked shelled lobster meat...........	4 servings
1 pound shucked oysters.....................	3 servings
1 pound shucked clams......................	4 to 6 servings

FISH UNITS PER POUND

1 pound fish filets..........................	3 ⅓ slices, depending on size and thickness of fish
1 pound fish steaks..........................	3 steaks, depending on size and thickness of fish
1 pound clams in shell.......................	12
1 pound oysters in shell......................	12
1 pound small shrimp in shell................	36 to 40
1 pound medium shrimp in shell..............	24 to 26
1 pound jumbo shrimp in shell...............	16 to 20

VEGETABLES

½ pound (1 large) Chinese turnip, cut in thin strips	2 cups
½ pound (1 large) Chinese turnip, cut in ½-inch dice................................	2 cups

½ pound (1 medium) cucumber, cut in ½-inch dice   1 cup

½ pound (1 medium-large) zucchini, cut in ½-inch dice. . . . .   1 cup

½ pound (2 large) leeks, cut in ¼-inch rounds. . .   2 cups

½ pound (3 large) carrots, sliced in 1½-inch diagonal or rolling cut slices. . . . .   1 cup

½ pound (3 large) carrots, cut in ½-inch dice. .   1¼ cups

½ pound (1 large) bamboo shoot, cut in ½-inch dice. . . . .   1 cup

½ pound (1 large) bamboo shoot, cut in 4 x 1 x ⅛-inch slices. . . . .   1 cup

½ pound (1 large) bamboo shoot, cut in 4 x ¼ x 1/16-inch shreds. . . . .   1⅓ cups

½ pound (1 medium-large) hairy melon, peeled and cut in thin strips.   2 cups

½ pound (1 medium-large) hairy melon, peeled and cut in ½-inch dice. . . . .   2 cups

½ pound (17 three-inch pods) okra, cut in half. .   1⅓ cups

½ pound (17 three-inch pods) okra, cut in 1½-inch diagonal slices. . . . .   2 cups

½ pound (2 medium) bitter melon, seeded and cut in thin strips. . . . .   2 cups

½ pound (2 medium) bitter melon, seeded and cut in ½-inch slices. . . . .   2 cups

½ pound (2 narrow) Chinese eggplants, quartered and cut in 1½-inch lengths. . . . .   2 cups

½ pound (2 narrow) Chinese eggplants, cut in ½-inch dice. . . . .   slightly more than 2 cups

½ pound American eggplant, peeled and cut in ½-inch dice. . . . .   1½ cups

½ pound spinach with roots, cut in 1½-inch lengths. . . . .   slightly more than 4 cups

1 pound (4 large stalks) celery, cut in 1½-inch diagonal slices. . . . .   2 cups

1 pound (1 bunch) asparagus, coarse stalks trimmed, cut in 1½-inch diagonal or rolling slices. . . . .   3 cups

1 pound fava beans, shelled....................	1⅓ cups
1 pound lima beans, shelled....................	⅔ cup
1 pound green peas, shelled....................	slightly more than 1 cup
1 pound Chinese chard (*bok choy*), cut in 1½-inch lengths...............................	3 cups
1 pound Chinese cabbage, cut in 1½-inch lengths..	6 cups
1 pound bean sprouts.........................	3½ cups
1 pound pea sprouts..........................	6 cups
1 pound mushrooms, cut in straight slices.......	5 cups
1 pound snow peas, threaded, with ends snipped..	4 cups
1 pound string beans, threaded, with ends snipped	3½ cups
1 pound bean curd, cut in 3½-inch squares.......	5 cups
6 scallions, cut in 1½-inch diagonal slices.......	¾ cup
6 scallions, cut in ¼-inch rounds..............	⅔ cup
1 large scallion with 2 inches green, finely minced	1 tablespoon
1 eight-ounce can water chestnuts (about 30 water chestnuts)..............................	1 cup
6 water chestnuts, peeled and finely diced........	¼ cup
1 medium-large (6-ounce) bell pepper, cored, seeded and sliced in thin strips..............	1¼ cups
1 medium-large (6-ounce) bell pepper, cut in 2-inch squares................................	2 cups
1 medium-large (8-ounce) onion, cut in ½-inch dice...................................	½ cup

DRIED VEGETABLES

1 pound dried chestnuts (do not expand much on soaking)...............................	2⅔ cups
¼ pound (4 cups) dried mushrooms, soaked.....	8 cups
¼ cup dried wood ears, soaked.................	1 cup
1 tablespoon dried cloud ears, soaked..........	3 tablespoons
1 ounce dried tiger lilies, soaked..............	1 cup
½ pound bean thread noodles, soaked..........	5 cups

NUTS

1 pound shelled almonds.	3 cups
1 pound shelled cashews.	4 cups
1 pound shelled fresh chestnuts.	2 cups
1 pound shelled peanuts.	3½ cups
1 pound shelled walnuts.	4 cups

RICE

Allow about ⅓ cup uncooked rice
or 1 cup cooked rice per serving.

2¼ cups (1 pound) long-grain rice.	6¾ to 7¾ cups cooked
1 cup (6½ to 7 ounces) long-grain rice.	3 to 3½ cups cooked
1 cup glutinous rice.	2⅔ cups cooked
1 cup precooked rice (Uncle Ben's Minute Rice). .	2 cups cooked
¼ pound rice sticks.	2 cups soaked
¼ pound rice sticks.	4 cups deep-fried

NOODLES

1 to 1¼ cups (4 ounces) uncooked spaghetti or thin noodles.	2½ cups cooked
2 cups (8 ounces) uncooked Chinese thin soft noodles.	3 cups cooked
2 cups (8 ounces) uncooked homemade egg noodles	2½ to 2⅔ cups cooked

MISCELLANEOUS MEASURES

1 pound lard.	2 cups
1 pint vegetable oil.	2 cups
1 pound flour, unsifted.	3½ cups
1 pound flour, sifted.	4 cups
1 pound cornstarch.	3 cups
1 pound brown sugar.	2¼ cups

1 pound granulated sugar.....................   2¼ cups
1 ounce salt..............................   2⅛ tablespoons
8 fluid ounces (16 tablespoons)................   1 cup
12 tablespoons (6 fluid ounces)...............   ¾ cup
10 tablespoons and 2 teaspoons...............   ⅔ cup
8 tablespoons (4 ounces).....................   ½ cup
5 tablespoons and 1 teaspoon................   ⅓ cup
4 tablespoons (2 ounces).....................   ¼ cup
1 fluid ounce (2 tablespoons)................   ⅛ cup
½ fluid ounce (3 teaspoons)................   1 tablespoon
60 drops..............................   1 teaspoon

HOW CHINESE COOKING TECHNIQUES RELATE TO WESTERN METHODS

╘╝╘╝╘╝╘╝╘╝╘╝╘╝╘╝╘╝╘╝╘╝╘╝╘╝╘╝

What are Chinese cooking techniques? How many are there, and how do they differ from Western methods? This subject involves many points of view. One writer stretches the ways of cooking in the Chinese manner to twenty-one! Most authorities, however, seem agreed on eight to a dozen techniques. As I see it, clarification is necessary. In reviewing these "Chinese" methods, some very familiar terms such as boiling, deep-frying and braising crop up. We have already acknowledged that most cooking techniques we use in the Western world probably originated in China. But when you consider, for instance, that deep-fat frying is applied every day in the United States to potatoes and doughnuts, it would seem to me fatuous to discuss it as a uniquely Chinese technique.

With one or two exceptions, the techniques are basically the same for Chinese and Americans. What makes the difference is the Chinese cook's approach to them, what he will cook using each method and his versatility and flexibility. To explain further, the Chinese approach to what we consider standard methods has been influenced by endemic and economic factors. Scarcity of fuel dictated rapid cooking at intense heat, whereas smoldering embers provided the means for long, slow cooking. Climatic and transportation problems caused the development of preserved, salted and dried foodstuffs. These had to be treated and cooked in certain fashions. With the growth of Chinese culture, Chinese epicures sought a harmonious balance of flavors at each meal. A Chinese chef was required to become adept at incorporating the entire spectrum of techniques into the framework of a single meal. Thus, by necessity, timing became an integral part of his curriculum. It is these nuances of heat levels, ingredients and time factors which distinguish the art of Chinese cuisine from ordinary Western cooking practices.

CHINESE COOKING TECHNIQUES

STIR-FRY-TOSS

A uniquely Chinese method of cooking. High heat is almost always required throughout the cooking.

TIME: 5 to 10 minutes.
UTENSILS: Iron skillet or wok.
FAT: Peanut oil or corn oil.
MAIN INGREDIENTS: All types, thinly cut for even cooking.
PROCESS: Rapid frying, stirring and tossing.
FINISHED CHARACTERISTICS: Cooked-through but crunchy vegetables. Natural colors, textures, flavors. The integrity of each ingredient must be preserved.

BRAISING

A technique similar to Western braising except that the ingredients are nearly always pre-fried at medium-high heat, which is then turned to low.

TIME: 30 minutes to 2 hours.
UTENSILS: Iron or copper skillet, electric frypan (all with covers).
FAT: Peanut oil, corn oil, lard.
MAIN INGREDIENTS: Meat or poultry (cut up or whole) and vegetables (usually cut up). Braised whole fish is called "Red-Stewed Fish" when soy sauce is added and when the cornstarch thickening is omitted.
PROCESS: Ingredients fried, liquid and seasonings added, all covered and braised until done. Served hot or cold.
FINISHED CHARACTERISTICS: Well-cooked morsels, clear sauce neither too thick nor runny. Comparable to French ragouts or *daubes*.

RED-STEWING

Unlike Western stewing, the food is not browned in fat and thickeners are not used. The sauce is condensed by long, slow simmering in which soy sauce and sugar are always featured.

TIME: 1 to 3 hours.
UTENSILS: Dutch oven, soup pot, kettle, electric deep-fry cooker (all with covers).
FAT: None.

MAIN INGREDIENTS: Whole chicken, duck, shoulder of pork, leg of lamb, ham or other large cuts. Root-type vegetables.

PROCESS: Ingredients stewed in soy sauce with seasonings and spices.

FINISHED CHARACTERISTICS: Reddish-brown coloring, rich sauce. Dishes served either hot or cold and jellied. When served jellied, resembles French *boeuf à la mode*.

BOILING AND CLEAR-SIMMERING

Boiling may be compared to Western soupmaking in which individual or combined ingredients are cooked in stock or water. Clear-Simmering is comparable to poaching, when a single large cut is slowly simmered.

TIME: 2 to 4 hours.

UTENSILS: Dutch oven, heavy pot, kettle, double boiler, electric deep-fry cooker (all with covers). For whole fowl, roasting pan with foil cover.

FAT: None.

MAIN INGREDIENTS: Whole birds, fish, shoulder or leg of lamb or pork.

PROCESS: The meat portion is covered with water, brought to a boil and immediately lowered to simmer.

FINISHED CHARACTERISTICS: Ungarnished cooked-through meat and a sparkling-clear broth. Served with sauces, dips and condiments.

STEAMING

Used less in Western cooking than in Chinese, where it replaces baking. This technique is not to be confused with double-boiling.

TIME: Ranges from 10 minutes to 2 or 3 hours, depending on material being steamed.

UTENSILS: See pages 7–12.

FAT: Little or none.

MAIN INGREDIENTS: A wide range, including meat, poultry, fish and pastries.

PROCESS: The item is placed on a rack standing above boiling water in a pot. The pot is covered and the food is cooked by circulating steam.

FINISHED CHARACTERISTICS: Pastries are sheer, chewy yet delicate; fish is moist and flakes easily; fowl is juicy and tender. Steaming is the supreme test of the freshness of ingredients.

FRYING

Shallow-Frying
Comparable to sautéing or panfrying. The ingredients, often precooked, are browned in shallow oil on one side, then turned to finish the cooking.

TIME: Depends on the ingredients.
UTENSILS: Any skillet.
FAT: Peanut oil or corn oil; occasionally lard.
MAIN INGREDIENTS: Egg dishes, pre-steamed pastries, noodles, fish filets, shellfish and vegetables.
PROCESS: Ingredients fried over low-medium heat in a skillet, the bottom of which is just covered with oil.
FINISHED CHARACTERISTICS: Medium to low heat preserves flavor and avoids a heavy fried taste.

Semi–Deep-Frying and Deep-Frying
This process is similar to the French-frying used for potatoes, doughnuts and other Western foods. Deep-Frying uses more fat than Semi–Deep-Frying.

TIME: Usually 6 to 8 minutes.
UTENSILS: Deep skillet, electric frypan or deep-fry cooker.
FAT: Peanut oil or corn oil.
MAIN INGREDIENTS: A wide variety, including pastries, fish and chicken parts.
PROCESS: A minimum of 2 cups of oil is heated according to the recipe; food is cooked in small portions.
FINISHED CHARACTERISTICS: Crisp golden-brown exterior, juicy cooked-through interior.

OVEN BARBECUING (ROASTING),
OUTDOOR BARBECUING AND SMOKE-COOKING

Oven Barbecuing
Meat and poultry marinated, then hung in the oven from hooks or spitted on a rotisserie or placed on racks to permit dripping of fat without causing steam.

TIME: From 1 to 3 hours.

UTENSILS: Hooks made from 6-inch skewers, roasting pans and racks or rotisserie equipment, drip pans.

FAT: None.

MAIN INGREDIENTS: Pork loin strips, spareribs, short ribs, poultry (parts and whole).

PROCESS: Slow roasting in circulating heat over indirect fire. No broiling.

FINAL CHARACTERISTICS: Evenly cooked crisp exteriors without charring, moist interiors. Rich flavor.

Outdoor-Barbecuing

Meat, poultry and fish (parts and whole) is marinated (sometimes steamed), then brushed with glaze or basted during cooking. Barbecuing done on grill over hot coals at even temperature.

TIME: 20 minutes to 3 hours.

EQUIPMENT: Any barbecue unit, charcoal briquets. (See page 260.)

FAT: Little or none.

MAIN INGREDIENTS: Pork loin strips, spareribs, short ribs, skewered lamb and beef, chicken and duck (parts and whole), fish (steaks or whole).

PROCESS: Food is cooked by direct infrared radiation from thoroughly heated coals (not by flame).

FINAL CHARACTERISTICS: Crisply textured exteriors with unique flavor, cooked-through and moist interiors.

Outdoor Smoke-Cooking

Not comparable to Western smoke-cooking or barbecuing, but is essentially the same as Chinese barbecuing—with minor but significant additions.

TIME: 20 minutes to 3 hours.

EQUIPMENT: Smoke-cooker or any barbecue unit with a hood or cover.

FAT: Little or none.

MAIN INGREDIENTS: Pork loin strips, spareribs, short ribs, skewered lamb or beef, chicken or duck (parts or whole), fish (steaks or whole).

PROCESS: Food cooked by heat and flavored by smoke in covered unit. Smoke flavor controlled by the addition of certain ingredients, either early or late in the cooking.

FINAL CHARACTERISTICS: Deep, rich exterior glaze. Smoke flavor accented by tea leaves, anise or whatever spice is added.

Indoor Smoke-Cooking
There is no comparable Western technique. The ingredients are marinated and sometimes pre-steamed or fried to minimize smoke-cooking time. (Short, intense smoke-cooking is characteristic of this method.)

TIME: Approximately 20 minutes per pound of chicken, 15 minutes per pound of fish.
UTENSILS: Heavy foil-lined skillet with cover.
FAT: Little or none.
MAIN INGREDIENTS: Primarily poultry parts or fish steaks. Meats seldom sugar-smoked.
PROCESS: Ingredients cooked in smoke generated by burning sugar in a closed skillet. Requires ventilated room.
FINISHED CHARACTERISTICS: Glazed exterior, unusual tangy flavor.

HOT POT COOKING

Of Mongolian origins, hot pot cooking consisted of "rinsing" strips of raw meat in boiling water and eating at once. Peking gourmets refined the dish to include all kinds of food and substituted stock for the water.

TIME: 1 or 2 minutes.
UTENSILS: Oriental chafing pot, any casserole with cover used over an electric burner, or an electric frypan.
FAT: None.
MAIN INGREDIENTS: Finely sliced pork, beef, lamb, chicken, duck, prawns, lobster, fish filets, squid, liver, mustard greens, watercress, celery, cabbage, chrysanthemum petals.
PROCESS: Food is dipped into boiling stock until just cooked, dipped into a sauce and eaten at once. The vegetables are then briefly cooked in the broth and served with it.
FINISHED CHARACTERISTICS: Very fresh food is cooked in boiling stock so that all juices and flavors are sealed in. Food must be attractively served; it is very finely sliced for uniform cooking. It is served with dipping sauces.

STIR-FRY-TOSS-TECHNIQUE 1

What is known as Stir-Fry or Toss-Fry Cooking is at once the most popular and yet the most difficult to achieve of all purely Chinese techniques. Since the three actions, stirring, frying and tossing, are mandatory for success, it is not an affectation on my part that I call it Stir-Fry-Toss Cooking. What is involved may sound deceptively simple. Quantities of thinly sliced food are fried rapidly in small amounts of oil over very high heat, tossed thoroughly to coat with the oil and stirred constantly to prevent scorching. The entire operation is accomplished in minutes. But the success or failure of this method depends on many incidentals—readiness, the correct precutting of ingredients, the correct cooking utensil and heat levels and, most important, timing. There are three fundamental requirements to keep in mind for preparing a stir-fry-toss recipe.

THE INGREDIENTS: These must be cut to match in size and should be ready to use in the cooking sequence of the recipes. Meat, poultry, fish and vegetables are always either sliced on the diagonal, cut into strips or shreds, diced or minced to insure evenness of cooking. Seasonings and liquids must be measured in advance of cooking. Thickeners should not be combined with water or stock ahead of time unless the combination is stirred before adding—the cornstarch tends to settle and harden and must be re-blended.

THE COOKING UTENSIL: Cast-iron skillets and woks are best suited to this active type of cooking.

THE COOKING FAT: The choice of fat is of primary importance. It must have a flavor entirely compatible with Chinese food and have a high enough smoking point to withstand intense heat—a minimum temperature of 350° F. is required for the stir-fry-toss technique. Lard is compatible with Chinese ingredients, but the smoking point must be taken into account. The highest grade of leaf lard, which has a smoking point of 396° F., may be used, but lesser grades with smoking points of 350° F. to 365° F. could cause trouble. It is advisable to use lard in braised recipes, where intense heat is not a requirement. Peanut oil is by far the best fat for stir-fry-toss cooking. It has a fine nutty flavor which enhances Chinese ingredients and it can be heated to high degrees (450° F. to 470° F.) without burning. Next in order of preference come corn oil (440° F. to 460° F.) and cottonseed oil (450° F.). Sesame oil has a good flavor but a low smoking point and it is expensive to use in large amounts. Do not use butter or olive oil—the former has too low a smoking point and the latter is not compatible in taste with Chinese food.

Before starting to cook, examine the following instructions which you will find in the stir-fry-toss recipes.

TURN HEAT UNDER SKILLET OR WOK TO HIGH: This means that the control on your stove should be set for maximum heat.

THE HEAT REMAINS HIGH THROUGHOUT THE COOKING: This holds true for nearly all the recipes in this technique. Some recipes do call for a change in temperature so always read recipes carefully.

WHEN THE PAN IS HOT, ADD THE OIL: The pan is hot enough to add the oil if a drop of water on its surface bubbles into steam.

THE OIL SHOULD SIZZLE AT ONCE: The heated pan will cause the oil to sizzle immediately, but allow a minute or two (depending on the amount of oil) for it to become very hot.

BEFORE THE OIL BEGINS TO SMOKE: Since there is no way in which you can attach a thermometer to an ordinary skillet or wok, and since an electric frypan cannot provide the high heat necessary for the rapid searing of ingredients, you must watch this stage carefully. If you miscalculate and the oil begins to smoke (you will notice a thin bluish wisp rising), remove the pan from the heat at once and wait until the smoke disappears before adding ingredients. (Should the fat you are using happen to be lard, discard it at once. The chemical changes that occur in lard which has reached the smoking point cause it to become acrid and unsuitable.) If you have let this go too long and the oil has burned (it will turn dark and become odorous), discard it. Wash out the pan and start again. All this sounds complex. It really isn't. Heat the oil until it is very hot, but don't let it burn.

ADD INGREDIENTS: Vegetables, meat, fish and poultry are added and stir-fried and tossed according to the times specified in each recipe. Read the notes on stir-fry-toss cooking of meat, poultry and fish to learn in what order they must be combined in the pan.

ADD SEASONINGS: In "Classic" recipes, the seasonings (soy sauce, salt, sugar and liquor) are added immediately after the vegetables and meats have been cooked. If a thickener (cornstarch) is used, it is dissolved in stock or water and stirred into the mixture in the pan. The sauce is cooked for a minute or two to allow the cornstarch to develop (it will make the sauce thick and clear) and the dish is ready to serve at once. In "Dredged" recipes, the meat, fish or poultry ingredients are dredged before cooking with the cornstarch and then tossed with the seasonings and allowed to stand for a period of time. This has the effect of coating the meats as well as tenderizing them. The dredged ingredients are turned into the pan and stir-fried together. Stock or water is added, depending on the recipe (if leafy or moisture-producing vegetables are used, additional liquid is often unnecessary). The mixture is stirred until the sauce has thickened and the dish is ready. Both methods are shown in the drawings on pages 75, 76, 82 and 83.

POINTS TO REMEMBER IN STIR-FRY-TOSS COOKING OF VEGETABLES

The Chinese cook vegetables almost entirely by the stir-fry-toss technique. Occasionally root-type or dried vegetables are braised slightly for tenderness. Chinese cooks consider our methods of boiling or even steaming vegetables both insipid and wasteful of nutritive elements. Vegetables prepared in the Chinese manner, while cooked through, remain crisp on the exterior and vividly bright in color. This can only be accomplished by strictly observing the basic requirements of stir-fry-toss cooking: a utensil which conducts heat evenly; a small amount of very hot oil; rapid stirring for a short period of time; proper preparation of the ingredients. Stir-fry-toss vegetables are seldom cooked longer than 5 minutes, depending of course on the quantity and combination of vegetables being cooked.

Vegetables should always be thinly cut to achieve maximum cooking in the least time possible. Stalky or root vegetables should be sliced diagonally; round vegetables must be sliced straight or diced. Pulpy vegetables should be cut in wedges; melon-type vegetables can be sliced diagonally, rolling cut or diced. Leafy vegetables should be straight cut. Do not wash, peel or slice vegetables until just before using. Light, moisture, heat and air all tend to rob vegetables of their natural vitamins. After washing, drain and dry vegetables as thoroughly as possible before cooking. Gently wipe between kitchen or paper towels. Chinese chefs have special moisture-extracting presses for this purpose.

When adding vegetables to the sizzling oil, be very careful of hot fat splattering. Even the most carefully wiped vegetables have enough moisture left to cause the oil to splatter. Asbestos gloves and long tongs will protect your hands and provide distance between you and the pan.

Never add a large quantity all at once to the pan. When cooking leafy vegetables with stalks (Chinese chard, mustard greens or Chinese cabbage), always fry the stalk or heart sections for a minute or two before adding the leaf portions.

Do not forget to taste-test vegetables for doneness. In spite of the fact that cooking times are specified in the recipes, every stove has its own idiosyncrasies, every skillet its own degree of heating intensity.

To avoid needless waste, be sure to check pages 38–40 to determine how many vegetables to buy.

VEGETABLE CATEGORIES AND PRECOOKING INSTRUCTIONS

For the sake of simplifying the approach to vegetables, I have divided them into five arbitrary groups based on how they are prepared and treated in cooking. In the first category are Fresh Vegetables (those most commonly used), followed by Leafy, Melon-Type, Root-Type, Dried, and Salted, Preserved and Pickled Vegetables. The Fresh Vegetable group includes some Root- and Melon-Type vegetables as well as some frozen and canned vegetables. So please look upon this category as a group of commonly used vegetables. Also, it is true that both Leafy and Melon-Type vegetables produce moisture on cooking. My reason for separating them is because they are treated differently in cooking.

The designation White-Cooked means that the vegetables are stir-fry-tossed without the addition of soy sauce, alcohol or condiment sauces. The term Red-Cooked indicates that soy sauce is used to flavor and color the dish.

It is assumed that all vegetables will have been washed and dried before cutting Chinese style.

FRESH VEGETABLES

Unless otherwise indicated, vegetables are not parboiled. Frozen and canned vegetables are never parboiled and are always carefully wiped dry. They are cut the
same way as fresh vegetables. If no preparation out of the ordinary is needed, the
vegetable is listed without further comment.

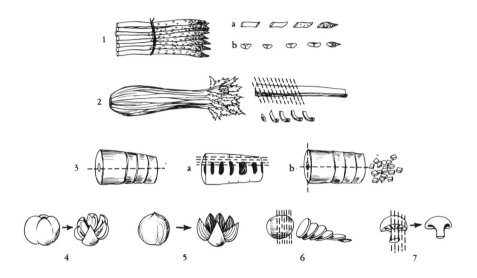

Cutting Vegetables
1. Asparagus—cut diagonally or in rolling cut (a. diagonal cut; b. rolling cut).   2. Celery—
cut diagonally.   3. Bamboo shoot—cut in half, then cut in long strips or quarter and dice
(a. cut in strips; b. quartered and diced).   4. Tomato—cut in six wedges.   5. Onion—
cut in six wedges.   6. Water chestnut—cut in thin rounds.   7. Mushrooms—cut in T slices.

ASPARAGUS: Snap off tough stems. Parboil 3 minutes. Slice diagonally into 1½-inch
lengths or rolling knife cut.
BAMBOO SHOOTS: Peel away outer covering. Parboil 10 minutes and drain. Cut into
thin strips, shreds or dice. If using canned bamboo shoots, drain and remove the
whitish residue, if any, on shoots. Cut into thin strips, shreds or dice. The canned
bamboo shoots are uniformly tender yet still crunchy and are more convenient to
use than the fresh.
BEANS, FAVA
BEANS, LIMA
BROCCOLI: Trim coarse outer stems. Split stalks lengthwise. Parboil 3 minutes.
Slice diagonally into 1½-inch lengths.

CARROTS: Cut in strips, shreds or dice. Parboil strips and shreds 2 minutes. Parboil dice 3 minutes.

CAULIFLOWER: Cut stalks into ½-inch diagonal slices. Break flowerets into small clusters. Parboil stalks 3 minutes, clusters 1 minute.

LEEKS: Wash very carefully. They are full of sand. Retain 1 to 1½ inches of green. Split in half lengthwise. Cut into ½- to 1½-inch diagonal slices.

LOTUS ROOT: Peel and cut into thin rounds.

PEAS, GREEN: Parboil 3 minutes.

PEPPERS, GREEN OR RED: Halve, core and remove seeds. Cut in thin strips or 1-inch squares or dice.

ONIONS: Cut small onions into wedges or thin rounds. Dice large onions. Onions are rarely served alone as a vegetable.

SCALLIONS: Retain 1 to 1½ inches of green. Cut into ¼-inch rounds or ½- to 1½-inch diagonal slices. Scallions are never served as a vegetable in and of themselves but are often part of a vegetable mixture.

SNOW PEAS: Break off tips and remove thread along length of pod. Leave whole.

STRING BEANS: Cut diagonally into 1½-inch lengths, shreds (julienne strips) or dice.

WATER CHESTNUTS: Peel and cut into thin rounds or dice.

LEAFY VEGETABLES

Do not parboil any of these. In almost every case (bean and pea sprouts and Chinese parsley are the exceptions) the stalk ends are separated from the leaf ends and cooked different lengths of time.

BEAN OR PEA SPROUTS: Wash; pick out green hulls, which cause bitterness. Drain well. For faster cooking, blanch by pouring boiling water over them. Drain well. Do not cut bean or pea sprouts. If canned bean sprouts are used, they must be well soaked in cold water before using.

CHINESE CABBAGE: Split in half lengthwise. Rinse and cut into ½- to 1½-inch diagonal slices.

CHINESE CHARD: Wash well, trim coarse root end. Discard yellow center flowerets. Cut into ½- to 1½-inch slices.

CHINESE PARSLEY or CORIANDER: Wash and drain; pick off leaves. Chop or leave whole. Chinese parsley is never cooked as a vegetable. It is used mostly to add zest to bland dishes or as a garnish.

MUSTARD CABBAGE: Wash and drain well. Cut curved stalks into ½- to 1½-inch pieces. Cut leaves into strips ½x1½ inches.

MUSTARD GREENS (YOUNG): Wash, drain and dry. Cut stalks in $1\frac{1}{2}$-inch lengths. Cut leaves into strips $\frac{1}{2}$x$1\frac{1}{2}$ inches.

PEA SPROUTS: See Bean Sprouts.

SPINACH: Soak in warm water to remove dirt. Rinse in cold water and drain very well. Scrape pink roots, trim threads but do not remove roots. Cut each cluster into 3 portions, separating the root ends from the leafy sections.

WATERCRESS: Soak to remove dirt. Rinse and drain well. Cut into $1\frac{1}{2}$- to 2-inch sections.

MELON-TYPE VEGETABLES

Do not parboil any of these except Bitter Melon.

BITTER MELON: Remove long stem. Do not pare. Cut in half and remove pulp and seeds. Cut into $\frac{1}{2}$-inch slices or strips. Parboil 3 minutes to minimize bitterness. Drain well.

CUCUMBERS: Pare older cucumbers but not young ones. Quarter lengthwise and remove seeds. Cut into $\frac{1}{4}$- to $\frac{1}{2}$-inch slices, $\frac{1}{2}$-inch dice or strips or shreds.

HAIRY OR FUZZY MELON: Peel. Quarter lengthwise. Cut into $\frac{1}{2}$-inch slices or dice or thin strips or shreds.

OKRA: Cut stem ends and slice each pod diagonally into 2 or 3 pieces.

TOMATOES: Use firm, small, just-ripe tomatoes. Do not peel. Cut each one into 6 wedges.

WINTER MELON: Remove seeds and peel. Cut into $\frac{1}{2}$-inch dice.

ZUCCHINI: Do not peel. Quarter lengthwise and remove seeds. Cut into $\frac{1}{4}$- to $\frac{1}{2}$-inch slices, $\frac{1}{2}$-inch dice or strips or shreds.

ROOT-TYPE VEGETABLES

Do not parboil any of these.

CHINESE EGGPLANT: Do not peel the narrow white or purple eggplants. Using a stainless steel knife, cut into $\frac{1}{2}$-inch diagonal slices or $\frac{1}{2}$-inch dice. For larger American eggplant, remove cap and quarter lengthwise. Peel. Cut into $\frac{1}{2}$-inch slices or $\frac{1}{2}$-inch dice.

CHINESE TURNIPS: Trim ends, scrape and quarter. Cut into thin strips or $\frac{1}{2}$-inch dice.

MUSHROOMS: Scrub. Trim tough bases of stems but do not separate from caps. Cut in $\frac{1}{8}$-inch T slices. A slender-bladed knife, like a French vegetable knife, is better than a Chinese cutting knife for cutting mushrooms.

DRIED VEGETABLES AND VEGETABLE DERIVATIVES

With the exception of mushrooms, which are sometimes cooked alone, dried vegetables are nearly always combined with garden vegetables—say, about half and half. Keep the expansion of dried vegetables in mind when substituting dried for fresh in any given recipe. (See White-Cooked, Leafy, Dried and Melon-Type Vegetables, pages 71–72, for some suggested combinations.) When dried vegetables are braised or cooked for a longer time than in the stir-fry-toss method, presoaking time is reduced.

BAMBOO-SHOOT TIPS: Soak in warm water at least 2 hours. Drain well. They will about double in size and change color from brown to creamy ivory. They have a somewhat more intense flavor than the canned or fresh bamboo shoots and are also used in combination with other vegetables. Since they are already cut into strips when packaged, you may suit yourself or the pattern of the other ingredients when cutting.

BEAN CURD SHEETS: Break off 2-inch pieces from the curved, boardlike sheets. Soak 2 hours in warm water. Drain well before using. Combine with vegetables of crunchy texture.

BEAN THREAD NOODLES: A dried derivative of mung beans, they require soaking. They are never stir-fried alone but are sometimes added to Stir-Fry-Toss dishes as a base. As such, they are first soaked 15 to 30 minutes in boiling water, well drained and snipped with scissors for easier handling. They are then simmered in a seasoned stock or liquid for a given time. Bean threads must not be overcooked or they lose their glossy look and satiny texture.

CHINESE CHESTNUTS: Rinse well and soak in warm water 1 hour. Using the same water in which the chestnuts have soaked, cook over low heat 1 hour. The chestnuts will expand slightly. Drain well before using. They should be tender, but not to the point of crumbling. They have a true chestnut flavor combined with a slight smokiness which is quite palatable. Dried chestnuts may be used alone or cooked with vegetables of contrasting texture.

CLOUD EARS: Rinse well in cold water several times. Cover with warm water and let stand at least 30 minutes. Rinse again under running cold water and rub between fingers to dislodge grit and twigs. Cloud ears will about triple in size after soaking. They will seem like very dark, shiny little ears. Cloud ears are used primarily for their texture in combination with other ingredients.

DRIED CHINESE MUSHROOMS (LARGE TO SMALL) and GRASS MUSHROOMS: Rinse well in cold water. Cover with warm water and let stand at least 10 minutes. They will expand to roughly double their volume. After soaking, the mushrooms will look velvety and feel fleshy. Drain, gently squeezing out the liquid with the fingers. Cut away hard centers. Leave whole if they are small mushrooms or grass mushrooms; cut into strips if they are large. Reserve the liquid to use in place of water or stock if it is called for in the recipe. Dried mushrooms are usually braised after being stir-fry-tossed to enable the vegetables to absorb the seasonings.

TIGER LILIES (also known as GOLDEN NEEDLES): Soak in warm water 30 minutes. The lilies will soften and expand somewhat—the difference is not appreciable. Drain well and snip each lily into 2 or 3 pieces. Tiger lilies have a mild flavor and delicate stalklike texture. They are used in combination with other vegetables.

WOOD EARS: Rinse well in cold water. Cover with warm water and soak at least 30 minutes. Rinse again under cold water and rub to dislodge grit and twigs. After soaking, wood ears will expand to about four times their original size. They become like large, floppy ears with a dark reddish-brown cast, slightly translucent. Like cloud ears, they are used in combination with other vegetables for their crunchy texture.

SALTED, PRESERVED OR PICKLED VEGETABLES

When cooking any of the vegetables in this category, watch for excessive saltiness. Soy sauce should be used minimally and salt omitted. Like dried vegetables, these preserved or pickled ingredients are seldom cooked alone but are used to spike up the flavors of other ingredients, mostly meat or fish. No recipes are given for them as individual vegetables.

BAMBOO SHOOTS PICKLED IN BRINE: Drain. If not already sliced, cut into strips or shreds. Rinse in cold water if you prefer less brininess.

MUSTARD GREENS PICKLED IN BRINE: Wash thoroughly in cold water. Soaking is unnecessary. Cut into shreds, strips, dice or chop.

PRESERVED OR SALTED TURNIPS: Untie small individual packages. Rinse well in cold water and soak in hot water at least 1 hour. Drain. Cut stalk portions into thin strips or shreds. Cut leaves into strips or chop.

SALTED OR PICKLED GREENS (Kohlrabi or other greens indigenous to China): Rinse and chop or slice. Some of these greens—Red in Snow, for example—are available canned in oil. Do not rinse or soak any oil-packed greens.

SPICED PICKLED MUSTARD GREENS: These are most often to be found in jars or cans, pickled with peppers and sometimes packed in condiment sauces. Do not wash. Cut into shreds, strips, dice or chop.

SPICED TURNIPS: Do not wash or soak. Cut into strips, shreds or fine dice. These are spiced with peppers and are extremely hot.

HOW TO PARBOIL VEGETABLES

Bring 1 cup of water to a boil in an uncovered 2-quart saucepan over medium heat. Add 4 cups vegetables prepared for cooking (sliced or diced, tough portions trimmed). Shake pan to distribute vegetables evenly. Allow water to come to a boil again; boil 3 minutes. Drain at once. Greens precooked in an open saucepan with just enough water to cover will be brilliant in color. To parboil vegetables with both stalky and tender or budlike portions (broccoli, asparagus, cauliflower), place whole or in stalks in a coffee percolator or the upper section of a double boiler containing enough boiling water to reach the top of the vegetable stalks. Parboil in an upright position 2 minutes, then tilt or bend vegetables so that the floweret or tender portions are submerged and boil 1 minute longer. Drain at once.

NOTE: Do not use baking soda for additional brightness of color. It tends to give certain vegetables a slippery quality and is not necessary.

WHITE-COOKED FRESH VEGETABLES
Parboiled

Cooking Time: 4 minutes

Utensils
Chinese cutting knife
2-quart enameled saucepan or upper portion of double boiler
12-inch skillet or wok
Tongs or chopsticks

Ingredients

4 cups vegetables, mixed or unmixed (asparagus, canned or fresh bamboo shoots, broccoli, carrots, cauliflower, peas)	$\frac{1}{2}$ teaspoon salt $\frac{1}{4}$ teaspoon sugar 2 tablespoons peanut oil or corn oil

Before Cooking
Prepare vegetables as directed on pages 53–54 and measure. Parboil in 1 cup of water 3 minutes. Drain at once and dry well. Do not parboil canned bamboo shoots. Combine salt and sugar. Set aside. Have oil ready to go.

Cooking Instructions

Turn heat under skillet or wok to high. (The heat remains high throughout the cooking.) When the pan is hot, add the oil. It should sizzle at once. Before the oil begins to smoke, add the vegetables. Stir-fry-toss rapidly 3 minutes. In the case of broccoli and cauliflower, add the clusters after 2 minutes of frying, then continue frying 1 minute longer. Sprinkle with salt and sugar and toss 1 minute to blend. Remove from heat. The colors of the vegetables should be brilliant, the texture crisp but cooked through and the surface barely glazed with oil. There should be no excess liquid in the pan.

SERVINGS: Enough for 2 to 3 as a single course with rice or for 4 to 6 in a full menu.

RED-COOKED FRESH VEGETABLES (PARBOILED): Decrease salt to ¼ teaspoon and add 1 tablespoon soy sauce with the seasonings.

WHITE-COOKED FRESH VEGETABLES

Not Parboiled

Cooking Time: 4 minutes

Utensils
Chinese cutting knife
12-inch skillet or wok
Tongs or chopsticks

Ingredients

4 cups sliced vegetables, mixed or unmixed (green beans, celery, bell peppers, lotus root, water chestnuts, whole snow peas)

½ teaspoon salt
¼ teaspoon sugar
2 tablespoons peanut oil or corn oil

Before Cooking

Slice vegetables as desired, selecting cut from listing of Fresh Vegetables (pages 53–54). Combine salt and sugar; set aside. Have oil ready to go.

Cooking Instructions

Turn heat under skillet or wok to high. (The heat remains high throughout the cooking.) When the pan is hot, add the oil. It should sizzle at once. Before the oil begins to smoke, add the vegetables. Stir-fry-toss rapidly 3 minutes. Sprinkle with salt and sugar. Toss 1 minute to blend. Remove from heat. The vegetables should be crunchy yet cooked through, the colors still vivid. If you prefer slightly softer vegetables with more liquid, cover pan during the last 2 minutes of cooking, lifting the cover to stir and toss at 30-second intervals to prevent scorching.

SERVINGS: Enough for 2 to 3 as a single course with rice or for 4 to 6 in a full menu.

RED-COOKED FRESH VEGETABLES (NOT PARBOILED): Decrease salt to ¼ teaspoon and add 1 tablespoon soy sauce with the seasonings.

WHITE-COOKED FRESH VEGETABLES

Bean Variety

Cooking Time: 5½ to 6½ minutes

Utensils
Chinese cutting knife
Bowls for ingredients
12-inch skillet or wok—with cover
Tongs or chopsticks

Ingredients

2	scallions, each with 1½ inches of green, cut in ¼-inch rounds	1½ teaspoon sugar
4	cups shelled lima or fava beans	⅓ cup water
½	teaspoon salt	2½ tablespoons peanut oil or corn oil

Before Cooking

Prepare the vegetables. Combine salt and sugar. Measure water. Have oil ready.

Cooking Instructions

Turn heat under skillet or wok to high. When the pan is hot, add the oil. It should sizzle at once. Before the oil begins to smoke, add the scallions. Stir-fry-toss no more than 30 seconds. Do not allow the scallions to burn. Add the beans and stir-fry-toss with the scallions 3 minutes. Add salt and sugar; blend well 1 minute. Add water. Reduce heat to medium. Cover the pan and cook 2 to 3 minutes, stirring at 30-second intervals. Remove from heat. The beans should be tender and slightly darkened in color. The combination of scallions with the beans and sugar produces a subtle flavor. These are popular served either hot or cold.

SERVINGS: Enough for 2 to 3 as a single course with rice or for 4 to 6 in a full menu.

RED-COOKED FRESH VEGETABLES (BEAN VARIETY): Decrease salt to ¼ teaspoon and add 1 tablespoon soy sauce with the seasonings.

WHITE-COOKED LEAFY VEGETABLES
Stalk Variety

Cooking Time: 4 to 7 minutes

Utensils
Chinese cutting knife
2 soup plates
Small bowl for seasonings
12-inch skillet or wok
Tongs or chopsticks

Ingredients

1	slice ginger root (2x1x⅛ inch)	½	teaspoon salt
4	cups sliced Chinese cabbage, Chinese chard, mustard cabbage or mustard greens	1	teaspoon sugar
		2	tablespoons peanut oil or corn oil

Before Cooking

Prepare ginger root. Slice vegetables, following directions for Leafy Vegetables (pages 54–55). After cutting, separate the stalk sections from the leaf sections into 2 soup plates. Combine salt and sugar; set aside. Have oil ready to go.

Cooking Instructions

Turn heat under skillet or wok to high. (The heat remains high throughout the cooking.) When the pan is hot, add the oil. It should sizzle at once. Before the oil begins to smoke, add the ginger root and stir-fry 1 minute. Add the stalk sections of the vegetables; stir-fry-toss 2 minutes. Add the salt and sugar and toss with vegetables quickly to blend. Add the leaf sections and stir-fry-toss 1 minute. Remove from heat. Remove ginger slice. The stalk portions should be very crisp and the leaf sections just wilted. The natural colors of the vegetables will be retained. There should not be much liquid in the pan. If you prefer softer vegetables with more pan juices, cover the pan after frying the stalk portions and fry 2 minutes longer, stirring every 30 seconds. Remove cover; add leaf sections and continue stirring 1 minute.

SERVINGS: Enough for 2 as a single course with rice or for 4 in a full menu.

RED-COOKED LEAFY VEGETABLES (STALK VARIETY): Decrease salt to $\frac{1}{4}$ teaspoon and add 1 tablespoon soy sauce with the seasonings.

WHITE-COOKED LEAFY VEGETABLES

Bunchy Variety

Cooking Time: 4 minutes

Utensils
Chinese cutting knife
Strainer to blanch sprouts
2 soup plates
Small bowl for seasonings
12-inch skillet or wok

Ingredients

2	cloves garlic, peeled and split (for spinach or watercress only)	$\frac{1}{2}$	teaspoon salt
		1	teaspoon sugar
4	cups cut spinach, watercress, bean sprouts or pea sprouts	2	tablespoons peanut oil or corn oil

Before Cooking

Prepare garlic; set aside. Prepare spinach or watercress or blanch sprouts following directions for Leafy Vegetables (pages 54–55). Separate the root ends of spinach and cress from the leafy clusters into 2 soup plates. Combine salt and sugar; set aside. Have oil ready to go.

Cooking Instructions

Turn heat under skillet or wok to high. (The heat remains high throughout the cooking.) When the pan is hot, add the oil. It should sizzle at once. Before the oil begins to smoke, add the garlic and stir-fry 1 minute. Add the stalk and root sections of the spinach or cress or add all of the sprouts. Add the salt and sugar. If using spinach or cress, stir-fry the stalk and root sections 3 minutes, then add the leaf sections and stir-fry-toss 1 minute. If using sprouts, stir-fry-toss 4 minutes. Remove from heat. Remove garlic. The spinach or cress should be crisp in the root and stalk sections and slightly limp in the leaf portions. The colors should be bright. The bean or pea sprouts should retain their crunchiness and have an "alive" color to them. Overcooked sprouts have a grayish cast and are watery.

SERVINGS: Enough for 2 as a single course with rice or for 4 in a full menu.

NOTE: Garlic, salt and sugar combined with spinach create a harmonious blend of flavors. Garlic may be omitted when using watercress or sprouts.

RED-COOKED LEAFY VEGETABLES (BUNCHY VARIETY): Decrease salt to $\frac{1}{4}$ teaspoon and add 1 tablespoon soy sauce with the seasonings.

WHITE-COOKED MELON-TYPE VEGETABLES

Cooking Time: 6 to 8 minutes

Utensils
Chinese cutting knife
Small bowl for seasonings
12-inch skillet or wok
Wooden spoon

Ingredients

4	cups sliced or diced cucumbers, zucchini, hairy melon, bitter melon, winter melon or okra	½	teaspoon salt
		½	teaspoon sugar
		2	tablespoons peanut oil or corn oil

Before Cooking
Prepare vegetables as directed on page 55. If using bitter melon, parboil. Combine salt and sugar; set aside. Have oil ready to go.

Cooking Instructions
Turn heat under skillet or wok to high. When the pan is hot, add the oil. It should sizzle at once. Before the oil begins to smoke, add the vegetables and stir-fry-toss rapidly 3 minutes. Add salt and sugar. Reduce heat to medium and stir-fry gently with the wooden spoon 3 to 5 minutes longer. The cucumbers and melons should be translucent, the okra quite tender. There will be some pan juices.

SERVINGS: Enough for 2 as a single course with rice or for 4 in a full menu.

NOTE: Tomatoes are rarely stir-fry-tossed alone. If you choose to cook them this way, substitute 4 cups of unpeeled tomato wedges for the other vegetables. Follow the recipe but cut the final cooking time to 3 minutes. Be gentle with the stirring to avoid breaking the tomato wedges.

RED-COOKED MELON-TYPE VEGETABLES: Decrease salt to ¼ teaspoon and add 1 tablespoon soy sauce with the seasonings.

WHITE-COOKED FRESH MUSHROOMS

Cooking Time: 4 to 5 minutes

Utensils
Slender-bladed knife for cutting mushrooms
Small bowl for seasonings
12-inch skillet or wok
Tongs or chopsticks

Ingredients

4   cups sliced mushrooms, ⅛- to   ⅛   teaspoon five-spice seasoning (op-
     ¼-inch thick   tional)
½   teaspoon salt   2½   tablespoons peanut oil or corn oil
¾   teaspoon sugar

Before Cooking

Prepare mushrooms. Combine salt, sugar and five-spice seasoning; set aside. Have
oil ready to go.

Cooking Instructions

Turn heat under skillet or wok to high. When the pan is hot, add the oil. It
should sizzle at once. Before the oil begins to smoke, add the mushroom slices and
stir-fry-toss 2 minutes. Add salt, sugar and five-spice seasoning. Reduce heat to medium and cook 2 to 3 minutes longer. The mushrooms should have lost any
wooden look and be just translucent.

SERVINGS: Enough for 2 to 3 as a single course with rice or for 4 to 6 in a full
menu.

RED-COOKED MUSHROOMS: Decrease salt to ¼ teaspoon and add 1 tablespoon soy
sauce with the seasonings.

WHITE-COOKED CHINESE TURNIPS

Cooking Time: 6 minutes

Utensils

Chinese cutting knife
Small bowl for seasonings
12-inch skillet or wok
Tongs or chopsticks

Ingredients

4   cups cut Chinese turnips, in thin   ¾   teaspoon sugar
     strips or ½-inch dice   2½   tablespoons peanut oil or corn oil
½   teaspoon salt

Before Cooking
Prepare turnips. Combine salt and sugar; set aside. Have oil ready to go.

Cooking Instructions
Turn heat under skillet or wok to high. When the pan is hot, add the oil. It should sizzle at once. Before the oil begins to smoke, add the turnips and stir-fry-toss 3 minutes. Add salt and sugar. Reduce heat to medium and stir-fry-toss the turnips 3 minutes longer. They should be crisp but tender and cooked through.

SERVINGS: Enough for 2 to 3 as a single course with rice or for 4 to 6 in a full menu.

RED-COOKED CHINESE TURNIPS: Decrease salt to $\frac{1}{4}$ teaspoon and add 1 tablespoon soy sauce with the seasonings.

WHITE-COOKED EGGPLANT

Cooking Time: 5 minutes

Utensils
Stainless steel cutting knife
Small bowl for seasonings
12-inch enameled or stainless-steel skillet
   or wok—with cover
Tongs or chopsticks

Ingredients

2	cloves garlic, minced	$\frac{1}{2}$	teaspoon salt
4	cups unpeeled Chinese eggplant or peeled ordinary eggplant in $\frac{1}{2}$-inch diagonal slices or dice	$\frac{1}{2}$	teaspoon sugar
		3	tablespoons peanut oil or corn oil

Before Cooking
Prepare garlic and eggplant. Combine salt and sugar; set aside. Have oil ready to go.

Cooking Instructions
Turn heat to high under skillet or wok. When the pan is hot, add the oil. It should sizzle at once. Before the oil begins to smoke, add the minced garlic. Stir

once quickly and add the eggplant. Stir-fry-toss 2 minutes. Add salt and sugar. Reduce heat to medium. Cover and cook 3 minutes, stirring at 1-minute intervals. The eggplant should be translucent but not pulpy.

SERVINGS: Enough for 2 as a single course with rice or for 4 in a full menu.

NOTE: Enameled or stainless utensils are best for cooking eggplant. It tends to discolor when it comes into contact with iron.

RED-COOKED EGGPLANT: Decrease salt to $\frac{1}{8}$ teaspoon and add $1\frac{1}{2}$ tablespoons soy sauce with the seasonings.

DRIED CHINESE MUSHROOMS

Cooking Time: 20 to 21 minutes

Utensils
Bowl for soaking mushrooms
Small bowl for seasonings
12-inch skillet or wok—with cover
Tongs or chopsticks

Ingredients

2	cups small dried Chinese or grass mushrooms	$\frac{1}{2}$	cup chicken stock
$2\frac{1}{2}$	tablespoons soy sauce	1	tablespoon cornstarch
1	tablespoon brown sugar	1	cup mushroom liquid
$\frac{1}{4}$	teaspoon salt	$\frac{1}{4}$	teaspoon sesame oil (optional)
$\frac{1}{4}$	teaspoon five-spice seasoning	2	tablespoons peanut oil or corn oil

Before Cooking
Rinse the dried mushrooms in cold water. Place in a bowl and add just enough warm water to cover. Let stand 15 minutes to soften. Drain and squeeze with fingers to remove excess moisture. Cut away the hard centers but leave the mushrooms whole. Reserve 1 cup of the liquid in which the mushrooms have soaked. Combine the soy sauce, brown sugar, salt and five-spice seasoning in the small bowl. Measure the chicken stock and set aside. Combine the cornstarch and mushroom liquid. Have both oils ready to go.

Cooking Instructions

Turn heat under skillet or wok to high. When the pan is hot, add the oil. It should sizzle at once. Before the oil begins to smoke, add the mushrooms and stir-fry-toss 3 minutes. Add the seasoning mixture, stir to blend. Add the chicken stock. Reduce heat to medium-low. Cover pan and braise 15 minutes. Give the cornstarch-mushroom liquid a quick stir and add to mushrooms in pan. Turn heat up to medium-high and stir uncovered 2 to 3 minutes or until the sauce is thick and clear. Sprinkle with sesame oil. The mushrooms should still be firm but tender and juicy. The sauce will be fragrant and a clear velvety brown in color.

SERVINGS: Enough for 3 to 4 as a single course with rice or for 6 to 8 in a full menu.

DRIED CHINESE MUSHROOMS AND OYSTER SAUCE: Follow the preceding recipe for Dried Chinese Mushrooms but decrease soy sauce to 2 tablespoons and omit the salt. After braising the mushrooms, stir in 1½ tablespoons oyster sauce and blend with the mushrooms and seasonings. Add the cornstarch dissolved in mushroom liquid and cook 2 to 3 minutes or until the sauce has thickened. Oyster sauce and dried mushrooms are exceptionally harmonious in combination.

DRIED CHINESE MUSHROOMS, BAMBOO-SHOOT TIPS AND CHESTNUTS WITH BEAN THREAD NOODLES

Mixed Dried Vegetables and Vegetable Derivatives

Cooking Time: 10½ minutes

Utensils
5 bowls for soaking ingredients
Chinese cutting knife
Small bowl for seasonings
12-inch skillet or wok
Tongs or chopsticks
Pancake turner

Ingredients
½ cup dried chestnuts
½ cup dried bamboo-shoot tips

1 cup small dried Chinese or grass mushrooms

1	tablespoon wood ears	$\frac{1}{4}$	teaspoon salt
1	package ($\frac{1}{4}$ pound) bean thread noodles	$\frac{1}{2}$	teaspoon brown sugar
		1	cup chicken stock
1	teaspoon minced ginger root	1	teaspoon soy sauce
1	tablespoon soy sauce	2	tablespoons peanut oil or corn oil

Before Cooking

Two hours before starting to cook, soak chestnuts and bamboo-shoot tips separately in warm water. After soaking the chestnuts 1 hour, drain and boil gently in 1 cup water 1 hour. Drain and set aside. Drain bamboo-shoot tips after 2 hours. Rinse dried mushrooms and wood ears. Soak separately in warm water 30 minutes. Drain well. Cover the bean threads with boiling water and soak 30 minutes. Drain well. Mince the ginger root and set aside. Combine the 1 tablespoon soy sauce with the salt and brown sugar; set aside. Combine the chicken stock with the 1 teaspoon soy sauce. Have oil ready to go.

Cooking Instructions

Turn heat under skillet or wok to high. When the pan is hot, add the oil. It should sizzle at once. Before the oil begins to smoke, add the minced ginger and stir-fry 30 seconds. Add the bamboo-shoot tips; stir-fry-toss 2 minutes. Add the chestnuts; stir-fry-toss 1 minute. Add mushrooms and wood ears and stir-fry together 2 minutes. Add the seasonings and stir to blend. Remove the vegetables to a heated plate with the pancake turner. Reduce heat to medium. Add the bean threads to the pan. Pour in the seasoned stock and simmer 5 minutes. Remove from heat. Put the bean threads in a heated serving bowl and top with the mixed vegetables. This dish offers an intriguing combination of textures: crisp bamboo-shoot tips, tender chestnuts, crunchy wood ears, velvety mushrooms and resilient bean threads.

SERVINGS: Enough for 3 as a single course with rice or for 6 in a full menu.

COMBINED VEGETABLES

Although the vegetables have been presented in separate categories up to this point, they are, in fact, most often combined in recipes. Once you have mastered the preparation and cooking of each group of vegetables, it is then only a matter of observing which vegetables must be parboiled, which need to be soaked, which require more oil or longer cooking in order to produce any desired mixture of ingredients. The possible combinations are infinite. The following are just a couple of examples.

WHITE-COOKED ASPARAGUS, BAMBOO SHOOTS, CHINESE TURNIPS AND CHINESE CHARD

Fresh, Root-Type and Leafy Vegetables

Cooking Time: 5 minutes

Utensils
Chinese cutting knife
Bowls for vegetables and seasoning
12-inch skillet or wok
Tongs or chopsticks

Ingredients

1	cup parboiled sliced asparagus (1½-inch pieces)	1	cup sliced Chinese chard (1½-inch pieces)
1	cup shredded bamboo shoots, canned or fresh (parboil fresh)	½	teaspoon salt
1	cup shredded Chinese turnips	¾	teaspoon sugar
		2½	tablespoons peanut oil or corn oil

Before Cooking
Prepare vegetables. Separate the stalk sections of the chard from the leaf sections in 2 bowls. Combine the salt and sugar. Have oil ready to go.

Cooking Instructions
Turn heat under skillet or wok to high. (The heat remains high throughout the cooking.) When the pan is hot, add the oil. It should sizzle at once. Before the oil begins to smoke, add the asparagus and stir-fry-toss 1 minute. Add the bamboo shoots and turnips; stir-fry-toss 1 minute. Add the stalk sections of chard and the salt and sugar. Blend well with the other vegetables and stir-fry-toss 2 minutes. Add the leaf sections of chard and stir-fry 1 minute. Remove from heat. In this dish, each vegetable has been prepared and cooked according to its individual group specifications. The asparagus should be crisp but tender, and the bamboo shoots, turnips and chard stalks should still be crunchy. The leaf portions will be just limp, still brilliant in color.

SERVINGS: Enough for 2 as a single course with rice or for 4 in a full menu.

SUBSTITUTIONS:
    For the asparagus and bamboo shoots, use broccoli, cauliflower or water chestnuts.

For the turnips, use fresh mushrooms or eggplant.

For the chard, use mustard greens or Chinese cabbage.

RED-COOKED ASPARAGUS, BAMBOO SHOOTS, CHINESE TURNIPS AND CHINESE CHARD: Decrease salt to $\frac{1}{4}$ teaspoon and add 1 tablespoon soy sauce before adding the leaf portions of the chard to the pan.

WHITE-COOKED FRESH, LEAFY, DRIED AND MELON-TYPE VEGETABLES

Cooking Time: 5 to 6 minutes

Utensils
Chinese cutting knife
Small bowls for vegetables and seasoning
Strainer
12-inch skillet or wok
Tongs or chopsticks

Ingredients

$\frac{1}{3}$ cup sliced scallions ($\frac{1}{4}$-inch rounds)	1 tablespoon wood ears
	$\frac{1}{2}$ cup hairy melon strips
$\frac{1}{3}$ cup sliced celery ($\frac{1}{2}$-inch diagonal)	1 cup bean sprouts or pea sprouts
	$\frac{1}{2}$ teaspoon salt
$\frac{1}{2}$ cup snow peas	$\frac{3}{4}$ teaspoon sugar
$\frac{1}{3}$ cup sliced water chestnuts	2 tablespoons peanut oil or corn oil
$\frac{1}{3}$ cup tiger lilies	

Before Cooking
Prepare the scallions, celery, snow peas and water chestnuts. Soak tiger lilies in warm water 15 minutes. Drain and snip each tiger lily into 2 pieces. Rinse wood ears and soak in warm water 15 minutes; drain and set aside. Peel hairy melon and cut into thin strips. Pick over bean or pea sprouts and remove pale green hoods. Put in a strainer and blanch by pouring boiling water over them. Drain well. Combine salt and sugar; set aside. Have oil ready to go.

Cooking Instructions

Turn heat under skillet or wok to high. (The heat remains high throughout the cooking.) When the pan is hot, add the oil. It should sizzle at once. Before the oil begins to smoke, add the scallions and stir-fry 30 seconds. Add the celery; stir-fry-toss 30 seconds. Add the snow peas and water chestnuts and stir-fry-toss 1 minute. Add the tiger lilies and wood ears; stir 1 minute. Add the hairy melon slices, sprinkle with salt and sugar and stir-fry-toss 1 minute. Add the sprouts. Toss all the vegetables together 1 to 2 minutes. Remove from heat. Though four categories of vegetables are combined in this recipe, the final texture is one of crispness.

SERVINGS: Enough for 2 as a single course with rice or for 4 in a full menu.

SUBSTITUTIONS:

For the scallions, celery, snow peas and water chestnuts, use leeks, green peppers, string beans and lotus roots.

For the tiger lilies and wood ears, use dried mushrooms or cloud ears.

For the hairy melon, use cucumber, bitter melon or tomato wedges.

For the sprouts, use spinach or watercress.

RED-COOKED FRESH, LEAFY, DRIED AND MELON-TYPE VEGETABLES: Decrease salt to $\frac{1}{4}$ teaspoon and add 1 tablespoon soy sauce with the seasonings.

BEAN CURD

This unusual product of the soy bean is bland tasting and resembles cream cheese in texture. It is compatible with nearly every ingredient and can be incorporated in practically every technique. It is best treated as a category by itself. Because it is extremely fragile, bean curd must never be tossed. In fact, it almost should not be stirred but gently fried by shaking the pan and basting with oil. You will notice that the cooking instructions here differ slightly.

BEAN CURD

Cooking Time: 3 to 4½ minutes

Utensils
Chinese cutting knife
Small bowl for seasonings
12-inch skillet or wok
Spoon for basting
Small spatula

Ingredients

5	squares bean curd (1 pound)	¼	teaspoon sugar
1	scallion with 1½ inches of green, cut in ¼-inch rounds	1½	tablespoons soy sauce
½	teaspoon salt	3	tablespoons peanut oil or corn oil

Before Cooking
Cut each 3-inch square of bean curd into 9 pieces; set aside. Prepare scallion. Combine the salt, sugar and soy sauce; set aside. Have oil ready to go.

Cooking Instructions
Turn heat under skillet or wok to medium. (The heat remains at medium throughout the cooking.) When the pan is hot, add the oil. The oil should sizzle at once. Before the oil begins to smoke, add the diced bean curd. Let the cubes brown on one side, then turn them over with the small spatula and brown on the other, a total of 3 to 4 minutes. Shake the pan during the frying to baste the uppermost sides. Sprinkle with the soy-salt-sugar mixture and cook 30 seconds longer. Top with the scallion rounds and serve.

NOTE: Some of the bean curd dice will undoubtedly fall apart in the cooking no matter how careful you are. Don't worry about it. The main point is to avoid mashing them all together.

BEAN CURD WITH DICED HAM
Cut 2 ounces Virginia ham into ½-inch dice. Follow the recipe for Bean Curd but before the oil begins to smoke, add the ham and toss 2 minutes. Remove ham to a warm plate. Fry bean curd and return ham to pan. Continue as directed.

BEAN CURD WITH SHRIMP AND GREEN PEAS
Cut 6 raw small shrimp in half and measure ⅓ cup shelled green peas, parboiled 3 minutes. Follow the recipe for Bean Curd but before the oil begins to smoke, add the peas and stir-fry 1 minute. Add the shrimp and toss together 2 minutes. Remove to a warm plate. Fry bean curd and return peas and shrimp to the pan. Continue as directed.

BEAN CURD WITH SALTED MUSTARD GREENS
Rinse a stalk of mustard green pickled in brine in cold water. Chop coarsely and measure ½ cup. Follow the recipe for Bean Curd but before the oil begins to smoke, add the greens and stir-fry-toss 2 minutes. Remove to a warm plate. Fry bean curd and return the mustard greens to the pan. Add soy sauce and sugar but omit salt. Cook a full minute. Top with scallion rounds and serve.

BEAN CURD WITH DRIED CHINESE MUSHROOMS
Prepare Dried Chinese Mushrooms as directed in the recipe on page 67. In a separate skillet or wok, follow the recipe for Bean Curd but omit seasonings. Add the stir-fried Bean Curd to the stir-fried Dried Chinese Mushrooms, stirring gently to mix without mashing.

BEAN CURD WITH OYSTER SAUCE
Follow any of the preceding recipes for Bean Curd but omit the salt. Add 1 tablespoon oyster sauce with the soy sauce and sugar.

STIR-FRY-TOSS VEGETABLES WITH SAUCES

STIR-FRY-TOSS VEGETABLES WITH THICKENED SAUCE
Follow any recipe for white- or red-cooked vegetables but first mix 1½ teaspoons cornstarch with ½ cup liquid (chicken stock, water or the liquid in which the vegetables were parboiled). Immediately after adding the seasonings, stir in the cornstarch-liquid mixture and cook 1 to 2 minutes, until the sauce becomes thick and clear. Do not use a thickener with starchy vegetables, such as lima or fava beans.

STIR-FRY-TOSS VEGETABLES WITH OYSTER SAUCE

Follow any recipe for white- or red-cooked vegetables. When the seasonings are added, stir in 2 tablespoons oyster sauce and blend well. Cook 1 minute and remove from heat. This is especially good with asparagus, turnips or dried mushrooms.

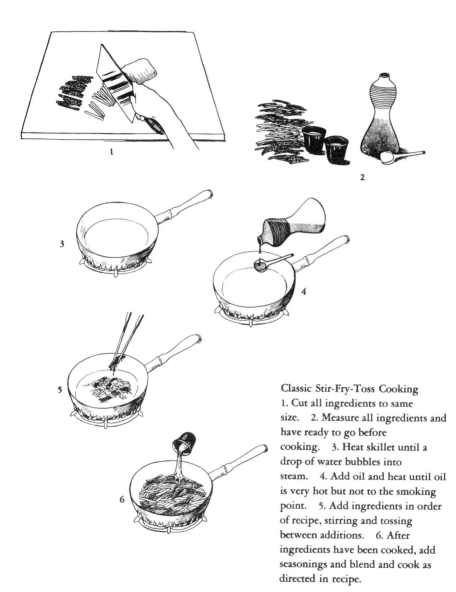

Classic Stir-Fry-Toss Cooking
1. Cut all ingredients to same size.   2. Measure all ingredients and have ready to go before cooking.   3. Heat skillet until a drop of water bubbles into steam.   4. Add oil and heat until oil is very hot but not to the smoking point.   5. Add ingredients in order of recipe, stirring and tossing between additions.   6. After ingredients have been cooked, add seasonings and blend and cook as directed in recipe.

Classic Stir-Fry-Toss Cooking (cont.)
7. If dish is to be served with a thickened sauce, have cornstarch and water ready to go.   8. Stir thickener quickly before adding and stir ingredients while adding.   9. Stir rapidly until sauce thickens. Remove from fire.

STIR-FRY-TOSS VEGETABLES WITH BEAN CURD CHEESE SAUCE
Blend 2 cakes of wined bean curd cheese (*Foo Yu*) with ¼ teaspoon sugar and 2 teaspoons liquid from the bean curd cheese bottle. Mash into a smooth, creamy paste. Follow any recipe for white-cooked vegetables. After adding the salt and sugar, stir in the bean cheese paste. Blend well and serve. This is delicious over crisp cooked greens of any category.

STIR-FRY-TOSS VEGETABLES WITH BROWN BEAN SAUCE
Follow any recipe for white-cooked vegetables but omit the salt. When the sugar is added, stir 1 tablespoon brown bean sauce into the vegetables and blend well. Let cook 1 minute and remove from heat. Crisp vegetables, such as bamboo shoots, water chestnuts and lotus root, are excellent with this sauce.

STIR-FRY-TOSS VEGETABLES WITH HOISIN SAUCE

Follow any recipe for white-cooked vegetables. When the seasonings are added, stir in 1 tablespoon Hoisin sauce. Blend well and cook 1 minute. Remove from heat. This is best with vegetables of the melon family, such as cucumbers, zucchini and hairy melon.

POINTS TO REMEMBER IN STIR-FRY-TOSS COOKING OF MEAT

In recipes that combine meat with vegetables, always stir-fry the meat first. Remove the cooked meat to a warm plate and then fry the vegetables in the fat remaining in the pan, adding more oil if needed. It is not necessary to wash the pan out after frying the meat, although some cooks prefer to do so in order to preserve the bright colors of the vegetables. This step requires the addition of more oil and the flavor of the drippings would then go to waste. Never fry the meat after the vegetables in the same pan. Moisture released from the cooked vegetables causes toughness in the meat. Since the stir-fry-toss recipes call for 1 pound of meat, it is safe to fry it all at once without fear of the meat being steamed by overcrowding in the pan. If you are going to increase the meat portions of these recipes, be sure to fry in more than one lot, thus insuring evenly browned rather than steamed and pallid meat.

In the preliminary frying, beef strips or dice should be about one-half to three-quarters done, with raw portions of the meat still showing. Fry only 2 to 3 minutes maximum so that after the vegetables have been cooked and the meat is returned to the pan it can cook with the seasonings for another minute or so without toughening. Never overcook beef—it will toughen.

It is proper at this point to caution you about overcooking anything in this technique. The natural integrity of all ingredients and flavors must be retained. Overcooked vegetables will be soggy and threadlike; overcooked meat, fish or poultry will be dry or tough and tasteless.

Pork strips, shreds or dice, must be cooked slightly longer than beef, about 5 minutes in all. No traces of pink should show after the preliminary frying. Pork remains tender regardless of cooking time, but should not be overcooked to the point of dryness.

The same rules for pork apply to lamb slices or shreds.

Liver should be fried until no blood spots appear and kidneys, cut in thin comb-like slices, must be cooked only until crisply tender.

Large pieces of meat are never stir-fried.

Suitable cuts of meat for the stir-fry-toss technique are:

BEEF: Flank steak, sirloin or filet of beef, sliced diagonally or in strips or shreds. Filet of beef or top round steak, diced. Minced or ground beef.

PORK: Butt, lean shoulder or loin, boned and trimmed of fat and bone and cut the same as beef. Minced or ground pork.

LAMB: Shoulder or leg, boned and trimmed of fat. Cut the same as beef. Minced or ground lamb.

CLASSIC SLICED PORK

Cooking Time: 4 minutes

Utensils
Chinese cutting knife
Small bowl for seasonings
Long tongs or chopsticks for tossing
12-inch skillet or wok

Ingredients

1	pound pork shoulder, butt or loin, trimmed and cut in thin diagonal slices	2	teaspoons sherry
		½	teaspoon salt
		½	teaspoon sugar
1½	tablespoons soy sauce	2	tablespoons peanut oil or corn oil

Before Cooking
Prepare pork. Combine soy sauce, sherry, salt and sugar in the small bowl. Have oil ready to go.

Cooking Instructions
Turn heat under skillet or wok to high. (The heat remains high throughout the cooking.) When the pan is hot, add the oil. It should sizzle at once. Before the oil begins to smoke, add the pork slices and stir-fry-toss 3 minutes. The pork should begin to lose its pinkness. Add the soy-sherry-salt-sugar mixture. Toss rapidly 1 minute. Remove from heat. The meat should be just cooked, with no pinkness. The general color of the dish should be a dark, rich brown. The sauce should be scant and clear.

SERVINGS: Enough for 2 as a single course with rice or for 4 to 6 in a full menu.

CLASSIC SLICED BEEF: Substitute 1 pound beef sirloin or filet for the pork. Stir-fry the beef slices only 2 minutes (the meat should be partially cooked with raw portions still showing) before adding the seasonings. The cooked beef should be slightly rare but not raw.

NOTE: This is the Classic manner for preparing stir-fried sliced pork or beef—without thickening agents, spices, stock or other embellishments.

SLICED PORK WITH FRESH MUSHROOMS

Cooking Time: 8 to 10 minutes

Utensils
Chinese cutting knife
Small dish for seasonings
12-inch skillet or wok
Slotted spatula
Soup plate

Ingredients

1	pound pork shoulder, butt or loin, trimmed and cut in diagonal slices	½	teaspoon salt
		½	teaspoon brown sugar
		1	tablespoon soy sauce
2	scallions, chopped	1	teaspoon sherry
½	pound medium mushrooms, cut in ⅛-inch T slices	2	tablespoons peanut oil or corn oil
		1	tablespoon peanut oil or corn oil

Before Cooking
Prepare pork and vegetables. Combine salt, brown sugar, soy sauce and sherry in the small dish. Have both portions of oil ready to go.

Cooking Instructions
Turn heat under skillet or wok to high. (The heat remains high throughout the cooking.) When the pan is hot, add the 2 tablespoons oil. It should sizzle at once. Before the oil begins to smoke, add the pork slices and stir-fry-toss 3 minutes. Remove with slotted spatula to the soup plate. Add the 1 tablespoon oil to the pan. When the oil is hot, add the chopped scallions. Toss-fry 30 seconds. Add the mushroom slices; stir-fry-toss 3 minutes or until the mushrooms lose their wooden

look and begin to become tender. Return the pork to the scallions and mushrooms in the pan. Stir just to mix. Add the salt-sugar-soy-sherry mixture. Stir gently 2 minutes. The pork slices should be just cooked, the mushrooms tender but not rubbery and overcooked. The dish should be a medium brown color with not much sauce. If you prefer more liquid, cover pan the last 2 minutes, stirring at 30-second intervals.

SERVINGS: Enough for 3 as a single course with rice or for 6 in a full menu.

SLICED BEEF WITH FRESH MUSHROOMS: Substitute 1 pound beef sirloin or filet for the pork. Stir-fry the beef slices only 2 minutes. Continue as directed.

SLICED PORK WITH BEAN THREAD NOODLES

Cooking Time: 3 minutes to stir-fry-toss
                5 minutes to simmer

Utensils
4-quart casserole or pot
Small bowls for soaking mushrooms and
    shrimp
Chinese cutting knife
Large wire strainer or sieve for draining
    bean threads
Small wire strainer for draining mush-
    rooms
Scissors
12-inch skillet or wok
Slotted spatula

Ingredients

$\frac{1}{4}$	pound bean thread noodles	1	teaspoon soy sauce
6	medium dried Chinese mush-rooms	2	cups chicken stock
		$\frac{1}{2}$	teaspoon salt
1	tablespoon dried Chinese shrimp (optional)	$\frac{1}{2}$	teaspoon brown sugar
		1	tablespoon soy sauce
1	pound pork shoulder, butt or loin, trimmed and cut in diagonal slices	$\frac{1}{2}$	teaspoon sesame oil
		2	tablespoons peanut oil or corn oil

Before Cooking

Place bean threads in the casserole or pot. Add enough boiling water to cover and let stand 15 minutes. Rinse dried mushrooms and shrimp in cold water. Place in separate small bowls and cover with warm water. Let stand 15 minutes to soften. Prepare pork. Drain bean threads thoroughly and snip with scissors into 4-inch lengths. Drain mushrooms and shrimp. Cut hard center out of each mushroom, then cut each mushroom into thin strips. Measure the remaining ingredients and set aside separately.

Cooking Instructions

Turn heat under skillet or wok to high. When the pan is hot, add the peanut oil. It should sizzle at once. Before the oil begins to smoke, add the pork slices and stir-fry-toss 3 minutes. Add the 1 teaspoon soy sauce. Stir to blend and remove from pan with slotted spatula. Pour the chicken stock into the casserole or pot. Add the bean threads, mushroom strips, shrimp, salt, sugar and the 1 tablespoon soy sauce. Bring to a boil. Reduce heat to low and simmer 5 minutes. Add pork slices and stir to blend. Top with sesame oil and remove from heat.

SERVINGS: Enough for 3 as a single course or for 6 to 8 in a full menu.

SLICED BEEF WITH BEAN THREAD NOODLES: Substitute 1 pound beef sirloin or filet for the pork. Stir-fry-toss the beef slices only 2 minutes before adding the soy sauce. Continue as directed.

DREDGED SLICED PORK

Cooking Time: 6 to 7 minutes

Utensils
Chinese cutting knife
Soup plate
Chopsticks
12-inch skillet or wok

Ingredients

1 pound pork shoulder, butt or loin, trimmed and cut in diagonal slices	1½ tablespoons soy sauce
	1 teaspoon sherry
	½ teaspoon minced ginger root
1 tablespoon cornstarch	2 tablespoons chicken stock or water
½ teaspoon salt	
½ teaspoon sugar	2 tablespoons peanut oil or corn oil

Before Cooking

Prepare pork. Place the pork slices in the soup plate and dredge with the cornstarch, salt and sugar. Sprinkle with the soy sauce and sherry. Toss well with chopsticks to coat slices evenly. Let stand 15 minutes. Mince ginger root. Measure chicken stock or water. Have oil ready to go.

Cooking Instructions

Turn heat under skillet or wok to high. (The heat remains high throughout the cooking.) When the pan is hot, add the oil. It should sizzle at once. Before the oil begins to smoke, add the minced ginger root and stir-fry 30 seconds. Add the dredged pork, giving it a quick stir first. Stir-fry-toss 3 minutes. The meat should be two-thirds done at this point. Add the stock or water and stir-fry 2 to 3 minutes longer. The dish should be an even, rich brown with a scant but thick sauce. The pork strips should be just done, with no pink portions.

SERVINGS: Enough for 2 as a single course with rice or for 4 to 6 in a full menu.

DREDGED SLICED BEEF: Substitute 1 pound flank steak, beef sirloin or filet for the pork. If you like, add ¼ teaspoon anise seed to the cornstarch mixture. Stir-fry-toss the beef slices only 2 minutes before adding the stock or water. Then stir-fry only 1 to 2 minutes.

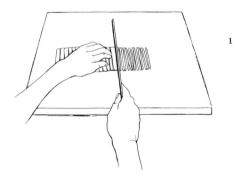

1

Dredged Stir-Fry-Toss Cooking
1. Cut meat in straight slices, then in strips.

Dredged Stir-Fry-Toss Cooking (cont.)
2. Add cornstarch, salt and sugar.   3. Sprinkle with soy sauce and sherry and toss to
blend.   4. Heat skillet until a drop of water bubbles into steam. Add oil and heat until oil is
very hot but not to the smoking point.   5. Add ingredients in order of recipe, stirring and
tossing between additions.   6. Add stock or water.   7. Stir-fry-toss until sauce thickens and
is clear. Remove from fire.

DREDGED SLICED PORK WITH FRESH VEGETABLES

Cooking Time: 9 to 11 minutes

Utensils
Chinese cutting knife
Soup plate
Chopsticks
12-inch skillet or wok
Slotted spatula

Ingredients

1 pound pork shoulder, butt or loin, cut in thin diagonal slices or strips	½ teaspoon salt
	½ teaspoon sugar
	1½ tablespoons soy sauce
1 tablespoon cornstarch	1 teaspoon sherry

Continued on next page

2 cups Fresh Vegetables (pages 53–54), mixed or unmixed

1 teaspoon finely minced ginger root

3 tablespoons chicken stock or water

2 tablespoons peanut oil or corn oil

1½ tablespoons peanut oil or corn oil

Before Cooking

Prepare pork. Place the pork in a soup plate and dredge with the cornstarch, salt and sugar. Sprinkle with soy sauce and sherry. Toss well with chopsticks to coat the slices evenly. Let stand at least 10 minutes while you prepare the Fresh Vegetables as directed. (Do not use lima or fava beans.) Mince ginger root. Measure stock or water. Have both portions of oil ready to go.

Cooking Instructions

Turn heat under skillet or wok to high. (The heat remains high throughout the cooking.) When the pan is hot, add the 2 tablespoons oil. It should sizzle at once. Before the oil begins to smoke, add the dredged pork, giving it a quick stir first. Stir-fry-toss 3 minutes. The pork should be two-thirds done at this point. Remove with slotted spatula to the soup plate. Add the 1½ tablespoons oil to the pan. When the oil is hot, add the vegetables and minced ginger root. Stir-fry-toss 2 to 3 minutes. (Pulpy vegetables will require 2 minutes; rooty vegetables, 3 minutes.) Return the pork to the pan. Add the stock or water. Stir-fry-toss 2 minutes. Remove from heat. The pork should be just done, with no pinkness; the sauce should be scant but thick and the vegetables crisp but cooked through.

SERVINGS: Enough for 3 as a single course with rice or for 6 to 8 in a full menu.

DREDGED SLICED BEEF WITH FRESH VEGETABLES: Substitute 1 pound flank steak, beef sirloin or filet for the pork. Stir-fry-toss the beef slices only 1½ minutes and stir-fry-toss the vegetables and ginger root only 2 minutes. Proceed as directed.

DREDGED SLICED LAMB WITH FRESH VEGETABLES: Substitute 1 pound boned shoulder or leg of lamb for the pork. The addition of stock is optional.

DREDGED SLICED PORK WITH LEAFY VEGETABLES

Follow the recipe for Dredged Sliced Pork with Fresh Vegetables but omit the stock or water. Substitute 2 cups of any of the Leafy Vegetables (pages 54–55) for the Fresh Vegetables and prepare as directed. When the partially cooked pork is removed from the pan, add the 1½ tablespoons oil. When the oil is hot, add the stalk portions of the vegetables and the ginger root. Stir-fry-toss 2 minutes. Add the leaf portions (and/or bean or pea sprouts, if using). Stir-fry-toss 1 minute. Return the pork to the pan. Stir for 1 minute. Remove from heat. If you prefer more liquid and softer vegetables, cover the pan for 1 to 2 minutes, stirring at 30-second intervals.

SERVINGS: Enough for 3 as a single course with rice or for 6 to 8 in a full menu.

DREDGED SLICED BEEF WITH LEAFY VEGETABLES: Follow the directions above, making the substitutions in the recipe for Dredged Sliced Beef with Fresh Vegetables.

DREDGED SLICED LAMB WITH LEAFY VEGETABLES: Follow the directions above, making the substitutions in the recipe for Dredged Sliced Lamb with Fresh Vegetables.

DREDGED SLICED PORK WITH MELON-TYPE VEGETABLES
Follow the recipe for Dredged Sliced Pork with Fresh Vegetables but decrease the stock or water to $1\frac{1}{2}$ tablespoons. Substitute 2 cups of any of the Melon-Type Vegetables (page 55) for the Fresh Vegetables and prepare as directed. When the partially cooked pork is removed from the pan, add the $1\frac{1}{2}$ tablespoons oil. When it is hot, add the vegetables and ginger root. Stir-fry-toss 2 minutes (gently in the case of tomatoes and okra). Return the pork to the pan. Add the $1\frac{1}{2}$ tablespoons stock or water. Stir gently 1 minute. More liquid will be produced as the dish stands.

SERVINGS: Enough for 3 as a single course with rice or for 6 to 8 in a full menu.

DREDGED SLICED BEEF WITH MELON-TYPE VEGETABLES: Follow the directions above, making the substitutions in the recipe for Dredged Sliced Beef with Fresh Vegetables.

DREDGED SLICED LAMB WITH MELON-TYPE VEGETABLES: Follow the directions above, making the substitutions in the recipe for Dredged Sliced Beef with Fresh Vegetables.

DREDGED SLICED PORK WITH ROOT-TYPE VEGETABLES
Follow the recipe for Dredged Sliced Pork with Fresh Vegetables but increase the second amount of oil to 2 tablespoons and increase the stock or water to $\frac{1}{4}$ cup. Substitute 2 cups of sliced mushrooms, eggplant or Chinese turnip for the Fresh Vegetables. (If in doubt about preparing the vegetables, see Root-Type Vegetables, page 55.) When the partially cooked pork is removed from the pan, add the 2 tablespoons oil. When the oil is hot, add the vegetables and ginger root. Cook 3 to 5

minutes or until the vegetables lose their wooden look and become somewhat transparent. Add more oil if the vegetables appear to absorb it too rapidly. Return the pork to the pan. Blend well with the vegetables. Add the ¼ cup stock or water and cook 2 minutes.

SERVINGS: Enough for 3 as a single course with rice or for 6 to 8 in a full menu.

DREDGED SLICED BEEF WITH ROOT-TYPE VEGETABLES: Follow the directions above, making the substitutions in the recipe for Dredged Sliced Beef with Fresh Vegetables.

DREDGED SLICED LAMB WITH ROOT-TYPE VEGETABLES: Follow the directions above, making the substitutions in the recipe for Dredged Sliced Lamb with Fresh Vegetables.

DREDGED SLICED PORK WITH DRIED VEGETABLES
OR VEGETABLE DERIVATIVES
Follow the recipe for Dredged Sliced Pork with Fresh Vegetables but substitute ½ to 1 cup of any of the Dried Vegetables (pages 56–57) for ½ to 1 cup of the Fresh Vegetables and prepare as directed. (Do not use bean thread noodles.) When the partially cooked pork is removed from the pan, add the 1½ tablespoons oil to the pan. When the oil is hot, add the Fresh Vegetables and ginger root. Stir-fry-toss 2 minutes. Add the Dried Vegetables and stir-fry-toss 1 to 2 minutes. Return the pork to the pan. Add the 3 tablespoons stock or water. Stir 1 minute. Remove from heat.

SERVINGS: Enough for 3 as a single course with rice or for 6 to 8 in a full menu.

DREDGED SLICED BEEF WITH DRIED VEGETABLES OR VEGETABLE DERIVATIVES: Follow the directions above, making the substitutions in the recipe for Dredged Sliced Beef with Fresh Vegetables.

DREDGED SLICED LAMB WITH DRIED VEGETABLES OR VEGETABLE DERIVATIVES: Follow the directions above, making the substitutions in the recipe for Dredged Sliced Lamb with Fresh Vegetables.

DREDGED SLICED PORK WITH SALTED, PRESERVED OR PICKLED VEGETABLES
Follow any of the preceding recipes for Dredged Sliced Pork with Vegetables but decrease the amount of soy sauce to 2 teaspoons and omit the salt entirely when using salted or preserved ingredients. Taste pickled ingredients for saltiness—some

are salted, some are not. Use ½ to 1 cup of Salted, Preserved or Pickled Vegetables (page 57) prepared as directed. Use enough of the vegetables in any of the previous recipes to make up 2 cups. When the partially cooked pork is removed from the pan, add the salted, preserved or pickled ingredients. Stir-fry 1 to 2 minutes. Add the Fresh, Leafy, Melon-Type, Root-Type or Dried Vegetables that you are using. Follow the timing specified in those recipes.

SERVINGS: Enough for 3 as a single course with rice or for 6 to 8 in a full menu.

DREDGED SLICED BEEF WITH SALTED, PRESERVED OR PICKLED VEGETABLES: Follow the directions above in any of the preceding recipes for Dredged Sliced Beef with Vegetables.

DREDGED SLICED LAMB WITH SALTED, PRESERVED OR PICKLED VEGETABLES: Follow the directions above in any of the preceding recipes for Dredged Sliced Lamb with Vegetables.

CLASSIC SLICED PORK LIVER

Cooking Time: 4½ minutes

Utensils
Chinese cutting knife
Small bowl for seasonings
12-inch skillet or wok
Long tongs, chopsticks or spatula for stir-
     ring

Ingredients

1	pound pork liver	½	teaspoon sugar
1	tablespoon sherry, gin or vodka	1½	tablespoons soy sauce
½	teaspoon salt	2	tablespoons peanut oil or corn oil

Before Cooking
Rinse liver. Split liver in half lengthwise. Cut into 1-inch diagonal slices. Measure liquor and set aside. Combine salt, sugar and soy sauce in the small bowl. Have oil ready to go.

Cooking Instructions
Turn heat under skillet or wok to high. (The heat remains high throughout the cooking.) When the pan is hot, add the oil. It should sizzle at once. Before the oil begins to smoke, add the liver slices and stir-fry-toss 3 minutes. Add sherry, gin or vodka; stir 1 minute. Add the salt-sugar-soy mixture. Give a quick stir to blend and fry no longer than 30 seconds. Remove from heat. The liver should be smooth, still fairly resilient but not bloody. The sauce will be dark and clear but scant.

SERVINGS: Enough for 2 as a single course with rice or for 3 to 4 in a full menu.

DREDGED SLICED PORK LIVER WITH LEEKS

Cooking Time: 6 minutes

Utensils
Chinese cutting knife
Soup plate for liver
Chopsticks
12-inch skillet or wok
Slotted spatula

Ingredients

1	pound pork liver, split and cut into 1-inch slices	$1\frac{1}{2}$	tablespoons soy sauce
2	teaspoons cornstarch	1	medium leek, split and cut into 2-inch pieces
$\frac{1}{2}$	teaspoon salt	2	tablespoons peanut oil or corn oil
$\frac{1}{2}$	teaspoon brown sugar	$1\frac{1}{2}$	tablespoons peanut oil or corn oil
1	tablespoon sherry, gin or vodka		

Before Cooking
Rinse liver. Split liver in half lengthwise. Cut into 1-inch diagonal slices. Place the slices in the soup plate and dredge with cornstarch, salt and brown sugar. Sprinkle with the sherry, gin or vodka and soy sauce. Toss well with chopsticks to coat slices evenly. Let stand 15 minutes. Prepare the leek. Have both portions of oil ready.

Cooking Instructions
Turn heat under skillet or wok to high. (The heat remains high throughout cooking.) When the pan is hot, add the 2 tablespoons oil. It should sizzle at once. Be-

fore the oil begins to smoke, add the dredged liver slices, giving them a quick stir first. Stir-fry-toss 3 minutes. Remove liver slices with slotted spatula to the soup plate. Add the 1½ tablespoons oil to the pan. When it is hot, add the leeks and stir-fry-toss 2 minutes. Return the liver to the leeks in the pan. Stir-fry 1 minute. Remove from heat. The liver should be smooth in texture, but not bloody. The sauce should be dark and thick, but not plentiful. The leeks should be only just cooked.

SERVINGS: Enough for 2 as a single course with rice or for 3 to 4 in a full menu.

DREDGED SLICED PORK LIVER WITH VEGETABLES: Follow the procedures for Dredged Sliced Pork with Fresh, Leafy, Melon-Type, Root-Type or Dried Vegetables (see pages 83–86) but substitute pork liver for the pork. The addition of stock is optional.

SLICED PORK KIDNEYS

Cooking Time: 4 minutes

Utensils
Chinese cutting knife
Large bowl for soaking kidneys
Small bowl for seasonings
Long tongs or chopsticks
12-inch skillet or wok

Ingredients

4	pork kidneys	1	tablespoon soy sauce
4	scallions with unwilted greens, cut in 1½-inch diagonal rounds	¼	teaspoon salt
		½	teaspoon brown sugar
1	tablespoon gin or vodka	2	tablespoons peanut oil or corn oil

Before Cooking
Wash kidneys thoroughly; discard the core and remove membranes and white veins. Cut into thin comblike slices. Soak 1 hour in cold water, changing the water twice. Drain kidney slices on paper towels and blot well. The kidneys must be as

dry as possible before cooking. Prepare the scallions. Measure the gin or vodka and set aside. Combine the soy sauce, salt and sugar in the small bowl. Have oil ready to go.

Cooking Instructions

Turn heat under skillet or wok to high. (The heat remains high throughout the cooking.) When the pan is hot, add the oil. It should sizzle at once. Before the oil begins to smoke, add the scallions and stir-fry-toss 1 minute. Add the kidney slices; stir-fry no longer than 1 minute. Add the gin or vodka. Stir once rapidly. Then pour in the soy-salt-sugar mixture. Stir-fry-toss 2 minutes. Remove from heat. The kidneys should be just done and not overcooked. There will be a scant, dark, clear sauce.

SERVINGS: Enough for 2 as a single course with rice or for 3 in a full menu.

NOTE: Gin or vodka is used in this recipe as a substitute for *Kaoliang,* a clear po-tent Chinese liquor distilled from a type of grain by that name.

GROUND PORK AND WATER CHESTNUTS

Cooking Time: 6 minutes

Utensils
Chinese cutting knife
Meat grinder
Soup plate
Small bowl for cornstarch and stock
12-inch skillet or wok
Tongs, chopsticks or spatula for stirring

Ingredients

1	pound pork shoulder, butt or loin, ground	½	teaspoon sugar
9	water chestnuts, finely minced	1	tablespoon sherry, gin or vodka
1	teaspoon finely minced ginger root	3	teaspoons cornstarch
		¼	cup chicken stock
2	teaspoons soy sauce	2	to 4 whole Boston (butter) let-tuce leaves
½	teaspoon salt	1½	tablespoons peanut oil or corn oil

Before Cooking
Mince pork finely, using 2 Chinese cutting knives, or put pork through medium blade of the meat grinder twice. Place in the soup plate. Combine the minced water chestnuts and ginger root with the ground pork. Blend soy sauce, salt and sugar; add to pork mixture. Measure liquor and set aside. Combine cornstarch and stock. Rinse the tender whole leaves of lettuce and blot dry. Have oil ready to go.

Cooking Instructions
Turn heat under skillet or wok to high. (The heat remains high throughout the cooking.) When the pan is hot, add the oil. It should sizzle at once. Before the oil begins to smoke, add the seasoned ground pork mixture. Stir-fry-toss about 3 minutes or until the meat loses its pinkness. Add sherry, gin or vodka. Stir just to blend. Give the cornstarch-stock mixture a quick stir and add to the pan. Stir and toss about 3 minutes or until the mixture thickens and there is little liquid remaining. Remove from heat. Serve with lettuce leaves on separate dishes. The pork mixture is spooned into each leaf and rolled up like a pancake.

SERVINGS: Enough for 2 as a single course with rice or for 3 to 4 in a full menu.

NOTE: This recipe is a variation of a banquet dish usually made with squab (see Squab Soong, page 114). In this more plebeian version, you may substitute $\frac{1}{4}$ cup finely minced celery or bamboo shoots (or a mixture of both) for the water chestnuts.

GROUND PORK WITH BAMBOO SHOOTS, MUSHROOMS AND EGGS

Cooking Time: 6 to 7 minutes

Utensils
Chinese cutting knives or meat grinder
Soup plate
Bowl for beaten eggs
12-inch skillet or wok
Slotted spatula for stirring and removing
    ingredients

Ingredients

1	pound pork shoulder, butt or loin, ground	3	medium eggs
½	teaspoon salt	2	tablespoons cold water
½	teaspoon brown sugar	½	cup canned button mushrooms, drained
1	tablespoon soy sauce	1½	tablespoons peanut oil or corn oil
1	large bamboo shoot (8 ounces)	1	tablespoon peanut oil or corn oil

Before Cooking

Mince pork finely, using 2 Chinese cutting knives, or put pork through medium blade of the meat grinder twice. Combine in the soup plate with the salt, sugar and soy sauce. Drain bamboo shoot and slice very thinly. Beat eggs with water until they are frothy; set aside. Have mushrooms and both portions of oil ready to go.

Cooking Instructions

Turn heat under skillet or wok to high. (The heat remains high throughout the cooking.) When the pan is hot, add the 1½ tablespoons oil. It should sizzle at once. Before the oil begins to smoke, add the seasoned ground pork mixture. Stir-fry-toss 3 to 4 minutes. Remove pork to the soup plate. Add the remaining 1 table-spoon oil to the pan and heat. Add bamboo shoots and stir-fry-toss 1½ minutes. Add button mushrooms and stir with bamboo shoots 1 minute. Return the pork to the pan. Blend well with the vegetables. Pour egg-water mixture over pork and vegetables. Let stand 30 seconds to set slightly, then stir-fry to create fine egg shreds. The pork should be just done, somewhat crumbly, with no pinkness. The vegetables should be tender, the egg shreds firm but not dry. There should be little or no liquid in the pan.

SERVINGS: Enough for 3 as a single course with rice or for 4 to 6 in a full menu.

SLICED BEEF AND SALTED GREENS

Cooking Time: 5 to 6 minutes

Utensils
Chinese cutting knife
12-inch skillet or wok
Small bowl for cornstarch-stock mixture
Pancake turner for stirring and removing
   meat
Saucer for seasonings

Ingredients

1	pound flank steak, sirloin or filet, cut in diagonal slices	½	teaspoon salt
½	large onion, chopped	1	tablespoon cornstarch
1	cup chopped salted mustard greens, rinsed and drained	⅓	cup cold chicken stock or cold water
1	teaspoon sugar	2	tablespoons peanut oil or corn oil
		1	tablespoon peanut oil or corn oil

Before Cooking
Slice beef and chop vegetables. Combine salt and sugar in the saucer. Combine cornstarch and stock or water. Have both portions of oil ready to go.

Cooking Instructions
Turn heat under skillet or wok to high. (The heat remains high throughout the cooking.) When the pan is hot, add the 2 tablespoons oil. It should sizzle at once. Before the oil begins to smoke, add the meat slices and stir-fry-toss rapidly 1 to 2 minutes. The meat should be generally pinkish, with raw portions still showing. Remove the meat with the turner to a plate. Add the 1 tablespoon oil to the fat remaining in the pan. Stir in the onions and toss-fry 2 minutes. The onions should be slightly brown at the edges. Add the salted greens; stir-fry-toss 1 minute. Return the beef to the pan. Add salt and sugar. Give the cornstarch-stock mixture a quick stir and add to the pan. Stir rapidly 1 minute. The meat should be just cooked, the vegetables tender and the sauce scant and clear.

SERVINGS: Enough for 2 as a single course with rice or for 4 to 6 in a full menu.

GROUND BEEF, PICKLED GREENS AND EGG SCRAMBLE

Cooking Time: 8 to 9 minutes

Utensils
Chinese cutting knife
Small bowl for seasonings
12-inch skillet or wok
Slotted spatula

Ingredients

1	can (8 ounces) chopped pickled mustard greens or 1 cup salted mustard greens	3	teaspoons soy sauce
		½	teaspoon sugar
		3	medium eggs
1	cup coarsely chopped young spinach (with roots)	1	pound ground beef
		1	tablespoon peanut oil
½	large onion, chopped	1	tablespoon sesame oil
2	teaspoons minced ginger root		

Before Cooking
Prepare the vegetables. If you use salted mustard greens, rinse first in cold water to remove excess salt. Mince ginger root. Combine the soy sauce and sugar in the small bowl. Beat eggs until they are frothy. Have meat and both portions of oil ready to go.

Cooking Instructions
Turn heat under skillet or wok to high. (The heat remains high throughout the cooking.) When the pan is hot, add the 1 tablespoon peanut oil. It should sizzle at once. Before the oil begins to smoke, add the meat, breaking up the chunks with the sharp end of the spatula. Stir-fry-toss to brown the meat. This should take 3 to 4 minutes. Remove the meat to a warm plate. Add the 1 tablespoon sesame oil to the oil remaining in the pan. When the oil is hot, but before it smokes, add the onion. Sesame oil burns quickly, so do not overheat. Stir-fry 1 minute. Add the ginger and toss with the onion 30 seconds. Add the pickled greens and stir-fry-toss 2 minutes. Add spinach and stir-toss 1 minute longer. Return the cooked meat to the pan, sprinkle with the soy-sugar mixture and toss well to blend with the meat and vegetables. Add the beaten eggs and let the pan stand over the heat without stirring 30 seconds. Then toss to scramble the partially set eggs with the other ingre-

dients. The finished dish should be a rich brown in color, crumbly in texture and without sauce. Since the greens are very salty, no salt is used in this recipe.

SERVINGS: Enough for 3 as a single course with rice or for 4 to 6 in a full menu.

OYSTER BEEF SLICES

Cooking Time: 3 minutes

Utensils
Chinese cutting knife
Chopsticks
Long tongs for tossing meat during cook-
ing
12-inch skillet or wok
Soup plate

Ingredients

1	pound flank steak, sirloin or filet, cut in ⅛-inch diagonal slices	1	tablespoon sherry
1	tablespoon cornstarch	2	scallions, each with 1½ inches of green, cut in 1½-inch rounds
½	teaspoon salt	2	tablespoons oyster sauce
1	teaspoon brown sugar	2	tablespoons peanut oil or corn oil
1½	tablespoons soy sauce		

Before Cooking
Prepare beef slices. Place in the soup plate and dredge with the cornstarch, salt and sugar. Sprinkle with soy sauce and sherry. Toss well with chopsticks to coat slices evenly. Let stand at least 10 minutes. Slice scallions. Have oyster sauce and oil ready to go.

Cooking Instructions
Turn heat under skillet or wok to high. (The heat remains high throughout the cooking.) When the pan is hot, add the oil. It should sizzle at once. Before the oil begins to burn, add the beef slices, giving them a quick stir first. Stir-fry-toss 1 minute. Add the scallions and stir-fry 1 minute. Add the oyster sauce. Stir well 1 minute to blend. Remove from heat.

SERVINGS: Enough for 2 as a single course with rice or for 4 to 6 in a full menu.

TOMATO BEEF SLICES

Cooking Time: 9 minutes

Utensils
Chinese cutting knife
Soup plate
12-inch skillet or wok
Chopsticks
Slotted spatula for stirring and
    removing meat

Ingredients

1	pound flank steak, sirloin or filet, cut in diagonal slices or strips	1	small onion (size of a plum), quartered
1	tablespoon cornstarch	½	stalk celery, cut in thin strips
1	teaspoon salt	1	small green pepper, cut in average strips
2	teaspoons brown sugar		
2	teaspoons vinegar	3	small firm tomatoes, quartered
1	teaspoon sesame oil	¼	cup chicken stock or water
1	tablespoon soy sauce	2	tablespoons peanut oil or corn oil
1	slice ginger root (2x1x⅛ inch)	1	tablespoon peanut oil or corn oil

Before Cooking
Prepare beef slices. Place in the soup plate and dredge with the cornstarch, salt and brown sugar. Sprinkle with the vinegar, sesame oil and soy sauce. Toss well with chopsticks to coat slices evenly. Let stand at least 10 minutes while you prepare vegetables. Have stock or water and both portions of oil ready to go.

Cooking Instructions
Turn heat under skillet or wok to high. (The heat remains high throughout the cooking.) When the pan is hot, add the 2 tablespoons oil. It should sizzle at once. Before the oil begins to smoke, add the meat slices, giving them a quick stir first. Stir-fry-toss 2 minutes. Remove with slotted spatula to a warm dish. Add the 1 tablespoon oil to the pan. When it is hot, add the ginger root. Stir-fry 1 minute. Add the onions, celery and green pepper; stir-fry-toss 2 minutes. The onion should be transparent and golden brown at the edges. Add the tomatoes and stir 3 minutes. Return the meat to the pan. Add the stock and stir to blend 1 minute. Remove the ginger. The general color of this dish will be light brown with the peppers and

tomatoes bright in color and still crisp. The sauce should be of medium thickness —it will become thinner and more plentiful on standing. The flavor is delicately sweet-and-sour. Served cold on noodles, this is a popular hot-weather dish in China.

SERVINGS: Enough for 2 as a single course with rice or for 4 to 6 in a full menu.

NOTE: Be sure that the tomatoes used are not too ripe or they will purée in the cooking.

PEPPERED STEAK STRIPS

Cooking Time: 2½ minutes

Utensils
Chinese cutting knife
Mortar and pestle
Small bowl for soy sauce and sherry
12-inch skillet or wok
Long tongs or chopsticks for tossing

Ingredients

1	pound flank steak, sirloin or filet	2	tablespoons soy sauce
1	teaspoon salt	1	tablespoon sherry
¼	teaspoon sugar	2	tablespoons peanut oil or corn oil
1	tablespoon coarsely ground black pepper		

Before Cooking
Pound beef with the blunt edge of the cutting knife. Grind the salt, sugar and pepper together in a mortar with a pestle. Sprinkle the meat with the seasonings and pound into the meat with the blunt edge of the cutting knife. Cut meat into diagonal slices. Combine the soy sauce and sherry in the small bowl. Have oil ready to go.

Cooking Instructions
Turn heat under skillet or wok to high. (The heat remains high throughout the cooking.) When the pan is hot, add the oil. It should sizzle at once. Before the oil

begins to smoke, add the beef slices and stir-fry-toss rapidly 2 minutes. Add the soy sauce and sherry. Stir just 30 seconds to blend. The dish will be light brown with a thin sauce.

SERVINGS: Enough for 2 as a single course with rice or for 4 to 6 in a full menu.

BEEF LIVER,
Shanghai Style

Cooking Time: 4 minutes

Utensils
Chinese cutting knife
Soup plate
Chopsticks
12-inch skillet or wok
Slotted spatula

Ingredients

1	pound baby beef liver, halved and cut in 1½-inch diagonal slices	2	teaspoons sherry
2	teaspoons cornstarch	¼	teaspoon sesame oil
½	teaspoon salt	2	scallions with 1½ inches of green, cut in 1½-inch diagonal slices
½	teaspoon brown sugar	¼	cup chicken stock
⅛	teaspoon five-spice seasoning	2	tablespoons peanut oil or corn oil
1	tablespoon soy sauce		

Before Cooking
Prepare liver. Place in the soup plate and dredge with the cornstarch, salt, brown sugar and five-spice seasoning. Sprinkle with soy sauce, sherry, sesame oil and sliced scallions. Toss well with chopsticks to coat the slices evenly. Have stock and oil ready to go.

Cooking Instructions
Turn heat under skillet or wok to high. (The heat remains high throughout the cooking.) When the pan is hot, add the oil. It should sizzle at once. Before the oil begins to smoke, add liver mixture, giving it a quick stir first. Stir-fry-toss rapidly 3

minutes, using the spatula to turn slices. Add the stock and continue stirring 1 minute. The dish should be dark brown in color with a velvety, rich sauce. The liver should be tender—not overcooked, but not bloody either.

SERVINGS: Enough for 3 as a single course with rice or for 6 in a full menu.

CLASSIC SLICED LAMB,
Peking Style

Cooking Time: 4 minutes

Utensils
Chinese cutting knife
Small bowls for seasonings
12-inch skillet or wok
Tongs or chopsticks for stirring

Ingredients

1	pound boned shoulder or leg of lamb, cut into thin diagonal slices	1	teaspoon salt
		½	teaspoon sugar
3	young scallions, each with 1½ inches of greens, cut in 1-inch diagonal slices	2	teaspoons gin, vodka or sherry
		2	tablespoons peanut oil or corn oil

Before Cooking
Prepare the lamb and scallions. Measure the salt, sugar and liquor. Have oil ready to go.

Cooking Instructions
Turn heat under skillet or wok to high. (The heat remains high throughout the cooking.) When the pan is hot, add the oil. It should sizzle at once. Before the oil begins to smoke, add the lamb and stir-fry-toss 2 minutes. Add the sliced scallions; stir-fry-toss 1 minute. Add the salt and sugar and stir just to mix. Add the liquor. Stir rapidly to let some of the alcohol evaporate, less than 1 minute. Remove from heat. The lamb should be just cooked and fairly pale in color. What liquid remains should be clear.

SERVINGS: Enough for 2 as a single course with Mandarin Pancakes or rice or for 4 to 6 in a full menu.

NOTE: This is a basic Northern dish—without embellishments, spices or condiments. A strip or two of lamb is usually rolled into a Mandarin Pancake. Condiments such as mustard, Hoisin sauce, soy sauce or bean curd cheese may be served separately in small dishes for dipping.

DREDGED SLICED LAMB AND LEEKS,
Peking Style

Cooking Time: 6 minutes

Utensils
Chinese cutting knife
Soup plate
Chopsticks
12-inch skillet or wok
**Slotted spatula for stirring and removing
     ingredients**

Ingredients

1	pound boned shoulder or leg of lamb, cut in thin diagonal slices or strips	3	young leeks, split lengthwise and cut into 1½-inch slices
1	tablespoon cornstarch	¼	teaspoon five-spice seasoning
½	teaspoon salt	1½	tablespoons gin, vodka or sherry
1	teaspoon brown sugar	2	tablespoons peanut oil or corn oil
1½	tablespoons soy sauce	1	tablespoon peanut oil or corn oil

Before Cooking
Prepare lamb. Place in the soup plate and dredge with the cornstarch, salt and brown sugar. Sprinkle with soy sauce. Toss well with chopsticks to coat slices evenly. Let stand 10 to 15 minutes. Wash, trim and cut the leeks. Have seasoning, liquor and both portions of oil ready to go.

Cooking Instructions

Turn heat under skillet or wok to high. (The heat remains high throughout the cooking.) When the pan is hot, add the 2 tablespoons oil. It should sizzle at once. Before the oil begins to smoke, add the lamb, giving it a quick stir first. Stir-fry-toss 3 minutes. Remove lamb to soup plate with slotted spatula. Add the 1 table-spoon oil to the pan. When it is very hot, add the leeks. Stir-fry-toss 2 minutes. Return the lamb to the pan and sprinkle with five-spice seasoning. Blend well 30 seconds. Add the gin, vodka or sherry. Stir rapidly to allow some of the alcohol to evaporate, about 30 seconds. Remove from heat. The lamb should be only just done, the leeks just brown at the edges. There will be almost no liquid and the dish will be dark brown in color.

SERVINGS: Enough for 2 as a single course with Mandarin Pancakes or rice or for 4 to 6 in a full menu.

NOTE: For variations of Dredged Sliced Lamb with Vegetables, see the Dredged Sliced Pork recipes (pages 81–86).

GROUND LAMB WITH GARLIC,·

Peking Style

Cooking Time: 5 to 6 minutes

Utensils
Chinese cutting knives or meat grinder
Soup plate
Small bowl for seasonings
12-inch skillet or wok
Tongs, chopsticks or spatula for stirring

Ingredients

1	pound lean boned shoulder or leg of lamb	1	teaspoon soy sauce
3	large cloves garlic, minced	1	tablespoon gin or vodka
½	teaspoon minced ginger root	¼	cup chicken stock
½	teaspoon salt	1	tablespoon cornstarch
½	teaspoon sugar	2	tablespoons peanut oil or corn oil

Before Cooking
Trim fat from lamb. Mince, using 2 Chinese cutting knives, or put lamb through medium blade of meat grinder twice. Place in the soup plate. Combine the minced garlic and ginger root with the ground lamb. Blend salt, sugar and soy sauce; add to lamb mixture. Measure the liquor. Combine the cornstarch and stock. Have the liquor and oil ready to go.

Cooking Instructions
Turn heat under skillet or wok to high. (The heat remains high throughout the cooking.) When the pan is hot, add the oil. It should sizzle at once. Before the oil begins to smoke, add the ground lamb mixture and stir-fry-toss 3 minutes. Add the gin or vodka and stir just to blend. Give the cornstarch-stock mixture a quick stir and add to the pan. Stir until the mixture thickens and there is not much liquid remaining, 2 to 3 minutes at the most. Remove from heat. The dish should be fairly light in color and smooth in texture.

SERVINGS: Enough for 2 as a single course with Mandarin Pancakes or rice, or for 3 to 4 in a full menu.

GROUND LAMB SCRAMBLE,

Peking Style

Cooking Time: 7½ to 8½ minutes

Utensils
2 Chinese cutting knives or meat grinder
    with medium blade
Soup plate
Bowls for soaking dried ingredients
Bowl for beaten egg
12-inch skillet or wok
Slotted spatula for removing and stirring
    ingredients

Ingredients

¾ pound lean boned shoulder or leg of lamb	4 medium dried mushrooms
1 tablespoon dried wood ears	2 scallions with green, cut in ½-inch diagonal slices
6 dried tiger lilies	1 teaspoon minced ginger root

½ cup pea sprouts

3 medium eggs

2 tablespoons cold water

½ teaspoon salt

1 teaspoon brown sugar

2 tablespoons soy sauce

1 tablespoon peanut oil or corn oil

2 tablespoons peanut oil or corn oil

Before Cooking

Trim fat from lamb. Mince, using 2 Chinese cutting knives, or put lamb through medium blade of meat grinder twice. Soak the wood ears, tiger lilies and dried mushrooms in warm water 20 minutes. Drain well. It is important that they be squeezed dry. Leave the wood ears whole. Cut the tiger lilies into 1-inch pieces. Remove the hard center from the mushrooms and cut them into thin strips. Prepare the scallions and ginger root. Wash the pea sprouts and remove the pale green hoods; drain well. Combine the eggs and cold water and beat until frothy. Have salt, sugar, soy sauce and both portions of oil ready to go.

Cooking Instructions

Turn heat under skillet or wok to high. (The heat remains high throughout the cooking.) When the pan is hot, add the 2 tablespoons oil. It should sizzle at once. Before the oil begins to smoke, add the ground lamb and stir-fry-toss 3 minutes. Sprinkle with the salt, sugar and soy sauce. Blend well and remove from pan to warm soup plate. Add the 1 tablespoon oil to the pan. When the oil is hot, add the scallions and ginger root. Stir-fry 30 seconds. Add the wood ears, tiger lilies and mushroom strips. Stir-fry-toss 1 minute. Add the pea sprouts and toss with the vegetables in the pan 1 minute. Return the lamb to the pan. Stir to blend 30 seconds. Pour the egg-water mixture over all. Let stand 30 seconds, then stir-fry and scramble 1 to 2 minutes. The lamb should be just done and the vegetables crisp but cooked through. The eggs should be in shreds. This dish is generally quite dry and fairly crumbly in texture. If the soaked ingredients have been squeezed dry and the pea sprouts properly drained, there should be little liquid in the pan.

SERVINGS: Enough for 2 to 3 as a single course with Mandarin Pancakes or for 4 to 6 in a full menu.

NOTE: This Mandarin dish is usually made with pork or lamb shreds. If you prefer to use the fine strips of meat, simply shred the same amount of either lamb or pork and proceed accordingly. When it is made with pork strips, it is called *Mo-shu-ro* in Chinese. It is made classically without pea sprouts or mushrooms. While these are restaurant innovations, they enhance the interest of this essentially simple dish.

POINTS TO REMEMBER IN STIR-FRY-TOSS COOKING OF POULTRY

Chicken, duck or squab are never stir-fried whole. Chicken and duck are cut into ½- to 2-inch portions. Squab is quartered and sometimes boned. Raw chicken breasts and thighs may be boned and cut into strips, shreds or dice. Chicken wings and drumsticks are usually cut across in 3 sections. Liver is sliced thinly on the diagonal.

In contrast to Stir-Fry-Toss meat dishes, raw chicken should be added after the vegetables have been cooked. Moisture released from the cooked vegetables keeps the chicken from browning and sticking to the pan. Since chicken strips are very tender and cook rapidly, there is little danger of the moisture causing toughness. Chicken strips should be cooked no longer than it takes for the meat to turn from pinkish to white, or from translucent to opaque. If a thick sauce, such as Hoisin, brown bean or oyster, is not one of the ingredients, cornstarch is always used to prevent the chicken from becoming stringy and to ensure a smooth sauce. Sometimes egg whites are added for a velvety texture. Thus, whether the cornstarch is used to dredge the chicken or added at the end of the cooking, Classic Stir-Fry-Toss Chicken is synonymous with Dredged Sliced Chicken. The difference between the two lies only in the procedure.

CLASSIC SLICED CHICKEN BREAST

Cooking Time: 3 to 4 minutes

Utensils
Chinese cutting knife
Soup plate
Chopsticks
12-inch skillet or wok
Tongs or chopsticks

Ingredients

2	whole fryer breasts (¾ pound each), skinned, boned and cut lengthwise in thin strips	2	teaspoons cornstarch
		½	teaspoon salt
		½	teaspoon brown sugar

1½ tablespoons soy sauce
2 teaspoons gin, vodka or sherry
1 scallion with green, cut in ¼-inch rounds

1 teaspoon minced ginger root
2 tablespoons chicken stock or water
3 tablespoons peanut oil or corn oil

Before Cooking
Prepare chicken. Place the chicken strips in the soup plate and dredge with the cornstarch, salt and brown sugar. Sprinkle with the soy sauce and liquor. Toss well with chopsticks to coat the strips evenly. Let stand 10 to 15 minutes. Prepare scallion and ginger root. Have the stock or water and the oil ready to go.

Cooking Instructions
Turn heat under skillet or wok to high. (The heat remains high throughout the cooking.) When the pan is hot, add the oil. It should sizzle at once. Before the oil begins to smoke, add the scallion and ginger root. Stir-fry 30 seconds. Add the dredged chicken strips, giving them a quick stir first. Stir-fry-toss 1½ minutes. The chicken should lose its pinkness. Add the stock or water and stir to blend 1 to 2 minutes. Remove from heat. The chicken strips should be separate but not overcooked and stringy. They will be lightly glazed with a delicate, scant sauce.

SERVINGS: Enough for 3 as a single course with rice or for 6 in a full menu.

SLICED CHICKEN BREAST WITH FRESH VEGETABLES

Cooking Time: 5 minutes

Utensils
Chinese cutting knife
Measuring cups and spoons
Soup plate
Chopsticks
12-inch skillet or wok
Tongs or chopsticks

Ingredients

2 whole fryer breasts (¾ pound each), skinned, boned and cut lengthwise in thin strips
1 tablespoon cornstarch
1 teaspoon brown sugar
2 tablespoons soy sauce
1 tablespoon gin, vodka or sherry
2 cups Fresh Vegetables (pages 53–54), mixed or unmixed

1 scallion with green, cut in ¼-inch rounds
1 teaspoon minced ginger root
½ teaspoon salt
3 tablespoons chicken stock or water
3 tablespoons peanut oil or corn oil

Before Cooking

Prepare chicken. Place the chicken strips in the soup plate and dredge with the cornstarch and brown sugar. Sprinkle with the soy sauce and liquor. Toss well with chopsticks to coat the strips evenly. Let stand while preparing the Fresh Vegetables as directed. (Do not use lima or fava beans.) Prepare the scallion and ginger root. Have the salt, stock and oil ready to go.

Cooking Instructions

Turn heat under skillet or wok to high. (The heat remains high throughout the cooking.) When the pan is hot, add the oil. It should sizzle at once. Before the oil begins to smoke, add the scallion and ginger root. Give a quick stir. Add the vegetables and stir-fry-toss 2 minutes. (Root vegetables will require slightly more time, pulpy vegetables slightly less.) Sprinkle the vegetables with salt; mix well. Add the dredged chicken and stir-fry-toss 2 minutes or until there is no pinkness in the chicken strips. Add the stock or water. Stir 1 minute or until the sauce is thickened. Remove from heat. The chicken strips should be tender and just done, the vegetables crisply cooked through, the sauce scant but golden brown and thick.

SERVINGS: Enough for 4 as a single course with rice or for 8 in a full menu.

SLICED CHICKEN BREAST WITH LEAFY VEGETABLES

Follow the recipe for Sliced Chicken Breast with Fresh Vegetables but omit the stock or water. Substitute 2 cups of any of the Leafy Vegetables (pages 54–55) for the Fresh Vegetables and prepare as directed. Add the stalk portions of the vegetables first and stir-fry-toss 2 minutes. Add the leaf portions (and/or bean or pea sprouts, if using) and stir-fry-toss 1 minute.

SERVINGS: Enough for 4 as a single course with rice or for 8 in a full menu.

SLICED CHICKEN BREAST WITH MELON-TYPE VEGETABLES

Follow the recipe for Sliced Chicken Breast with Fresh Vegetables but substitute 2 cups of any of the Melon-Type Vegetables (page 55) for the Fresh Vegetables and prepare as directed. Stir-fry-toss 2 minutes, gently in the case of easily squashed vegetables such as tomatoes and okra.

SERVINGS: Enough for 4 as a single course with rice or for 8 in a full menu.

SLICED CHICKEN BREAST WITH ROOT-TYPE VEGETABLES

Follow the recipe for Sliced Chicken Breast with Fresh Vegetables but increase the oil and stock or water to $\frac{1}{4}$ cup. Substitute 2 cups of any of the Root-Type Vegetables (page 55) for the Fresh Vegetables and prepare as directed. Cook 3 to 5 minutes or until the vegetables lose their wooden look and become somewhat transparent.

SERVINGS: Enough for 4 as a single course with rice or for 8 in a full menu.

SLICED CHICKEN BREAST WITH DRIED VEGETABLES OR
VEGETABLE DERIVATIVES

Follow the recipe for Sliced Chicken Breast with Fresh Vegetables but substitute $\frac{1}{2}$ to 1 cup of any of the Dried Vegetables (pages 56–57) for $\frac{1}{2}$ to 1 cup of the Fresh Vegetables and prepare as directed. (Do not use bean thread noodles.) Stir-fry-toss Fresh Vegetables 2 minutes. Add the Dried Vegetables and stir-fry-toss 1 to 2 minutes.

SERVINGS: Enough for 4 as a single course with rice or for 8 in a full menu.

SLICED CHICKEN BREAST WITH SALTED, PRESERVED OR
PICKLED INGREDIENTS

Follow any of the preceding recipes for Sliced Chicken Breast with Vegetables but decrease the amount of soy sauce to 2 teaspoons and omit the salt entirely if using salted or preserved ingredients. Taste pickled ingredients for saltiness—some are salted, some are not. Use $\frac{1}{2}$ to 1 cup of Salted Preserved or Pickled Vegetables (page 57) prepared as directed. Use enough of the vegetables in any of the previous recipes to make up 2 cups. Stir-fry the salted, preserved or pickled ingredients 1 to 2 minutes. Add the Fresh, Leafy, Melon-Type, Root-Type or Dried Vegetables that you are using. Follow the timing specified in those recipes.

SERVINGS: Enough for 4 as a single course with rice or for 8 in a full menu.

CURRIED BREAST OF CHICKEN WITH WALNUTS AND GREEN PEPPERS

Cooking Time: 5½ minutes

Utensils
Chinese cutting knife
Soup plate
12-inch skillet or wok
Tongs or slotted spatula

Ingredients

2   whole fryer breasts (¾ pound each), boned, skinned and cut in ½-inch dice

2   teaspoons cornstarch

4   scallions, each with 1 inch of green, minced

½   large green pepper, finely diced

2   tablespoons coarsely chopped walnuts

2   teaspoons curry paste or 1 tablespoon curry powder

½   teaspoon salt

1   teaspoon sugar

¼   cup chicken stock or water

2   tablespoons peanut oil or corn oil

Before Cooking
Prepare chicken. Place the chicken in the soup plate and dredge with cornstarch. Let stand while preparing the vegetables and walnuts and measuring the rest of the ingredients. Have oil ready to go.

Cooking Instructions
Turn heat under skillet or wok to high. When the pan is hot, add the oil. It should sizzle at once. Before the oil begins to smoke, add the minced scallions. Give a quick stir (less than 30 seconds) and add the green pepper and walnuts. Stir-fry-toss 1 minute. Add the curry paste, salt and sugar. Reduce heat to medium-low and stir rapidly 1 minute to blend and prevent scorching. Add the chicken. Turn heat to medium-high and stir-fry-toss 2 minutes or until the chicken loses its pinkness. Add the stock or water and blend well 1 minute. Remove from heat. The chicken will be tender, just-cooked morsels in a thick piquant sauce.

SERVINGS: Enough for 4 as a single course with rice or for 6 in a full menu.

CURRIED SHRIMP WITH WALNUTS AND GREEN PEPPERS: Substitute 1½ pounds raw medium shrimp for the chicken. Shell, wash and devein the shrimp; cut into ½-inch dice. Proceed as in the recipe above.

NOTE: Curried dishes are not traditionally Chinese. But typically, the Chinese assert their own personality on this Indian specialty. Chinese curried foods are usually stir-fried, rather than braised or stewed, and the result is a lighter curry flavor. Try to use curry paste rather than powder, which has a tendency to retain a "raw" taste in quick-cooked recipes. Curry paste is available in most specialty food stores.

DICED CHICKEN WITH BLACK AND WHITE MUSHROOMS

Cooking Time: 5 to 6 minutes

Utensils
Chinese cutting knife
Soup plate
Chopsticks
Small bowl for chicken stock
12-inch skillet or wok
Slotted spatula

Ingredients

1 cup small dried mushrooms	1½ tablespoons soy sauce
1½ pounds chicken breast and thigh, skinned, boned, cut in ½-inch dice	2 teaspoons sherry
	⅛ teaspoon five-spice seasoning
1 tablespoon cornstarch	1 cup canned button mushrooms
½ teaspoon salt	¼ cup chicken stock
½ teaspoon brown sugar	3 tablespoons peanut oil or corn oil

Before Cooking
Rinse the dried mushrooms in cold water and soak in 2 cups warm water 30 minutes. Prepare the chicken. Place in the soup plate and dredge with the cornstarch, salt and brown sugar. Sprinkle with soy sauce, sherry and five-spice seasoning. Toss well with chopsticks to coat the chicken evenly. Drain the soaked dried mushroom; trim away the hard centers but leave the mushrooms whole. Have the button mushrooms, stock and oil ready to go.

Cooking Instructions

Turn heat under skillet or wok to high. (The heat remains high throughout the cooking.) When the pan is hot, add the oil. It should sizzle at once. Before the oil begins to smoke, add the drained mushrooms. Stir-fry-toss 1 minute. Add the button mushrooms and stir-fry 1 minute. Remove the mushrooms with the slotted spatula. Add the dredged chicken to the pan. Stir-fry-toss 2 minutes, scraping up any particles sticking to the pan. Return the mushrooms to the pan and mix with the chicken. Add the stock and stir 1 to 2 minutes or until the sauce is thickened. Remove from heat. The chicken will be only just cooked. Both types of mushrooms will be tender. Crispness is not a factor in this recipe. The general appearance of this dish will be golden brown with a scant but rich and thick sauce.

SERVINGS: Enough for 3 as a single course with rice or for 6 to 8 in a full menu.

DICED CHICKEN WITH PEPPERS AND OYSTER SAUCE

Cooking Time: 6 to 7 minutes

Utensils
Chinese cutting knife
Soup plate
Small bowl for seasonings
12-inch skillet or wok
Tongs or slotted spatula for stirring

Ingredients

1½	pounds chicken breasts and thighs, skinned, boned and cut in ½-inch dice	½	teaspoon sugar
		¼	teaspoon salt
2	teaspoons cornstarch	1	teaspoon soy sauce
2	scallions with 1 inch of green, cut in ½-inch rounds	1	teaspoon sherry, gin or vodka
		2	tablespoons oyster sauce
1	green bell pepper, cut in ½-inch squares	⅛	teaspoon crushed red pepper flakes
1	red bell pepper, cut in ½-inch squares	2	tablespoons chicken stock or water
		2	tablespoons peanut oil or corn oil

Before Cooking
Prepare the chicken. Place in the soup plate and sprinkle with the cornstarch. Prepare the scallions and peppers. Combine the sugar, salt, soy sauce, liquor and oyster sauce in the small bowl. Have the red pepper flakes, chicken stock or water and oil ready to go.

Cooking Instructions
Turn heat under skillet or wok to high. (The heat remains high throughout the cooking.) When the pan is hot, add the oil. It should sizzle at once. Before the oil begins to smoke, add the scallions, green and red pepper squares and crushed red pepper flakes. Stir-fry-toss 2 minutes. Add the dredged chicken and stir-fry rapidly 2 to 3 minutes or until the chicken pieces just turn white. Add the seasoning-liquor-sauce mixture; stir 1 minute to blend. Add the stock or water and stir 1 minute. Remove from heat. The chicken dice should be tender and just done in a velvety golden brown sauce. The peppers will still be bright in color and crisp in texture.

SERVINGS: Enough for 3 to 4 as a single course with rice or for 6 in a full menu.

DICED CHICKEN WITH ZUCCHINI AND HOISIN SAUCE

Cooking Time: 4 to 5 minutes

Utensils
Chinese cutting knife
12-inch skillet or wok
Tongs or chopsticks

Ingredients

1½ pounds chicken breast and thigh, skinned, boned and cut in ½-inch dice	2 cups diced unpared zucchini
	3 teaspoons Hoisin sauce
	2 tablespoons peanut oil or corn oil
1 teaspoon minced ginger root	

Before Cooking
Prepare chicken and zucchini. Mince ginger root. Have Hoisin sauce and oil ready to go.

Cooking Instructions

Turn heat under skillet or wok to high. (The heat remains high throughout the cooking.) When the pan is hot, add the oil. It should sizzle at once. Before the oil begins to smoke, add the ginger root and zucchini; stir-fry-toss 1 minute. Add the chicken and stir 2 to 3 minutes or until the pieces just turn white. Add Hoisin sauce and stir well 1 minute to blend. The dish will be a pinkish red, with cooked but juicy chicken and crisp bright-green zucchini.

SERVINGS: Enough for 3 as a single course with rice or for 6 in a full menu.

DICED CHICKEN WITH CUCUMBERS AND HOISIN SAUCE: Substitute 2 cups diced seeded cucumbers for the zucchini.

DICED CHICKEN WITH HAIRY MELON AND HOISIN SAUCE: Substitute an 8-ounce hairy melon, peeled and diced, for the zucchini.

SLICED CHICKEN LIVERS WITH BAMBOO SHOOTS AND WATER CHESTNUTS

Cooking Time: 6½ to 7½ minutes

Utensils
Chinese cutting knife
Soup plate
Chopsticks
Small bowl for stock
12-inch skillet or wok
Slotted spatula

Ingredients

¾	pound chicken livers, cut in ½-inch diagonal slices	⅛	teaspoon five-spice seasoning
3	teaspoons cornstarch	1	teaspoon minced ginger root
½	teaspoon brown sugar	1½	cups bamboo shoots in thin strips
¼	teaspoon salt	½	cup thinly sliced water chestnuts
2	tablespoons soy sauce	¼	cup chicken stock
1	teaspoon sherry	3	tablespoons peanut oil or corn oil

Before cooking
Prepare chicken livers. Place the slices in the soup plate and dredge with the cornstarch, sugar and salt. Sprinkle with the soy sauce, sherry and five-spice seasoning. Mix well with chopsticks to coat the slices evenly. Prepare the ginger root, bamboo shoots and water chestnuts. Have stock and oil ready to go.

Cooking Instructions
Turn heat under skillet or wok to high. (The heat remains high throughout the cooking.) When the pan is hot, add the oil. It should sizzle at once. Before the oil begins to smoke, add the minced ginger. Give a stir and add the bamboo shoots and water chestnuts. Stir-fry-toss 2 minutes. Remove with slotted spatula. Add the dredged liver slices to the pan and stir-fry-toss about 3 minutes or until there are no blood specks on the liver and the slices seem firm. Add the stock and stir 30 seconds. Return the vegetables to the pan. Stir together 1 minute or until the sauce thickens. Remove from heat. The dish will be a rich, dark brown, with the livers just cooked and the vegetables still crisp. The flavor is a subtle blending of soy, wine and spice.

SERVINGS: Enough for 2 as a single course with rice or for 4 to 6 in a full menu.

SWEET-AND-SOUR SLICED CHICKEN LIVERS

Cooking Time: 8 to 9 minutes

Utensils
Chinese cutting knife
Soup plate
Chopsticks
Pint-size bowl or measuring cup
12-inch skillet or wok
Slotted spatula for stirring and removing
ingredients

Ingredients

¾	pound chicken livers, cut in ½-inch slices	¼	teaspoon salt
2	teaspoons cornstarch	1	tablespoon soy sauce
		1	small onion, cut in 6 wedges

Continued on next page

1 medium green pepper, halved crosswise, each half cut in 3 pieces	4 tablespoons brown sugar
	1 tablespoon tomato purée
	¼ cup chicken stock
1 slice ginger root (2x1x⅛ inch)	1 tablespoon cornstarch
3 tablespoons rice vinegar or cider vinegar	3 tablespoons peanut oil or corn oil

Before Cooking

Place the liver slices in the soup plate and dredge with the 2 teaspoons cornstarch and salt. Sprinkle with soy sauce. Toss well with chopsticks to coat the slices evenly. Prepare the vegetables and ginger root. Combine the vinegar, brown sugar, tomato purée and chicken stock in the pint-size bowl or measuring cup. Add the 1 tablespoon cornstarch and stir to dissolve; set aside. Have oil ready to go.

Cooking Instructions

Turn heat under skillet or wok to high. (The heat remains high throughout the cooking.) When the pan is hot, add the oil. It should sizzle at once. Before the oil begins to smoke, add the ginger root and stir-fry-toss 1 minute. Add the onion wedges; stir-fry 1 minute. Add green pepper pieces and stir-fry 1 minute. Remove vegetables with the slotted spatula. Add the dredged liver slices to the oil remaining in the pan. Stir-fry-toss 3 to 4 minutes, scraping up any particles sticking to the pan. The liver should be firm and without blood specks. Add the vinegar, brown sugar, tomato and cornstarch mixture. Stir 1 minute to mix. Return the vegetables to the pan. Stir about 1 minute or until the sauce thickens. Remove from heat. The dish will be a russet color, the vegetables bright and very crisp. The sauce will be thick and clear.

SERVINGS: Enough for 2 as a single course with rice or for 4 to 6 in a full menu.

SQUAB SOONG
Minced Squab

Cooking Time: 9 to 10 minutes

Utensils
2 Chinese cutting knives
Soup plate
Chopsticks
12-inch skillet or wok
Slotted spatula for stirring

Ingredients

3   squabs (1 pound each), skinned and boned
1   teaspoon minced ginger root
⅓   cup minced celery
⅓   cup minced bamboo shoots
⅓   cup minced water chestnuts
⅓   cup minced canned button mushrooms

2   teaspoons cornstarch
¼   cup chicken stock
½   teaspoon salt
¼   teaspoon sugar
3   teaspoons gin, vodka or sherry
3   tablespoons peanut oil or corn oil
    Inner leaves of 1 head Boston (butter) lettuce (refrigerated)

Before Cooking
Place the skinned and boned squabs on a cutting board and cut them into small pieces for easier mincing. Using the 2 cutting knives, chop until the squab meat is finely minced; place in the soup plate. Mince the ginger root, celery, bamboo shoots, water chestnuts and button mushrooms as finely as possible. (Mince them separately.) Combine the vegetables with the squab. Combine the cornstarch and stock. Have the salt, sugar, liquor and oil ready to go.

Cooking Instructions
Turn heat under skillet or wok to high. (The heat remains high throughout the cooking.) When the pan is hot, add the oil. It should sizzle at once. Before the oil begins to smoke, add the squab mixture and stir-fry-toss 5 minutes. Add the salt and sugar and stir 1 minute to blend. Add the liquor. Stir-fry 1 minute. Give the cornstarch-stock mixture a quick stir and add, stirring 2 to 3 minutes or until the mixture thickens. Remove from heat. The texture of the squab mince should be velvety, the color somewhat pale. The mince is passed on one serving dish, the chilled lettuce leaves on another. The mince is spooned onto a lettuce leaf, folded like a tortilla and eaten with the fingers.

SERVINGS: Enough for 2 as a single course or for 4 in a full menu.

CHOP SUEY
Sub Gum

Every writer of Chinese cookbooks lays claim to a story about this particular dish. Most are agreed that Chop Suey, as we know it, is an American adaptation of an old Cantonese standby called *Sub Gum*. My own cook served *Sub Gum* with many variations, sometimes substituting duck or pheasant for the chicken, at other times adding thinly sliced liver or kidneys. When he was in a Northern mood, he added garlic and wine; when he felt Szechuanese, he spiked up the dish with hot peppers. As it is served in the United States, Chop Suey usually features only one kind of meat or shellfish.

Cooking Time: 13 minutes

Utensils
Chinese cutting knife
Small bowl for seasonings
12-inch skillet or wok
Tongs or chopsticks

Ingredients

¼	cup dried mushrooms	1	teaspoon minced ginger root
⅓	cup pea sprouts	6	water chestnuts, thinly sliced
¼	pound lean pork, cut in thin strips	2	tablespoons soy sauce
¼	pound Virginia ham, cut in thin strips	1	teaspoon sugar
¼	pound chicken breast, cut in thin strips	½	teaspoon salt
¼	pound tiny shrimp, peeled	2	teaspoons cornstarch
2	scallions, each with 1 inch of green, cut in ½-inch rounds	1	tablespoon chicken stock or water
		2	tablespoons peanut oil or corn oil

Before Cooking
Soak the dried mushrooms in warm water 15 minutes. Drain well; cut out the hard centers and cut into thin strips. Rinse the pea sprouts and pick off green hoods. Prepare the pork, ham, chicken, shrimp, scallions, ginger root and water chestnuts. Combine the soy sauce, sugar and salt in the small bowl; set aside. Combine the cornstarch and chicken stock or water. Have oil ready to go.

Cooking Instructions
Turn heat under skillet or wok to high. (The heat remains high throughout the cooking.) When the pan is hot, add the oil. It should sizzle at once. Before the oil

begins to smoke, add the scallions and ginger. Stir rapidly, no longer than 30 seconds. Add the pork strips and stir-fry-toss 5 minutes. Add the ham, chicken and shrimp. Stir-fry-toss 3 minutes. Add the water chestnuts, mushrooms and sprouts. Stir-fry 2 minutes. Stir in the seasoning mixture and blend well 30 seconds. Give the cornstarch-stock mixture a quick stir and add to the pan; stir-fry-toss 2 minutes. The meats, chicken and shrimp should be done, the vegetables still bright in color and crisp to the taste. The sauce should be scant and not too thick. A mark of inferior Chop Suey is the overuse of cornstarch.

SERVINGS: Enough for 2 to 3 as a single course with rice or for 4 to 5 in a full menu.

POINTS TO REMEMBER IN STIR-FRY-TOSS
COOKING OF FISH

Only seafood with a firm texture, such as scallops, crabs, lobsters, prawns and shrimp, are suited to the intense heat and rapid stirring of this technique. Fish filets with flaky, delicate texture are inclined to disintegrate with this technique; they are usually semi–deep-fried. Shellfish must always be cooked raw and crabs and lobsters freshly killed at home if possible. Crabs, lobsters, prawns or shrimp which have been previously cooked toughen on reheating and the juices essential to the finished flavor of the dish are lost. There is no hard and fast rule about when the shellfish should be added to the pan; follow the instructions in each recipe. Other rules, however, remain unchangeable: the oil must always be extremely hot and the shellfish cooked only a few minutes—no longer than the time required for the flesh to change color.

FRESH SCALLOPS WITH VEGETABLES

Cooking Time: $6\frac{1}{2}$ to $7\frac{1}{2}$ minutes

Utensils
Chinese cutting knife
Small bowl for seasonings
Measuring cup
12-inch skillet or wok
Tongs or chopsticks

Ingredients

1 tablespoon dried shrimp	2 ounces snow peas
6 medium dried mushrooms	1 teaspoon salt
1 pound fresh scallops	½ teaspoon sugar
2 teaspoons finely minced ginger root	2 teaspoons soy sauce
	1 teaspoon vodka, gin or sherry
1 scallion with 1 inch of green, cut in 1-inch rounds	1 tablespoon cornstarch
	¾ cup chicken stock
½ cup water chestnuts, cut in ¼-inch slices	½ cup canned button mushrooms, drained
½ cup bamboo shoots in ½-inch dice	3 tablespoons peanut oil or corn oil

Before Cooking

Soak the dried shrimp in warm water 1 hour. Drain and set aside. Soak the dried mushrooms in warm water at least 20 minutes. Drain well. Remove hard centers from soaked mushrooms and cut in ½-inch dice. Trim away the small, hard muscle on the side of each scallop. Straight-cut each scallop into 2 coins. Prepare the ginger root, scallion, water chestnuts and bamboo shoots. Thread snow peas; snip off ends but leave whole. Combine the salt, sugar, soy sauce and liquor. Combine the cornstarch and chicken stock in the measuring cup. Have button mushrooms and oil ready to go.

Cooking Instructions

Turn heat under skillet or wok to high. (The heat remains high throughout the cooking.) When the pan is hot, add the oil. It should sizzle at once. Before the oil begins to smoke, add the ginger root and scallion. Stir-fry-toss 50 seconds. Add the water chestnuts and bamboo shoots and stir-fry 1 minute. Add the snow peas and stir-fry 1 minute longer. Next add the drained button mushrooms, the diced dried mushrooms and the dried shrimp. Stir-fry 1 minute. Add the scallops and stir together with the vegetables 1 minute. Pour in the soy sauce mixture. Toss to blend. Add the cornstarch-stock mixture, giving it a quick stir first, and stir well 2 to 3 minutes or until the sauce has thickened. The vegetables must be crunchy in texture and still bright in color. The scallops should be just done and glazed with a semi-thick but clear sauce. Do not overcook or the scallops will toughen.

SERVINGS: Enough for 4 as a single course with rice or for 6 to 8 in a full menu.

SHRIMP,
Chungking Style

Cooking Time: 4 minutes

Utensils
Chinese cutting knife
Small bowls for seasonings
12-inch skillet or wok
Long tongs or chopsticks
Slotted spoon or spatula

Ingredients

1	pound small shrimp (36 to 40), shelled and deveined	2	teaspoons brown sugar
		½	teaspoon salt
2	scallions with 1 inch of green, minced	2	tablespoons canned or fresh tomato purée
2	cloves garlic, minced	¼	teaspoon crushed Szechuan pepper or crushed red pepper flakes
1	tablespoon minced ginger root		
1	tablespoon soy sauce	2	tablespoons peanut oil or corn oil
1	tablespoon pale dry sherry	2	tablespoons peanut oil or corn oil
1	teaspoon cider vinegar		

Before Cooking
Prepare the shrimp, scallions, garlic and ginger root. Combine the soy sauce, sherry, vinegar, brown sugar and salt in a small bowl. Measure the tomato purée into another. Have the pepper and both portions of oil ready to go.

Cooking Instructions
Turn heat under skillet or wok to high. (The heat remains high throughout the cooking.) When the pan is hot, add 2 tablespoons of the oil. It should sizzle at once. Before the oil begins to smoke, stir in the shrimp and stir-fry-toss 2 minutes. Remove with slotted spoon or spatula. Add the remaining 2 tablespoons oil to the pan. Heat until it sizzles. Stir in the scallions, garlic and ginger root. Toss 1 minute. Return the shrimp to the pan and toss quickly to mix. Add the combined seasonings and stir well. Blend in the tomato purée and the Szechuan pepper or the crushed red pepper flakes. Stir-fry-toss 30 seconds. The shrimp should be crisp, the sauce a rich red and not too plentiful.

SERVINGS: Enough for 2 as a single course with rice or for 4 to 6 in a full menu.

NOTE: There is a tendency in the United States to use catsup in place of the tomato purée. If you choose to do so, reduce the sugar and vinegar by half. This dish is of Szechuanese origin; consequently, it's meant to be peppery. Increase or decrease the amount of pepper to suit your own taste.

DICED SHRIMP AND CUCUMBERS

Cooking Time: 4½ to 5½ minutes

Utensils
Chinese cutting knife
12-inch skillet or wok
Chopsticks or long tongs
Slotted spoon or spatula
Soup plate

Ingredients

1	pound medium shrimp (24 to 26), shelled and deveined, cut in ½-inch dice	2	scallions, minced
		2	medium cucumbers, seeded and cut in ½-inch dice
2	teaspoons cornstarch	2	tablespoons peanut oil or corn oil
½	teaspoon salt		

Before Cooking
Place the shrimp in the soup plate, sprinkle with the cornstarch and salt and toss together with chopsticks. Prepare the scallions and cucumbers. Have the oil ready to go.

Cooking Instructions
Turn heat under skillet or wok to high. (The heat remains high throughout the cooking.) When the pan is hot, add the oil. It should sizzle at once. Before the oil begins to smoke, add minced scallions and toss rapidly 30 seconds. Add the cucumbers and stir-fry-toss 2 minutes. Add the shrimp mixture, blend well and stir-fry-toss 2 to 3 minutes or only until the shrimp becomes pink. This dish must not be overcooked. The colors should be contrastingly bright and the cucumbers just translucent. No soy sauce is used with this dish.

SERVINGS: Enough for 2 as a single course with rice or for 4 to 6 in a full menu.

PRAWNS IN SHELLS

Cooking Time: 4½ to 5½ minutes

Utensils
Chinese cutting knife
Small bowl for seasonings
12-inch skillet or wok
Tongs or chopsticks for tossing

Ingredients

1	pound large prawns with shells (16 to 20), feelers removed	1	tablespoon pale dry sherry
1	teaspoon minced ginger root	½	teaspoon salt
1	clove garlic, minced	1	teaspoon sugar
1	teaspoon minced Chinese parsley (optional)	¼	teaspoon crushed Szechuan pepper or crushed black pepper
2	tablespoons soy sauce	2	tablespoons peanut oil or corn oil

Before Cooking
Prepare the prawns, ginger root, garlic and parsley. Combine the soy sauce, sherry, salt, sugar and pepper in the small bowl. Have oil ready to go.

Cooking Instructions
Turn heat under skillet or wok to high. (The heat remains high throughout the cooking.) When the pan is hot, add the oil. It should sizzle at once. Before the oil begins to smoke, add the ginger root and garlic. Stir-fry 30 seconds. Add the prawns and stir-fry-toss 2 minutes. Stir in the combined seasonings and blend well. Stir 2 to 3 minutes. Top with minced parsley. The prawns should be cooked through, pinkish in color and coated with a brown glaze. The scant juices in the pan are characterized by the lack of thickening agents. Cooking prawns by this method helps to keep them tender and moist; the prawn shell acts as a steamer.

SERVINGS: Enough for 2 as a single course with rice or for 4 to 6 in a full menu.

PRAWNS IN SHELLS WITH SNOW PEAS
Follow the recipe for Prawns in Shells but add ½ cup chopped celery, 1 cup snow peas (threaded and ends snipped) and 1 tablespoon peanut oil or corn oil. When

the garlic and ginger root have been stir-fried 30 seconds, add the celery. Stir-fry-toss 1 minute. Add the snow peas and stir and toss 2 to 3 minutes. Remove the vegetables and keep warm. Add the 1 tablespoon oil to the pan. When the oil is hot, add the prawns and continue cooking as directed. Before removing from heat, return the vegetables to the pan and stir well to blend.

SERVINGS: Enough for 2 as a single course with rice or for 4 to 6 in a full menu.

PRAWNS WITH DICED HAM

Cooking Time: 6 to 7 minutes

Utensils
Chinese cutting knife
Soup plate
Chopsticks for tossing
12-inch skillet or wok
Slotted spatula for stirring and scraping

Ingredients

1	pound medium prawns (24 to 26), shelled and deveined	2	tablespoons carrots in ¼-inch dice
1	egg white	2	tablespoons green peas
2	teaspoons cornstarch	⅛	pound Virginia ham, cut in ¼-inch dice
1	teaspoon sugar	1	tablespoon sherry
½	teaspoon salt	¼	cup chicken stock
2	teaspoons gin or vodka	3	tablespoons peanut oil or corn oil
2	tablespoons water chestnuts in ¼-inch dice		

Before Cooking
Combine the prawns, egg white, cornstarch, sugar, salt and gin or vodka in the soup plate. Let the prawns stand while you prepare the vegetables and ham. Parboil carrots and peas 3 minutes each. Drain well. Have the remaining ingredients ready to go.

Cooking Instructions

Turn heat under skillet or wok to high. (The heat remains high throughout the cooking.) When the pan is hot, add the oil. It should sizzle at once. Before the oil begins to smoke, add the water chestnuts and stir-fry-toss 1 minute. Add carrots and peas. Stir-fry-toss 1 minute. Add the diced ham and stir-fry with vegetables 1 minute. Pour in the prawn mixture and stir-fry, tossing well to mix. Scrape the bottom of the pan to prevent scorching. Stir 2 minutes or just until the prawns turn pinkish. Add the sherry, giving 1 or 2 quick stirs to allow the alcohol to evaporate. Add the stock and stir rapidly 1 to 2 minutes or until the sauce thickens. Do not overcook the prawns. This dish contains no soy sauce. It is noted for its color contrasts—curled pink prawns with jade-green peas, white water chestnuts, orange carrots and reddish ham. The sauce should be semi-thick and fairly clear.

SERVINGS: Enough for 3 as a single course with rice or for 6 in a full menu.

PRAWNS WITH OYSTER SAUCE

Cooking Time: 4½ minutes

Utensils
Chinese cutting knife
Small bowl for seasonings
12-inch skillet or wok
Tongs or chopsticks

Ingredients

2	pounds jumbo prawns (32 to 40), shelled and deveined, feelers removed	2	teaspoons sherry
		2	cloves garlic, finely minced
		2	teaspoons finely minced ginger root
½	teaspoon salt		
1	teaspoon brown sugar	2	tablespoons oyster sauce
1½	tablespoons soy sauce	3	tablespoons peanut oil or corn oil

Before Cooking

Prepare the prawns. Combine the salt, brown sugar, soy sauce and sherry in the small bowl. Prepare the garlic and ginger root. Have the oyster sauce and oil ready to go.

Cooking Instructions
Turn heat under skillet or wok to high. (The heat remains high throughout the cooking.) When the pan is hot, add the oil. It should sizzle at once. Before the oil begins to smoke, add the minced garlic and ginger root and stir 30 seconds. Add the prawns and stir-fry-toss 2 minutes. Add the soy sauce mixture and stir just to blend. Pour in the oyster sauce and stir 2 minutes. Remove from heat. The prawns will be coral-pink swirls in a velvety but scant golden brown sauce.

SERVINGS: Enough for 4 as a single course with rice or for 6 to 8 in a full menu.

LOBSTER WITH BLACK BEAN SAUCE,

Canton Style

Cooking Time: 16 minutes

Utensils
Chinese cutting knife
1-pint bowl for meat and seasonings
Bowl for cornstarch and stock
12-inch skillet or wok
Tongs or chopsticks

Ingredients

2	lobsters (1½ pounds each)	2	teaspoons brown sugar
⅛	pound ground lean pork	1	teaspoon cornstarch
⅛	pound Virginia ham, minced	1	tablespoon sesame oil
2	cloves garlic, minced	1	tablespoon cornstarch
1	teaspoon minced ginger root	1	cup chicken stock
2	tablespoons soft black beans, rinsed, drained and mashed	2	eggs, beaten until frothy
		½	cup sherry
½	teaspoon salt	2	tablespoons peanut oil or corn oil

Before Cooking
Kill each lobster by making an incision in the back, where the chest and tail meet. Discard the stomach (in the head), intestinal vein and legs and antennae. Remove

the feathery gill-like portions under the sides of the shell. Crack claws. Cut body into about 14 pieces. Rinse the lobster portions in cold water and blot dry. Combine the pork, ham, garlic, ginger root, black beans, salt, brown sugar, the 1 teaspoon cornstarch and sesame oil. Combine the 1 tablespoon cornstarch with the chicken stock. Beat eggs until foamy. Have the sherry and oil ready to go.

Cooking Instructions
Turn heat under skillet or wok to medium. When the pan is hot, add the oil. It should sizzle at once. Before the oil begins to smoke, add the pork-ham-bean mixture and stir-fry-toss 3 minutes. Add the lobster pieces and stir-fry 2 minutes. Add the sherry and stir 1 minute to allow the alcohol to evaporate. Give the cornstarch-stock mixture a quick stir and add to the pan. Reduce heat to low and simmer about 5 minutes or until the lobster shells are bright red. The lobster meat should be just opaque in a thick and creamy sauce specked with bits of black bean.

SERVINGS: Enough for 4 as a single course with rice or for 6 to 8 in a full menu.

CRAB WITH LOBSTER SAUCE,
Canton Style

Cooking Time: 11 minutes

Utensils
Chinese cutting knife
Small bowls for ingredients and seasonings
Bowl for beaten egg
12-inch skillet or wok
Tongs or chopsticks for stirring

Ingredients

2	Dungeness crabs (1 to 1½ pounds each) or 2 Maryland crabs with additional blue claws to make 3 pounds	¼	cup soy sauce
		½	teaspoon salt
		1	teaspoon brown sugar
2	cloves garlic, finely minced	3	teaspoons cornstarch
2	teaspoons finely minced ginger root	¼	cup chicken stock
		1	egg
2	tablespoons soft black beans, rinsed, drained and finely chopped	¾	cup sherry
		3	tablespoons peanut oil or corn oil

Before Cooking

Kill, clean and prepare crabs (page 29). If this seems too difficult, have your fish dealer kill and clean them. They should be used as soon as possible after killing. Combine the minced garlic and ginger root with the black beans. Combine the soy sauce, salt and brown sugar. Combine the cornstarch and chicken stock. Beat the egg until frothy. Have sherry and oil ready to go.

Cooking Instructions

Turn heat under skillet or wok to high. When the pan is hot, add the oil. It should sizzle at once. Before the oil begins to smoke, add the crab chunks, claws and legs. Stir-fry-toss 3 minutes. Add bean-garlic-ginger mixture. Stir-fry rapidly 2 minutes. Add the sherry and stir 1 minute to allow some of the alcohol to evaporate. Give the cornstarch and stock mixture a quick stir and add. Allow to boil, then reduce heat to medium and cook 5 minutes or until the shrimp are pink. Remove from heat and add beaten egg. Blend thoroughly. The crab shells will be bright red, the sauce thick and creamy with black specks.

SERVINGS: Enough for 4 as a single course with rice or for 6 to 8 in a full menu.

NOTE: This dish is called Crab with Lobster Sauce presumably because the bean-sherry-egg combination originated as a sauce for lobster.

PRAWNS OR SHRIMP IN SHELLS WITH LOBSTER SAUCE: Substitute 2 pounds jumbo prawns or shrimp for the crab. Wash and remove feelers but do not shell. Drain well before cooking.

BRAISING—
TECHNIQUE 2

Braising is a traditional method of Chinese cooking. However, its lengthy cooking requirements, which tie up a burner for long periods, make it unsuitable for small restaurant kitchens—probably the reason why most people are unfamiliar with braising in Chinese cuisine.

Braised dishes are extremely convenient for entertaining—once the preliminaries are taken care of, the dish cooks itself. Unlike Stir-Fry-Toss foods, these dishes do not suffer noticeably when they are slightly overcooked. They keep well and, in the manner of all stews, actually improve by standing a day or two.

If you stop to think about it, you will realize that braising is a technique you often use. Every time you brown ingredients in fat, add a small amount of liquid, cover the pan and cook over low heat, you are braising or fricasseeing. Chinese braising is much the same—but with these differences: The meat, fish or fowl is almost never dredged before frying; small amounts of cornstarch dissolved in water or stock are added in the final stages of cooking; and soy sauce and liquor are often included with the stock or water. In sum, a Chinese braised dish is quite similar to a French ragout or daube.

The technique of Braising is a natural sequence to Stir-Fry-Toss cooking since the preliminary step in braising employs frying over relatively high heat. If you use an electric frypan, turn the dial anywhere from 340° F. to 380° F. (usually 360° F.), depending on the specific recipe and the type of fat being used. If a skillet or wok is used, the heat should be between medium-high and high. The signal on an electric pan will indicate when the desired temperature has been reached; or

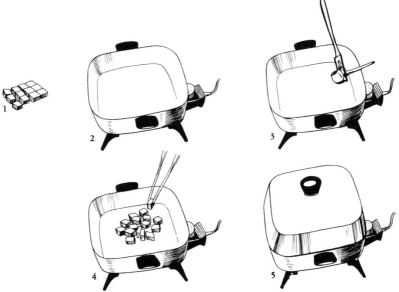

Braising
1. Cut ingredients to uniform size.   2. Heat electric frypan or skillet or wok to temperature specified in recipe until a drop of water bubbles into steam.   3. Add lard or oil and heat in electric frypan until correct temperature is reached or until just before the smoking point in skillet or wok. 4. Add meat, cook until brown and add liquor and seasonings.   5. Add liquid and let come to a boil. Reduce heat, cover, and braise until done.

a drop of water should bubble into steam on the surface of a skillet or wok. Fat is then added and heated in the electric pan to the temperature specified in the recipe. (The fat in the skillet or wok should be sizzling and almost, but not quite, at the smoking point.) If the fat in the skillet or wok should begin to smoke, remove the pan at once from the stove and wait until it has stopped smoking. If the fat used is lard, be very careful not to let it smoke. Burnt lard has an acrid flavor and must be replaced. Again, as in Stir-Fry-Toss cooking, the meat must be added to the fat before the vegetables to ensure proper browning.

Even though the soy sauce in these recipes enhances the color of the finished dish, the moist heat used in this method tends to fade the ingredients. Even when ingredients are not subject to fading, it is not advisable to attempt browning more than $\frac{3}{4}$ to 1 pound of meat or poultry at a time in a $10\frac{1}{2}$x$10\frac{1}{2}$-inch electric frypan or a 12-inch skillet or wok. Since the recipes in this section call for $1\frac{1}{2}$ pounds of meat, it is better to brown the pork, beef or lamb in two lots. To attempt to fry the entire amount at one time will result in an overcrowded steaming pan in which nothing browns.

Chicken, duck and squab are usually cut into chopstick-size pieces before frying; therefore these should be browned in more than one lot. One fryer does not sound like very much, but in weight and volume a 3-pound bird, no matter how it is cut up, takes up plenty of frying space. Therefore, fry the poultry pieces in three lots.

Whole fish is treated in a slightly different manner. You may be able to fit a 2-pound fish in your electric frypan, skillet or wok—in which case, of course, do so. In the case of a larger whole fish, either use an enameled iron roasting pan which will accommodate the whole fish or cut the fish in half or into 3 equal parts. Place the parts in the hot fat at the same time and turn them at the same time. If you are using a whole 3-pound fish and you don't want to cut it, the roasting pan should be 15x10x3 inches. For the braising, make a cover of double-thickness aluminum foil to fit over the top of the roasting pan.

As to the cooking itself, the tempo of stirring here is quite different from that of the Stir-Fry-Toss technique. Meat and poultry pieces should be allowed to rest on each side a few minutes to allow browning of that side before turning. Using a spatula scrape up the meat or poultry, making sure that you collect portions which may have stuck to the pan; turn over and brown. Continue until all sides are browned. Braising employs less of the constant tossing and stirring associated with Stir-Fry-Toss cooking.

Whole fish is fried on one side, while the top is basted with hot fat. It is then turned over and allowed to brown on the other side, while the previously browned side is basted. The time allocated for browning varies with the cooking utensil. The times given in the recipes relate to electric frypans. Ingredients browned on a gas stove should take somewhat less time. The important factor is that the ingredients being cooked are browned. If this takes you slightly longer than indicated in the recipes, adjust by braising for a shorter period. If, on the other hand, the browning takes less time, you might require additional braising time.

After the principal ingredient is browned, the liquor is added—alone or in conjunction with the seasonings. When adding liquor to meat or poultry, stir quickly for 30 seconds to allow the alcohol to evaporate and to permit the flavor of the liquor to be absorbed by the other ingredients.

Since whole fish obviously cannot be stirred, the liquor in this case should be combined with the seasoning mixture (soy sauce, salt, sugar), stirred around and spooned over the fish. Allow a minute or two for the flavors to merge and develop, then add the hot water or hot stock. Let the ingredients in the pan come to a boil, then reduce the heat to 200° F. to 220° F. on an electric frypan (depending on the recipe) or to low under the skillet or wok.

Cover the utensil and braise for the time specified in the recipe. If you are using more than 2 teaspoons of sugar, add it during the last 15 minutes of braising. Any amount of sugar over 2 teaspoons tends to scorch during long periods of cooking. In the case of meat and poultry, a few minutes before the cooking time is up, pour in the cornstarch dissolved in water or stock. Continue cooking 2 to 4 minutes, stirring until the sauce is thickened and clear. In the case of whole fish, braise the full time indicated on the recipe. Remove the fish to a heated platter and then add the dissolved cornstarch to the liquid in the pan. Stir until the sauce is thickened (2 to 4 minutes) and pour over the fish. The dish may be served at once in the manner suggested in each variation or it may be poured into a flat pan, chilled and served jellied. As a rule, the jellied braised dishes are made with a minimum of vegetables and must have the top layer of congealed fat removed before serving.

In buying meat for braising, make allowances for waste. For example, if you are using pork blade steaks and your recipe calls for 1½ pounds of pork, count on anywhere from ¾ to 1 pound of waste in bone and fat. Buy 2½ pounds of pork steak. This holds true for chuck roasts with bone and lamb shoulder or leg. Use the discarded bones to make an unsalted stock (except with beef). The Chinese preference for chicken and pork stocks is discussed more fully in the section on stocks (page 168).

Unless otherwise specified, the weights of chicken, duck and squab are reckoned with bones. Waste in these ingredients amounts to wing and drumstick tips. These, along with the neck, gizzard and heart (feet also, if they are available) should be simmered into a stock. Whole-fish weight includes bones, head and tail. Fish filets are rarely used in this method of cooking. On the whole, braising is an ideal technique for ingredients which require longer cooking than Stir-Fry-Toss cooking involves, but not quite so long as the Clear-Simmering or Red-Stewing techniques.

The following meats, poultry and fish are best suited to braising:
PORK: Fresh shoulder, butt, arm steaks, blade steaks, loin chops, tenderloin, unsalted belly, fresh ham.
BEEF: Round steak, top round, bottom round, heel of round, standing rump, chuck steaks, flank steak, plate beef.
LAMB: Shoulder, breast, boned leg, riblets, neck slices.
POULTRY: Chicken, duck, squab, quail, pheasant.
WHOLE FISH: Carp, perch, butterfish, sea bass, scup, mullet.

Fresh shellfish are seldom braised because they toughen when cooked a long time. Abalone, crab, oysters, prawns and shrimp may be added during the last minutes of braising if you like.

Fats used in braising may include any vegetable oil with the exception of olive oil, which has too definite a flavor of its own. Peanut oil and corn oil are preferred; sometimes sesame oil is used in conjunction with peanut oil or corn oil. When using sesame oil, be careful—it may burn. Lard works quite well in this type of cooking and is true to authentic origins. The smoking point of lesser grades of lard is 350° F. to 365° F. The highest temperature it should reach is about 340° F. Be sure to ascertain the burning point of the lard you are using and vary your temperatures accordingly. Do not use lard in braised dishes which you plan to serve cold. Butter is never used in Chinese cooking.

CLASSIC BRAISED DICED PORK

Cooking Time: Approximately 1 hour, 15 minutes

Utensils
Chinese cutting knife
1½-pint saucepan
12-inch skillet, wok or electric frypan—
    with cover
Tongs, chopsticks or spatula for turning
    meat

Ingredients

1½ pounds pork (butt, shoulder, un-
    salted belly or ham)
1   cup hot unsalted chicken stock or
    hot water
2   teaspoons cornstarch
2   tablespoons cold water or cold
    stock

2   teaspoons sherry
3   tablespoons soy sauce
¼   teaspoon salt
2   teaspoons brown sugar
2   tablespoons peanut oil, corn oil
    or lard

Before Cooking
Trim pork of excess fat and gristle (unless using pork belly, where fat predominates and is desirable). Cut into 1½-inch dice. Gently heat the 1 cup stock or water in the saucepan. Combine the cornstarch and 2 tablespoons of cold water. Measure the remaining ingredients.

Cooking Instructions

Turn heat under skillet or wok to medium-high (360° F. on electric frypan; 340° F. if using lard). When a drop of water on the skillet or wok bubbles into steam (signal on frypan will go off), add the oil. Just before the oil begins to smoke (signal on frypan will go off again), add diced pork. Fry half the meat at a time. When the meat is browned all over (about 10 minutes), add the sherry and toss 30 seconds. Add the soy sauce, salt and sugar. Stir 30 seconds to blend. Add the hot stock or water and let the mixture come to a boil. Reduce heat to low (200° F. on frypan). Cover and braise 1 hour, turning the meat from time to time. Five minutes before removing from heat, give the cornstarch-water mixture a quick stir and add. Stir until the sauce is thickened and clear. The pork should be fork-tender, the sauce thick, brown and clear, and it should be savory with the flavor of the meat. Serve at once as the sauce thins on standing. Or serve cold and jellied.

SERVINGS: Enough for 3 as a single course with rice or for 4 to 6 in a full menu.

NOTE: If you are using chicken bouillon cubes or canned broth, omit the salt.

CLASSIC BRAISED DICED BEEF: Substitute $1\frac{1}{2}$ pounds beef (chuck or top or bottom round), cut in $1\frac{1}{2}$-inch dice, for the pork.

CLASSIC BRAISED DICED LAMB: Substitute $1\frac{1}{2}$ pounds lamb (lean boned shoulder or leg, cut in $1\frac{1}{2}$-inch dice, riblets or neck slices) for the pork.

REGIONAL VARIATIONS OF CLASSIC BRAISED
DICED PORK, BEEF AND LAMB

PEKING: Just after browning meat, add the stalky portions of 2 leeks, cut in $\frac{1}{4}$-inch slices, and 1 clove garlic, finely minced. Substitute gin or vodka for the sherry and increase to 1 tablespoon. Proceed as directed in the Classic recipe.

CANTON: Just after browning meat, add 2 teaspoons finely minced ginger root and 1 tablespoon finely minced scallion. Proceed as directed in the Classic recipe.

SHANGHAI: Increase soy sauce to $\frac{1}{4}$ cup and omit salt. Increase brown sugar to 1 tablespoon. Proceed as directed in the Classic recipe but do not add brown sugar until the last 30 minutes of cooking.

SZECHUAN: Just after browning meat, add 1 tablespoon minced ginger root, 3 scallions, cut in $\frac{1}{2}$-inch slices, and either $\frac{1}{4}$ teaspoon ground Szechuan pepper or crushed red pepper flakes. Fry 1 minute. Proceed as directed in the Classic recipe, adding 2 teaspoons rice vinegar or cider vinegar with the soy sauce.

BRAISED DICED GINGER PORK

Follow the Canton variation for Classic Braised Diced Pork but increase the minced ginger root and sherry to 1 tablespoon each. Proceed as directed. One to 2 cups vegetables may be added according to the instructions given in any of the following braised pork and vegetable recipes.

SERVINGS: Enough for 3 to 4 as a single course with rice or for 6 in a full menu.

BRAISED DICED GINGER BEEF: Follow the directions above using the Canton variation for Classic Braised Diced Beef.

BRAISED DICED GINGER LAMB: Follow the directions above using the Canton variation for Classic Braised Diced Lamb.

BRAISED SPICED PORK

Follow the Peking or Shanghai variation for Classic Braised Diced Pork. After adding stock or water, add 1 star anise and $\frac{1}{2}$ teaspoon five-spice seasoning. Then add 6 dried Chinese red dates and 1 piece dried tangerine peel (2 inches in diameter), which have been soaked in warm water 15 minutes. Cover, lower heat and braise as directed. One to 2 cups of any vegetable may be added according to the instructions given in any of the following braised pork and vegetable recipes.

SERVINGS: Enough for 3 to 4 as a single course with rice or for 6 in a full menu.

BRAISED SPICED BEEF: Follow the directions above using the Peking or Shanghai variation for Classic Braised Diced Beef.

BRAISED SPICED LAMB: Follow the directions above using the Peking or Shanghai variation for Classic Braised Diced Lamb.

BRAISED DICED PORK WITH DRIED CHESTNUTS

Boil $\frac{1}{2}$ pound dried chestnuts in 3 cups water 1 hour; drain well. Peel off thin, brownish skins. Reserve the chestnut liquid (about $\frac{1}{3}$ cup) and use in place of, or in combination with, the water or stock. Prepare the Peking variation for Classic Braised Diced Pork, adding the drained chestnuts to the pan just after adding the liquid. Cover, lower heat and braise as directed. To serve, pile pork and chestnuts on a serving dish.

SERVINGS: Enough for 3 to 4 as a single course with rice or for 6 in a full menu.

BRAISED DICED BEEF WITH DRIED CHESTNUTS: Follow the directions above using the Peking variation for Classic Braised Diced Beef.

BRAISED DICED LAMB WITH DRIED CHESTNUTS: Follow the directions above using the Peking variation for Classic Braised Lamb.

BRAISED DICED PORK WITH FRESH VEGETABLES

Follow the recipe for Classic Braised Diced Pork or any of the regional variations. Prepare 2 cups, mixed or unmixed, of any of the Fresh Vegetables (except lima and fava beans, broccoli, lotus root, leeks and scallions) as directed on pages 53–54 and add to the pork for the last 30 minutes of braising. Two to 3 minutes before removing from heat, add the cornstarch dissolved in stock or water. Stir until sauce is thickened. To serve, mix the meat and vegetables together and arrange on a platter.

SERVINGS: Enough for 3 to 4 as a single course with rice or for 6 in a full menu.

BRAISED DICED BEEF WITH FRESH VEGETABLES: Follow the directions above using the recipe for Classic Braised Diced Beef or any of the regional variations.

BRAISED DICED LAMB WITH FRESH VEGETABLES: Follow the directions above using the recipe for Classic Braised Diced Lamb or any of the regional variations.

BRAISED DICED PORK WITH LEAFY VEGETABLES

Follow the recipe for Classic Braised Diced Pork or any of the regional variations but decrease the stock or water to ⅔ cup. Prepare 2 cups, mixed or unmixed, of any of the Leafy Vegetables (except Chinese parsley and mustard cabbage) as directed on pages 54–55. Fifteen minutes before the end of the braising time, add the stalk sections of the vegetables. Cover and continue braising. Remove ingredients from pan. Add the leaf portions to the pan juices (spinach and watercress would be added only at this point). Cover and braise 3 minutes. Remove from pan. Add cornstarch dissolved in cold water or stock to the pan and cook until sauce thickens, 2 to 3 minutes. To serve, arrange the vegetables on a platter and place pork on top. Pour thickened sauce over all.

SERVINGS: Enough for 3 to 4 as a single course with rice or for 6 in a full menu.

BRAISED DICED BEEF WITH LEAFY VEGETABLES: Follow the directions above using the recipe for Classic Braised Diced Beef or any of the regional variations.

BRAISED DICED LAMB WITH LEAFY VEGETABLES: Follow the directions above using the recipe for Classic Braised Diced Lamb or any of the regional variations.

BRAISED DICED PORK WITH MELON-TYPE VEGETABLES
Follow the recipe for Classic Braised Diced Pork or any of the regional variations, but decrease stock or water to ⅔ cup. Thirty minutes before the pork has finished braising, add 2 cups of any of the Melon-Type Vegetables (page 55) and continue braising until done. Remove ingredients from pan, add cornstarch dissolved in water or stock to juices in pan and stir uncovered 2 to 3 minutes until the sauce has thickened. To serve, arrange braised pork and vegetables on a platter and pour sauce over.

SERVINGS: Enough for 3 to 4 as a single course with rice or for 6 in a full menu.

BRAISED DICED BEEF WITH MELON-TYPE VEGETABLES: Follow the directions above using the recipe for Classic Braised Diced Beef or any of the regional variations.

BRAISED DICED LAMB WITH MELON-TYPE VEGETABLES: Follow the directions above using the recipe for Classic Braised Diced Lamb or any of the regional variations.

BRAISED DICED PORK WITH ROOT-TYPE VEGETABLES
Follow the recipe for Classic Braised Diced Pork or any of the regional variations. Thirty minutes before the pork has finished braising, add 2 cups of any of the Root-Type Vegetables (page 55) cut in 1½-inch dice unless using mushrooms, which are sliced and not added until 15 minutes before the pork has finished braising. (Sweet potatoes or yams in 1½-inch dice may also be used.)
Cover and braise 15 minutes at 200° F. Then add ¼ cup additional hot stock. (If mushrooms are being used, the additional stock is added only if necessary.) Cover and continue to braise 15 minutes longer. To serve, pile braised pork and vegetables on a serving dish.

SERVINGS: Enough for 3 to 4 as a single course with rice or for 6 in a full menu.

BRAISED DICED BEEF WITH ROOT-TYPE VEGETABLES: Follow the directions above using the recipe for Classic Braised Diced Beef or any of the regional variations.

BRAISED DICED LAMB WITH ROOT-TYPE VEGETABLES: Follow the directions above using the recipe for Classic Braised Diced Lamb or any of the regional variations.

BRAISED DICED PORK WITH DRIED VEGETABLES OR
VEGETABLE DERIVATIVES

Follow the recipe for Classic Braised Diced Pork or any of the regional variations. In the last 30 minutes of braising, add 2 cups of any of the Dried Vegetables (pages 56–57), soaked and drained. Soaking time for dried vegetables in braising can be reduced to 10 minutes or until hard stems and twiglike matter can be easily cut away. Three minutes before removing from heat, add cornstarch dissolved in water or stock. Cook uncovered until sauce has thickened. To serve, pour mixed pork and vegetables into a serving dish.

SERVINGS: Enough for 3 to 4 as a single course with rice or for 6 in a full menu.

BRAISED DICED BEEF WITH DRIED VEGETABLES OR VEGETABLE DERIVATIVES: Follow the directions above using the recipe for Classic Braised Diced Beef or any of the regional variations.

BRAISED DICED LAMB WITH DRIED VEGETABLES OR VEGETABLE DERIVATIVES: Follow the directions above using the recipe for Classic Braised Diced Lamb or any of the regional variations.

BRAISED DICED PORK WITH SALTED, PRESERVED OR PICKLED INGREDIENTS

Follow the classic recipe or the Canton variation for Braised Diced Pork, reducing the soy sauce to 2 teaspoons. Omit salt. In the last 30 minutes of cooking add 1 to 1½ cups of Fresh, Leafy, Melon-Type, Root-Type or Dried Vegetables prepared according to the instructions on pages 53–57. Then add ½ to 1 cup of the sliced or chopped Salted, Preserved or Pickled Ingredients (page 57). Add the cornstarch dissolved in water or stock 3 minutes before removing from fire. Cook uncovered, stirring until sauce has thickened. To serve, pile pork and vegetables onto a serving dish.

SERVINGS: Enough for 3 to 4 as a single course with rice or for 6 in a full menu.

BRAISED DICED BEEF WITH SALTED, PRESERVED OR PICKLED INGREDIENTS: Follow the directions above using the recipe for Classic Braised Diced Beef or the Canton variation.

BRAISED DICED LAMB WITH SALTED, PRESERVED OR PICKLED INGREDIENTS: Follow the directions above using the recipe for Classic Braised Diced Lamb or the Canton variation.

BRAISED OXTAILS

Follow the recipe for Classic Braised Diced Pork or any of the regional variations. Substitute 2 pounds oxtails, cut in 2-inch lengths, for the pork. Fry half the oxtails at a time until they are all browned. Pour off excess fat in pan. Add sherry, seasonings and water or stock. After the heat has been lowered to a simmer, braise 3 to 4 hours. Three minutes before turning off heat, add cornstarch dissolved in water or stock.

SERVINGS: Enough for 3 to 4 as a single course with rice or for 4 to 6 in a full menu.

NOTE: Oxtails may be used in combination with any of the vegetable categories presented in this chapter.

BRAISED FIVE-FLOWERED PORK WITH CHESTNUTS AND RED BEAN CHEESE

Cooking Time: Approximately 1½ hours

Utensils
Chinese cutting knife
Soup plate
8-ounce measure or bowl
Chopsticks
1½-pint saucepan
12-inch skillet, wok or electric frypan—
    with cover

Ingredients

1⅓ cups dried Chinese chestnuts or
    1½ cups fresh chestnuts
1   pound pork belly
2   tablespoons red bean cheese
    (*naam yu* sauce)
2   cloves garlic, finely minced
1½ teaspoons soy sauce

½   teaspoon sherry
½   teaspoon brown sugar
1   teaspoon sesame oil
1   teaspoon cornstarch
1   cup chicken stock
1   tablespoon peanut oil or corn oil

Before Cooking
One hour before cooking starts, rinse dried chestnuts in cold water and soak with enough warm water to cover. If using fresh chestnuts, boil 30 minutes and peel, reserving 1 cup of the liquid in which the chestnuts were cooked. Cut the pork into approximately 2-inch dice. Place in the soup plate. In the 8-ounce measure or bowl, mash the red bean cheese with the minced garlic, soy sauce, sherry, brown sugar, sesame oil and cornstarch. Combine with diced pork and toss with chopsticks to coat meat evenly. Let stand 15 minutes. Drain the soaked chestnuts, reserving 1 cup of liquid in which they were soaked. Combine the chestnut liquid with the chicken stock in the 1½-pint saucepan and heat gently. Measure peanut oil or corn oil and have ready to go.

Cooking Instructions
Turn heat under skillet or wok to medium-high (360° F. on electric frypan). When a drop of water on the skillet or wok bubbles into steam (signal on frypan will go off), add the oil. Just before the oil begins to smoke (signal on frypan will go off again), add the seasoned pork mixture. Stir-fry-toss 3 to 5 minutes. Add the drained chestnuts and stir-fry 2 minutes. Add the heated stock and reserved 1 cup chestnut liquid. Let the mixture come to a boil. Cover and reduce heat to low (200° F. on electric frypan). Simmer 1½ hours, until the pork is clear, somewhat glutinous in texture and easily pierced with a fork. The chestnuts will be very tender but still whole; the sauce will be medium thick, pungent and slightly sweet.

SERVINGS: Enough for 3 as a single course with rice or for 4 to 6 in a full menu.

ONE HUNDRED ABDOMEN OF BEEF WITH RED BEAN CHEESE
Follow the recipe for Five-Flowered Pork with Chestnuts and Red Bean Cheese but substitute 1 pound beef plate for the pork belly. Instead of chestnuts, soak 1½ cups dried bamboo shoot tips or ¾ cup each dried bamboo shoots and dried chestnuts.

SERVINGS: Enough for 3 as a single course with rice or for 4 to 6 in a full menu.

BRAISED DICED PORK AND BEAN CURDS,

Soochow Style

Cooking Time: 20 minutes

Utensils
Chinese cutting knife
Bowls for ingredients
Soup plate for pork
12-inch skillet, wok or electric frypan—
    with cover
Slotted spatula for stirring and removing
    ingredients

Ingredients

1	tablespoon dried shrimp	2	tablespoons Hoisin sauce
1	pound lean pork (shoulder, butt or loin), trimmed of fat and bone	2	teaspoons brown bean sauce
1	medium bamboo shoot	½	cup drained button mushrooms
½	bell pepper	½	cup chicken stock
2	squares bean curd	1	tablespoon gin or vodka
1	tablespoon brown sugar	3	tablespoons peanut oil or corn oil

Before Cooking

Soak the dried shrimp in warm water 1 hour. Drain well. Cut pork and bamboo shoot into ½-inch dice. Cut the bell pepper into ½-inch squares. Cut each bean curd into 8 squares. Combine the brown sugar, Hoisin sauce and brown bean sauce. Have the other ingredients ready to go.

Cooking Instructions

Turn heat under skillet or wok to high (380° F. on electric frypan). When a drop of water on the skillet or wok bubbles into steam (signal on frypan will go off), add the oil. Just before the oil begins to smoke (signal on frypan will go off again), add diced pork. Stir-fry-toss 3 minutes. Remove pork with slotted spatula to the soup plate. Add the bamboo shoots to the pan; stir-fry 1 minute. Add the button mushrooms and shrimp; stir 1 minute longer. Pour in the gin or vodka and give a quick stir to blend. Add the brown sugar, Hoisin sauce and brown bean sauce. Blend well. Pour in the chicken stock and let mixture come to a boil. Add the bell pepper squares and bean curd. Handle the bean curd gently. It must remain intact throughout the cooking. Lower heat to medium (360° F. on frypan). Cover pan and cook 15 minutes. Turn off heat. This is a rich, spicy and somewhat salty dish. Use no salt or soy sauce with it. The pork cubes should be tender, the vegetables slightly overdone by Chinese standards. There should be a rich, thick sauce.

SERVINGS: Enough for 2 as a single course with rice or for 4 to 6 in a full menu.

YANGCHOW LION'S HEAD

Cooking Time: 20 to 25 minutes to shallow-fry
1½ hours to braise

Utensils
2 Chinese cutting knives or meat grinder
Large bowl for pork
Wooden spoon
12-inch skillet, wok or electric frypan
5-quart enameled casserole or electric deep-
    fry cooker—with cover
Slotted spatula

Ingredients

2	pounds medium-fat pork butt or 4 cups ground pork	¼	cup cold water
½	cup cooked crab meat, picked over for cartilage (optional)	2	small Chinese cabbages (¾ to 1 pound each)
1	teaspoon finely minced ginger root	6	medium dried mushrooms
¼	cup soy sauce	¾	cup chicken stock
½	tablespoon sherry	1	tablespoon soy sauce
1	teaspoon salt	1	teaspoon brown sugar
1	teaspoon brown sugar	2	tablespoons peanut oil or corn oil
1	tablespoon cornstarch	1	tablespoon peanut oil or corn oil combined with 1 tablespoon sesame oil
1	egg, beaten		

Before Cooking
Select a cut of pork with about 25 percent fat. Cut the pork into 2-inch chunks and feed through the medium blade on the meat grinder. After all the pork has been ground, divide into 2 equal parts. Put 1 part back through the grinder with the picked-over crab and grind a second time. Combine all in the large bowl. (If you mince the pork by hand, chop half of it semifinely and the other half very finely.) Add the ginger root to the pork mixture. Combine the ¼ cup soy sauce, the sherry, salt and brown sugar and stir it into the pork mixture. Blend lightly with a wooden spoon. (Do not pack the meat fibers together. That will make the balls heavy.) Add the cornstarch and blend again carefully. Beat the egg with the cold water until frothy; add to the pork mixture. Fold the meat gently with the wooden

spoon until the mass is cohesive and all the ingredients are well blended. Cut each Chinese cabbage lengthwise in fourths. When cooked, the cabbage quarters will resemble the manes of lions. Rinse the cabbage and drain well. Rinse the dried mushrooms in cold water and soak in warm water at least 10 minutes. Drain and trim the hard center stems. Combine the chicken stock with the sugar and 1 tablespoon soy sauce. Measure the first portion of oil. Measure and combine the second portions of oil.

Cooking Instructions

Turn heat under skillet or wok to medium (360° F. on electric frypan). When a drop of water on the skillet or wok bubbles into steam (signal on frypan will go off), add the 2 tablespoons peanut oil or corn oil. Just before the oil begins to smoke (signal on frypan will go off again), shape the ground pork mixture into 6 balls the size of tennis balls. Brown on all sides, shaping them with the wooden spoon. Do not press or flatten the balls, but pat lightly to preserve their shapes. To turn the balls, use the back of a spatula, prying gently. The browning should take between 10 and 15 minutes. Pour the combined chicken stock, soy sauce and sugar in the 5-quart casserole or electric deep-fry cooker. Bring to a boil; reduce heat to simmer. As the balls are done, very gently place them in the casserole or cooker. Cover and simmer 1½ hours. Meanwhile, without rinsing the skillet, wok or electric frypan, add the combined peanut oil and sesame oil. When the oil is hot (380° F. on frypan), add the cabbage quarters. Fry 5 minutes, turning the cabbage on all sides. (Unless you are using a wok, you will probably have to do this in 2 shifts.) Cover and fry 3 minutes, turning the cabbage at 30-second intervals. Turn off heat; set cabbage aside. Twenty minutes before the pork balls are done, lift cover, gently shift balls and line the casserole or cooker with the cabbage quarters. Add the drained soaked mushrooms and replace the balls. Cover and continue simmering until done. The balls should be brown on the exterior and firm but tender. The cabbage must be cooked through, with crisp stems and flowing leaves, its shape retained. There should be some sauce, but not a soup. Serve directly from the casserole, using a large spoon to ladle out the Lion's Head.

SERVINGS: Enough for 6 as a single course with rice or for 12 in a full menu.

NOTE: This essentially simple dish is a specialty of Yangchow City, in the same province as Shanghai. Like most slow-cooked or casserole dishes, Lion's Head is more a home-style dish than a restaurant dish. There are a number of versions of this recipe, one of which calls for poaching the pork balls without prefrying and serving them with the cabbage in a kind of soupy concoction. Regardless of the fact that it is a home-cooked dish, correctly prepared Lion's Head can be quite elegant—but there's a big difference between a meatball-and-cabbage stew and crusty but tender pork balls on a bed of crisply cooked Chinese cabbage.

CLASSIC BRAISED CHICKEN

Cooking Time: 55 to 60 minutes

Utensils
Chinese cutting knife
1½-pint saucepan
Small bowls
12-inch skillet, wok or electric frypan—
    with cover
Tongs, chopsticks or spatula for turning

Ingredients

1	frying chicken (2 to 3 pounds)	1½	tablespoons sherry
4	tablespoons soy sauce	2	teaspoons cornstarch
¼	teaspoon salt	2	tablespoons cold water or cold chicken stock
2	teaspoons brown sugar		
1	cup unsalted hot chicken stock or hot water	3	tablespoons peanut oil, corn oil or lard

Before Cooking
Chop the drumsticks into ½-inch rounds. Cut each wing into 3 parts, saving bony tips for making stock. Divide the breast and thigh portions into 2x3-inch pieces. Combine back, giblets and wing tips with 2 cups cold water in the saucepan and prepare stock (see page 168). Combine soy sauce, salt and brown sugar in a small bowl. Measure the remaining ingredients and have ready to go.

Cooking Instructions
Turn heat under skillet or wok to medium-high (360° F. on electric frypan; 340° F. if using lard). When a drop of water on the skillet or wok bubbles into steam (signal on frypan will go off), add the fat. Just before the fat begins to smoke (signal on frypan will go off again), add the meaty parts of the chicken. Fry chicken until golden brown (about 10 minutes). Remove and add less meaty

pieces, wings and drumsticks and fry another 10 minutes. Return the first lot of chicken to the pan. Add the sherry and stir 30 seconds. Add soy sauce, salt and sugar mixture. Stir to blend. Add hot stock and let come to a boil. Turn heat to low (220° F. on frypan). Cover and braise 35 minutes, stirring from time to time. Combine the cornstarch and cold water or stock. Stir into pan. Cook 2 to 3 minutes, until the sauce has thickened and is clear, dark and velvety. The pure flavor and fragrance of chicken will predominate. Arrange chicken pieces on platter and pour sauce over.

SERVINGS: Enough for 3 as a single course with rice or for 6 in a full menu.

CLASSIC BRAISED DUCK: Substitute 1 duckling (4 to 5 pounds) for the chicken. If using fresh duck, be sure to remove the oil sacs above the tail. While the skin of frozen duck does not take to roasting nearly as well as fresh duck, it is very well suited to braised or stewed dishes. Increase the soy sauce to 5 tablespoons and water or stock to 2 cups.

CLASSIC BRAISED SQUAB: Substitute 3 squabs (1 pound each) for the chicken. Wash and drain squabs and cut each into quarters.

REGIONAL VARIATIONS OF CLASSIC BRAISED CHICKEN, DUCK AND SQUAB

PEKING: Just after browning chicken, duckling or squabs, add 1 large leek, trimmed and cut in $\frac{1}{4}$-inch rounds, and 1 clove garlic, finely minced. Substitute gin or vodka for sherry. Proceed as directed in the Classic recipe.

CANTON: Just after browning chicken, duckling or squabs, add 2 tablespoons finely minced ginger root and 1 tablespoon finely minced scallion. Proceed as directed in the Classic recipe.

SHANGHAI: Increase soy sauce to $\frac{1}{3}$ cup and decrease salt to $\frac{1}{8}$ teaspoon. Proceed as directed in the Classic recipe but do not add brown sugar until the last 15 minutes of cooking.

SZECHUAN: Just after browning chicken, duckling or squabs, add 1 tablespoon minced ginger root, $\frac{1}{3}$ cup sliced scallions ($\frac{1}{4}$-inch rounds) and either $\frac{1}{4}$ teaspoon crushed red pepper flakes or ground Szechuan pepper. Fry together 1 minute. Proceed as directed in the Classic recipe but add 2 teaspoons rice vinegar or cider vinegar with the soy sauce.

BRAISED GINGER CHICKEN

Follow the Canton variation for Classic Braised Chicken but increase finely minced ginger root to 1½ tablespoons and liquor to 2 tablespoons. Proceed as directed. Arrange chicken on a platter and pour sauce over.

SERVINGS: Enough for 3 as a single course with rice or for 6 in a full menu.

BRAISED GINGER DUCK: Follow the directions above using the Canton variation for Classic Braised Duck.

BRAISED GINGER SQUAB: Follow the directions above using the Canton variation for Classic Braised Squab.

BRAISED SPICED CHICKEN

Follow the Peking or Shanghai variation for Classic Braised Chicken. After the addition of stock or water, add 1 star anise and ½ teaspoon five-spice seasoning. Then add 6 dried Chinese red dates and 1 piece dried tangerine peel (2 inches in diameter) which have previously been soaked in warm water 15 minutes. Cover, lower heat and braise as directed. Arrange chicken on a platter and pour sauce over.

SERVINGS: Enough for 3 as a single course with rice or for 6 in a full menu.

BRAISED SPICED DUCK: Follow the directions above using the Peking or Shanghai variation for Classic Braised Duck.

BRAISED SPICED SQUAB: Follow the directions above using the Peking or Shanghai variation for Classic Braised Squab.

BRAISED SPICED HONEY CHICKEN

Follow the directions for Braised Spiced Chicken but add 2 tablespoons honey to the soy sauce mixture and omit sugar.

SERVINGS: Enough for 3 as a single course with rice or for 6 in a full menu.

BRAISED SPICED HONEY DUCK: Follow the directions above using Braised Spiced Duck.

BRAISED SPICED HONEY SQUAB: Follow the directions above using Braised Spiced Squab.

BRAISED CHICKEN WITH DRIED CHESTNUTS

Boil $\frac{1}{2}$ pound dried chestnuts in 3 cups water 1 hour. Drain well and reserve the chestnut liquid to combine with the hot water or stock to make 1 cup. Follow the Peking variation for Classic Braised Chicken. Just after adding the chestnut water or stock, add the drained chestnuts to the pan. Proceed as directed.

An unusual flavor is sometimes given to this dish by the addition of pork or smoked ham. Add $\frac{1}{4}$ pound ground or shredded lean pork or $\frac{1}{8}$ pound shredded smoked ham just after the chicken has been browned. Toss the chicken with the pork or ham until the pork loses its pinkness, about 3 minutes. If you are using the smoked ham, toss about 2 minutes. Add the liquor, seasonings and chestnuts. Stir well to blend. Proceed as directed. Pour chicken and chestnuts into a serving dish.

SERVINGS: Enough for 3 to 4 as a single course or for 6 to 8 in a full menu.

BRAISED DUCK WITH DRIED CHESTNUTS: Follow the directions above using the Peking variation for Classic Braised Duck.

BRAISED SQUAB WITH DRIED CHESTNUTS: Follow the directions above using the Peking variation for Classic Braised Squab.

BRAISED CHICKEN WITH FRESH VEGETABLES

Follow the recipe for Classic Braised Chicken or any of the regional variations. Prepare 2 cups, mixed or unmixed, of any of the Fresh Vegetables (except lima and fava beans, broccoli, lotus root, leeks and scallions) as directed on pages 53–54 and add to the chicken for the last 15 minutes of braising. Proceed as directed. To serve, arrange vegetables and chicken on platter.

SERVINGS: Enough for 3 to 4 as a single course with rice or for 6 to 8 in a full menu.

BRAISED DUCK WITH FRESH VEGETABLES: Follow the directions above using the recipe for Classic Braised Duck or any of the regional variations.

BRAISED SQUAB WITH FRESH VEGETABLES: Follow the directions above using the recipe for Classic Braised Squab or any of the regional variations.

BRAISED CHICKEN WITH LEAFY VEGETABLES

Follow the recipe for Classic Braised Chicken or any of the regional variations but decrease the stock or water to $\frac{3}{4}$ cup. Prepare 2 cups, mixed or unmixed, of any of the Leafy Vegetables (except Chinese parsley and mustard cabbage) as directed on pages 54–55. Fifteen minutes before the end of the braising time, add the stalk sections to the chicken. Cover and continue braising 10 minutes. Add the leaf portions. Cover and braise 3 minutes. Proceed as directed. To serve, arrange the vegetables in a flat bowl or platter. Place chicken pieces on top and pour sauce over all.

SERVINGS: Enough for 4 as a single course with rice or for 6 to 8 in a full menu.

BRAISED DUCK WITH LEAFY VEGETABLES: Follow the directions above using the recipe for Classic Braised Duck or any of the regional variations.

BRAISED SQUAB WITH LEAFY VEGETABLES: Follow the directions above using the recipe for Classic Braised Squab or any of the regional variations.

BRAISED CHICKEN WITH MELON-TYPE VEGETABLES
Follow the recipe for Classic Braised Chicken or any of the regional variations. After browning chicken, add 2 cups of any of the cut-up Melon-Type Vegetables (page 55) and stir together 2 to 3 minutes. Add seasonings and proceed as directed but decrease water or stock to ¾ cup. To serve, arrange mixed chicken and vegetables on a platter.

SERVINGS: Enough for 3 to 4 as a single course with rice or for 6 to 8 in a full menu.

BRAISED DUCK WITH MELON-TYPE VEGETABLES: Follow the directions above using the recipe for Classic Braised Duck or any of the regional variations.

BRAISED SQUAB WITH MELON-TYPE VEGETABLES: Follow the directions above using the recipe for Classic Braised Squab or any of the regional variations.

BRAISED CHICKEN WITH ROOT-TYPE VEGETABLES
Follow the recipe for Classic Braised Chicken or any of the regional variations but increase fat to 4 tablespoons. After browning chicken, add 2 cups of any of the Root-Type Vegetables (page 55) cut in 1½-inch dice—unless using mushrooms, which are sliced and added later. (Sweet potatoes and yams cut in 1½-inch dice may also be used.) Add liquor, seasonings and stock or water. Cover and braise 15 minutes at 200° F. Then add ¼ cup more water or stock. Cover and continue braising 15 minutes longer. If using mushrooms, add to the chicken for the last 15 minutes of braising, adding hot water or stock if necessary. To serve, arrange chicken mixed with vegetables on a platter.

SERVINGS: Enough for 4 as a single course with rice or for 6 to 8 in a full menu.

BRAISED DUCK WITH ROOT-TYPE VEGETABLES: Follow the directions above using the recipe for Classic Braised Duck or any of the regional variations.

BRAISED SQUAB WITH ROOT-TYPE VEGETABLES: Follow the directions above using the recipe for Classic Braised Squab or any of the regional variations.

BRAISED CHICKEN WITH DRIED VEGETABLES OR VEGETABLE DERIVATIVES
Follow the recipe for Classic Braised Chicken or any of the regional variations. When ready to lower the heat to braise, add 2 cups of any of the Dried Vegetables (pages 56–57) prepared as directed. (The presoaking time may be reduced to 10 minutes.) To serve, arrange chicken mixed with vegetables on a platter.

SERVINGS: Enough for 4 as a single course with rice or for 6 to 8 in a full menu.

BRAISED DUCK WITH DRIED VEGETABLES OR VEGETABLE DERIVATIVES: Follow the directions above using the recipe for Classic Braised Duck or any of the regional variations.

BRAISED SQUAB WITH DRIED VEGETABLES OR VEGETABLE DERIVATIVES: Follow the directions above using the recipe for Classic Braised Squab or any of the regional variations.

BRAISED CHICKEN WITH SALTED, PRESERVED OR PICKLED INGREDIENTS
Follow the recipe for Classic Braised Chicken or the Canton variation. Reduce the soy sauce to 3 teaspoons and omit salt. After 15 minutes braising, add 1 to 1½ cups Fresh, Leafy, Melon-Type or Dried Vegetables. (Root-Type Vegetables, with the exception of mushrooms, must be added to the fried chicken as soon as it is brown.) Then add ½ to 1 cup of any of the Salted, Preserved or Pickled ingredients (page 57), sliced or chopped. Serve the chicken mixed with the vegetables on a platter.

SERVINGS: Enough for 4 as a single course with rice or for 6 to 8 in a full menu.

BRAISED DUCK WITH SALTED, PRESERVED OR PICKLED INGREDIENTS: Follow the directions above, using the recipe for Classic Braised Duck or the Canton variation.

BRAISED SQUAB WITH SALTED, PRESERVED OR PICKLED INGREDIENTS: Follow the directions above, using the recipe for Classic Braised Squab or the Canton variation.

CLASSIC BRAISED WHOLE FISH

Cooking Time: 25 to 30 minutes for large fish
                22 to 25 minutes for smaller fish

Utensils
Long sharp knife
Small bowl for seasoning
1-pint saucepan for stock
12-inch skillet, wok, electric frypan or
    15x10x3-inch roasting pan
Lined rubber gloves
Large spoon for basting fish
Spatula for turning fish

Ingredients

1	whole dressed carp or sea bass (2½ pounds) or 2 whole dressed perch or scup (1 to 1½ pounds each)	¼	teaspoon salt
		1	cup hot unsalted chicken stock or hot water
2	slices ginger root (3x1½x⅛ inch)	2	teaspoons cornstarch
1½	tablespoons sherry	2	tablespoons cold chicken stock or cold water
3	tablespoons soy sauce		
1	teaspoon brown sugar	⅓	cup peanut oil or corn oil

Before Cooking
Have the fish cleaned and scaled with the head and tail intact. Wash the fish thoroughly in cold water, making sure that all blood clots in the cavity are removed. Blot dry inside and out with paper towels. The fish should be as dry as possible before frying. Rub the whole fish with the ginger root; reserve the ginger slices. Using a long sharp knife, make 3 diagonal slashes on each side of the fish. If the fish is too big to cook whole in your pan, cut it into 2 or 3 equal parts. They can be carefully reassembled on a platter after cooking. Combine the sherry, soy sauce, brown sugar and salt in the small bowl. Gently heat the stock or water in the saucepan. Combine cornstarch and water or stock. Have oil ready to go.

Cooking Instructions

Turn heat under skillet, wok or roasting pan to medium-high (360° F. on electric frypan). When a drop of water on the skillet, wok or roasting pan bubbles into steam (signal on frypan will go off), add the oil. Just before the oil begins to smoke (signal on frypan will go off again), add the ginger slices. Fry 1 minute. Place fish in pan. If you are using the whole uncut fish, wear lined rubber gloves to prevent the fish from slipping out of your grasp. Hold by the tail and gently lower into the hot oil. Fry fish on one side 5 minutes, basting the top constantly with oil from the pan. Then turn the fish, using the spatula to help. Move the pan from the fire while you are doing this to prevent spattering. Fry on the other side 5 minutes, again basting with oil. Pour or siphon off oil. Sprinkle sherry-soy sauce mixture over fish. Then add the hot stock or water and let the mixture come to a boil. Reduce heat to medium-low (260° F. on frypan). Cover and braise 15 to 20 minutes for large fish, 12 to 15 minutes for small. Turn fish at least once during braising, being careful not to break it. To cover the roasting pan, use a double thickness of foil fitted over the top of the pan. Test for doneness with a fork; the meat should be opaque and flake easily. Carefully remove to a heated platter. Remove the ginger slices from the pan. Combine the cornstarch and cold water or stock and add to the juices in the pan. Stir uncovered 2 to 3 minutes, until the sauce becomes thick, dark and clear. Pour the sauce over the fish. This dish may be served hot or cold.

SERVINGS: Enough for 3 to 4 as a single course with rice or for 6 in a full menu.

REGIONAL VARIATIONS OF CLASSIC BRAISED WHOLE FISH

PEKING: Substitute gin or vodka for the sherry and increase to 2 tablespoons. After frying the fish on both sides, drain or siphon off all but 2 tablespoons oil. Add the stalky portions of 2 leeks, cut in 1/4-inch slices, and 1 clove garlic, finely minced. Fry along with fish 2 minutes. Proceed as directed in the Classic recipe.

CANTON: After frying the fish on both sides, drain or siphon off all but 1 tablespoon oil. Add 3 scallion stalks, cut in 1/4-inch rounds. Fry along with fish 2 minutes. If you like, add 2 tablespoons fresh or canned tomato purée to the sherry, soy, salt and sugar mixture. Proceed as directed in the Classic recipe.

SHANGHAI: Increase soy sauce to 1/3 cup and omit salt. Increase brown sugar to 1 tablespoon. Proceed as directed in the Classic recipe.

SZECHUAN: After frying the fish on both sides, drain or siphon off all but 1 tablespoon oil. Add 3 scallion stalks, cut in 1/4-inch slices. Fry scallions along with fish 2 minutes. To liquor-soy sauce mixture, add 2 teaspoons rice vinegar or cider vinegar and ¼ teaspoon either crushed red pepper flakes or ground Szechuan pepper. Proceed as directed in the Classic recipe.

BRAISED GINGER FISH

Follow the Canton variation for Classic Braised Whole Fish but increase the ginger root to 4 slices (do not remove until just before serving) and increase the sherry to 2 tablespoons. One-half to 1 cup vegetables may be added according to the instructions given in any of the following braised fish and vegetable recipes.

SERVINGS: Enough for 3 to 4 as a single course with rice or for 6 in a full menu.

BRAISED SPICED WHOLE FISH

Follow the Peking or Shanghai variation for Classic Braised Whole Fish up to the point of adding water or stock. Add 1 star anise and ½ teaspoon five-spice seasoning. Then add 6 dried mushrooms, 4 dried Chinese red dates and 1 piece dried tangerine peel (2 inches in diameter), all of which have been separately soaked in warm water 30 minutes. Drain well before adding to the fish and cut out woody sections in mushrooms. Proceed as directed.

SERVINGS: Enough for 3 to 4 as a single course with rice or for 6 in a full menu.

BRAISED SPICED HONEY FISH

Follow the directions for Braised Spiced Whole Fish but omit tomato purée and add 2 tablespoons honey to the soy sauce mixture.

SERVINGS: Enough for 3 to 4 as a single course with rice or for 6 in a full menu.

BRAISED WHOLE FISH WITH DRIED CHESTNUTS

Boil ½ pound dried chestnuts in 3 cups water 1 hour. Drain well and reserve chestnut liquid to combine with the hot water or stock to make 2 cups. Follow the Peking variation for Classic Braised Whole Fish, adding the drained chestnuts to the pan after adding the chestnut water and stock. Cover, lower heat and braise until the fish is done. Remove fish to a platter and keep warm in a 170° F. oven. Continue braising the chestnuts until they are tender. Thicken sauce by adding the cornstarch mixture. Cook uncovered 2 to 3 minutes. Pour the chestnuts and sauce over the fish and serve.

SERVINGS: Enough for 4 as a single course with rice or for 6 to 8 in a full menu.

BRAISED WHOLE FISH WITH FRESH VEGETABLES

Follow the recipe for Classic Braised Whole Fish or any of the regional variations. Prepare 1 cup, mixed or unmixed, of any of the Fresh Vegetables (except lima and fava beans, broccoli, lotus root, leeks and scallions) as directed on pages 53–54. After frying the fish on one side, add vegetables to the pan. Turn the fish over, scooping the vegetables to the sides of the pan in the process. Fry the fish on the other side. Drain or siphon off the oil. Add seasoning mixtures and water or stock. Proceed as directed in the Classic recipe or any of the regional variations.

SERVINGS: Enough for 4 as a single course with rice or for 6 to 8 in a full menu.

BRAISED WHOLE FISH WITH LEAFY VEGETABLES

Follow the recipe for Classic Braised Whole Fish or any of the regional variations. Drain off all but 1 tablespoon oil. Decrease the stock or water to $\frac{3}{4}$ cup. Prepare 1 cup, mixed or unmixed, of any of the Leafy Vegetables (except Chinese parsley and mustard cabbage) as directed on pages 54–55.

In the final 10 minutes of braising, add the stalky sections of the vegetables. Continue braising until done. Carefully remove fish and stalk sections. To the juices in the pan, add the leaf sections, cover and braise 2 to 3 minutes. To serve, arrange a bed of vegetables on a platter. Lay the fish on top. Thicken sauce in pan with cornstarch mixture and pour over fish and vegetables.

SERVINGS: Enough for 4 as a single course with rice or for 6 to 8 in a full menu.

BRAISED WHOLE FISH WITH MELON-TYPE VEGETABLES

Follow the recipe for Classic Braised Whole Fish or any of the regional variations. When the fish has been browned on both sides, pour off all but 3 tablespoons of oil and add 1 cup of any of the cut-up Melon-Type Vegetables (page 55). Fry the vegetables alongside of the fish (be careful not to squash tomatoes or okra). Add the seasonings, water or stock decreased to $\frac{2}{3}$ cup and continue braising as directed. When fish and vegetables are done, place fish on a platter and arrange the vegetables on both sides. Add the cornstarch mixture to juices in the pan. Cook and stir 3 minutes or until the sauce thickens and is clear. Pour over the fish and vegetables.

SERVINGS: Enough for 4 as a single course with rice or for 6 to 8 in a full menu.

BRAISED WHOLE FISH WITH ROOT-TYPE VEGETABLES

Follow the recipe for Classic Braised Whole Fish or any of the regional variations. When the fish has been browned on both sides, drain or siphon off all but 3 tablespoons of the oil. Add 1 cup of any of the cut-up Root-Type Vegetables (page 55)—unless using mushrooms, which are not added until the last 15 minutes of braising. Fry the vegetables beside the fish 2 to 3 minutes. Add seasonings, water or stock and continue braising as directed. Test vegetables when fish is done. The fish cooks rapidly, the vegetables will require further braising in most cases. Remove fish to a heated platter; add $\frac{1}{4}$ cup hot water or stock to the vegetables and liquid in the pan, cover and braise 15 minutes longer. Add cornstarch mixture and cook uncovered 2 to 3 minutes until sauce has thickened. Pour vegetables and sauce over fish.

SERVINGS: Enough for 4 as a single course with rice or for 6 to 8 in a full menu.

BRAISED WHOLE FISH WITH DRIED VEGETABLES OR
VEGETABLE DERIVATIVES

Follow the recipe for Classic Braised Whole Fish or any of the regional variations. When the fish is browned on both sides, add 1 cup of any of the Dried Vegetables (pages 56–57), soaked and drained, or a combination of Fresh, Leafy or Root-Type Vegetables and Dried Vegetables to make 1 cup. (The presoaking time may be reduced to 10 minutes.) Fry with the fish 2 to 3 minutes. Add seasonings and water or stock. Proceed as in Classic or regional recipe. To serve, arrange the fish on a platter and pour vegetables and sauce over.

SERVINGS: Enough for 4 as a single course with rice or for 6 to 8 in a full menu.

BRAISED WHOLE FISH WITH SALTED, PRESERVED OR
PICKLED INGREDIENTS

Follow the recipe for Classic Braised Whole Fish or the Canton variation. Fry the fish on both sides as directed and remove all but 2 tablespoons oil from the pan. Add $\frac{1}{2}$ cup prepared Salted, Preserved or Pickled ingredients (page 57). At the same time, add $\frac{1}{2}$ cup Fresh, Leafy, Melon-Type, Root-Type Vegetables or Dried ingredients prepared according to the instructions on pages 53–57. Fry together with fish 2 to 3 minutes. Reduce soy sauce to 3 teaspoons and omit salt. Add water or stock. Cover, braise and thicken as directed.

SERVINGS: Enough for 4 as a single course with rice or for 6 to 8 in a full menu.

BRAISED ABALONE WITH VEGETABLES

Cooking Time: 19 minutes

Utensils
Chinese cutting knife
Small bowls for seasonings, abalone liquid
  and cornstarch mixture
12-inch skillet, wok or electric frypan—
  with cover

Ingredients

¼ cup salted turnip in ½-inch dice
1 pound canned abalone, drained
   (reserve liquid) and cut in ½-inch
   dice
2 teaspoons finely minced ginger
   root
1 clove garlic, finely minced
½ cup onions in ½-inch dice
½ cup bamboo shoots in ½-inch dice
½ cup water chestnuts in ½-inch
   dice

½ cup Virginia ham in ½-inch dice
1 tablespoon soy sauce
1 tablespoon vodka, gin or sherry
¼ teaspoon salt
1 teaspoon brown sugar
2½ teaspoons cornstarch
¼ cup drained, canned button mushrooms
2 tablespoons peanut oil or corn oil

Before Cooking

One hour ahead of time, soak salted turnip in hot water. Drain and rinse thoroughly in cool water before dicing. Put ¼ cup of the reserved abalone liquid in one small bowl and ½ cup in another. With the blunt edge of a Chinese cutting knife, separately mince ginger root and garlic; set aside. Dice the onions, bamboo shoots and water chestnuts and ham. Combine soy sauce, liquor, salt and brown sugar in a small bowl. Combine the cornstarch with the ¼ cup abalone liquid. Have the mushrooms and oil ready to go.

Cooking Instructions

Turn heat under skillet or wok to medium-high (360° F. on electric frypan). When a drop of water on the skillet or wok bubbles into steam (signal on frypan will go off), add the oil. Just before the oil begins to smoke (signal on frypan will go off again), add ginger root and garlic. Stir-fry 30 seconds. Add salted turnip and stir and toss 1 minute. Add onions; stir-fry-toss 2 minutes. Then add bamboo shoot and water chestnuts. Stir-fry 1 minute. Add button mushrooms and diced ham; stir 1 minute. Add combined soy sauce, liquor and seasonings; stir 30 seconds. Add the ½ cup abalone liquid. Stir to blend. Reduce heat to very low (220° F. on frypan). Cover and braise 10 minutes. Turn heat up again to medium-high (360° F. on frypan). Remove cover and add abalone. Stir just 30 seconds. Add the cornstarch-abalone liquid mixture, stirring well before adding to the pan. Blend with ingredients. Cover pan and turn off heat at once. Allow to remain in pan no longer than 2 minutes. Serve at once. This is a dish of widely varying textures. The extreme crunchiness of salted turnips and the crispness of bamboo shoots and water chestnuts are complemented by the soft button mushrooms and the slightly resilient abalone. The sauce will be scant but thick and a rich brown in color.

SERVINGS: Enough for 3 as a single course with rice or for 4 to 6 in a full menu.

BRAISED ABALONE WITH OYSTER SAUCE: Omit the cornstarch-abalone liquid mixture and add 2 tablespoons oyster sauce at the end of the cooking.

NOTE: In either recipe, use the best canned abalone available and do not overcook. Canned abalone is already cooked and will toughen if heated longer than a minute or two.

RED-STEWING— TECHNIQUE 3

㲋㲋㲋㲋㲋㲋㲋㲋㲋㲋㲋

Red-Stewing simply means the slow simmering of food in water containing soy sauce and sugar; the end product is a richly condensed stew with a deep reddish hue. The techniques of Red-Stewing and Braising are sometimes confusingly lumped together. Here are the ways to distinguish the basic differences between the two.

Red-Stewed dishes are always made with comparatively large amounts of soy sauce, whereas Braised dishes are usually prepared with little or no soy. To offset the saltiness of the soy sauce and to enhance the flavor and color, greater quantities of sugar are used in Red-Stewing than in Braising. Meat or poultry that is Red-Stewed is never browned by prefrying; with Braised dishes, the main ingredients always are. Thickening agents, such as cornstarch or flour, are never added in Red-Stewing. The gravy is condensed solely by long, covered simmering. Large cuts and older, fibrous or muscled ingredients, such as fowl, legs of fresh ham and lamb and shanks of beef, lend themselves well to this slow-cooking technique. Fish does not, with the exception of dried ingredients such as dried oysters, clams or scallops. Fresh fish subjected to the long cooking process of Red-Stewing disintegrates and becomes tasteless.

Fish is probably the cause of the most common confusion between these two techniques. We are told on all sides that Red-Stewed Fish is a most popular Chinese repast. But on studying recipes for "Red-Stewed" Fish, one discovers, in most instances, that the methods of preparation include dredging, browning and simmering. Correct—but these are the steps of Braising. And braised fish without the added cornstarch thickening at the end of cooking is what the Chinese mean when they discuss fish in terms of stewing.

Any of the recipes or their variations and combinations under the heading of Braised Whole Fish (pages 148–152) can be served as Red-Stewed Fish. Prepared in this way, fish is highly esteemed served cold. In the cold form, omit the vegetables.

Since the main ingredients used in Red-Stewing cause these dishes to jell easily —and the dishes are liked equally well hot or cold—vegetables are usually kept to a minimum. (For those who enjoy vegetables with everything and who might prefer to serve these dishes hot, I recommend 1 to 2 cups of any of those which appear on pages 53–57, with the exception of the salted, preserved or pickled vegetables. These are too salty to be compatible with the large quantities of soy used in Red-Stewing (follow the Braised Diced Pork recipes, pages 131–136, for cooking time of vegetables). As a matter of preference and logic, the Chinese stay with the Root-Type Vegetables, such as turnips, potatoes, taro root and lotus roots, which are enhanced by the stewing process.

Because of the long hours required to produce such concentrated food, Red-Stewed dishes are not found too often in restaurants. Nevertheless, this technique of cooking is a mainstay in China, particularly in Shanghai, where sugar is used quite liberally in conjunction with the soy sauce. The Chinese prefer rock sugar over our refined product, claiming that it gives a richer, shinier glaze to the finished product. I have found that brown sugar (and occasionally honey) works out quite well.

POINTS TO REMEMBER IN RED-STEWING

For successful Red-Stewing, use a sturdy Dutch oven or a cast-iron enameled casserole (a tight-fitting cover is essential whichever you use). If you prefer, use an electric deep-fry cooker—it will produce excellent results. Long tongs or chopsticks are necessary for turning the ingredients. In Red-Stewing, the meat or fowl can be cooked whole, until it is chopstick-tender; or it may be cut into 2-inch dice or odd-shaped chunks that are roughly the same size.

The meat is placed in the pot with hot water, the heat of which seals in the flavor. The resulting liquid will be a gravy (rather than a soup) which complements the main ingredient. This kind of long-term cooking allows for sufficient expression of juices without draining the meat of all flavor.

Turn the heat under the Dutch oven or casserole to medium or set the deep-fry cooker at 300° F. When the liquid begins to boil, add aromatic ingredients—such as ginger root, garlic or leeks. Then add all seasonings except sugar, which when

Red-Stewing Large Cuts and Whole Poultry
1. Place main ingredient in pot.   2. Add hot water and seasonings.   3. Cover and bring to a boil. Reduce heat and simmer until done.

cooked in any quantity is inclined to become scorched. The heat should at once be reduced to very low on the stove or reset at 200° F. to 220° F. on the electric cooker. Cover the pot tightly and simmer for the length of time designated in the recipe. Thirty minutes before the dish has finished cooking, add the sugar, stirring well to blend. The ingredients should be turned at least twice during the simmering process. To test if the meat is done, prod it with a chopstick. The chopstick should pierce through the fibers of the meat easily. For chicken, duck or squab, prod the chopstick through the fleshiest part of the drumstick.

The regional variations are merely a matter of ingredient adjustments and, in some cases, supplementation; the fundamentals of the technique remain unchanged. If you plan to vary the recipe by using beef or lamb instead of pork, be sure to note that the cuts of beef best suited to this method of cooking take longer to simmer than pork. More specific details regarding time are given in the recipes. When substituting duck for chicken in the poultry recipes, remember that more liquid is required—and the duck may need longer simmering. The cuts of pork, beef, lamb and types of poultry best suited to this method of cooking are described in the recipes.

Informally, a Red-Stewed dish served with rice can constitute the whole meal. It has more importance if it follows a Chinese cold plate, a light soup, a steamed dish and one or two contrasting stir-fried dishes. If you are serving Red-Stewed Duck, your stir-fried dishes might possibly be shrimp or pork or a vegetable.

CLASSIC RED-STEWED PORK

Cooking Time: 2 hours

Utensils
Chinese cutting knife
Small bowl for seasonings
Dutch oven, 4-quart cast-iron casserole or
    electric deep-fry cooker—with tight-
    fitting cover
Tongs or chopsticks to turn meat

Ingredients

4	pounds pork (shoulder, butt, tenderloin, unsalted belly, fresh ham or fresh shoulder hock)	$\frac{1}{3}$	cup soy sauce
		$\frac{1}{2}$	teaspoon salt
		2	teaspoons brown sugar
3	slices ginger root ($3x1\frac{1}{2}x\frac{1}{8}$ inch)	$1\frac{1}{2}$	cups hot water
$1\frac{1}{2}$	tablespoons sherry		

Before Cooking
Wipe the meat with a damp cloth. If you are using pork belly, fresh ham or hocks, leave the rind on. With a sharp knife, make several gashes in the fleshy part of the meat so that it will better absorb the flavors. The meat is now ready to be cooked whole or, if you prefer, it can be cut into odd-sized chunks or 2-inch dice. Prepare the ginger root. Combine the sherry, soy sauce and salt in the small bowl. Have brown sugar and hot water ready to go.

Cooking Instructions
Place pork in the pot; add hot water. Turn heat to medium (300° F. on electric cooker). When the liquid begins to boil, add the ginger root and sherry-soy-salt mixture. Reduce heat to very low (200° F. to 220° F. on cooker). Cover tightly and simmer $1\frac{1}{2}$ hours. Add the brown sugar and stir well to blend, turning the whole pork or pork chunks. Cover again and simmer 30 minutes longer. (Pork with skin will take longer.) Test meat for tenderness by piercing with a fork or chopstick. If you have left the pork whole, carve it into chunks or dice before serving. Arrange on a platter and pour gravy over all. This dish may be eaten either hot or cold. If served cold and jellied, remove the top layer of fat.

SERVINGS: Enough for 6 to 8 as a single course with rice or for 10 to 12 in a full menu.

Red-Stewing Cut Up Ingredients
1. Combine cut up meat or poultry with hot water in pot.   2. Bring to a boil and add spices and seasonings.   3. Cover, reduce heat and simmer for time specified in recipe.   4. Remove food to heated serving dish or platter.   5. Add vegetables to juices in pan and cook until tender.

CLASSIC RED-STEWED BEEF: Substitute 4 pounds of beef (shin or shank, chuck, heel of round, rolled or standing rump, plate or brisket) for the pork. Simmer a total of about 3 hours, depending on the cut of beef used. Test for tenderness with a chopstick—it should pierce the meat easily.

CLASSIC RED-STEWED LAMB: Substitute 4 pounds lamb (leg or shoulder, cut into 2-inch dice, or riblets or neck slices) for the pork. The Northern Chinese favor mutton, which has too pronounced a flavor for unaccustomed palates. Stewing the lamb with the bone in increases the jelling properties when served cold.

REGIONAL VARIATIONS OF CLASSIC RED-STEWED PORK,
BEEF AND LAMB

PEKING: Omit ginger root and substitute gin or vodka for the sherry. When the liquid begins to boil, add 2 leeks, trimmed and cut in ¼-inch slices, and 2 cloves garlic, finely minced. Proceed as directed in the Classic recipe.

CANTON: Same as the Classic recipe.

SHANGHAI: Increase the soy sauce to ½ cup and the brown sugar to 1 tablespoon. Proceed as directed in the Classic recipe.

SZECHUAN: Add 3 scallions, cut in ¼-inch rounds, along with the ginger. Add ¼ teaspoon either ground Szechuan pepper or crushed red pepper flakes and 2 teaspoons rice vinegar or cider vinegar with the sherry-soy-salt mixture. Proceed as directed in the Classic recipe.

RED-STEWED PORK WITH ROOT-TYPE VEGETABLES

Follow the recipe for Classic Red-Stewed Pork but 30 minutes before the stewing is completed, add 2 cups of any (except mushrooms, which are added later) of the Root-Type Vegetables (page 55), cut in 2-inch chunks or dice. Add the sugar and stir well to blend. Cover and continue to stew 15 minutes. If fresh mushrooms are being used, they should be cut into T-shaped slices and added at this time. Cover and continue stewing 15 minutes or until the ingredients are done. Serve hot only.

SERVINGS: Enough for 6 to 8 as a single course with rice or for 10 to 12 in a full menu.

RED-STEWED BEEF WITH ROOT-TYPE VEGETABLES: Follow the directions above using the recipe for Classic Red-Stewed Beef.

RED-STEWED LAMB WITH ROOT-TYPE VEGETABLES: Follow the directions above using the recipe for Classic Red-Stewed Lamb.

RED-STEWED SPICED PORK

Follow the Peking or Shanghai variation for Classic Red-Stewed Pork. When the mixture boils, add 1 teaspoon star anise, 1 piece dried tangerine peel (2 inches in diameter) and 4 dried Chinese red dates (the peel and dates soaked in warm water 15 minutes) and 1½-inch stick cinnamon with the liquor-soy-salt combination.

SERVINGS: Enough for 6 to 8 as a single course with rice or for 10 to 12 in a full menu.

RED-STEWED SPICED BEEF: Follow the directions above using the Peking or Shanghai variation for Classic Red-Stewed Beef. Red Stewed Spiced Beef without the dried dates, chilled and cut in wafer-thin slices, makes an excellent hors d'oeuvre. Or, along with barbecued ham and White-Cut Chicken, it can be part of a Chinese cold meat platter.

RED-STEWED SPICED LAMB: Follow the directions above using the Peking or Shanghai variation for Classic Red-Stewed Spiced Lamb.

RED-STEWED PORK WITH DRIED CHESTNUTS

Soak ½ pound dried chestnuts in 3 cups water 30 minutes. Boil in the same water 30 minutes. Drain well. Peel off the thin brownish skins. Follow the Shanghai variation for Classic Red-Stewed Pork but add the chestnuts for the last hour of stewing. Try this recipe with fresh ham or pork belly (with rind), cut into 2-inch chunks or dice.

SERVINGS: Enough for 6 to 8 as a single course with rice or for 10 to 12 in a full menu.

RED-STEWED BEEF WITH DRIED CHESTNUTS: Follow the directions above using the Shanghai variation for Classic Red-Stewed Beef.

RED-STEWED LAMB WITH DRIED CHESTNUTS: Follow the above recipe using the Shanghai variation for Classic Red-Stewed Lamb.

RED-STEWED OXTAILS
Follow the recipe for Classic Red-Stewed Pork or any of the regional variations but substitute 4 to 5 pounds oxtails, cut into 2-inch lengths, for the pork. Increase soy sauce to $\frac{1}{2}$ cup and hot water to 4 to 5 cups. Increase simmering time to $3\frac{1}{2}$ to 4 hours. Skim off surface fat before serving.

SERVINGS: Enough for 4 to 6 as a single course with rice or for 6 to 8 in a full menu.

CLASSIC RED-STEWED CHICKEN

Cooking Time: $1\frac{1}{2}$ to 2 hours

Utensils
Chinese cutting knife
Small bowl for seasonings
Dutch oven, 4-quart cast-iron casserole or
    electric deep-fry cooker—with tight-
    fitting cover
Tongs or chopsticks for turning hen

Ingredients

1	stewing hen (4 to 6 pounds)	$\frac{1}{3}$	cup soy sauce
2 to 3	cups hot water	$\frac{1}{4}$	teaspoon salt
3	slices ginger root (3x1½x⅛ inch)	2	teaspoons brown sugar
2	tablespoons sherry		

Before Cooking

Wash hen thoroughly inside and out. Pull away threadlike matter in cavity but retain fat which clings to skin. Do not disjoint the bird. Use 2 cups water for a 4-pound hen, 3 cups for a 6-pound hen. Prepare ginger root. Combine the sherry, soy sauce and salt in the small bowl. Have brown sugar ready to go.

Cooking Instructions

Place the hen in the pot; add the hot water. Turn heat to medium (300° F. on electric cooker). When the liquid begins to boil, add the ginger root and sherry-soy-salt mixture. Reduce heat to very low (200° F. to 220° F. on electric cooker). Cover tightly and stew gently 1 to 1½ hours, depending on the age of the bird. Turn the hen over once or twice during the cooking. Add the brown sugar and simmer 30 minutes longer. Test for tenderness by piercing the thick portion of the drumstick with a chopstick. Slight overcooking in this technique is not considered a disadvantage; it makes serving easier. The bird will be dark brown with a scant gravy richly aromatic of chicken and soy sauce. To serve, place bird on a platter, pour sauce over and bring to the table. "Carve" with chopsticks by pulling away fairly large portions, or cut before bringing to the table.

SERVINGS: Enough for 6 to 8 as a single course with rice or for 8 to 10 in a full menu.

CLASSIC RED-STEWED DUCK: Substitute 1 duckling (5 pounds) for the chicken. If you are using fresh duck, be sure to remove the oil sacs above the tail. Use 3 cups water. Cook either whole or cut in Chinese-style serving pieces. The duck may require a longer cooking time than the chicken.

CLASSIC RED-STEWED SQUAB: Substitute 4 squabs (1 pound each) for the chicken. Leave the squab whole or cut each into quarters.

RED-STEWED FRYING CHICKEN

Follow the recipe for Classic Red-Stewed Chicken but substitute 2 fryers (2½ pounds each) for the hen. Cut chicken into Chinese-style serving pieces, retaining the fat that clings to the skin. Use 3 cups hot water and increase the soy sauce to 5 tablespoons. Proceed as directed, stewing 45 minutes to 1 hour. Serve on a platter with sauce poured over.

SERVINGS: Enough for 6 to 8 as a single course with rice or for 8 to 10 in a full menu.

REGIONAL VARIATIONS OF CLASSIC RED-STEWED CHICKEN, DUCK OR SQUAB

PEKING: Decrease ginger root to 1 slice. Substitute gin or vodka for the sherry. When the liquid begins to boil, add 1 large leek, trimmed and cut in ¼-inch slices, and 1 clove garlic, finely minced, along with the ginger root. Proceed as directed in the Classic recipe or variation using fryers.

CANTON: Decrease ginger root to 2 slices. When the liquid begins to boil, add 3 scallions, trimmed and cut diagonally in 1½-inch lengths, along with the ginger root. Proceed as in the Classic recipe or variation using fryers.

SHANGHAI: Increase soy sauce to ½ cup and decrease salt to ⅛ teaspoon. Proceed as directed in the Classic recipe or variation using fryers, increasing brown sugar to 1 tablespoon.

SZECHUAN: Add 3 scallions, cut in 1½-inch slices, and either ¼ teaspoon ground Szechuan pepper or crushed red pepper flakes with the ginger root. Add 2 teaspoons rice vinegar or cider vinegar with the sherry-soy-salt mixture. Proceed as directed in the Classic recipe or variation using fryers.

RED-STEWED CHICKEN WITH ROOT-TYPE VEGETABLES
Follow the recipe for Classic Red-Stewed Chicken but 30 minutes before stewing is completed, add 2 cups of any of the Root-Type Vegetables (page 55) cut into 2-inch chunks or dice. (If using mushrooms, they should be cut in T-shape slices and not added until 15 minutes before the stewing is completed.) Cover and continue stewing until ingredients are done. Serve hot only.

SERVINGS: Enough for 6 to 8 as a single course with rice or for 8 to 10 in a full menu.

RED-STEWED DUCK WITH ROOT-TYPE VEGETABLES: Follow the directions above using the recipe for Classic Red-Stewed Duck.

RED-STEWED SQUAB WITH ROOT-TYPE VEGETABLES: Follow the directions above using the recipe for Classic Red-Stewed Squab.

RED-STEWED SPICED CHICKEN
Follow the Peking, Shanghai or Szechuan variation for Classic Red-Stewed Chicken. At the same time that the ginger root and other aromatics (depending on

which regional variation you are working from) are added, also add 1 teaspoon star anise with 1 piece dried tangerine peel (2 inches in diameter) and 4 dried Chinese dates (the peel and dates soaked in warm water 15 minutes) and a $1\frac{1}{2}$-inch stick cinnamon or $\frac{1}{4}$ teaspoon five-spice seasoning.

SERVINGS: Enough for 6 to 8 as a single course with rice or for 8 to 10 in a full menu.

RED-STEWED SPICED DUCK: Follow the directions above using the Peking, Shanghai or Szechuan variation for Classic Red-Stewed Duck.

RED-STEWED SQUAB: Follow the directions above using the Peking, Shanghai or Szechuan variation for Classic Red-Stewed Squab.

RED-STEWED SPICED HONEY CHICKEN, DUCK OR SQUAB
Substitute or add 1 tablespoon honey for the brown sugar in any of the variations used.

RED-STEWED CHICKEN WITH DRIED CHESTNUTS
Soak $1\frac{1}{3}$ cups dried chestnuts in 3 cups warm water 30 minutes. Drain well and scrape off the thin brownish skin. Add to chicken just before covering to simmer. Proceed as directed in recipe for Classic Red-Stewed Chicken. If you are using fryers instead of a hen, follow ingredient variations and instructions for Red-Stewed Frying Chicken and boil the chestnuts in water 1 hour before draining them and adding to the pan. Cover and simmer as directed. Serve hot. If you are using the whole chicken, arrange the bird on a platter and spoon the chestnuts and gravy around it. If you are using the fryers cut into Chinese serving pieces, pour combined chicken, chestnuts and gravy into a bowl. Serve hot only.

SERVINGS: Enough for 6 to 8 as a single course with rice or for 8 to 10 in a full menu.

RED-STEWED DUCK WITH DRIED CHESTNUTS: Follow the directions above using the recipe for Classic Red-Stewed Duck.

RED-STEWED SQUAB: Follow the directions above using the recipe for Classic Red-Stewed Squab.

BOILING AND CLEAR-SIMMERING— TECHNIQUE 4

ꙸꙸꙸꙸꙸꙸꙸꙸꙸꙸꙸꙸꙸꙸꙸꙸꙸꙸꙸ

BOILING

As in Western cooking, boiling is the technique used for most Chinese soups. Apart from handling certain fast-cooking ingredients which require short, intense boiling, the process is usually one of bringing a liquid to the boiling point and then lowering it to a simmer. In most cuisines, soup is divided into two classes. The French have their clear and thick soups, *consommés* and *potages,* as do the Japanese with their *suimono* and *misoshiru.*

Contrarily, Chinese soup categories are defined as light or heavy rather than clear or thick. What is in appearance a thick soup, such as Hot and Pungent Soup, is actually considered light because of its refreshing qualities. It is a safe assumption that a stock cooked with greens, with or without the addition of cornstarch, is a Light Soup and that a soup containing large quantities of meat, fish or fowl, along with additional fresh or dried ingredients, may be termed Heavy. However, when the Light Soup contains more ingredients, the distinction between the two Chinese soup categories is not always obvious. The best way to determine the category is to see how the soup is served. Light Soups are served after rich courses or in warm weather; Heavy Soups are considered gourmet fare—or in family-style meals may represent the main course or the entire meal.

LIGHT SOUPS

PROCESS: Relatively short cooking time. Ingredients are boiled up quickly or, when dried ingredients are used, the stock is brought to a boil and the ingredients simmered until done. The principle behind these soups is to retain the natural flavors and textures of the ingredients.

MAIN INGREDIENTS: Cool water or stock. Tender cuts of pork, beef, lamb, chicken, duckling or squab. Small whole fish or fish steaks.

SUBSIDIARY INGREDIENTS: Fresh Vegetables (tougher ones parboiled before they are added). Leafy Vegetables, Melon-Type Vegetables, Root-Type Vegetables (parboiled before they are added), dried ingredients (soaked before they are added), a thickener (cornstarch), eggs, seasonings, garnishes.

CHARACTERISTICS: The broth may be clear or thickened, but is light and almost astringent in taste. The essential quality of vegetables—crunchiness and color—must be intact. Dried ingredients are gently expressed of flavor and tender. Meats, fish or poultry must be barely cooked—just enough to infuse the broth with subtle flavor. Fish should be cooked in large pieces to prevent disintegration; meat and poultry should be cut in slivers. Light Soups should have the character of essences, or teas, even though they may be thickened with cornstarch or enriched with eggs, bean curd or other ingredients.

HEAVY SOUPS

PROCESS: Long, slow simmering. Ingredients are brought to a boil, then heat is reduced at once to a simmer.

MAIN INGREDIENTS: Cool water and a vast range of meats and poultry are used, generally in substantial portions. Usually, fresh fish belongs in Light Soups, since fish disintegrates with long simmering. In some Heavy Soups, though, fish may be added during the final stage of cooking. These soups are sometimes treated (on informal occasions) as meals in themselves. In a family-style dinner, for example, a Heavy Soup might be served with a Chinese cold plate and one or two contrasting stir-fry-toss dishes. At a banquet which consists of a myriad of courses, the Heavy Soup is served for the sheer luxury of it in the latter stages of the meal.

SUBSIDIARY INGREDIENTS: Any and all types of vegetables, added in progression according to the length of time required for their cooking. While these should retain their individual characteristics and must never be mushy, they are often cooked considerably longer than in Light Soups. Stalky or Root-Type Vegetables need not be parboiled. Delicacies such as bird's nest, shark's fins and snow fungus are often featured as the principal ingredient—or added for unique flavor. More commonplace dried ingredients, such as shrimp, abalone, ducks' feet, gizzards, tiger lilies, mushrooms, wood and cloud ears, may be added as well. Enrichments and garnishes may include eggs, bean curd, cornstarch, wine, sesame oil, Chinese parsley, Szechuan pepper, vinegar, gingko nuts, lotus seeds and occasionally a touch of condiment sauces.

CHARACTERISTICS: Richly endowed with choice and varied ingredients. Served formally as a *pièce de résistance* towards or at the end of the meal.

POINTS TO OBSERVE WHEN MAKING CHINESE SOUPS

When making soup, unlike Braising and Red-Stewing, meat, fish or poultry are brought to a boil with cool water, or, in the case of Light Soups, with cool stock. When the main ingredient and the liquid are at the same temperature, brought to a boil and afterward simmered, the maximum flavor of the main ingredient is incorporated into the broth.

If you are using an electric deep-fry cooker, it should be set at 300° F. The heat on a stove should be at medium. When large bubbles appear in the liquid, the soup is boiling. Remove all scum with a slotted spoon. Reset the cooker at 200° F. or turn the heat under an ordinary burner to very low. When the liquid is simmering, it will scarcely bubble at all; the surface should merely dimple occasionally (the French call it smiling). At this point, depending on how long each ingredient takes to cook, you may begin to add additional items. During the simmering process, the cover of the pot should be partially ajar.

Never use too much water in proportion to the main ingredient. No amount of skill can compensate for a watery soup. (The exception is making stock where you may use more water.) To ensure a rich broth, use 2 cups of water to 1 pound of meat, fish or poultry. Increase the amount of water when adding highly flavored ingredients such as dried scallops or dried oysters. More water is also needed if you use ingredients such as bean threads, which tend to absorb liquid. If you are using cornstarch as a thickener, always dissolve it in cold water before adding it to the soup. Lumps in a smooth soup are inexcusable.

Soup is indispensable to the Chinese way of eating. A guest can determine whether the meal is going to be family-style or a banquet by the soup the host places before him. Three or four soups in an elegant dinner are not uncommon in Chinese entertaining.

Begin with simpler recipes such as Egg Flower or Easy Winter Melon Soup rather than, say, Bird's Nest or Szechuan Watermelon Soup. As you acquire experience and confidence, advance to the more exotic recipes.

NOTE: Since water plays a predominant part in the preparation of any soup, be it a simple stock or a recipe involving many ingredients, consider using bottled spring water. The difference in smoothness and taste is well worth the few extra pennies involved.

STOCK

Because stock is an essential ingredient in so much of Chinese cooking, it becomes very important. One can, of course, take a purist attitude towards producing a rich stock, which amounts in the long run to producing a soup in itself. In my opinion, the value of being a purist is related directly to the end result, and because stock is primarily a component ingredient, I am inclined to compromise. This is not to say that I recommend a watery stock tinged with meat or poultry flavor (why not use water?) but instead, make stock with what might ordinarily amount to waste. That is, instead of using a whole chicken or a generous cut of pork in making stock, use backs, necks, feet, carcasses, bones, gizzards and trimmings—but with less water. In the final reckoning, this will give you a stock which, if not equal, is certainly adequate.

The Chinese favor the delicacy of chicken followed by, and often combined with, pork. Beef is much too intense for their tastes as well as for their sense of smell. * This sensitivity towards odor is also extended to fish. Fish stock, while mandatory for French cuisine and a basic of Japanese cooking, is never used in Chinese dishes. The Chinese chef, while treating fish with all his culinary ingenuity (the *taste* of fish being highly acceptable), will go to great lengths to mask even the slightest vestige of fishy odor and would not dream of emphasizing it with a concentrate.

* The Chinese become quite personal in this aversion to beef odors. I recall a young Chinese woman expressing her distaste for a popular American bachelor who was courting her. She claimed that, like most Westerners, he exuded the smell of beef.

Boiling (Soups)
1. Put main ingredient in electric deep-fry cooker or soup kettle, add cold water and bring to a boil.   2. Remove scum, reduce heat to a simmer.   3. Simmer, partially uncovered, and add additional ingredients according to time specified in recipe. Thickeners and garnishes are added just before turning off heat.

If even the idea of making a stock of trimmings seems like too much trouble (and frankly, if you plan one or two Stir-Fry-Toss dishes, I agree that it might well'be), there are acceptable substitutes. Use them in this order of preference: 1) Canned chicken broth (not chicken consommé). Buy a good quality, the less salty the better. Chill cans before using and remove the layer of congealed fat on the surface. 2) Chicken base, in compressed powdered form, sold in jars or cans. This makes a fairly good stock with a fine golden color. Watch out for oversaltiness. 3) Chicken granules, much the same as chicken base. 4) And finally, chicken bouillon cubes. These are convenient but are generally overly accented with salt and vegetable flavorings.

If you use any of these substitutes in place of stock, reserve the salt called for in the recipe until after the stock has been added. Then taste. If it is salty enough, omit the salt from the recipe. If not, add the salt called for, but in reduced amounts, tasting after each addition.

I have earlier expressed my distaste for the overall uniformity of flavor created by the injudicious use of monosodium glutamate. The making of stock with waste material and bones is the one area where I feel that a small amount of monosodium glutamate is an improvement, as it tends to enliven the flavor of less-mature ingredients.

POINTS TO REMEMBER WHEN MAKING STOCK

The truism "Old chickens make the best soup" applies as well to making stock. Use carcasses of stewing hens rather than those of broilers or fryers. Use ham bones and pork neckbones. Use the coarse outer stalks of celery and older carrots. Avoid starchy vegetables as these will affect the clarity of the stock. When using bones entirely, be sure to simmer the stock for a long time (up to 8 hours) to allow the maximum extraction of gelatinous properties. Do not combine cooked bones with raw ones; this will cause the stock to be cloudy. Be sure to skim the stock when the scum rises to the surface; otherwise the foamy matter will discolor the stock. So that the flavors remain, the simmering stock should be partially covered with the lid of the utensil after the first hour or so of simmering. Salt must be added only at the end of simmering; the long cooking reduces the amount of stock and intensifies the seasonings. If you are making stock for the purpose of adding it to other recipes or as a soup base, either decrease the salt or omit it entirely. Remember to cool stock before refrigerating. Then store covered. Remove the surface layer of congealed fat when ready to use, not before; the fat acts as a protective coating.

CHICKEN STOCK

Cooking Time: 3 to 4 hours

Utensils
6-quart enameled casserole or electric deep-
    fry cooker—with cover
Slotted spoon
Sieve
Bowl for strained stock

Ingredients

4	pounds raw chicken carcasses, backs, necks, feet, wing tips and gizzards	1	large carrot
		1	large leek with some of green or 1 onion
10	cups bottled spring water	½	teaspoon monosodium glutamate
1	outer stalk celery	½	teaspoon salt

Before Cooking

Rinse the chicken parts. Trim claws on chicken feet and scrub feet with brush. Let come to room temperature. Measure water and let come to room temperature. Clean and trim vegetables. Have monosodium glutamate and salt ready to go.

Cooking Instructions

Place chicken parts in casserole or electric deep-fry cooker. Add water. Turn heat to medium (300° F. on cooker). Bring water and chicken to a boil. At once begin skimming the surface with a slotted spoon to remove scum. Reduce heat to very low (200° F. on cooker). Simmer uncovered 1 hour. Add monosodium glutamate. Then partially cover casserole or cooker by placing lid on at an angle; continue simmering 2 to 3 hours. (If you are only using chicken carcasses and feet and no chicken parts, simmer a total of 6 to 8 hours). If you find during the simmering that your stock is reducing too rapidly or too much, you may add hot water, ½ cup at a time. Add the celery, carrot and leek or onion for the last hour of simmering. Ten minutes before turning off the heat, add the salt. Strain stock through sieve into a bowl. For an even clearer stock, first line the sieve with a double layer of damp cheesecloth (dipped in water and wrung out). Allow stock to cool. Cover and refrigerate. Just before using, scrape off the congealed layer of surface fat.

NOTE: If you live in a part of the country where they are available, by all means use chicken feet in the making of stock. They are high in gelatinous properties and will jell the stock perfectly when it is chilled. Most poultry dealers will gladly give them to you when you make regular purchases.

PORK STOCK

Cooking Time: 3 to 4 hours

Utensils
4-quart enameled casserole or electric deep-
    fry cooker—with cover
Slotted spoon
Sieve
Bowl for strained stock

Ingredients

1	pound lean pork (scraps or cheap cut)	8	cups bottled spring water
1	pound pork neckbones or 1 raw ham bone, cracked	1	slice ginger root (2x1x⅛ inch)
		½	teaspoon monosodium glutamate
		½	teaspoon salt

Before Cooking

Trim fat from pork. Rinse pork bones or ham bone. Measure water. Allow meat and water to come to room temperature. Have other ingredients ready to go.

Cooking Instructions

Place pork and bones in casserole or electric deep-fry cooker. Add water. Turn heat to medium (300° F. on cooker). Bring stock to a boil. Skim surface with slotted spoon to remove scum. Turn heat to very low (200° F. on cooker). Simmer uncovered 1 hour. Add ginger root and monosodium glutamate. Then partially cover casserole or cooker by placing lid on at an angle; continue simmering 2 to 3 hours. If you find during the simmering that your stock is reducing too rapidly or too much, you may add hot water, ½ cup at a time. Ten minutes before turning off the heat, add salt. Strain stock through sieve into a bowl. For an even clearer stock, first line the sieve with a double layer of damp cheesecloth (dipped in water and wrung out). Allow stock to cool. Cover and refrigerate. Just before using, scrape off the congealed layer of surface fat.

CHICKEN OR PORK SOUP WITH VEGETABLES

Any of the following 5 Light Soups may be thickened as instructed below or served with any of the optional garnishes, singly or in combination. Add the chicken shreds to the pork stock and the pork shreds to the chicken stock.

OPTIONAL THICKENER: Dissolve 1 tablespoon cornstarch in 3 tablespoons cold water. Add to soup and allow to boil 3 minutes.

OPTIONAL GARNISHES: 2 teaspoons chopped scallions, 1 tablespoon shredded Virginia ham, 1 tablespoon shredded Egg Threads (page 235) or 2 tablespoons Deep-Fried Rice Sticks (page 315).

SERVINGS: Enough for 6.

BOILED CHICKEN OR PORK SOUP WITH FRESH VEGETABLES

Measure 6 cups strained chicken or pork stock into a 2½-quart enameled saucepan. Bring to a boil. Add 1½ cups of any of the Fresh Vegetables on pages 53–54. Boil 5 minutes. Add ¼ cup shredded chicken breast or pork. Boil 5 minutes. Taste for seasoning. Add ½ teaspoon sesame oil and serve.

BOILED CHICKEN OR PORK SOUP WITH LEAFY VEGETABLES

Measure 6 cups strained chicken or pork stock into a 2½-quart enameled saucepan. Bring to a boil. Add ¼ cup shredded chicken breast or pork. Boil 5 minutes. Add 1½ cups of any of the Leafy Vegetables on pages 54–55. Boil stalk portions 3 minutes. Add leaf portions and boil 2 minutes. Taste for seasoning. Add ½ teaspoon sesame oil and serve.

BOILED CHICKEN OR PORK SOUP WITH
MELON-TYPE VEGETABLES

Measure 6 cups strained chicken or pork stock into a 2½-quart enameled saucepan. Bring to a boil. Add ¼ cup shredded chicken breast or pork. Boil 5 minutes. Add 1½ cups of any of the Melon-Type Vegetables on page 55 except tomatoes. Boil 10 minutes. Add ½ teaspoon sesame oil and serve.

BOILED CHICKEN OR PORK SOUP WITH
ROOT-TYPE VEGETABLES

Measure 6 cups strained chicken or pork stock into a 2½-quart enameled saucepan. Bring to a boil. Add ¼ cup shredded chicken breast or pork. Boil 5 minutes. Add 1½ cups of any of the following vegetables cooked in this manner: Fresh mushrooms, sliced; boil 5 minutes. Eggplant, thinly sliced; boil 10 minutes; Chinese turnips, cut into shreds; boil 10 minutes. Taste for seasoning. Add ½ teaspoon sesame oil and serve.

BOILED CHICKEN OR PORK SOUP WITH DRIED VEGETABLES

Measure 6 cups strained chicken or pork stock into a 2½-quart enameled saucepan. Bring to a boil. Add one of the following dried vegetables: ¼ cup dried mushrooms or tiger lilies (snipped in two) or 1 tablespoon cloud ears or wood ears (all well rinsed in cold water and soaked in warm water 15 minutes). Drain and add to stock. Reduce heat and simmer 15 minutes. Add ¼ cup shredded chicken breast or pork and simmer 5 minutes longer. Taste for seasoning. Add ½ teaspoon sesame oil and serve.

NOTE: Dried vegetables may be used in combination, with the amounts reduced, or with any of the other vegetable categories. In this case, simmer the dried ingredients and then turn up the heat before adding the shorter-cooking vegetables. Additional dried ingredients, all rinsed in cold water and soaked in warm, for Boiled Chicken and Pork Soup include: 6 red dates (soaked 30 minutes), 2-inch-wide piece of tangerine peel (soaked 30 minutes), 1 tablespoon shrimp (soaked 1 hour) or 2 tablespoons lotus seeds (soaked 1 hour).

EGG FLOWER SOUP

Cooking Time: 2 to 3 minutes

Utensils
Chinese cutting knife
2-quart enameled saucepan or electric deep-
fry cooker
Small bowls
Bowl for eggs

Ingredients

$1\frac{1}{2}$	tablespoons cornstarch	6	cups unsalted chicken or pork
$\frac{1}{3}$	cup cold water		stock or canned chicken broth*
$\frac{1}{2}$	square bean curd, shredded	$\frac{3}{4}$	teaspoon salt
1	slice ginger root ($2 \times 1 \times \frac{1}{8}$ inch)	$\frac{1}{2}$	teaspoon sugar
1	scallion, minced	$\frac{1}{8}$	teaspoon pepper
3	eggs, beaten until frothy	1	teaspoon sesame oil

Before Cooking
Combine cornstarch and water. Prepare bean curd, ginger root and scallion. Beat eggs. Measure stock or broth and pour into saucepan or electric deep-fry cooker. Have salt, sugar, pepper and sesame oil ready to go.

Cooking Instructions
Turn heat under saucepan to medium (300° F. on cooker). Bring stock to a boil. Add bean curd, ginger root, salt, sugar and pepper. Boil together 1 minute. Give

* If you are using canned chicken broth, either decrease or omit salt.

the cornstarch-water mixture a quick stir and add it to the stock. Boil 1 minute. Stir in the beaten eggs and remove from heat at once or turn off cooker. Top with sesame oil and minced scallion. The eggs will give the effect of lacy shreds floating in a delicate broth.

SERVINGS: Enough for 6.

NOTE: Whenever eggs are added to a liquid containing cornstarch, this threading effect occurs. If you wish to poach an egg in a soup, either add cornstarch after the egg has been poached or omit it entirely. Egg Flower Soup is a Light Soup, suitable for informal meals or meals with rich main dishes.

HOT AND PUNGENT SOUP

Cooking Time: 10 minutes

Utensils
Chinese cutting knife
**2-quart enameled saucepan or electric deep-
fry cooker**
Small bowls
Bowl for eggs

Ingredients

6	cups unsalted chicken stock or canned chicken broth*	¾	teaspoon salt
¼	pound raw pork, finely shredded	1	teaspoon sugar
⅓	cup finely shredded bamboo shoots	¼	teaspoon pepper
½	cup finely shredded bean curd	2	tablespoons rice vinegar or cider vinegar
⅓	cup canned button mushrooms	2½	tablespoons cornstarch
4	teaspoons light soy sauce	¼	cup cold water
1	teaspoon gin, vodka or sherry	2	small eggs, beaten
		2	teaspoons sesame oil

* If you are using canned chicken broth, either decrease or omit salt.

Before Cooking
Measure stock or broth and pour into the saucepan or electric deep-fry cooker. Add pork, bamboo shoots and bean curd, all in similar-size shred, and mushrooms. Combine soy sauce, liquor, salt, sugar, pepper and vinegar in a small bowl. Combine cornstarch and cold water. Beat eggs until frothy and light in color. Have sesame oil ready.

Cooking Instructions
Turn heat under saucepan to medium (300° F. on cooker). Bring stock mixture to a boil. Reduce heat to low (200° F. on cooker). Simmer 10 minutes. Add seasonings and stir to blend. Give the cornstarch-water mixture a quick stir and add to soup. Stir and remove from heat or turn off cooker. Pour in beaten eggs, stirring rapidly. Top with sesame oil and serve.

SERVINGS: Enough for 6.

NOTE: Hot and Pungent Soup, also called Hot and Sour Soup, is popular in the North of China. While it might seem quite exotic to Western tastes, this soup is not considered gourmet rare in China and falls under the category of Light Soups. Various ingredients such as wood ears, tiger lilies, dried mushrooms and dried tangerine peel are sometimes added. I have omitted them as I feel the soup is more subtle without. For those who wish to add them, consider these proportions: 1 tablespoon wood ears, 6 tiger lilies (snipped in thirds), 6 small or 3 large dried mushrooms (shredded after soaking), 1 piece tangerine peel (2 inches wide). All these ingredients must first be rinsed in cold water, then soaked in warm water 30 minutes. An authentic addition to this soup is chicken blood curdled with salt water and steamed until the blood develops a custard-like consistency. I have not found this to be popular with Westerners.

SQUAB AND HAIRY MELON SOUP

Cooking Time: 1 hour, 15 minutes

Utensils
Chinese cutting knife
3½-quart saucepan or electric deep-fry cooker—with cover
Sieve
Bowl for soup

Ingredients

1	piece dried tangerine peel (2 inches in diameter)	2	scallions
8	cups unsalted chicken stock or canned chicken broth*	2	medium hairy melons
		1	teaspoon sherry
1	squab	1	teaspoon salt
		$\frac{1}{4}$	teaspoon sugar

Before Cooking

Soak tangerine peel in water 15 minutes. Measure stock and pour into saucepan or electric deep-fry cooker. Rinse squab and cut in half. Trim scallions but leave whole. Peel hairy melons and cut into quarters, then slice each quarter into $1\frac{1}{2}$-inch rolling cut or dice. Have sherry, salt and sugar ready to go.

Cooking Instructions

Add the squab, scallions and tangerine peel to stock. Turn heat to medium (300° F. on cooker). Bring to a boil. Reduce heat to low (200° F. on cooker). Cover and simmer 30 minutes. Add hairy melon, sherry, salt and sugar. Cover and simmer 30 minutes longer or until squab is very tender. Strain through sieve into a bowl. Pick squab meat from bones, and add with hairy melon pieces to the clear broth. Although this is rich, it is considered a Light Soup.

SERVINGS: Enough for 6 to 8.

* If you are using canned chicken broth, either decrease or omit salt.

FISH AND VEGETABLE SOUP

Cooking Time: 30 minutes

Utensils
Chinese cutting knife
Small bowl
Soup plate for fish
Chopsticks
$2\frac{1}{2}$-quart enameled saucepan or electric deep-fry cooker—with cover

Ingredients

2	tablespoons light soy sauce	
1	tablespoon sesame oil	
1	teaspoon cornstarch	
½	teaspoon salt	
½	teaspoon sugar	
¼	teaspoon pepper	
½	pound carp, halibut or cod steaks	
2	slices ginger root (2x1x⅛ inch)	
2	cups of any of the following: Thinly sliced Chinese cabbage,	

chard, watercress, dandelion greens or spinach, cucumbers (peeled, seeded and cut in ½-inch slices), zucchini (seeded and cut in ½-inch slices) or hairy melon (peeled, seeded and cut in ½-inch slices)

6   cups unsalted chicken stock or canned chicken broth*

Before Cooking

Blend light soy sauce, sesame oil, cornstarch, salt, sugar and pepper in the small bowl. Cut fish steaks into fingerlike bars and place in the soup plate. Add seasonings to fish slices and gently toss with chopsticks to coat thoroughly. Let stand 15 minutes. Prepare ginger root and vegetables. Pour stock or broth into the saucepan or electric deep-fry cooker.

Cooking Instructions

Turn heat under saucepan to medium (300° F. on cooker). Bring stock to a boil. This will take about 15 minutes. Add ginger root and vegetables. Reduce heat to very low (200° F. on cooker). Partially cover saucepan or cooker by placing lid on at a slant. Simmer 5 minutes. Gently add the marinated fish slices and seasoning mixture. Simmer 10 minutes. Although this is hearty, it is considered a Light Soup. The vegetables used will naturally contribute to the flavor of the finished dish.

SERVINGS: Enough for 8.

NOTE: The following additional ingredients may be added with the vegetables: ½ tablespoon dried wood ears, rinsed and soaked 15 minutes; ¼ cup snipped tiger lilies, soaked 15 minutes; ¼ cup dried mushrooms, rinsed and soaked 15 minutes; ½ tablespoon small dried shrimp, soaked 1 hour; 1 square bean curd, cut into ½-inch dice.

*   If you are using canned chicken broth, either decrease or omit salt.

SIZZLING RICE SOUP

Cooking Time: Approximately 30 minutes to prepare Rice Crusts
Approximately 15 minutes to boil and simmer stock

Utensils
Chinese cutting knife
2-quart enameled saucepan

Ingredients

1 scallion with green, minced	4 cups unsalted chicken stock or canned chicken broth*
½ teaspoon salt	
⅛ teaspoon pepper	1 recipe Rice Crusts (page 311)

Before Cooking
Mince the scallion. Measure salt and pepper; set aside. Measure stock or broth and pour into the saucepan. Prepare Rice Crusts just before serving soup.

Cooking Instructions
Turn heat under saucepan to medium. Bring stock to a boil. Reduce heat to low and add seasonings. Simmer 5 minutes. Bring the soup to the table in a tureen or bowl; serve the Rice Crusts in a separate dish. Drop pieces of hot deep-fried Rice Crusts into soup. It will sizzle explosively.

SERVINGS: Enough for 4.

NOTE: This simple recipe was a standby for leftover rice in China and was quite common among the poorer classes. In certain restaurants in this country it is featured as a gourmet specialty. During the Japanese occupation of China, this soup took on nationalistic popularity and was called Bomb Tokyo Soup. It should be considered a Light Soup.

* If you are using canned chicken broth, either decrease or omit salt.

EASY WINTER MELON SOUP

Cooking Time: 1 hour, 15 minutes

Utensils
Chinese cutting knife
2½-quart enameled saucepan or electric deep-
**   fry cooker**

Ingredients

¼ pound lean pork, shredded	½ teaspoon sugar
3 large dried mushrooms	½ teaspoon sherry
½ pound winter melon	6 cups unsalted chicken stock or
¾ teaspoon salt	canned chicken broth*

Before Cooking
Cut pork into fine shreds. Rinse mushrooms in cold water and soak in warm water 10 minutes. Drain; remove hard centers and cut into shreds to match pork. Peel and seed winter melon and cut into 2-inch dice. Measure salt, sugar and sherry; set aside. Measure stock or broth into the saucepan or electric deep-fry cooker.

Cooking Instructions
Turn heat under saucepan to medium (300° F. on cooker). Bring stock to a boil. Reduce heat to low (200° F. on cooker). Add winter melon and simmer 30 minutes. Add pork and mushrooms. Simmer 30 minutes. Fifteen minutes before turning off heat, add salt, sugar and sherry. Stir gently to blend. The soup should be light and clear, the melon very tender and translucent. This is a very simplified version of what is normally a banquet soup, and would be classified as a Light Soup.

SERVINGS: Enough for 6.

*   If you are using canned chicken broth, either decrease or omit salt.

WINTER MELON LAKE

Cooking Time: 5 to 6 hours

Utensils

Sharp pointed knife
Chinese cutting knife
Soup kettle or pot (12 inches tall, 10 inches
    diameter)
Rack or trivet to fit base of pot
Twine
Kettle for boiling water
Small bowl
2½-quart saucepan
Bowl or 1½-quart soufflé dish to support
    melon

Ingredients

1	winter melon (10 pounds)	¼	cup diced Virginia ham
	Boiling water	1	whole chicken breast or 1-pound
4	cups unsalted chicken stock		squab
4	cups unsalted pork stock	1	tablespoon sherry
1	slice ginger root (3x1½x⅛ inch)	1	teaspoon salt
10	small dried mushrooms	1	teaspoon sugar
½	cup dried lotus seeds	⅛	teaspoon pepper
½	cup diced water chestnuts	¼	cup diced canned abalone
½	cup diced bamboo shoots	½	cup Chinese parsley (optional)

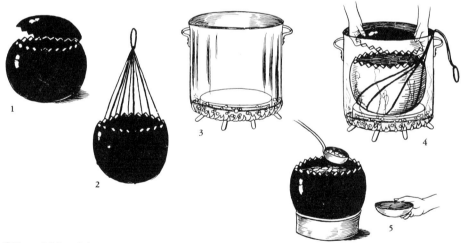

Winter Melon Lake
1. Cut lid in serrated pattern.   2. Make sling.   3. Add water to 1-inch level in pot and bring
to a boil.   4. Pour heated stock into melon shell, cover with lid and steam.   5. Place melon
on a soufflé dish for support and serve.

Before Cooking
Place the rack or trivet in the kettle. Wash and scrub the melon. Make a lid by cutting off the top fourth of the melon, making a zigzag pattern for a serrated edge. Scrape the insides of the melon, including the lid, removing all seeds, stringy material and most of the pulp. Leave a 1½-inch wall of pulp within the shell of the melon. Set the lid aside. Now, using 4 lengths of twine, make a sling, knotted under the melon shell and tied with a loop on top. Lower the melon by the twine into the kettle. Begin steaming the melon (see Cooking Instructions) before proceeding with preparations. Peel and slice ginger root. Rinse mushrooms, soak 10 minutes in warm water and drain. Measure lotus seeds and dice water chestnuts, bamboo shoots and ham. Bone chicken breast or rinse out squab. Combine sherry, salt, sugar, and pepper in the small bowl. During the final cooking period of the soup, dice abalone. Rinse, pick over and measure Chinese parsley.

Cooking Instructions
Bring water in a kettle to a boil. Meanwhile, also bring chicken and pork stock to a boil in the saucepan. Carefully pour 1 inch of boiling water around the melon. Put the heated stock into the melon shell. It should be no more than ¾ full. Save any additional stock for adding later if desired. Turn heat under pot to medium. Cover melon with its own lid and steam 4 hours, adding boiling water as needed. Remove lid and add ginger root, mushrooms, lotus seeds, water chestnuts, bamboo shoots, ham, chicken breast or squab, and combined seasonings. Cover again and simmer 1 to 2 hours, or until melon pulp is soft and translucent. Five minutes before the soup is ready, remove chicken breast or squab, dice the meat and return it to the melon along with the diced abalone. Top with Chinese parsley. To serve, lift melon out of pot with strings and place on a bowl or soufflé dish for support. Remove twine and ladle soup into bowls, scooping up some of the cooked melon. This rich soup served in its own melon bowl is a favorite banquet dish and, because of its wealth of ingredients, is classified as a Heavy Soup.

SERVINGS: Enough for 6 to 8.

WATERMELON SOUP,
Szechuan Style

Cooking Time: 2 to 3 hours to precook melon
2 hours to simmer soup

Utensils

Sharp pointed knife
Chinese cutting knife
Roasting pan
3½-quart enameled saucepan or electric deep-
**   fry cooker—with cover**
Roasting rack
Kettle for boiling water
Small bowl

Ingredients

1	oval red-fleshed watermelon (8x12 inches)
	Boiling water
½	cup shredded lean raw pork
1½	cups shredded raw chicken breast
½	cup shredded raw duck
½	cup shredded lean raw lamb
½	cup shredded Virginia ham
1	slice ginger root (2x1x⅛ inch)
½	cup shredded celery
½	cup shredded bamboo shoots
½	cup small dried or grass mushrooms
4	scallions, minced
½	teaspoon salt
1	teaspoon sugar
⅛	teaspoon crushed Szechuan pepper or crushed red pepper flakes
½	teaspoon rice or cider vinegar
1	tablespoon light soy sauce
1	tablespoon dry mustard
1	teaspoon fennel seeds
2½	cups chicken stock or canned chicken broth*
1	cup shredded crab meat
½	cup shredded canned abalone
2	teaspoons sesame oil
½	cup Chinese parsley or watercress

Before Cooking

Wash and scrub the melon. Set the melon on a table horizontally. Make a lid by cutting off an oval-shaped piece about 6 to 8 inches long, making a zigzag pattern for a serrated edge. Scrape away the pulp and seeds from the lid and set it aside. Then scoop out the seeds and most of the pulp from the walls of the melon, leaving 1½ inch of pink pulp within the shell. (Do not scoop away to the green; some melon pulp is necessary to flavor the soup.) Place the roasting rack as flat as possible in the roasting pan. Put the melon on rack. Add 2 inches of boiling water to the pan. Replace the melon lid and place the pan over low heat. Allow the melon to steam 2 hours, adding boiling water to the pan to maintain the 2-inch level. Prepare the remaining ingredients. Finely shred the pork, chicken breast,

---

*   If you are using canned chicken broth, decrease the salt.

duck, lamb and ham. Peel ginger root and slice. Shred the celery and bamboo shoots. Rinse and soak the dried or grass mushrooms in warm water 10 minutes; drain. Trim and mince the scallions. Combine the salt, sugar, Szechuan pepper or red pepper flakes, vinegar and soy sauce in the small bowl. Add the dry mustard and fennel seeds. Measure stock or broth and pour into the saucepan or electric deep-fry cooker. Prepare the crab meat and abalone; set aside. Have sesame oil ready. Wash and pick over the parsley.

Cooking Instructions
Add the pork, chicken, duck, lamb, ham and ginger root to the stock in the saucepan or cooker. Turn heat under saucepan to medium (300° F. on cooker). Let mixture come to a boil. Reduce heat to low (200° F. on cooker). Cover and simmer 1 hour. Remove lid from melon shell and ladle in soup. Add the celery, bamboo shoots, mushrooms, scallions and seasoning-spice mixture. Replace melon lid and continue simmering 1 hour. Add crab meat and abalone for the last 5 minutes of simmering. Lift melon shell from roasting pan and place on a large oval platter. Remove lid from melon and top soup with sesame oil and parsley. This spicy and pungent soup is considered a gourmet dish, and is therefore a Heavy Soup, really a meal in itself. It is served in small bowls with pieces of melon scooped from the shell.

SERVINGS: Enough for 6 to 8.

NOTE: Shrimp or lobster may be substituted for the crab. Scallops or clams may be used in place of the abalone. Button mushrooms, canned gingko nuts or dried soaked lotus seeds may be added if you desire; in which case decrease some of the other ingredients.

BIRD'S NEST SOUP

Cooking Time: 2½ hours to soak and precook bird's nest
             30 minutes to simmer soup

Utensils
Tweezers
Chinese cutting knife
2½-quart enameled saucepan or electric deep-
    fry cooker
Sieve

Ingredients

2	ounces bird's nest (see note)	2	teaspoons sherry
4	cups cold water	½	teaspoon salt
¼	teaspoon baking soda	⅛	teaspoon pepper
¼	cup grass mushrooms or 8 small dried mushrooms	1	tablespoon cornstarch (optional)
¼	cup shredded raw chicken breast	1½	tablespoons cold water (optional)
1	tablespoon shredded Virginia ham	4	cups unsalted chicken stock or canned chicken broth*

Before Cooking

Soak bird's nest in warm water 2 hours. It will become somewhat gelatinous in appearance. Drain; using tweezers, pick out any feathers and foreign matter which have been dislodged. Place the drained nest in saucepan with 4 cups cold water and baking soda. Boil over medium heat 20 to 30 minutes. During this precooking process, more feathers and particles will rise to the surface. Remove as many of them as possible. You will not be able to get all of them, so don't be concerned. The nest will become more of a mass by now. Drain in sieve and rinse with cold water. Soak mushrooms in warm water at least 15 minutes; drain and rinse. Finely shred chicken breast and ham. Measure sherry, salt and pepper. If you are using a thickener, combine cornstarch and cold water. Measure stock or broth and pour into saucepan or electric deep-fry cooker.

Cooking Instructions

Add drained bird's nest to the stock in the saucepan or cooker. Turn heat to medium (350° F. on cooker). Bring stock to a boil. Reduce heat to low (200° F. on cooker). Add the mushrooms, chicken, ham, sherry, salt, and pepper. Simmer 30 minutes. Five minutes before turning off heat, give the cornstarch-water mixture a quick stir to blend and stir into the stock. The soup will be a medium-pale brown, delicate in flavor. If you do not use cornstarch, the soup will be clear, and if you do, it will be only slightly cloudy. The texture will be light, although this is considered a Banquet, or Heavy Soup.

SERVINGS: Enough for 6 to 8.

NOTE: Buy the bird's nest in 3½-ounce rectangular packages. Use ½ package for this recipe. See page 19 for description.

*   If you are using canned chicken broth, decrease salt in the recipe.

CLASSIC SHARK'S FIN SOUP

Cooking Time: 5 hours to soak and precook shark's fin
2 hours to simmer soup

Utensils
Chinese cutting knife
2½-quart enameled saucepan or electric deep-
    fry cooker—with cover
Sieve

Ingredients

4	ounces treated shark's fin (see note)	⅛	teaspoon pepper
2	cups cold water	2	teaspoons sesame oil
¼	teaspoon baking soda	1	small scallion, minced
2	teaspoons sherry	4	cups unsalted chicken stock or canned chicken broth*
½	teaspoon salt		

Before Cooking
Wash treated fins in cold water and then soak 4 hours in enough cold water to cover. They will become somewhat curly and gelatinous. Rinse several times in cold water to eliminate all foreign particles; you will find a considerable amount. Drain the fins. Combine fins with 2 cups cold water and baking soda in saucepan and bring to a boil. Simmer covered 1 hour. The fins should now have swelled and softened. Drain in sieve and rinse, again removing particles you may have missed before. While fins are simmering, measure and set aside sherry, salt, pepper and sesame oil. Trim and finely mince the scallion, including some of the green. Measure stock or broth and pour into saucepan or electric deep-fry cooker.

Cooking Instructions
Add fins to the stock in the saucepan or cooker. Turn heat to medium (300° F. on cooker). Bring to a boil. Reduce heat to low (200° F. on cooker). Simmer 1½ hours. Add sherry, salt and pepper. Cover and simmer 30 minutes. Top with sesame oil and minced scallion. The soup will be rich and clear, with tendrils of transparent fins floating in it. This is a gourmet specialty and is classified as a Heavy Soup.

* If you are using canned chicken broth, decrease salt in the recipe.

SERVINGS: Enough for 6 to 8.

NOTE: Buy treated shark's fin rather than the dried whole fin, with or without skin. The treated come in ½-pound packages and resemble crystallized wavy locks of pale blonde hair. See page 18 for further information on shark's fin.

SHARK'S FIN SOUP WITH CHICKEN

Soak and precook 4 ounces shark's fin as directed in the Classic recipe. Add drained fins to 4 cups chicken stock. Cover and bring to a boil; simmer 1¾ hours. Add 1 boned raw breast of chicken, cut in fine shreds, 1 tablespoon shredded Virginia ham, 2 teaspoons sherry, ½ teaspoon salt and ⅛ teaspoon pepper. Cover and simmer 30 minutes.

OPTIONAL: Thicken with 1 tablespoon cornstarch dissolved in ¼ cup cold water. Stir to blend over low heat 5 minutes. Top with 1 tablespoon finely minced scallions and 2 teaspoons sesame oil.

SERVINGS: Enough for 6 to 8.

SHARK'S FIN SOUP WITH CRAB

Soak and precook 4 ounces shark's fin as directed in the Classic recipe. Add drained fins to 4 cups chicken stock. Cover and bring to a boil; simmer 1¾ hours. Add 1 cup crab meat, 1 tablespoon shredded Virginia ham, ½ cup sliced water chestnuts, 2 teaspoons sherry, ½ teaspoon salt and ⅛ teaspoon pepper. Simmer 10 minutes.

OPTIONAL: Thicken with 1 tablespoon cornstarch dissolved in ¼ cup cold water. Stir to blend over low heat 5 minutes. Top with 1 tablespoon finely minced scallions and 2 teaspoons sesame oil.

SERVINGS: Enough for 6 to 8.

CLEAR-SIMMERING

At a glance, Clear-Simmering appears identical with Red-Stewing. The differences, though minor, are significant. In Red-Stewing, the main ingredients are cooked with quantities of soy sauce and sugar. The final product is stewlike in consistency, with what amounts to a reduced sauce or gravy. Clear-Simmered dishes, on the other hand, provide the heartiness of cooked meat followed by the lightness of a clear broth. With the exception of Drunken dishes, in which Clear-Simmered ingredients are later marinated in wine, little or no seasoning is used. Soy sauce is never used. The blandness of the Clear-Simmered meat, poultry or fish is usually offset by condiment sauces which are served along with the main dish. Close examples of this technique in Western cooking are New England boiled dinners and *pot au feu*. But in Clear-Simmered dishes, fresh vegetables are rarely added; the intrinsic flavor of the principal ingredient is preserved. Occasionally, for the sake of variety, small amounts of dried ingredients—mushrooms, tiger lilies, tangerine peel, shrimp, scallops—may be included.

The differences between Clear-Simmering and Boiling (as in the making of soups) are these: 1) In soups, clarity is not always the objective; any number of ingredients, including soy sauce, may be added. Clarity is essential in Clear-Simmered dishes. 2) A soup mixture may boil and simmer anywhere from 10 minutes (if you are using a stock base) to several hours. With the exception of fish, Clear-Simmered dishes invariably require long periods of cooking. 3) In Clear-Simmering, the water added to the main ingredients should always be hot; in soups, the water used must be cool. As in Red-Stewing, the purpose of the hot water is to leave the flavor of the meat, poultry or fish sealed within itself.

When done, Clear-Simmered meat or poultry may be served hot and cut into slices and accompanied by a variety of spicy sauces; or they may be chilled (the surface fat removed just before serving), thinly sliced and accompanied by condiments and pickles.

I have not supplied too many of these recipes since the difference between one Clear-Simmered dish and another lies primarily in the choice of the main ingredient. Although someone from Szechuan might enjoy pepper and vinegar with his Clear-Simmered dish while another, from Peking, might prefer scallions and a touch of wine, there are to my knowledge no established regional variations to these recipes. Regional tastes are best satisfied by supplementing the cooked food with extra garnishes and condiment sauces.

POINTS TO REMEMBER IN CLEAR-SIMMERING

You will need a 4- to 6-quart soup kettle, double boiler, Dutch oven or electric deep-fry cooker to accommodate whole fowl or large cuts of meat and water. Whole fish approximately 3 pounds in weight will require a 15x10x3-inch roasting pan. Whichever utensil is used, it must have a cover. (Aluminum foil makes a good roasting-pan cover.)

With the exception of fish, ingredients and hot water are brought to a boil (300° F. on electric cooker). With fish, water is first brought to a boil, then reduced to a simmer—at which point the fish is added. As soon as the water boils, remove scum with a slotted spoon. Reduce heat to very low or reset electric cooker to 200° F. Spices, ginger root or other aromatics are added next. The pot is covered and the ingredients are allowed to simmer for the time indicated in each recipe. Fifteen to 30 minutes before turning off the heat, seasonings are added. Meats and poultry cooked in this manner are usually cut into fairly large pieces and may be followed by a bowl of the hot clear broth. When these ingredients are served cold and sliced, they are called "white-cut."

CLEAR-SIMMERED PORK

Cooking Time: 2 to 2½ hours

Utensils
6-quart soup kettle or electric deep-fry
    cooker—with cover
Slotted spoon
Tongs

Ingredients

4   pounds pork (shoulder, butt, un-   2   slices ginger root (2x1x⅛ inch)
    salted belly or fresh ham)   1½ teaspoons salt
8   cups hot water

Procedure
Place pork in kettle and add hot water. Turn heat to medium (300° F. on electric deep-fry cooker). Let meat and water come to a boil. Skim surface with slotted spoon to remove scum. Reduce heat to very low (200° F. on cooker). Add the ginger root. Cover and simmer 2 to 2½ hours, depending on the cut of pork used. Pork belly with skin or large cuts of ham with skin will take longer. Add salt during the last 15 minutes of simmering. Turn pork with tongs once or twice during the cooking. Test meat for doneness by prodding with a chopstick. It should pierce the meat easily and there should be no trace of blood. Allow the meat to cool slightly, then drain, reserving broth, and slice. Serve meat followed by bowls of broth.

Clear-Simmering
Put whole bird or large cut of meat in soup kettle or electric deep-fry cooker, add hot water and bring to a boil. Reduce heat at once and simmer covered 2½ hours or for time specified in recipe.

WHITE-SLICED PORK: Cool meat and broth, then cover and refrigerate. Before serving, remove top layer of fat on broth and cut meat into wafer-thin slices. Arrange on a platter and serve with small dishes of Chinese-style Mustard or "Chekiang" Vinegar (page 351).

SERVINGS: Enough for 8 as a single hot course with broth or for 12 as a cold platter of White-Sliced Pork.

CLEAR-SIMMERED BEEF: Substitute 4 pounds beef (shin, shank, brisket or lean meaty short ribs) for the pork. Simmer anywhere from 30 minutes to 1 hour longer than the pork. Mild corned beef brisket clear-simmered with grass mushrooms, dried bamboo shoots and Chinese cabbage is an exceedingly good combination. It may also be served cold with dishes of spicy dips.

CLEAR-SIMMERED LAMB: Substitute 3 to 4 pounds boned lamb shoulder or leg for the pork. At the simmering stage, add 1 whole leek, washed and trimmed, along with the ginger root. The finished lamb should be sliced tissue-thin and served with bowls of broth. It may be served cold and thinly cut with small bowls of spicy sauces.

DRUNKEN PORK

Cooking Time: Approximately 2 hours

Utensils
6-quart soup kettle or electric deep-fry
    cooker—with cover

Slotted spoon
2-quart bowl or crock
Cheesecloth

Ingredients

3 to 4 pounds pork tenderloin or any
  lean cut of pork
6 to 8 cups hot water
2   slices ginger root (2x1x⅛ inch)
1   scallion, trimmed, with some
    green left

2½ teaspoons salt
⅛   teaspoon white pepper
2   cups pale dry sherry
    Salt and pepper

Procedure

Place the meat in the kettle; cover with the hot water. Turn heat to medium
(300° F. on electric deep-fry cooker). Allow pork and water to come to a boil.
Skim surface with slotted spoon to remove scum. Add ginger root and scallion. Reduce heat to very low (200° F. on cooker). Cover and simmer 1½ hours. Add salt
and pepper and simmer covered 30 minutes. Allow meat to cool in liquid, then
drain and save liquid to use as stock. Dry meat well with paper towels. Cover in
plastic wrap and refrigerate overnight or at least 8 hours. Slice the refrigerated pork
into thick pieces and line the bowl or crock. Pour the sherry over the pork slices. It
should cover the meat completely. Cover the bowl or crock with a double thickness of cheesecloth and tie with string. Return to the refrigerator and marinate 3
days.

To serve, drain the sherry, slice the pork thinly, arrange on a platter and sprinkle with salt and pepper. In Drunken dishes, the water in which the main ingredient is cooked is usually very heavily salted. While this eliminates the final dusting
with salt and pepper, it ruins what is otherwise an excellent stock. Drunken Pork
makes a zesty appetizer; it may also be served as a cold platter with condiments.

SERVINGS: Enough for 6 to 8 as a cold platter or for 12 as an appetizer.

NOTE: Beef and lamb are not used in Drunken dishes.

TWICE-COOKED PORK,

Szechuan Style

Cooking Time: 20 to 30 minutes to clear-simmer
            7 minutes to stir-fry-toss

Utensils
2½-quart enameled saucepan
Chinese cutting knife
Small strainer or sieve
Large strainer or sieve
12-inch skillet or wok
Large slotted spatula

Ingredients

1	pound boned lean pork (shoulder steaks, butt or chops)
2	scallions, trimmed
3	slices ginger root (2x1x⅛ inch)
2	cups hot water or hot chicken stock
2	teaspoons sherry
½	large green pepper, cut in 2-inch squares
½	medium bamboo shoot, cut in 2-inch squares

3	cloves garlic, minced
⅓	cup soft black beans, minced
1	teaspoon crushed red pepper flakes
2	tablespoons soy sauce
½	teaspoon sugar
2	tablespoons peanut oil or corn oil
1	tablespoon peanut oil or corn oil

Before Cooking
Trim all fat from the pork. If you are using chops or a cut with a bone, allow about ½ pound for the bone and buy 1½ pounds pork. I suggest pork steaks cut from the shoulder, as this makes the final cutting easier; there is generally less waste, since the steaks are usually trimmed of most fat beforehand. Prepare scallions and ginger root. Begin the Clear-Simmering. Meanwhile, cut the green pepper and the bamboo shoot. You should have about ½ cup of each. Mince the garlic with the Chinese cutting knife. Rinse the black beans in cold water; drain well in the small strainer. Then mince beans with the blunt edge of the Chinese cutting knife. Combine the garlic, beans and crushed pepper flakes. Combine soy sauce and sugar. Measure both portions of oil and have ready to go.

Clear-Simmer Cooking Instructions
Pour the 2 cups hot water or stock into the saucepan. Add the sherry, scallions and 1 slice of the ginger root. Add the whole pork piece or steaks. Cook over medium heat until boiling. Reduce heat to simmer at once. Simmer gently 30 minutes for whole piece of pork, 20 minutes for steaks. When done, drain pork in large strainer or sieve and reserve ¼ cup stock. The remaining stock may be used as a soup base. Allow pork to cool thoroughly 30 minutes. When the pork is cool, trim the bone and cut meat into 2-inch squares, ¼ inch thick. Set aside.

Stir-Fry-Toss Instructions

Turn heat under skillet or wok to high. (The heat remains high throughout the cooking.) When the pan is hot, add the 2 tablespoons oil. It should sizzle at once. Before the oil begins to smoke, add the remaining 2 slices of ginger root. Stir-fry-toss 1 minute. Add the green pepper and bamboo-shoot squares. Stir-fry-toss 2 minutes. Remove with slotted spatula to a dish. Pour the 1 tablespoon oil into the pan. When the oil sizzles, add the black beans, garlic and the red pepper flakes. Stir-fry-toss 1 minute. Add the pork squares and stir-fry-toss 3 minutes. Add the soy sauce and sugar; stir just to blend. Add the stock, blend and remove from heat. Remove ginger slices. The pork should be fried golden brown, the sauce scant, almost black and thick. The vegetables should be just done and part of the whole dish rather than separate entities. This dish is sometimes erroneously prepared with Hoisin sauce instead of the fermented black beans. And while it is delicious, it is not authentic.

SERVINGS: Enough for 2 as a single course with rice or for 4 to 6 in a full menu.

NOTE: I use chicken stock rather than water to simmer the pork. This produces a richer flavor and a rich soup base.

CLEAR-SIMMERED CHICKEN

Cooking Time: 2½ hours

Utensils
**6-quart soup kettle, Dutch oven or electric
    deep-fry cooker—with cover
Slotted spoon
Tongs**

Ingredients

1	stewing hen (4 pounds), washed, with stringy matter removed from cavity	8	cups hot water
		2	slices ginger root (2x1x⅛ inch)
		2	teaspoons salt

Procedure

Place hen in soup kettle, Dutch oven or electric deep-fry cooker; add the 8 cups hot water to pot. Turn heat to medium (300° F. on cooker). Bring chicken and water to a boil. Skim surface with slotted spoon to remove scum. Reduce heat to very low (200° F. on cooker). Add ginger root. Cover and simmer 2 hours, or until chopstick pierces the thickest part of chicken leg easily and no traces of pink appear. Add salt, cover and simmer 30 minutes. The chicken will be very tender and the stock absolutely clear. Cut chicken into Chinese-style serving pieces and arrange on a platter. Follow with bowls of broth.

SERVINGS: Enough for 8 served hot with broth and rice or for 8 to 10 served as a cold platter with condiments.

CLEAR-SIMMERED DUCK: Substitute 1 duckling (5 pounds) for the chicken and add a piece of dried tangerine (2 inches in diameter) during the simmering. You may have to break the duck's back or cut it in half to fit it into the pot. Or you may want to use a heavy roasting pan covered with foil instead. Simmer 2 to 2½ hours, until duck's leg pierces easily with chopstick. Serve either hot or cold, cut into bite-size pieces.

CLEAR-SIMMERED SQUAB: Substitute 4 squabs (1 pound each) for the chicken and simmer 1½ hours.

WHITE-CUT CHICKEN: When served cold, Clear-Simmered Chicken is known as White-Cut Chicken. It is usually prepared with a younger bird. For the hen, substitute a 3½- to 4-pound fryer with a good coating of fat under the skin. Decrease the cooking time to 1½ hours. Let the chicken cool in the stock, then cover and refrigerate. Before serving, chop the chicken into bite-size pieces, arrange on a platter and serve with small bowls of "Chekiang" Vinegar (page 351), Garlic-Soy Dip (page 351) or oyster sauce. Reserve broth for another occasion.

DRUNKEN CHICKEN

Follow the recipe for Clear-Simmered Chicken, but use a 3½- to 4-pound fryer. Simmer covered only 30 minutes. Allow bird to remain in stock to cool another 30 minutes. Remove chicken from stock and dry thoroughly. Wrap in plastic and refrigerate at least 8 hours. Split chicken in two. Place in a 2-quart bowl and cover with 2 cups sherry. Tie a kitchen towel over the bowl containing the chicken and let it marinate in the refrigerator 3 days. Drain chicken and chop into bite-size pieces. Sprinkle with salt and pepper to taste and serve with assorted dips and condiments (pages 22–23).

SERVINGS: Enough for 8 to 10 as a cold platter or for 16 as an appetizer.

DRUNKEN DUCK: Substitute 1 thawed frozen duckling (5 pounds) for the chicken, but simmer at least 2 hours. After marinating in sherry 3 days, drain duck and chop into bite-size pieces. Serve with trimmed scallions and assorted condiment sauces.

DRUNKEN SQUAB: Substitute 4 squabs (1 pound each) for the fryer. After marinating in sherry 3 days, cut each squab into quarters. Serve with assorted condiment sauces.

ANGEL CHICKEN

Cooking Time: 1½ to 2 hours

Utensils
Chinese cutting knife
Small bowl for seasonings
Soup plate
Chopsticks
5-quart double boiler with cover

Ingredients

1	tablespoon small dried shrimp	1	tablespoon soy sauce
1	fryer (3 to 3½ pounds)	2	teaspoons sherry, gin or vodka
½	ounce dried snow fungus	½	teaspoon sugar
½	tablespoon dried cloud ears	4	cups hot unsalted pork stock or
⅔	cup shredded bamboo shoots		hot water
½	cup shredded Virginia ham	¾	teaspoon salt
½	teaspoon minced ginger root		

Before Cooking
One hour ahead, soak the shrimp in hot water. Drain and reserve. Wash the fryer and pull out stringy matter from the cavity. Drain well. Blot outside and in with paper towels. Soak the snow fungus in warm water 15 minutes; drain. Rinse the cloud ears and soak in warm water 10 minutes. Rinse in cold water several times to remove grit and twigs; drain. Prepare the bamboo shoots, ham and ginger root. Combine soy sauce, liquor and sugar in the small bowl. Place the shrimp, snow

fungus, cloud ears, bamboo shoots, ham, ginger and seasonings in the soup plate and toss together with chopsticks to mix. Stuff this mixture into the bird's cavity. Sew or skewer and tie the opening. Skewer the neck cavity.

Cooking Instructions

Place the stuffed fryer in the top of the double boiler and add hot pork stock or water. Pour 2½ inches boiling water in the lower portion of the double boiler (see note). Place the top section of the double boiler over the lower and cover. Turn heat under double boiler to medium-low. Simmer 1½ to 2 hours. (Add more boiling water as needed to the lower portion of the double boiler.) In the last 30 minutes of cooking, add salt. The chicken should be chopstick-tender and have a glazed look. The broth should be amber colored and clear. Place the bird on a heated platter and remove skewers and string. Carve into large serving pieces at the table, spooning out filling with each serving. Provide small dishes of oyster sauce, soy sauce, mustard and rice or cider vinegar for dipping. Follow with steamed rice and bowls of broth.

SERVINGS: Enough for 4 to 6 as a single course with rice and broth or for 8 in a full menu.

JELLIED ANGEL CHICKEN: Place the cooked chicken breast-side-up in a deep Chinese-style bowl. Line a strainer with a kitchen towel wrung out in hot water. Pour the broth through the strainer over the chicken. Allow to cool, then refrigerate until the broth forms a firm jelly.

NOTE: This recipe may be cooked instead in any 6-quart pot, in which case you must increase the pork stock to 6 cups. Using a double boiler gives the finished food a steamed quality.

HIDDEN TREASURE CHICKEN

Cooking Time: 2½ hours to clear-simmer
30 minutes to deep-fry

Utensils
Chinese cutting knife
Bowl for mixing stuffing
5-quart double boiler with cover
2 spatulas for lifting cooked bird

Colander
Electric deep-fry cooker or large pot for
    deep-frying

Ingredients

$1\frac{1}{2}$	cups glutinous rice	2	slices ginger root ($3 \times 1\frac{1}{2} \times \frac{1}{8}$ inch)
1	stewing hen (4 pounds), boned*, with shape retained and skin undamaged	1	tablespoon sherry
		2	teaspoons salt
6	dried chestnuts	1	teaspoon granulated sugar
6	dried red dates	2	tablespoons light soy sauce
1	tablespoon raisins	1	teaspoon brown sugar
6	canned lotus seeds	4	cups hot unsalted chicken stock or hot water
6	canned gingko nuts	1	tablespoon cornstarch (optional)
$\frac{1}{4}$	cup diced Virginia ham	4	cups peanut oil or corn oil (optional)
$\frac{1}{4}$	cup diced Chinese sausage		
1	scallion, minced		

Before Cooking

Rinse the glutinous rice and cover with $1\frac{1}{2}$ cups cold water to soak 4 hours. Bone the hen if not already done. Soak the dried chestnuts in hot water 1 hour. Soak red dates in warm water 15 minutes; drain well. Measure the raisins. Drain and measure the canned lotus seeds and gingko nuts. Trim and mince scallion. Cut the ham and Chinese sausage into $\frac{1}{4}$-inch dice. Peel and slice the ginger root. Measure the sherry, salt and granulated sugar. Drain the glutinous rice thoroughly and add to it the light soy sauce, brown sugar and the minced scallion. Add the chestnuts, red dates, raisins, lotus seeds, gingko nuts, ham and Chinese sausage. Mix well to blend ingredients. Rinse the boned bird and blot dry, outside and in the cavity, with paper towels. Stuff cavity loosely with glutinous rice mixture and sew or skewer closed. Sew or skewer neck opening.

Cooking Instructions

Place the hot stock or hot water in the top of the double boiler. Add the sherry. Carefully lower the stuffed bird into the pot. Pour $2\frac{1}{2}$ inches of boiling water into

* If you are not experienced enough to bone a chicken without piercing the skin and are unable to find a poultry dealer willing to do this, you would be better off to use an unboned hen. However, the excellence of this Banquet treat is based on the contrast of boneless meat with savory stuffing, studded with dates, chestnuts, lotus seeds and gingko nuts. In China, this is prepared with a special black-skinned fowl.

the lower portion (about 2 quarts). Put top part of double boiler over the lower portion. Turn heat under double boiler to medium. Cover and simmer 2 hours. (Add more boiling water as needed to the lower portion of the double boiler.) Add salt and white sugar. Cover and simmer 30 minutes. Using two spatulas, carefully remove chicken to a heated platter. Reserve stock for another occasion. To serve, slice 3-inch strips across bird and cut each strip crosswise into squares.

OPTIONAL: When the bird has finished simmering, place it in a colander to drain. Lightly dust 1 tablespoon cornstarch over the cooked chicken. Allow it to cool. Place 4 cups peanut oil or corn oil in a clean deep pot or electric deep-fry cooker. Heat oil until it bubbles around a cube of fresh bread (375° F. on cooker). Gently lower the cooked stuffed bird into the hot oil and deep-fry until the skin is golden brown, 20 to 30 minutes. Drain and serve with small dishes of either Cantonese Salt or Spiced Salt (page 352).

SERVINGS: Enough for 4 to 6 as a single course or for 8 in a full menu.

NOTE: If you do not have a large enough double boiler, you may use any 6-quart pot with lid. Increase stock or hot water to 6 cups.

THREE IN ONE,
Peking Grand Fowl

Cooking Time: 3 hours to clear-simmer
              20 to 30 minutes to deep-fry

Utensils
Tweezers
1-quart saucepan
Strainer
String
4-quart Dutch oven or 14-inch wok—with
    cover
Large colander

Ingredients

$\frac{1}{2}$	ounce bird's nest	1	medium onion
2	teaspoons salt	4	slices ginger root (2x1x$\frac{1}{8}$ inch)
1	duck (4 to 6 pounds), boned*	$\frac{1}{4}$	cup shredded Virginia ham
1	fryer (2$\frac{1}{2}$ to 3$\frac{1}{2}$ pounds), boned*	1	tablespoon cornstarch (optional)
1	squab (1 pound), boned*	4	cups peanut oil or corn oil (op-
4	cups hot water		tional)
$\frac{1}{4}$	cup sherry		

Before Cooking

Soak the bird's nest in warm water 2 hours. (You will need about half a small nest.) The nest will become somewhat gelatinous in appearance after soaking. Drain. Using tweezers, pick out feathers and foreign matter which have become dislodged by the soaking. Place nest with 1$\frac{1}{2}$ cups cold water in the 1-quart saucepan and boil 10 to 15 minutes. Again remove any particles which rise to the surface. Place nest in a strainer and rinse with cold water. Drain well. Rinse and dry the boned birds, blotting gently inside and out with paper towels. Rub the salt in the cavities of the 3 birds. Stuff the squab with the drained bird's nest; sew closed. Fit the squab into the cavity of the fryer; sew the fryer closed. Then insert the squab-filled fryer into the duck's cavity; sew the duck closed. Tie the stuffed birds with string to retain their shape, making a loop on top for easier handling. Place in Dutch oven or wok, add hot water and sherry. Start cooking process. Meanwhile, prepare and measure remaining ingredients.

Cooking Instructions

Turn heat under Dutch oven or wok to medium-high. Let come to a boil. Reduce heat immediately and add onion and ginger root. Cover and simmer 3 hours. Test for doneness by prodding fleshiest part of leg with a chopstick. It should pierce easily and the juices should run clear, with no trace of pink. Remove bird to a heated platter. Remove strings. Sprinkle with shredded ham. Slice lengthwise down the middle, then across in 2$\frac{1}{2}$-inch squares. Serve with dishes of Cantonese Salt or Spiced Salt (page 352) and with plum, Hoisin or oyster sauce. When cross-sectioned, the meat will show the textures of duck, chicken and squab. The poultry will be succulent in a fragrant broth.

* The duck, chicken and squab must be boned in such a manner that the shape of each bird is retained and the skin is left intact. Chinese poultry dealers are adept at this.

OPTIONAL: When the birds have finished simmering, place in a colander to drain (do not remove strings). Lightly dust with cornstarch. Allow to cool. Reserve the cooking liquid for later use. Wash out Dutch oven or wok and dry. Add 4 cups peanut oil or corn oil. Heat oil until it sizzles around a cube of fresh bread. Carefully lower stuffed birds into oil. Deep-fry until golden brown, 20 to 30 minutes. Drain in colander and serve as directed above.

SERVINGS: Enough for 4 to 6 as a single course or for 6 to 8 in a full menu.

NOTE: Since most electric frypans are round rather than oval, the use of a Dutch oven or wok is more practical to accommodate the length of the duck.

CLEAR-SIMMERED FISH

Cooking Time: 15 minutes to simmer
              15 minutes to "steam"

Utensils
Roasting pan
Aluminum foil
Large spatula

Ingredients

2½	pounds bass, pike, mullet or shad, either whole or in large pieces	4	cups hot water
2	slices ginger root (2x1x⅛ inch)	¼	cup sherry
2	scallions, trimmed leaving some green	2	teaspoons salt

Before Cooking
Clean and scale fish, unless it is shad. If it is shad, leave the scales on to prevent the flesh from drying out. If the fish is too large to simmer whole, cut in half. Prepare the ginger slices and scallions. Pour hot water and sherry into roasting pan. Have salt ready.

Cooking Instructions
Turn heat under roasting pan to medium-high. Bring water and sherry to a boil. Add scallions and ginger root. Reduce heat to very low. When the boiling has subsided, carefully place fish in pan. Cover pan with aluminum foil and simmer gently

15 minutes. Turn fish, using the spatula. Add salt. Cover and turn off heat. Let fish stand 15 minutes. The steam circulating in the pan will continue to cook the fish. Place fish on a platter and serve with small dishes of "Chekiang" Vinegar (page 351), light soy sauce or Ginger-Soy Dip (page 352).

SERVINGS: Enough for 4 to 6 as a single course with steamed rice or for 6 to 8 in a full menu.

NOTE: Coarser-grained fish will take longer to cook. Test with a fork at the spine of the fish. The flesh should flake easily. Under no circumstances should the fish be overcooked.

VARIATION: Omit scallions from simmering process. Heat $\frac{1}{2}$ cup oil in a skillet. When the oil is very hot, add 3 scallions, trimmed and sliced. Fry until scallions begin to turn brown at the edges. After the fish has simmered and stood, drain carefully, arrange on a platter and pour oil and fried scallions over. Serve at once.

DRUNKEN FISH: Whole fish or fish steaks are not usually prepared in this manner.

CLEAR-SIMMERED SHRIMP

Cooking Time: 3 to 5 minutes

Utensils
2-quart enameled saucepan
Wire strainer

Ingredients

2	cups water	1	pound medium shrimp (24 to
$\frac{1}{4}$	cup pale dry sherry		26), washed but unshelled
2	slices ginger root (2x1x$\frac{1}{8}$ inch)	$\frac{3}{4}$	teaspoon salt

Procedure
Place water, sherry and ginger root in the saucepan and bring to a boil over medium-high heat. Reduce heat to low and add shrimp and salt. Simmer uncovered 3

minutes or until the shrimp turns bright coral. Drain. While still hot, shell and devein. Serve with Garlic-Soy Dip (page 351). To serve cold, drain cooked shrimp and pour ice water over. Drain. Shell and devein or leave in shells. Serve cold as an appetizer with Sesame-Soy Dip or "Chekiang" Vinegar (page 351) or Ginger-Soy Dip (page 352).

SERVINGS: Enough for 4 with rice as a single course or for 6 as an appetizer.

DRUNKEN SHRIMP

Follow the recipe for Clear-Simmered Shrimp but omit sherry and increase salt to 2 teaspoons. Simmer 3 minutes. Drain but do not shell. Allow shrimp to dry refrigerated. Place in a bowl. Pour ¾ cup pale dry sherry over shrimp. Cover bowl with plastic wrap. Refrigerate overnight. Drain and serve cold as either a cold platter or an appetizer with dips and sauces.

SERVINGS: Enough for 6.

STEAMING–
TECHNIQUE 5

己己己己己己己己己己

Steaming is a far more popular method of cooking among the Chinese than it is among Westerners. It is a technique applied to meats, poultry, fish, pastries and desserts, taking the place of baking for the last two, and was developed as a fuel- and space-saving device. The traditional bamboo tiers used in steaming allow for a variety and/or quantity of food to be cooked simultaneously over the same heat. When used as a precooking technique, it has the further advantage of cutting down the final stir-frying, barbecuing or smoking time. Since steamed food, cooked without the addition of liquid and with a minimum of seasoning, tends to retain its maximum flavor, the freshness of the ingredients is of ultimate importance.

While cooking in a double boiler is in a sense steaming, it is not interchangeable with the Chinese method. Double-boiler steaming is fine for cooking by dry steam and for reheating rice and pastries, but it lacks the intense moist heat required for Chinese or wet steaming.

HOW TO STEAM

Under the heading of Steaming Equipment and Instructions, I have explained how to set up equipment for steaming, using either everyday Western appliances or Chinese units specifically designed for steaming. I will attempt here to discuss certain fundamentals which apply, regardless of the utensil being used.

To moist-steam correctly, an outer vehicle—a soup pot, wok or skillet—is mandatory. It must have a proper-fitting, but not necessarily tight, lid. For long whole objects—a fish, for example—you will need a rectangular utensil, such as a roasting or baking pan, with an improvised cover of foil. A French fish-poaching pan, or *poissonière*, is ideal. Some kind of support is placed in the pot; this can be a trivet, cake rack, vegetable steamer, coffee can with perforated base, a heat-proof bowl or the ring of a springform cake pan. Boiling water is poured into the pot up to the full height of the trivet, rack or vegetable steamer—or up to $\frac{2}{3}$ the height of the coffee can, bowl or springform ring. Depending on the size of the ingredient to be steamed, it is arranged on a pie plate (lightly oiled if the food itself contains little or no fat) or placed in a heat-proof bowl or baking dish. The container is then placed on the support.

The heat is turned up to medium-high below the outer pot containing water. When the water begins to boil, the outer pot is covered, and the heat turned down to medium-low—but not to simmer. The water must actively boil if it is to generate enough steam to cook the food. Continue steaming covered for the time given in the recipe. Additional boiling water should be added to the pot to replace water that has evaporated. Care must be taken not to add too much nor to allow it to boil so vigorously that it splashes into the container of food.

Some sources feel that the food container should be covered with wax paper or foil to prevent condensed steam from pouring into the food. I believe that this defeats your purpose. In my experience, the moisture that collects on the domed covers of utensils tends to run down the sides of the cover rather than into the food. The paper cover just causes condensation in rather concentrated amounts; this liquid then runs directly into the food and at the same time impedes the circulation of steam.

When you steam individual foods such as pastries, meat balls, stuffed vegetables or fish filets, always place the food in single layers. Pastries and rice-coated foods should be placed about $\frac{1}{2}$ inch apart to allow for expansion. Meat, poultry, rice, noodles and pastries take to resteaming well. Seafood tends to toughen on reheating.

POINTS TO REMEMBER IN STEAMING

Before beginning to cook, assemble all the components of your steaming unit and make sure that they fit. A 9-inch cake rack won't squeeze into an 8-inch skillet. A trivet that is too tall or a steaming dish or bowl that is too high to enable you to cover the outer utensil won't work either. Stick to the utensils specified under

Steaming Equipment and Instructions or do your experimenting in advance. Be sure that your outer pot or pan is large enough to permit plenty of steam to circulate around the food.

The water level in the outer pot must be maintained so that the food being steamed won't dry out—but it must not be so high as to boil over and drench the food. The cover of the outer pan should fit snugly enough to retain the steam, but not so tightly that it will cause pressure buildup.

Steamed food should if anything be undercooked, since it tends to continue steaming after being removed from the steamer. The one exception to this rule is pork, which must always be steamed until it has no trace of pink.

Be very careful about removing steamed foods from the outer pot. Steam burns are extremely painful. When the food is cooked, turn off the heat. Wear a pair of asbestos or lined rubber gloves to remove the cover of the outer container; be sure to stand back and turn your face away from the steam. To remove the plate or bowl more easily, use a 3-tonged tension dish holder. (These tongs are available in Chinese hardware stores and are quite inexpensive.) Lower the tongs, allowing them to grasp the sides of the plate, then lift the plate from the steaming pot.

The following main-dish foods are best for steaming: minced pork, beef or lamb; minced chicken; minced prawns; fresh whole fish; chicken, duck or squab.

STEAMING EQUIPMENT AND INSTRUCTIONS

SKILLET OR ELECTRIC FRYPAN METHOD

Use a 10½- to 11½-inch electric frypan or skillet with a domed cover. Place a cake rack (9¾ inches) or a vegetable steaming basket (9 inches wide when opened flat) in the center of the pan as the steaming rack or support. Add boiling water up to the height of the support. Hold the food to be steamed on a heat-proof dish or pie plate. Use a 9-inch dish with a 10½-inch frypan and a 10-inch dish with an 11½-inch electric frypan or skillet. There should be a minimum clearance of ½ inch between all sides of the plate and the utensil. This method is ideal for steaming small amounts of food—meatballs or patties, stuffed vegetables and small whole ingredients.

WOK METHOD

Punch 6 holes in the bottom of a ½-pound coffee can with an ice pick. Place the can holes-side-up in the center of a 12-inch wok with a domed cover (the can acts as the steaming rack). Or use a 9¾-inch cake rack instead of the coffee can. Add

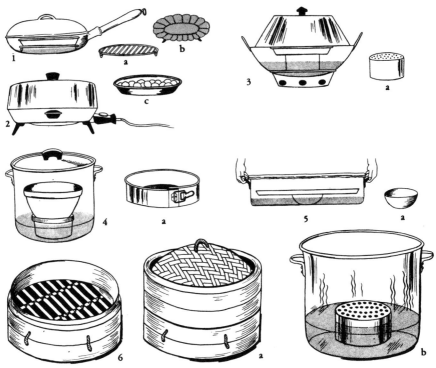

Steaming
1. Skillet with domed cover uses a cake rack (a) or opened steaming basket (b) and pie plate (c) to hold food to be steamed.   2. Electric frypan uses same steaming utensils as skillet. 3. Wok with domed cover uses perforated ½-pound coffee can (a) and pie plate to hold food to be steamed.   4. Soup kettle with cover uses Pyrex baking dish or ring of springform cake pan (a) and large bowl to hold ingredients to be steamed.   5. Foil-covered roasting pan uses small bowl or custard cup (a) and flat heatproof dish or shallow pan to hold food to be steamed.   6. Bamboo steamer has its own lid and may be used in a wok (a) or in a soup kettle (b).

boiling water up to ⅔ the height of the can or up to the height of the cake rack. A 10-inch Pyrex or metal pie plate is ideal for steaming small individual foods. To steam large cuts of meat or whole poultry, use the cake rack for support and place the food in a 2-quart bowl, Pyrex baking dish or soufflé dish.

SOUP KETTLE METHOD
Place a 2-quart Pyrex baking dish or the ring of a 9-inch springform cake pan in the center of a 12-quart soup kettle that is 12 inches in diameter. Use a 4-quart heat-proof bowl to hold the food to be steamed. This method is used to steam large cuts of meat and whole poultry.

ROASTING PAN METHOD

Place a 10-ounce custard cup in the center of a roasting pan (15x10x3 inches). The cup acts as the steaming rack. Add boiling water up to ⅔ the height of the cup. Arrange the food to be steamed either in a shallow pan (14x8x1 inch) or in a baking dish (14x9x2¼ inches). Improvise a cover for the roasting pan by using 12-inch-wide aluminum foil. Tear off a piece of foil 32 inches long and fold it over once so that you have a double thickness of foil 16 inches long by 12 inches wide. Fit the foil "cover" over the roasting pan. This method is used to steam whole small legs of ham, lamb, whole fryers or ducks or a whole fish.

BAMBOO TIERS METHOD

The classic Chinese method of steaming is by the use of bamboo tiers, one set upon the other and the top tier covered with a woven bamboo lid. Only one lid is needed, since the stacked tiers act as their own covers. The tiers have latticed bottoms to permit the free circulation of steam—but to prevent foods from becoming soggy, the tiers should be lined with kitchen towels wrung out in hot water. The food is placed on the tiers over the boiling water. The top tier is covered with its own bamboo lid; the outer pot does not need to be covered. A 12-inch wok can accommodate two 10-inch bamboo tiers. To steam three or more tiers a larger pot, such as a 12-quart soup kettle, is required. Aluminum steaming units with perforated tiers are also available in 10- to 12-inch sizes.

CLASSIC STEAMED MINCED PORK BALLS

Cooking Time: 35 to 45 minutes

Utensils
2 Chinese cutting knives or meat grinder
Bowl for ground pork
2 small bowls for seasonings and egg-water
    mixture
Wooden spoon or spatula
12-inch skillet, wok or electric frypan—
    with domed cover
9¾-inch cake rack, 9-inch vegetable steaming
    basket or ½-pound coffee can
9- or 10-inch Pyrex or metal pie plate

Ingredients

2	pounds medium-fat ground pork	1	teaspoon salt
1	teaspoon finely minced ginger root	1	teaspoon brown sugar
		1	egg, beaten
¼	cup soy sauce	¼	cup cold water
½	tablespoon sherry	1	tablespoon cornstarch

Before Cooking

Select a cut of pork with about 25% fat. Either mince by hand (page 34) or put through the medium blade of a meat grinder once, then put half of it through again. This uneven grinding approximates hand-mincing to some extent and results in juicier balls or patties. Place the minced pork in a bowl. Add the minced ginger root. Combine the soy sauce, sherry, salt and sugar in the small bowl. Stir well and blend lightly into the pork with a wooden spoon. (Be sure to blend lightly. Packing the meat fibers together will cause heaviness.) Combine the egg white and cold water in another small bowl. Beat well until blended. Add to the pork-ginger-soy mixture. Add the cornstarch. Again blend carefully with the wooden spoon, turning the meat over, under and over in a folding motion until the mass clings together and leaves the sides of the bowl. Pinch off the pork mixture and roll between palms to form marble- or golfball-size balls. Place the pork balls on an ungreased pie plate. (You should be able to get about 10 golfball-size balls on the 9-inch plate and 11 to 12 balls on the 10-inch plate. Do not let the balls touch.)

Cooking Instructions

Place the cake rack or steaming basket opened flat in the center of the skillet, wok or frypan. Add boiling water up to the height of the rack or ⅔ the height of the can if using a coffee can in the wok. Turn heat under skillet or wok to medium-high (360° F. on frypan). Bring the water to a boil. Place plate containing balls on rack. Cover the utensil with its own lid and reduce heat to medium (300° F. on frypan) or just high enough to keep the water actively boiling. Steam 25 minutes or until the meat appears only slightly pink when tested with a chopstick or fork. Remove balls to a heated plate and cover with foil. Keep warm in 170° F. oven. The balls will continue to steam in their foil covering while you steam the remaining balls 35 to 45 minutes. Serve with small dishes of mustard, Garlic-Soy Dip (page 351) and vinegar. To handle larger-size balls or patties or a large quantity of cocktail-size balls, you will require several steamings, or you may steam them all at one time with bamboo tiers. This recipe will produce succulent, savory meatballs, juicy and not too heavy.

AMOUNT: About 75 marble-size balls (for appetizers), about 24 golfball-size balls, 6 peach-size balls, 1 large ball or 4 patties.

CLASSIC STEAMED MINCED BEEF BALLS: Substitute 2 pounds medium-fat ground chuck for the pork. Steam 20 to 25 minutes. Test for doneness with fork or chopsticks—a slight pinkness in the beef is acceptable although not traditionally Chinese.

CLASSIC STEAMED MINCED LAMB BALLS: Substitute 2 pounds medium-fat ground lamb for the pork; reduce minced ginger to ½ teaspoon and add 2 cloves garlic, finely minced, to the meat mixture. Steam 25 to 30 minutes—slightly longer than beef but not quite so long as pork.

PORK BALLS WITH CRAB
Follow the recipe for Classic Steamed Minced Pork Balls but add ½ cup cooked crab meat to the second grinding of pork. Make sure that all pieces of cartilage have been removed from the crab. (Do not use beef or lamb in this variation.)

SERVINGS: Enough for 4 to 6 as a single course with rice or for 8 in a full menu.

PORK BALLS WITH SHRIMP
Follow the recipe for Classic Steamed Minced Pork Balls but add ½ cup shelled, finely minced raw shrimp to the second grinding of pork. (Do not use beef or lamb in this variation.)

SERVINGS: Enough for 4 to 6 as a single course with rice or for 8 in a full menu.

PORK PEARL BALLS
Four hours before preparing Classic Steamed Minced Pork Ball mixture, soak 2 cups glutinous rice in 2 cups cold water. Drain rice thoroughly and spread on a cookie sheet. Prepare and shape pork balls. Roll two at a time in glutinous rice, using the palms of your hands to roll and coat the balls with rice. Steam as directed in the Classic recipe until rice is translucent and tacky to the touch. The flavor and texture of the meat is surprisingly compatible with the bland rice. Both Pork Balls with Crab and Pork Balls with Shrimp can be used in this variation as well.

SERVINGS: Enough for 4 to 6 as a single course with rice or for 8 in a full menu.

BEEF PEARL BALLS: Follow the directions above using the recipe for Classic Steamed Minced Beef Balls.

LAMB PEARL BALLS: Follow the directions above using the recipe for Classic Steamed Minced Lamb Balls.

STEAMED CHINESE MUSHROOMS STUFFED WITH MINCED PORK

Prepare ½ recipe for Classic Steamed Minced Pork Balls or variations with crab or with shrimp. Rinse 24 medium-large dried mushrooms in cold water. Cover with warm water and soak 30 minutes. Drain well, squeezing out excess water with fingers. Using a grapefruit cutter or any small sharp knife, trim the hard centers but try not to cut through the mushrooms. Fill each mushroom cup with pork mixture, mounding it to a peak. Place half the filled mushrooms in a 9- or 10-inch lightly oiled Pyrex pie plate and steam 20 minutes or until the pork no longer shows pink when tested with a fork. Cover with foil and keep warm in a 170° F. oven while you steam the second lot of filled mushrooms. If you have bamboo steaming tiers, you may of course steam them all at once.

SERVINGS: Enough for 12 as an appetizer or for 6 as a course in a full menu.

NOTE: The following vegetables may also be filled with minced pork, beef or lamb and steamed:

Cucumbers: Peel six 8-inch cucumbers. Cut each into four 2-inch rounds. Core without piercing bottom of rounds.
Zucchini: Same as cucumbers, or cut lengthwise into boat shapes. Do not peel.
Eggplant: Use narrow Chinese eggplants; cut same as cucumbers or zucchini.
Onions: Use 24 smallish onions. Peel and core without piercing. Fill and steam until onions are very tender.

SERVINGS: Enough for 4 as a single course or 6 in a full menu.

STEAMED CHINESE MUSHROOMS STUFFED WITH MINCED BEEF: Prepare ½ recipe Classic Steamed Minced Beef Balls. Continue as directed above. Steam about 13 minutes.

STEAMED CHINESE MUSHROOMS STUFFED WITH MINCED LAMB: Prepare ½ recipe Classic Steamed Minced Lamb Balls. Continue as directed above. Steam about 16 minutes, slightly longer than beef but not quite so long as pork.

CLASSIC STEAMED SLICED OR DICED PORK

Cooking Time: 35 to 45 minutes

Utensils
Chinese cutting knife
9- or 10-inch Pyrex or metal pie plate
Chopsticks
12-inch skillet, wok or electric frypan—
    with domed cover
9¾-inch cake rack, 9-inch vegetable steaming
    basket or ½-pound coffee can

Ingredients

1½	pounds pork tenderloin	½	teaspoon salt
1	tablespoon soy sauce	2	teaspoons sugar
1	teaspoon sesame oil	½	teaspoon minced ginger root

Before Cooking
Cut the pork into very thin shreds or ½-inch dice. Place in pie plate. Add soy sauce, sesame oil, salt and sugar. Toss well with chopsticks to mix. Add minced ginger root to meat and seasonings. Let stand 30 minutes.

Cooking Instructions
Place the cake rack or steaming basket opened flat in the center of the skillet, wok or frypan. Add boiling water up to the height of the rack or ⅔ the height of the can if using a coffee can in the wok. Turn heat under skillet or wok to medium-high (360° F. on frypan). Bring the water to a boil. Place the pie plate containing the pork on the rack. Cover the utensil with its own lid. Reduce heat to medium (300° F. on frypan) or just high enough to keep the water actively boiling. Steam 35 to 45 minutes or until pork no longer shows pink. Toss with chopsticks once or twice during steaming so that the meat will cook evenly. This is a simple steamed pork, rather pale and uninteresting to any but Chinese tastes. It is served with condiments, pickles and steamed or congee rice.

SERVINGS: Enough for 2 to 3 as a single course with rice or for 4 in a full menu.

CLASSIC STEAMED SLICED OR DICED BEEF: Substitute 1½ pounds sirloin steak for the pork. Steam 20 to 25 minutes.

CLASSIC STEAMED SLICED OR DICED LAMB: Substitute $1\frac{1}{2}$ pounds lean boned lamb leg or shoulder, cut in thin shreds or $\frac{1}{2}$-inch dice, for the pork. Steam 25 to 30 minutes.

REGIONAL VARIATIONS OF CLASSIC STEAMED SLICED OR
DICED PORK, BEEF OR LAMB

PEKING: Add 1 tablespoon vodka, sherry or gin. Mix in $\frac{1}{2}$ cup sliced $\frac{1}{4}$-inch rounds of leeks or $\frac{1}{4}$ cup finely chopped scallions. Proceed as directed in the Classic recipe.

SHANGHAI: Increase soy sauce to 2 tablespoons and sugar to 5 teaspoons. Decrease salt to $\frac{1}{8}$ teaspoon. Add 1 teaspoon sherry. Proceed as directed in the Classic recipe.

CANTON: Increase ginger root to 2 teaspoons. Proceed as directed in the Classic recipe.

SZECHUAN: Add 1 teaspoon rice vinegar or cider vinegar and $\frac{1}{4}$ teaspoon ground Szechuan pepper or crushed red pepper flakes. Proceed as directed in the Classic recipe.

STEAMED SLICED OR DICED SPICED PORK
Follow the Peking or Shanghai variation for Classic Steamed Sliced or Diced Pork but add $\frac{1}{2}$ teaspoon five-spice seasoning.

SERVINGS: Enough for 2 to 3 as a single course with rice or for 4 in a full menu.

STEAMED SLICED OR DICED SPICED BEEF: Follow the Peking or Shanghai variation for Classic Steamed Sliced or Diced Beef but add $\frac{1}{2}$ teaspoon five-spice seasoning.

STEAMED SLICED OR DICED SPICED LAMB: Follow the Peking or Shanghai variation for Classic Steamed Sliced or Diced Lamb but add $\frac{1}{2}$ teaspoon five-spice seasoning.

STEAMED SLICED OR DICED PORK WITH VEGETABLES
Follow the recipe for Classic Steamed Sliced or Diced Pork but decrease pork to 1 pound and add 1 cup of any vegetables. Tough or root-type vegetables should be parboiled 3 minutes and drained well before adding. The most popular vegetables to use are preserved, pickled or salted—salted turnips, salted or spiced mustard greens and tea melons—or dried ingredients—tiger lilies, cloud ear fungus, mushrooms or dried bamboo shoot tips, all presoaked and drained.

SERVINGS: Enough for 2 to 3 as a single course with rice or for 4 in a full menu.

STEAMED SLICED OR DICED BEEF WITH VEGETABLES: Follow the directions above using the recipe for Classic Steamed Sliced or Diced Beef.

STEAMED SLICED OR DICED LAMB WITH VEGETABLES: Follow the directions above using the recipe for Classic Steamed Sliced or Diced Lamb.

STEAMED FIVE-FLOWER PORK

Follow the recipe for Classic Steamed Sliced or Diced Pork or any of the regional recipes but substitute 1½ pounds unsalted pork belly with rind for the pork tenderloin. Prick the pork belly and rind with a fork to allow for better absorption of the seasonings. Slice into strips, 2½x1½ inches. Marinate 30 minutes. Drain strips and place in the pie plate. Steam until the pork becomes translucent and the rind is easily pierced by a chopstick (about 1½ hours). Be sure to replenish boiling water as it evaporates from the steamer.

SERVINGS: Enough for 2 to 3 as a single course with rice or for 4 in a full menu.

STEAMED PORK PEARL SLICES

Four hours ahead of time, soak 1½ cups glutinous rice in 1½ cups cold water. Drain well and spread rice on a cookie sheet. Follow the recipe for Classic Steamed Sliced or Diced Pork or any of the regional variations but substitute 1½ pounds unsalted pork belly with rind for the pork tenderloin. Prick the pork belly and rind with a fork to allow for better absorption of the seasonings. Slice pork belly into strips, 2½x1½ inches. Marinate 30 minutes. Drain strips on paper towels. Roll strips in glutinous rice until well coated. Place in the pie plate and steam until pork is chopstick-tender.

SERVINGS: Enough for 2 to 3 as a single course or for 4 in a full menu.

STEAMED PORK SAND SLICES

Follow the recipe for Classic Steamed Sliced or Diced Pork or any of the regional variations but substitute 1½ pounds unsalted pork belly with rind for the pork tenderloin. Prick pork belly and rind with fork to allow for better absorption of the seasonings. Slice into strips, 2½x1½ inches. Marinate 30 minutes. While the slices are marinating, place 1 cup raw long-grain rice in a pie plate and toast in 350° F. oven 15 to 20 minutes. The rice should be a light golden brown. Using a rolling pin, crush rice coarsely between layers of wax paper. Drain pork slices and roll in crushed rice to coat. Place coated strips on a pie plate and steam until pork is chopstick-tender.

SERVINGS: Enough for 2 to 3 as a single course or for 4 in a full menu.

CLASSIC STEAMED MINCED CHICKEN BALLS

Cooking Time: 10 to 15 minutes

Utensils
2 Chinese cutting knives or meat grinder
Bowl for ground chicken
Small bowl for seasonings
Wooden spoon
Small bowl for egg white
Small bowl for oil
12-inch skillet, wok or electric frypan—
    with domed cover
9¾-inch cake rack, 9-inch vegetable steamer
    or ½ pound coffee can
9- or 10-inch Pyrex or metal pie plate

Ingredients

2½	cups ground raw chicken	1	teaspoon salt
6	water chestnuts, finely diced	¼	teaspoon sugar
1	large scallion with 1½ inches of green, finely minced	⅛	teaspoon white pepper
		1	egg white
1	tablespoon soy sauce	1	tablespoon cornstarch
2	teaspoons sherry, gin or vodka	1	tablespoon peanut oil

Before Cooking
Bone and skin a 3- to 3½-pound fryer or bone and skin 3 pounds of fryers' breasts and thighs. The chicken parts are preferable unless you want to make a stock of the waste portions. (Boning wings and drumsticks is tedious work.) Either mince by hand or put through the medium blade of a meat grinder once, then put half of it through again. This uneven grinding approximates hand-mincing to some extent and results in juicier balls and patties. Place the ground chicken (2½ cups) in a bowl. Add the diced water chestnuts and minced scallion. Combine the soy sauce,

liquor, salt, sugar and pepper in the small bowl. Stir well and blend lightly into the chicken with a wooden spoon. (Be sure to blend lightly. Packing the meat fibers together will cause heaviness.) Put the egg white in a bowl and beat until frothy. Add to the chicken mixture. Add the cornstarch. Again blend carefully with the wooden spoon, turning the meat over, under and over in a folding motion until the mass clings together and leaves the sides of the bowl. Pour about 1 tablespoon peanut oil into a small bowl. Dip fingertips in oil and rub a little oil on the palms of the hands. Pinch off the chicken mixture and roll between palms to form marble- or golfball-size balls. Place the chicken balls on an ungreased pie plate. (You should be able to get about 10 golfball-size balls on the 9-inch plate and 11 to 12 balls on the 10-inch plate. Do not let the balls touch.)

Cooking Instructions
Place the cake rack or steaming basket opened flat in the center of the pan. Add boiling water up to the height of the rack or $\frac{2}{3}$ the height of the can if using a coffee can in the wok. Turn heat under skillet or wok to medium-high (360° F. on electric frypan). Bring the water to a boil. Place the pie plate containing the chicken balls on the rack. Cover the utensil with its own lid and reduce heat to medium (300° F. on frypan) or just high enough to keep the water actively boiling. Steam 10 to 15 minutes or until the chicken is opaque when tested with a chopstick or fork. Serve hot with mustard, oyster sauce or Hoisin sauce or cover with Plum Sweet-and-Sour Sauce (page 355) or Brown Sauce (page 357).

SERVINGS: About 40 marble-size balls (for appetizers or soups) or about 10 golfball-size balls.

CLASSIC STEAMED MINCED DUCK BALLS: Substitute ground raw duckling for the chicken. (You will need a 4-pound duckling.)

CLASSIC STEAMED MINCED SQUAB BALLS: Substitute ground raw squab for the chicken. (You will need four 1-pound squabs.)

CHICKEN PEARL BALLS
Four hours before preparing the Classic Steamed Minced Chicken Ball mixture, soak $1\frac{1}{2}$ cups glutinous rice in $1\frac{1}{2}$ cups cold water. Drain rice thoroughly and spread on a cookie sheet. Prepare and shape pork balls. Roll two at a time in glutinous rice, using the palms of your hands to coat the balls with rice. Steam 15 to 20 minutes or until the rice is translucent and tacky to the touch.

SERVINGS: About 40 marble-size balls (for appetizers or soups) or about 10 golfball-size balls.

DUCK PEARL BALLS: Substitute Classic Steamed Minced Duck Ball mixture for the chicken mixture.

SQUAB PEARL BALLS: Substitute Classic Steamed Squab Ball mixture for the chicken mixture.

STEAMED CHINESE MUSHROOMS STUFFED WITH MINCED CHICKEN
Prepare Classic Minced Chicken Ball recipe. Rinse 24 medium-large dried mushrooms in cold water, then cover with warm water and soak 30 minutes. Drain well, squeezing out excess water with fingers. Using a grapefruit cutter or any small sharp knife, trim the hard centers but try not to cut through the mushrooms. Mound about a dessert-spoonful of minced chicken on each mushroom and place half the filled mushrooms on a lightly oiled 9- to 10-inch pie plate. Steam 10 to 15 minutes. The mushrooms should be very tender, the chicken opaque. Keep warm while you steam the second lot of filled mushrooms.

SERVINGS: Enough for 12 as an appetizer or 6 as a course in a full menu.

NOTE: The following vegetables may also be filled with minced chicken, duck or squab and steamed:

Cucumbers: Peel six 8-inch cucumbers. Cut each into four 2-inch rounds. Core without piercing bottom of rounds. Fill with pork ball mixture and steam as directed above.
Zucchini: Same as cucumbers, or cut lengthwise into boat shapes. Do not peel.
Eggplant: Use narrow eggplants; cut same as cucumbers or zucchini.
Onions: Use 24 smallish onions. Peel and core without piercing. Fill and steam until onions are very tender.

SERVINGS: Enough for 4 as a single course or 6 in a full menu.

STEAMED CHINESE MUSHROOMS STUFFED WITH MINCED DUCK: Substitute Classic Steamed Minced Duck Ball mixture for the chicken mixture. Continue as directed above.

STEAMED CHINESE MUSHROOMS STUFFED WITH MINCED SQUAB: Substitute Classic Steamed Minced Squab Ball mixture for the chicken mixture. Continue as directed above.

CLASSIC STEAMED WHOLE CHICKEN

Cooking Time: 2 to 3 hours

Utensils
4-quart heat-proof bowl
8-ounce measuring cup
12-quart soup kettle with cover
2-quart heat-proof bowl or ring of 9-inch
    springform cake pan

Ingredients

1	whole fryer (3 to 3½ pounds)	3	tablespoons sherry, gin or vodka
2	whole scallions, trimmed, each with 1½ inches of green	½	teaspoon brown sugar
½	cup soy sauce	¼	teaspoon salt

Before Cooking
Wash the chicken. Drain and blot it dry inside and out. Stuff scallions in the fryer's cavity. Place the bird in the 4-quart heat-proof bowl. Combine the soy sauce, liquor, sugar and salt in the measuring cup. Pour over the chicken. Let the bird stand in the marinade at least 2 hours, turning it every hour. Drain off marinade and reserve for another time.

Cooking Instructions
Place the 2-quart bowl or springform ring in the center of the soup kettle. Add boiling water up to ⅔ the height of the bowl. Turn heat under kettle to medium-high. Bring water to a boil. Place the bowl containing the chicken on the support. Cover the kettle and reduce heat to medium or just high enough to keep the water actively boiling. Steam 2 to 3 hours or until the thickest part of the drumstick pierces easily with a fork. Remove from heat and uncover. Take out the bowl containing the chicken. Serve either whole or cut into Chinese-style serving pieces. This is Chinese-seasoned Steamed Chicken. The chicken may also be steamed in 4 cups plain hot water without marinating beforehand; the results are much like Clear-Simmered Chicken.

SERVINGS: Enough for 4 as a single course with rice or for 6 to 8 in a full menu.

CLASSIC STEAMED WHOLE DUCK: Substitute 1 duckling (4 pounds) for the chicken. Steam 1 to 1½ hours longer.

CLASSIC STEAMED WHOLE SQUAB: Substitute 4 squabs (1 pound each) for the chicken.

STEAMED SPICED WHOLE CHICKEN

Follow the recipe for Classic Steamed Whole Chicken but add ¼ teaspoon five-spice seasoning, 2 star anise and 2-inch piece dried tangerine peel (previously soaked in hot water 15 minutes) to the marinade. Marinate and steam as directed.

SERVINGS: Enough for 4 as a single course with rice or for 6 to 8 in a full menu.

STEAMED SPICED WHOLE DUCK: Follow the recipe for Classic Steamed Whole Chicken but substitute 1 duckling (4 pounds) for the chicken and adapt the recipe as directed above.

STEAMED SPICED WHOLE SQUAB: Follow the recipe for Classic Steamed Whole Chicken but substitute 4 squabs (1 pound each) for the chicken and adapt the recipe as directed above.

STEAMED WHOLE CHICKEN WITH DRIED INGREDIENTS

Follow the recipe for Classic Steamed Whole Chicken or Steamed Spiced Whole Chicken. Before steaming, stuff the chicken with ½ cup dried small Chinese mushrooms or ⅓ cup grass mushrooms (rinsed, soaked in warm water 15 minutes and drained) and ¼ cup dried bamboo-shoot tips (soaked in hot water 1 hour and drained), ¼ cup tiger lilies (soaked in warm water 10 minutes and drained) and 2 slices ginger root (2x1x⅛ inch). Steam as directed. Serve either whole with vegetable garnish or chop into Chinese-style serving pieces and top with vegetables.

SERVINGS: Enough for 4 as a single course with rice or for 6 to 8 in a full menu.

STEAMED WHOLE DUCK WITH DRIED INGREDIENTS: Follow the recipe for Classic Steamed Whole Duck or Steamed Spiced Whole Duck and stuff as directed above.

STEAMED WHOLE SQUAB WITH DRIED INGREDIENTS: Follow the recipe for Classic Steamed Whole Squab or Steamed Spiced Whole Squab and stuff as directed above.

STEAMED GINGER CHICKEN WITH BLACK BEANS,

Cantonese Style

Cooking Time: 25 to 30 minutes

Utensils
Chinese cutting knife
Garlic press
1-pint bowl for seasonings
Wire strainer
10-inch pie plate
12-inch skillet, wok or electric frypan—
    with domed cover
9¾-inch cake rack, 9-inch vegetable steaming
    basket or ½-pound coffee can

Ingredients

1½ pounds fryer thighs and legs	2 teaspoons sesame oil
1½ pounds fryer breasts	2½ tablespoons soy sauce
2 teaspoons ginger root juice	2 tablespoons sherry, gin or vodka
2 teaspoons sugar	¼ cup salted black beans
¾ teaspoon salt	1 clove garlic, minced
3½ tablespoons cornstarch	

Before Cooking
Chop the fryer thighs, legs and breasts into 1½-inch Chinese-style serving pieces. Put enough slivers of peeled ginger root through a garlic press to make 2 teaspoons juice. Sprinkle the ginger juice over the sectioned chicken. Combine the sugar, salt, cornstarch, sesame oil, soy sauce and liquor in the pint bowl. Stir to a smooth paste. Put the black beans in the wire strainer and rinse under cold water until no salt is visible. Drain well. Place on a chopping board and mince finely, using the blunt edge of a Chinese cutting knife. Add the minced garlic and black beans to the seasoning-cornstarch mixture. Dip the chicken pieces in the bean-cornstarch paste to thoroughly coat them; arrange on the 10-inch pie plate.

Cooking Instructions

Place the cake rack or steaming basket opened flat in the center of the skillet, wok or frypan. Add boiling water up to the height of the rack or ⅔ the height of the can if using a coffee can in the wok. Turn heat under skillet or wok to medium-high (360° F. on frypan). Bring the water to a boil. Place the pie plate containing the chicken in pan. Cover the utensil with its own lid and reduce heat to medium (300° F. on frypan) or just high enough to keep the water actively boiling. Steam 25 to 30 minutes. The chicken pieces should be very tender, the sauce pungent and flecked with the black beans.

SERVINGS: Enough for 4 as a single course with rice or for 6 in a full menu.

GINGER DUCK WITH BLACK BEANS: Substitute 1 duckling (4 pounds) for the chicken. Steam 1 to 1½ hours longer.

GINGER SQUAB WITH BLACK BEANS: Substitute 4 squabs (1 pound each) for the chicken. (If you like, halve or quarter each squab.)

CLASSIC STEAMED MINCED SHRIMP BALLS

Cooking Time: 10 minutes

Utensils
Chinese cutting knife
Bowl for shrimp
Small bowl for egg white
Small bowl for oil
9- or 10-inch Pyrex or metal pie plate,
    lightly oiled
12-inch skillet, wok or electric frypan—
    with domed cover
9¾-inch cake rack, 9-inch vegetable steaming
    basket or ½-pound coffee can

Ingredients

1½ pounds raw jumbo shrimp	1½ teaspoons salt
½ teaspoon finely minced ginger root	⅛ teaspoon white pepper
	1½ teaspoons cornstarch
1 teaspoon finely minced scallion	1 egg white
1½ teaspoons sherry, vodka or gin	1 tablespoon oil for shaping balls

Before Cooking

Wash, shell and devein shrimp, removing feelers and tail. Drain the shrimp and place on a chopping board. Using a Chinese cutting knife, coarsely chop shrimp and then mince until it is a sticky paste. Place in a bowl. Add the minced ginger root. Add scallion, liquor, salt, pepper and cornstarch to shrimp paste. Stir until well blended. Put egg white in a small bowl and beat until entirely frothy. Fold into shrimp mixture and blend until the shrimp paste leaves the sides of the bowl. Put the oil in a small bowl and, dipping fingers into it, shape shrimp paste into balls. Place balls on a pie plate until ready to steam.

Cooking Instructions

Place the cake rack or steaming basket opened flat in the center of the skillet, wok or frypan. Add boiling water up to the height of the rack or ⅔ the height of the can if using a coffee can in the wok. Turn heat under skillet or wok to medium-high (360° F. on frypan). Bring the water to a boil. Place the pie plate containing the shrimp balls on the rack. Cover the utensil with its own lid and reduce heat to medium (300° F. on frypan) or just high enough to keep the water actively boiling. Steam about 10 minutes or until shrimp mixture shows pink when tested with chopstick or a fork. Serve hot with mustard, oyster sauce or Cantonese Salt (page 352) or Plum Sweet-and-Sour Sauce (page 355) or Brown Sauce (page 357).

SERVINGS: This amount will make about 40 marble-size balls (for soups or appetizers) or 16 golfball-size balls. As a single course with rice, the larger balls will be enough for 4.

OPTIONAL ADDITIONS: Add 6 finely diced water chestnuts or ¼ cup finely diced bamboo shoots and/or 1 tablespoon finely minced Virginia ham, and/or 2 to 3 teaspoons minced fresh parsley.

STEAMED CHINESE MUSHROOMS STUFFED WITH MINCED SHRIMP

Prepare Classic Steamed Minced Shrimp Ball mixture. Rinse 24 medium-large dried mushrooms in cold water, then cover with warm water and soak 30 minutes. Drain well, squeezing out excess water with fingers. Using a grapefruit cutter or any small sharp knife, trim the hard centers but try not to cut through the mushrooms. Mound about a dessert-spoonful of minced shrimp on each mushroom and place half the filled mushrooms on the lightly oiled pie plate. Steam about 10 minutes or until shrimp mixture shows pink when tested with chopsticks or a fork. The mushrooms should be very tender. Keep them warm while you steam the second lot of filled mushrooms.

SERVINGS: Enough for 12 as an appetizer or for 6 in a full menu.

NOTE: Minced shellfish is not usually cooked in variations such as pearl balls or sand balls—the longer steaming time required tends to toughen the fish.

CLASSIC STEAMED WHOLE FISH

Cooking Time: 25 to 30 minutes

Utensils
Baking dish (14x9x2¼ inches)
Roasting pan (15x10x3 inches)
10-ounce custard cup
Aluminum foil for cover (32x12 inches)

Ingredients

1 whole bass, carp, cod, mullet or shad (2 to 2½ pounds)	¼ teaspoon white pepper
2 slices ginger root (3x1½x⅛ inch)	1 large scallion with 1½ inches of green, minced
1½ teaspoon salt	

Before Cooking
Have the fish cleaned but with the head and tail intact. Scale (unless it is shad, which tends to dry out when scaled). Wash thoroughly in cold water, making sure to remove blood clots and stringiness inside the cavity. Drain and blot with paper towels. Rub fish from head to tail with ginger root. Place slices inside cavity. Sprinkle fish inside and out with salt and pepper. Place fish in the baking dish and sprinkle with minced scallion. Fold aluminum foil over once crosswise so that you have a 16x12-inch cover.

Cooking Instructions
Place the custard cup in the center of the roasting pan. Add boiling water up to ⅔ the height of the cup. Turn heat to medium-high. Bring the water to a boil. Put the baking dish containing the fish on the custard cup and fit the foil cover over the top and sides of the roasting pan. Reduce heat to medium or just high enough to keep the water actively boiling. Steam 25 to 30 minutes, adding more boiling water as required to replenish that which has evaporated from the roasting pan. Remove from heat; take off foil cover, making sure you stand away from the steam. The fish is cooked enough if the flesh at the spine near the head is opaque when tested with a fork and if the eyes have turned white and appear to bulge. Re-

move baking dish from roasting pan and serve fish at once with small dishes of Ginger-Soy Dip (page 352) and vinegar.

SERVINGS: Enough for 4 to 5 as a single course with rice or for 8 in a full menu.

NOTE: Fish steamed with such Spartan simplicity must be extremely fresh.

OPTIONAL ADDITIONS: One of the following may be sprinkled over the fish before steaming:

½   cup shredded Virginia ham.

1½ tablespoons black beans minced with 1 clove garlic.

¼   cup dried Chinese black olives soaked 30 minutes in warm water. Drain and mince with 1 clove garlic before adding.

½   cup bamboo shoots, cut in fine strips or shreds.

1   tablespoon cloud ears, rinsed, soaked in warm water 30 minutes and drained.

½   cup grass mushrooms or dried small mushrooms, rinsed, soaked in warm water 30 minutes and drained.

⅓   cup tiger lilies, soaked in hot water 15 minutes, drained and snipped in two.

6   dried Chinese dates, soaked in hot water 1 hour, drained and cut into strips.

1   tablespoon dried small shrimp, soaked 1 hour in hot water and drained.

¼   pound fresh or canned button mushrooms.

2   squares bean curd, diced or cut in strips.

STEAMED WHOLE HONEY SHAD

Follow the recipe for Classic Steamed Whole Fish but use a 2- to 2½-pound shad. Do not scale. After the fish has been sprinkled with salt and pepper, rub 2 tablespoons honey blended with 1 teaspoon sherry, gin or vodka over the entire surface of the shad. Omit the scallions.

SERVINGS: Enough for 4 to 5 as a single course with rice or for 8 in a full menu.

STEAMED WHOLE FISH WITH SAUCES

Follow the Classic recipe until the fish is steamed. Just before serving, cover with any of the following sauces: Mandarin Sweet-and-Sour Sauce, (page 354); Sweet-and-Sour Sauce, Cantonese Style (page 353); Plum Sweet-and-Sour Sauce (page 355); Brown Sauce (page 357).

SERVINGS: Enough for 4 to 5 as a single course with rice or for 8 in a full menu.

STEAMED WHOLE FISH WITH SOY SAUCE

Follow the recipe for Classic Steamed Whole Fish. After rubbing ginger root all over, place fish in baking dish. Combine 2 tablespoons soy sauce, 1 tablespoon vodka, gin or sherry, 2 teaspoons sesame oil, ¾ teaspoon salt and 1 teaspoon brown sugar in a small bowl. Sprinkle over the fish with minced scallion. Let stand 20 minutes, turning the fish once. Steam as directed.

NOTE: Any of the optional additions suggested for Classic Steamed Whole Fish may be used in this variation.

SERVINGS: Enough for 4 to 5 as a single course with rice or for 8 in a full menu.

STEAMED STUFFED WHOLE FISH

Cooking Time: 25 to 30 minutes

Utensils
Baking dish (14x9x2 inches)
Roasting pan (15x10x3 inches)
10-ounce custard cup
Aluminum foil for cover (32x12 inches)

Ingredients

1	whole carp or mullet (2 to 2½ pounds)		Steamed Minced Pork Balls with Crab (page 209), Steamed Minced Pork Balls with Shrimp (page 209) or Steamed Minced Shrimp Balls (page 220)
2	slices ginger root (2x1x⅛ inch)		
2	teaspoons sherry, vodka or gin		
½	teaspoon salt		
¾	cup uncooked mixture for Minced Pork Balls (page 207),	1	large scallion with 1½ inches of green, minced

Before Cooking
Have the fish cleaned but with the head and tail intact. Wash inside and out, removing any blood clots or foreign matter. Blot dry with paper towels. Lay the fish on the baking pan and rub with the ginger root. Sprinkle with the liquor, then dust with salt. Lightly pack the fish's cavity with one of the stuffing mixtures, patting the skin over it to make the filling adhere. Sprinkle with minced scallion.

Cooking Instructions
Place the custard cup in the center of the roasting pan. Add boiling water up to ⅔ the height of the cup. Turn heat to medium-high. Let the water come to a boil. Put the baking dish containing the fish on the custard cup and fit the foil cover over the top and sides of the roasting pan. Reduce heat to medium or just high enough to keep the water actively boiling. Steam 25 to 30 minutes or until fish flakes easily at the spine near the head and the eyes are white and bulging.

SERVINGS: Enough for 4 to 5 as a single course with rice or for 8 in a full menu.

NOTE: Any of the optional additions (page 223) suggested for Classic Steamed Whole Fish may be used here.

STEAMED FISH STEAKS

Cooking Time: 15 minutes

Utensils
12-inch skillet, wok or electric frypan—
   with domed cover
9¾-inch cake rack, 9-inch vegetable steamer
   or ½-pound coffee can
9- or 10-inch Pyrex or metal pie plate

Ingredients

2	pounds lean fish steaks, 1½ inches thick (rock cod, lingcod or carp)	2	teaspoons vodka, gin or sherry
		2	tablespoons sesame oil
2	teaspoons minced ginger root	½	teaspoon salt

Before Cooking
Place the fish steaks close together but not overlapping on the pie plate. Sprinkle minced ginger root over fish. Sprinkle with liquor, sesame oil and salt.

Cooking Instructions
Place the cake rack or steaming basket opened flat in the center of the skillet, wok or frypan. Add boiling water up to the height of the rack or ⅔ the height of the can if using a coffee can in the wok. Turn heat under skillet or wok to medium-

high (360° F. on frypan). Bring the water to a boil. Place the pie plate containing the fish steaks in pan. Cover the utensil with its own lid and reduce heat to medium (300° F. on frypan) or just high enough to keep the water actively boiling. Steam covered 15 minutes or until the fish flakes easily when tested with a fork in the thickest part. Serve with saucers of Garlic-Soy Dip, Ginger-Soy Dip or "Chekiang" Vinegar (page 351).

SERVINGS: Enough for 3 to 4 as a single course with rice or for 4 to 6 in a full menu.

NOTE: Fish Steaks may be prepared with the same optional additions (page 223) and sauces (pages 223–224) as Classic Steamed Whole Fish.

STEAMED LOBSTER
Fiery Dragon

Cooking Time: 20 minutes

Utensils
Chinese cutting knife
Bowl for ingredients
Baking dish (14x8x2½ inches), lightly oiled
Roasting pan (15x10x3 inches)
10-ounce custard cup
Aluminum foil for cover (32x12 inches)

Ingredients

2	live lobsters (1½ pounds each)	1	clove garlic, finely minced
1½	pounds pork tenderloin	1½	teaspoons salt
6	water chestnuts, finely diced	¼	teaspoon white pepper
¼	cup finely diced bamboo shoots	1	tablespoon sherry, gin or vodka
1	teaspoon minced ginger root		

Before Cooking
Have your fish dealer kill the lobsters and split them in half lengthwise. Discard stomach, intestinal vein, legs and antennae. Remove feathery gill-like portions under the shell. Crack the large claws. With a sharp knife, remove the meat from

the body of the lobster without breaking the shell. Cut into ¼-inch dice. Trim any fat from pork and cut into same size dice. Place lobster and pork in the bowl. Add diced water chestnuts, bamboo shoots, minced ginger root and garlic. Stir in the salt, pepper and liquor; toss ingredients to blend. Gently pack the 4 half-shells with the lobster-pork combination and place in the lightly oiled baking dish. Fold the aluminum foil over once crosswise so that you have a 16x12-inch cover.

Cooking Instructions
Place the custard cup in the center of the roasting pan. Add boiling water up to the height of the cup. Turn heat to medium-high. Bring the water to a boil. Put the baking pan containing the fish on the custard cup and fit the foil cover over the top and sides of the roasting pan. Reduce heat to medium or just high enough to keep the water actively boiling. Steam 20 minutes or until lobster is opaque and pork is cooked. Serve in the shell with small dishes of oyster sauce or shrimp sauce.

SERVINGS: Enough for 4 as a single course with rice or for 6 to 8 in a full menu.

OPTIONAL ADDITIONS: One of the following may be combined with the lobster-pork mixture before steaming:

1 tablespoon dried shrimp, soaked in hot water 1 hour and drained.

2 dried scallops, soaked in ½ cup hot water 1 hour, then simmered 1 hour, drained and shredded.

½ cup dried tiger lilies, soaked in warm water 15 minutes, drained and snipped in two.

10 tiny tea melons, sliced diagonally. These should be placed on top of the lobster-pork mixture.

NOTE: One tablespoon soy sauce may be added with any of the above additions. If you choose to do this, decrease the salt to ½ teaspoon.

FIERY DRAGON WITH BLACK BEANS
Follow the recipe for Steamed Lobster but first rinse 2 tablespoons soft black beans in cold water. Drain well and mince finely. Combine with ginger root, garlic and liquor before adding to lobster-pork mixture. Reduce salt to ½ teaspoon. Steam as directed. Serve without additional condiments.

SERVINGS: Enough for 4 as a single course with rice or for 6 to 8 in a full menu.

SHALLOW-FRYING, SEMI-DEEP-FRYING AND DEEP-FRYING-TECHNIQUE 6

Frying, as we know it in Western cuisines, is a technique unto itself. Western cooks generally fry flour-dredged or batter-coated fish, fowl and vegetables. In much of Chinese cooking, frying is a component method, and becomes either a starting or ending point for other techniques. For instance, the Chinese serve fried foods with a variety of extravagant sauces, sauces that are integral to the dish. Or meat, poultry, fish or pastries may be steamed or simmered first, then fried as a final, crowning touch.

The most satisfactory shortenings to use for shallow-, semi–deep- or deep-frying are, in this order: peanut oil, corn oil, cottonseed oil or leaf lard. The high smoking points of these fats, as well as their compatibility of flavor, make them superior for this method of cooking. Conversely, butter, margarine and olive oil are not suitable.

SHALLOW-FRYING

Shallow-frying is the equivalent of sautéing or pan-frying. With this method, the bottom of a skillet is just covered with oil and the ingredients are fried until they are cooked. The technique is often used for food which has been precooked by steaming or simmering, as is done for pan-fried noodles, dumplings and spring rolls. Shallow-frying is also employed for relatively simple egg dishes such as Egg

Shallow Frying
1. Add just enough oil to cover bottom of heated skillet.   2. When oil is hot, add ingredients. Brown slowly on one side and then on the other. There is not much stirring to this technique.   3. A sauce is added to the Egg Foo Yung.

Foo Yung. The rules of this technique adapt to the food that is being fried. Primarily shallow-frying is used for slow, crisp browning over a medium heat—neither much fat nor much stirring is entailed.

Heat skillet over low to medium heat or set electric frypan at temperature given in recipe. The pan is hot enough to use when a drop of water on its surface bubbles into steam. Add just enough oil or fat to cover the bottom of the skillet (see individual recipes for amounts of oil). When the oil in the skillet is very hot, it will begin to sizzle (the signal on the electric frypan goes off). Add ingredients, a few at a time. Too much food tends to lower the temperature of the fat, preventing proper crust formation.

Be sure any items to be fried are drained and quite dry. Steam caused by moist ingredients prevents the proper crisping of exteriors.

Brown slowly on one side, turn and brown on the other. The time needed depends on the ingredients being cooked.

SEMI–DEEP-FRYING AND DEEP-FRYING

Semi–deep-frying is a means of achieving a deep-fried taste and texture with less fat than is necessary for deep-frying. Basically it is a short but intense frying process, convenient for cooking smaller pieces of food such as meat, chicken or fish balls or

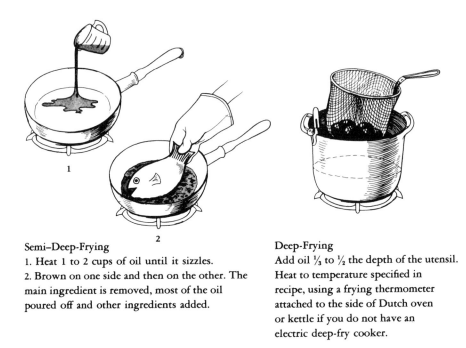

Semi–Deep-Frying
1. Heat 1 to 2 cups of oil until it sizzles.
2. Brown on one side and then on the other. The main ingredient is removed, most of the oil poured off and other ingredients added.

Deep-Frying
Add oil ⅓ to ½ the depth of the utensil. Heat to temperature specified in recipe, using a frying thermometer attached to the side of Dutch oven or kettle if you do not have an electric deep-fry cooker.

patties or meat or chicken shreds. Likewise, smaller whole fish or cut-up poultry are more easily cooked in a skillet or electric frypan containing 1 or 2 cups of oil than in larger utensils. For whole chicken, duck and larger fish, where depth or width are essential, soup kettles, electric deep-fry cookers or roasting pans are necessary.

Perfectly fried foods must have crisp golden brown exteriors, and be tender yet cooked through. This is assured by several means. Ingredients to be fried should not be chilled but kept at room temperature during the heating process of the fat or oil. Although some Chinese chefs suggest salting the oil, I would advise against it. Any impurities in the fat tend to lower the smoking point and make the fat less reusable. Instead of salting the oil, salt the food while it is still hot and is draining on paper towels.

As with shallow-frying, you should not attempt to fry too many ingredients at one time. If the oil is not hot enough or the ingredients are too moist, the crusting will take longer, causing the food to absorb grease. Soggy food is the result. When frying batter-coated foods, remove particles of batter which have broken off in the oil with a slotted spoon. Quality oils and fats used for deep-frying may be strained through a cheesecloth-lined strainer. They will keep indefinitely if stored in the re-frigerator when cooled. Oil in which fish has been fried is best used only once—twice at the most, and then only with fish.

POINTS TO REMEMBER IN SHALLOW-, SEMI–DEEP- AND DEEP-FRYING

As with the Stir-Fry-Toss Technique, preparation is essential. Be sure that your equipment and ingredients are within easy reach and that you have cleared enough space to drain the fried food on paper towels. Ingredients such as pastries must be as dry as possible and all ingredients should be at room temperature. Fillings for egg- or pastry-encased foods should be well drained before wrapping to prevent their leaking into the fat.

Shallow-fried foods require just enough oil to coat the bottom of the utensil. This amount of course varies with the type of food being cooked; refer to each rec-ipe for an exact quantity.

One to 2 cups of oil is usually sufficient for semi–deep-frying in a 10- to 12-inch skillet or electric frypan. Never use less than 3 cups of oil for deep-frying in these utensils or ones of similar size.

A good gauge for the amount of oil to use in deep-frying is to fill the utensil ⅓ to ½ full of fat. How deep the fat should be depends entirely on the size of the utensil. For instance, in a 6-quart pot or deep-fry cooker, you should use 2 to 3 quarts of oil, and in an 11-inch skillet with a 2½-quart capacity, 4 cups of oil would be correct for deep-frying.

Depending on what is being cooked, temperatures for semi–deep- and deep-frying range from 325° to 400° F. Actual temperatures are given with each recipe. When adding food to the fat, you may find a reduction of heat—increase the cook-ing temperature accordingly.

The most reliable way of determining the exact temperature is of course with a thermometer. If you are not using an electric frypan or deep-fry cooker, clip a frying thermometer to the side of the pot. Be sure that the bulb of the thermome-ter is below the surface of the oil, but that it is not touching the bottom of the pot. While ideal for determining exact temperatures, the frying thermometer is not practical for skillets. If you are not using electric appliances or a frying thermome-ter, cut a cube of fresh bread and drop it into the hot oil. If the fat sizzles and foams around the bread, it is hot enough for deep-frying.

PORK EGG FOO YUNG

Cooking Time: 4 minutes for each patty

Utensils
Bowl for combining ingredients
Chopsticks
8-inch skillet with rounded base
Spatula
9-inch heat-proof dish or pie plate

Ingredients

½   recipe Brown Sauce (page 357)
4   large eggs
2   egg whites
¾   cup shredded cooked pork
3   scallions with some green, cut in ¼-inch rounds
6   water chestnuts, cut in ¼-inch dice

¾   cup pea sprouts, washed and drained
¼   cup dried mushrooms
1   teaspoon salt
⅛   teaspoon white pepper
5   tablespoons peanut oil or corn oil

Before Cooking
Prepare Brown Sauce ahead of time. Gently reheat as you prepare the other ingredients. Place whole eggs and egg whites in bowl. Break yolks with chopsticks and stir slightly to blend. (Do not beat. The ingredients will adhere to each other better if eggs are unbeaten). Add the shredded pork to the eggs. Add scallions, water chestnuts and pea sprouts to egg-pork mixture. Rinse mushrooms and soak in warm water 15 minutes. Drain and shred finely. Add to eggs. Season mixture with salt and pepper. Have oil ready to go.

Cooking Instructions
Turn heat under skillet to medium. When it is hot enough for a drop of water to bubble into steam, add 3 tablespoons of the oil. When the oil begins to sizzle, pour half of the egg-meat-vegetable mixture into the skillet. Be careful of oil bubbling over the side of pan. Fry 2 minutes or until bottom of patty shows golden brown when lifted with spatula. Carefully flip egg patty over and brown other side. Remove browned egg patty to heated dish or pie plate. Add remaining 2 tablespoons oil to skillet and pour in remaining egg mixture. Repeat frying on both sides. Add to the first patty in the dish. Top with Brown Sauce and serve at once.

SERVINGS: Enough for 2 as a single course with rice or for 4 in a full menu.

BEEF EGG FOO YUNG: Substitute ¾ cup thinly shredded cooked fairly rare beef for the pork.

CHICKEN OR DUCK EGG FOO YUNG: Substitute ¾ cup thinly shredded cooked breast of chicken or duck for the pork.

SHRIMP EGG FOO YUNG: Substitute ¾ cup tiny shelled cooked shrimp for the pork.

CRAB OR LOBSTER EGG FOO YUNG: Substitute ¾ cup cooked fresh or canned crab or lobster for the pork. Remove cartilage.

NOTE: *Foo Yung* means hibiscus, and the egg patty is supposed to resemble the shade of the petals. Originally Chinese gourmets used only the white of the egg to achieve this effect. The addition of whole eggs to the whites allows for effective color and texture as well as body. When making chicken or shellfish Egg Foo Yung, ½ recipe Pouring Oyster Sauce (page 356) may be substituted for the Brown Sauce.

PORK SURPRISE PACKETS

Cooking Time: 1 minute to prefry each pancake
10 minutes to shallow-fry

Utensils
Bowl for egg mixture
Bowl for pork filling
8-inch skillet with rounded base
Spatula
12-inch skillet

.ents

recipe Brown Sauce (page 357),	4	eggs
Sweet-and-Sour Sauce (pages	2	tablespoons water
353–356) or Pouring Oyster	1	tablespoon flour
Sauce (page 356)	½	teaspoon salt

Continued on next page

$\frac{1}{4}$ teaspoon white pepper
$\frac{1}{2}$ pound ground pork
2 tablespoons soy sauce
1 teaspoon sherry
1 teaspoon cornstarch

$\frac{1}{2}$ teaspoon finely minced ginger root
1 scallion with $1\frac{1}{2}$ inches of green, finely minced
$\frac{1}{2}$ cup peanut oil or corn oil

Before Cooking

Prepare one of the listed sauces ahead of time. Place the eggs in a bowl. Add water. Beat until light, gradually adding flour, salt and pepper. Set aside. Place ground pork in another bowl. Add soy sauce, sherry, cornstarch, minced ginger root and scallion. Blend meat mixture well. Have oil ready to go.

Cooking Instructions

Place the 8-inch skillet over medium heat. When it is hot enough for a drop of water to bubble into steam add about 1 tablespoon of the oil. When the oil begins to sizzle, add 1 tablespoon of egg batter to the skillet and spread to form a round pancake. While the exposed surface is still moist (less than 1 minute), spoon 2 teaspoons of the meat mixture in the center of the pancake with spatula. Flip over the sides to form a half-moon, or turnover, shape. Gently press sides of the filled egg turnover with the flat edge of the spatula to seal. Remove to a warm plate. The underside of the pancake should just be cooked but not even slightly browned. If it is brown, the heat is too high. Repeat until all the packets have been fried and filled. Begin to reheat the sauce. Heat the larger skillet over medium-low heat. When it is hot enough for a drop of water to bubble into steam, add the remaining oil. When the oil begins to sizzle, add the partially fried egg packets and fry 5 minutes on each side or until they are golden brown. Place on a heated platter, cover with the reheated sauce and serve.

SERVINGS: Enough for 4 as a single course with rice or for 6 in a full menu.

VARIATIONS: Substitute mixture from $\frac{1}{2}$ recipe Classic Steamed Minced Pork Balls (page 207), Beef Balls (page 209), Chicken Balls (page 214), or Shrimp Balls (page 220) for the pork mixture given here.

EGG THREADS

(A Garnish)

Cooking Time: Approximately 1 minute for each batch

Utensils
Small bowl
8-inch flat-bottomed skillet

Ingredients

2	eggs	2	teaspoons peanut oil or corn oil
½	teaspoons salt		

Before Cooking
Place the eggs with the salt in the small bowl. Beat until thick and light colored. Have oil ready to go.

Cooking Instructions
Place skillet over medium-low heat. When the pan is hot enough for a drop of water to bubble into steam, add 1 teaspoon of the oil. Tilt the pan so that the oil covers the base, or spread it lightly over the surface with a piece of paper towel. Pour half the egg mixture into the skillet, again tilting the pan so that the base is covered with a thin layer of egg. Fry until edges become very light brown, then slip out of pan onto a plate. Repeat with the remaining oil and the remaining egg mixture. Place one thin circle of egg on top of the other; cut into four 2-inch strips. Then cut the strips into matchstick shreds. Toss them to separate. Use as a topping or garnish for any dish.

SEMI–DEEP-FRIED PORK BALLS

Cooking Time: 15 minutes for each batch

Utensils
12-inch skillet, wok or electric frypan
Slotted spatula

Ingredients

1	recipe Classic Steamed Minced Pork Balls (page 207)	2	cups peanut oil or corn oil

Before Cooking

Prepare minced pork as directed in recipe. Shape into marble-size balls for soups or appetizers or into golfball-size balls for main dishes.

Cooking Instructions

Heat oil in skillet or wok over medium-high heat until it foams around a cube of fresh bread (360° F. on electric frypan). Fry no more than 8 golfball-size balls at a time. Crowding results in soggy food. Shake the pan by the handle to keep the balls from sticking and to brown them evenly. Fry golfball-size balls uncovered 15 minutes, turning the balls on all sides until they are dark brown and crisp on the outside and show no pink on the inside when tested with a fork. (Marble-size balls take less time.) Remove balls with slotted spatula as they are done and drain on paper towels. Keep them warm, uncovered, in 170° F. oven while you fry the remaining balls. Serve with side dishes of Chinese-Style Mustard, Garlic-Soy Dip or Ginger-Soy Dip (pages 351–352).

SERVINGS: This amount will make about 75 marble-size balls or about 24 golfball-size balls; the larger size is enough for 6 as a single course with rice or for 8 to 12 in a full menu.

OPTIONAL SAUCES: Ahead of time prepare any one of the following sauces: Brown Sauce (page 357), Curry Sauce (page 358) or any of the Sweet-and-Sour Sauces (pages 353–356). Pour over the pork balls and serve with steamed rice.

SEMI–DEEP-FRIED BEEF BALLS: Use the recipe for Classic Steamed Minced Beef Balls (page 209). Follow the directions above but fry only 10 minutes. The Optional Sauces may also be used with beef balls.

SEMI–DEEP-FRIED LAMB BALLS: Use the recipe for Classic Steamed Minced Lamb Balls (page 209). Follow the directions above. The Optional Sauces may also be used with lamb balls.

SEMI–DEEP-FRIED PORK BALLS WITH VEGETABLES AND BROWN SAUCE

Prepare Brown Sauce (page 357) ahead of time. Prepare the pork ball mixture.

Shape into balls and using a skillet or wok fry as directed in the recipe for Semi-Deep-Fried Pork Balls. While the balls are frying, gently reheat the sauce. Drain the fried balls on paper towels. Pour off all but 2 tablespoons oil from the pan. Raise heat. Before the oil in the pan begins to smoke, add 1 cup threaded snow peas with ends snipped, ½ cup sliced water chestnuts or thinly sliced bamboo shoots and ⅓ cup dried mushrooms (rinsed, soaked in warm water 15 minutes and drained). Stir-fry-toss vegetables 2 to 3 minutes. Mix balls and vegetables together and arrange on a serving dish or in a bowl. Pour sauce over and serve with rice.

SERVINGS: Enough for 6 as a single course with rice or for 8 to 12 in a full menu.

SEMI–DEEP-FRIED BEEF BALLS WITH VEGETABLES AND BROWN SAUCE: Follow the recipe above but use Semi–Deep-Fried Beef Balls.

SEMI–DEEP-FRIED LAMB BALLS WITH VEGETABLES AND BROWN SAUCE: Follow the recipe above but use Semi–Deep-Fried Lamb Balls.

SEMI–DEEP-FRIED SPICED BEEF SHREDS

Cooking Time: 2 minutes to fry each batch of beef shreds
1 minute to fry vegetables

Utensils
Chinese cutting knife
Soup plate
Chopsticks to stir beef shreds
12-inch skillet, wok, or electric frypan
Slotted spatula
Wire strainer

Ingredients

1	pound flank steak, sirloin or filet, cut in shreds	2	teaspoons sherry
½	teaspoon salt	2	teaspoons finely minced ginger root
1	teaspoon brown sugar	⅓	cup shredded carrots
½	teaspoon crushed red pepper flakes	½	cup shredded celery
2	tablespoons soy sauce	⅓	cup shredded bamboo shoots
		2	cups peanut oil or corn oil

Before Cooking
Place beef in the soup plate and stir in the salt, brown sugar, pepper flakes, soy sauce and sherry. Let stand 10 minutes. Have ginger root, carrots, celery, bamboo shoots and oil ready to go.

Cooking Instructions
Heat oil in skillet or wok over medium-high heat until it foams around a cube of fresh bread (360° F. on electric frypan). Add a fourth of the seasoned beef shreds. Fry 2 minutes. With the slotted spatula remove the beef to the strainer. Fry and drain the remaining beef, in fourths. While the beef shreds are draining, pour off all but 1 tablespoon oil from the pan. Add the ginger root, carrot, celery and bamboo shoots. Fry 1 minute. Scoop up the vegetables with the slotted spatula and add them to the beef in the strainer. Serve at once on a warm platter. The uniqueness of this dish from Szechuan consists in the dryness of the beef contrasted with the crispness of the vegetables. Neither meat nor vegetables should be overcooked. What sauce there is will be thin but dark in color. You can control the peppery flavor in this dish by adding or decreasing the amount of pepper flakes.

SERVINGS: Enough for 2 as a single course with rice or for 4 to 6 in a full menu.

SEMI–DEEP-FRIED BEEF STRIPS WITH BLACK BEAN SAUCE,

Chungking Style

Cooking Time: 2 minutes to fry each batch of beef strips
1 minute to stir-fry vegetables

Utensils
Chinese cutting knife
Soup plate
Chopsticks for mixing
12-inch skillet, wok or electric frypan
Wire strainer or sieve
Slotted spatula

Ingredients

1	pound flank steak, sirloin or filet, cut in shreds	2	cloves garlic, minced
1	small egg, beaten	2	tablespoons soft black beans
1	teaspoon cornstarch	½	teaspoon crushed red pepper flakes
¼	cup shredded celery	2	teaspoons soy sauce
¼	cup shredded bamboo shoots	½	teaspoon brown sugar
¼	cup shredded cucumber	2	tablespoons chicken stock
1	teaspoon minced ginger root	2	cups peanut oil or corn oil

Before Cooking

Combine beef with beaten egg and cornstarch in soup plate. Set aside. Shred celery, bamboo shoots and cucumber. Mince ginger root and garlic. Rinse black beans in cold water. Drain well, then mince with the blunt edge of the Chinese cutting knife. Combine with garlic and red pepper flakes. Have soy sauce, sugar, stock and oil ready to go.

Cooking Instructions

Heat oil in skillet or wok over medium-high heat until it foams around a cube of fresh bread (360° F. on electric frypan). Add a fourth of the beef strips. Fry 2 minutes. With the slotted spatula, remove the beef to the wire strainer. Fry and drain the remaining beef, in fourths. Pour off all but 1 tablespoon oil from the pan. Add ginger root. Stir once quickly. Add the celery, bamboo shoots and cucumber. Stir-fry-toss 1 minute. Stir in the garlic, pepper flakes and black beans. Stir with vegetables 1 minute. Return meat to the pan. Add soy sauce, sugar and stock. Mix and remove from heat. Again, as in Spiced Beef Shreds, the desired quality is dryness of meat and crunchiness of vegetables.

SERVINGS: Enough for 2 as a single course with rice or for 4 to 6 in a full menu.

SEMI–DEEP-FRIED CHICKEN BALLS

Cooking Time: 10 minutes for each batch

Utensils
12-inch skillet, wok or electric frypan
Slotted spatula

Ingredients

1 recipe Classic Steamed Minced Chicken Balls (page 214)	2 cups peanut oil or corn oil

Before Cooking

Prepare minced chicken as directed in recipe. Shape into marble-size balls for soups or appetizers or into golfball-size balls for main dishes.

Cooking Instructions

Heat oil in skillet or wok over medium-high heat until it sizzles around a cube of fresh bread (360° F. on electric frypan). Fry no more than 8 golfball-size balls at a time. Crowding results in soggy foods. Shake the pan by the handle to keep the balls from sticking and to brown them evenly. Fry golfball-size balls uncovered 10 minutes until the balls are golden brown on the outside and show white inside when tested with a fork. (Marble-size balls take less time.) With slotted spatula remove balls as they are done and drain on paper towels. Keep them warm, uncovered, in 170° F. oven while you fry the remaining balls. Serve with side dishes of Chinese-Style Mustard, Garlic-Soy Dip or Ginger-Soy Dip (pages 351–352).

SERVINGS: This amount will make about 40 cocktail balls or 16 golfball-size balls; the larger size is enough for 3 to 4 as a single course with rice or for 6 in a full menu.

OPTIONAL SAUCES: Ahead of time prepare any one of the following sauces: Brown Sauce (page 357), Curry Sauce (page 358), Lichee Sauce (page 358), Pouring Oyster Sauce (page 356) or any of the Sweet-and-Sour Sauces (pages 353–356). Pour over the chicken balls and serve with steamed rice.

SEMI–DEEP-FRIED CHICKEN BALLS WITH VEGETABLES AND BROWN SAUCE

Prepare Brown Sauce (page 357) ahead of time. Prepare the chicken ball mixture. Shape into balls and using a skillet or wok fry as directed in the recipe for Semi–Deep-Fried Chicken Balls. While the balls are frying, gently reheat the sauce. Drain the fried balls on paper towels. Pour off all but 2 tablespoons oil from the pan. Raise the heat. Before the oil in the pan begins to smoke, add 1 cup threaded snow peas with ends snipped, ½ cup sliced water chestnuts or thinly sliced bamboo shoots and ⅓ cup dried mushrooms (rinsed, soaked in warm water 15 minutes and drained). Stir-fry-toss vegetables 2 to 3 minutes. Mix balls and vegetables together and arrange on a serving dish or in a bowl. Pour sauce over and serve with rice.

SERVINGS: Enough for 3 to 4 as a single course with rice or for 6 in a full menu.

SEMI–DEEP-FRIED WHITE CHICKEN SHREDS

Cooking Time: 2 minutes for each batch

Utensils
Chinese cutting knife
Soup plate
Small bowl for cornstarch mixture
Chopsticks for stirring
2-quart saucepan (8 inches in diameter)
Frying thermometer
Slotted spatula
Wire strainer

Ingredients

2	chicken breasts (¾ pound each)	¾	teaspoon salt
1	egg white	½	teaspoon sugar
1	tablespoon cornstarch	1	cup peanut oil or corn oil
2	teaspoons sherry, gin or vodka		

Before Cooking
Skin and bone the chicken breasts. Remove all connective tissue. Cut the chicken into fine shreds. You should have about 2 cups. Place shreds in the soup plate. Beat the egg white, cornstarch, liquor, salt and sugar in a small bowl. Pour over the chicken shreds and toss with chopsticks to blend. Let stand 10 minutes. Have oil ready to go.

Cooking Instructions
Heat oil in saucepan over medium-high heat until it foams around a cube of fresh bread (375° F. on thermometer). Add a third of the dredged seasoned chicken shreds. Stir with chopsticks to separate shreds. Fry just 2 minutes, until the shreds are crisp. With the slotted spatula, remove the cooked chicken to a wire strainer to drain off the oil. Fry and drain remaining chicken shreds, in thirds. Strain remaining oil and reserve for use another time. Chicken shreds cooked in this manner are tender-crisp, with the juices sealed in, as contrasted to Stir-Fry-Toss chicken shreds.

SERVINGS: Enough for 2 as a single course with rice or for 4 to 6 in a full menu.

SEMI–DEEP-FRIED RED CHICKEN SHREDS: Reduce salt to ½ teaspoon. Place fried and drained chicken shreds in a bowl or platter and toss with 1 tablespoon soy sauce until well mixed.

SEMI–DEEP-FRIED CHICKEN SHREDS WITH NUTS

Cooking Time: 2 minutes for each batch of chicken shreds
About 2 minutes for each batch of nuts

Utensils
Chinese cutting knife
Soup plate
Bowl or plate for vegetables
Small bowl for cornstarch mixture
Chopsticks
12-inch skillet, wok or electric frypan
Slotted spatula
Wire strainer

Ingredients

2	chicken breasts (¾ pound each)	½	teaspoon sugar
1	egg white	1	cup blanched almonds, cashews,
1½	tablespoons cornstarch		peanuts or walnuts
1	teaspoon sherry, gin or vodka	1	tablespoon soy sauce (optional)
¾	teaspoon salt	2	cups peanut oil or corn oil

Before Cooking
Skin and bone the chicken breasts. Remove all connective tissue. Cut the chicken into fine shreds. You should have about 2 cups. Place shreds in the soup plate. Combine the egg white, cornstarch, liquor, salt and sugar in the small bowl. Beat until foamy. Pour over chicken shreds and toss with chopsticks to blend. Let stand 10 minutes. Have nuts, soy sauce and oil ready to go.

Cooking Instructions
Heat oil in skillet or wok over medium-high heat until it foams around a cube of fresh bread (375° F. on electric frypan). Add a third of the chicken shreds. Separate the shreds with chopsticks, but do not stir and toss. Fry 2 minutes until the chicken strips change color and are crisp. With the slotted spatula, remove the

cooked chicken to the strainer. Fry and drain remaining chicken shreds, in thirds. Pour off all but ½ cup oil from the pan. Add nuts, ½ cup at a time, and fry about 2 minutes or until a pale golden brown, stirring constantly to prevent scorching. Place fried nuts on paper towels to drain and repeat frying process with remaining nuts. Drain nuts and combine with chicken strips in a heated bowl or platter. Sprinkle with soy sauce and toss to blend.

SERVINGS: Enough for 3 as a single course with rice or for 6 in a full menu.

SEMI–DEEP-FRIED DICED CHICKEN WITH PINEAPPLE

Cooking Time: 2 minutes for each batch of chicken
3 minutes for final cooking

Utensils
Chinese cutting knife
Soup plate
Small bowl for cornstarch mixture
Chopsticks
12-inch skillet, wok or electric frypan
Slotted spatula
Wire strainer

Ingredients

2	chicken breasts (¾ pound each)	¼	teaspoon salt
1	egg white	½	teaspoon brown sugar
1	tablespoon cornstarch	1	can (14 ounces) pineapple chunks
2	teaspoons soy sauce	2	cups peanut oil or corn oil
1	teaspoon vodka or gin		

Before Cooking
Skin and bone the chicken breasts. Remove all connective tissue. Cut chicken into ¾-inch dice. Place diced chicken in the soup plate. Beat the egg white, cornstarch, soy sauce, liquor, salt and brown sugar in the small bowl. Pour over chicken dice and toss with chopsticks to coat chicken. Let stand 10 minutes. Drain the pineapple and reserve ½ cup of the syrup. Set the fruit and the syrup aside. Have oil ready to go.

Cooking Instructions

Heat oil in skillet or wok over medium heat until it foams around a cube of fresh bread (360° F. on electric frypan). Add a third of the chicken. Stir with chopsticks to separate chicken, but do not toss. Fry 2 minutes, then remove with slotted spatula to the wire strainer. Fry and drain the remaining chicken dice, in thirds. Pour off all but 1 tablespoon oil from the skillet. Add the pineapple chunks and stir-fry-toss rapidly 1 minute. Return the chicken to the pan. Reduce heat to medium-low (300° F. on frypan). Add the reserved pineapple syrup. Stir gently to heat through and blend 1 to 2 minutes. The chicken should be fairly crisp and richly seasoned, contrasting with the tart sweetness of the pineapple.

SERVINGS: Enough for 3 as a single course with rice or for 6 in a full menu.

SEMI–DEEP-FRIED SHRIMP BALLS

Cooking Time: 10 minutes for each batch

Utensils
12-inch skillet, wok or electric frypan
Slotted spatula

Ingredients

1	recipe Classic Steamed Minced Shrimp Balls (page 220)	2	cups peanut oil or corn oil

Before Cooking
Prepare minced shrimp as directed in recipe. Shape into marble-size balls for soups or appetizers or into golfball-size balls for main dishes.

Cooking Instructions
Heat oil in skillet or wok until it foams around a cube of fresh bread (360° F. on electric frypan). Fry no more than 8 golfball-size balls at a time. Crowding results

in soggy foods. Shake the pan by the handle to keep the balls from sticking and to brown them evenly. Fry golfball-size balls uncovered 10 minutes. (Marble-size balls take less time.) The shrimp balls should be golden brown on the outside and pale pink on the inside when tested with a fork. Remove the balls as they are done with the slotted spatula. Place on paper towels to drain. Keep them warm, uncovered, in 170° F. oven while you fry the remaining balls. Serve with side dishes of Chinese-Style Mustard, Garlic-Soy Dip or Ginger-Soy Dip (pages 351–352).

SERVINGS: This amount will make about 40 cocktail balls or 16 golfball-size balls; the larger size is enough for 3 to 4 as a single course with rice or for 6 in a full menu.

OPTIONAL SAUCES: Ahead of time prepare any one of the following sauces: Brown Sauce (page 357), Curry Sauce (page 358) or any of the Sweet-and-Sour Sauces (pages 353–356). Pour over the shrimp balls and serve with rice.

SEMI–DEEP-FRIED CORAL AND JADE SHRIMP BALLS
Follow the recipe for Classic Steamed Minced Shrimp Balls but add 6 finely diced water chestnuts and 1 tablespoon finely minced parsley.

SERVINGS: Enough for 3 to 4 as a single course with rice or for 6 in a full menu.

SEMI–DEEP-FRIED SHRIMP BALLS WITH VEGETABLES
AND BROWN SAUCE
Prepare Brown Sauce (page 357) ahead of time. Prepare the shrimp ball mixture. Shape into balls and using a skillet or wok fry as directed in the recipe for Semi–Deep-Fried Shrimp Balls. While the balls are frying, gently reheat the sauce. Drain the fried balls on paper towels. Pour off all but 2 tablespoons oil from the pan. Turn the heat to high. Before oil in the pan begins to smoke, add 1 cup threaded snow peas with ends snipped, ½ cup sliced water chestnuts or thinly sliced bamboo shoots and ⅓ cup dried mushrooms (rinsed, soaked in warm water 15 minutes and drained). Stir-fry-toss vegetables 2 to 3 minutes. Mix the balls and vegetables together and arrange on a heated serving dish or in a bowl. Pour sauce over and serve with rice.

SERVINGS: Enough for 3 to 4 as a single serving with rice or for 6 in a full menu.

SEMI–DEEP-FRIED SWEET-AND-SOUR FISH,
Mandarin Style

Cooking Time: 26 to 30 minutes to fry fish
7 to 9 minutes to stir-fry vegetable-shrimp mixture

Utensils
Chinese cutting knife
Small bowls for vegetables, shrimp, sea-
    sonings
Heavy enameled roasting pan (15x10x3
    inches) or 14-inch wok
Frying thermometer (for roasting pan)
Lined rubber gloves
Wide spatula
Large oval platter for fish

Ingredients

1	drawn carp, bass or rock cod (3 pounds), with head and tail intact	½	cup cut-up small cleaned shrimp
⅓	cup small dried mushrooms	¼	cup soy sauce
2	cloves garlic, minced	¼	cup rice vinegar or cider vinegar
1	tablespoon finely minced ginger root	2	teaspoons sherry
		2	tablespoons brown sugar
4	scallions, with 1½ inches of green cut in ¼-inch slices	½	teaspoon salt
		¼	cup cornstarch
½	cup diced bamboo shoots	⅓	cup cold chicken stock
½	cup peas	1	tablespoon cornstarch
½	cup diced carrots	2	cups peanut oil or corn oil

Before Cooking
Have the fish cleaned and scaled but the head and tail left intact. Wash it thoroughly. Rinse in cold water and place on a bed of ice in a large pan (leave until 1
hour before cooking). Soak the dried mushrooms in warm water to cover 20 minutes. Combine the minced garlic and ginger root with the scallions in a small
bowl. Chop the bamboo shoot in ½-inch dice. Parboil peas and carrots 3 minutes
in ⅓ cup boiling water. (If you are using frozen vegetables, simply thaw, measure
and set aside.) Shell the shrimp, devein, rinse, drain and cut each into 3 pieces.
Combine soy sauce, vinegar, sherry and brown sugar in a bowl. Blend the salt into

the ¼ cup cornstarch. Measure the stock and the 1 tablespoon cornstarch but do not combine until just before adding to the pan. One hour before cooking, remove fish from refrigerator. Drain and blot outside and in with paper towels. Have oil ready to go.

Cooking Instructions

Turn heat under roasting pan or wok to high. When the pan is hot enough for a drop of water to bubble into steam, add the oil. If you are using a roasting pan with straight sides, attach the frying thermometer with the tip below the oil but not touching the bottom of the pan. While the oil is heating, sprinkle a counter or pastry board with half of the salted cornstarch. Roll one side of the fish in it. Turn the fish over and sprinkle the remaining salted cornstarch on the same side. Rub gently with fingers to coat the entire fish, head and tail too. Test to see if oil is hot enough (the oil should foam around a cube of fresh bread or register 375° F. on the thermometer). Now, pull on the lined rubber gloves and grasp the fish by the tail with the right hand and support the head and body with the left. Gently lower the fish by the tail into the pan. Be careful of spattering oil. Fry 3 to 5 minutes on one side. Then, using the wide spatula, turn fish and fry 3 to 5 minutes on the other. Reduce heat to medium and continue cooking 20 minutes, turning fish twice. Baste the top surface of fish with oil while the bottom is frying. Fish is done when a fork easily pierces the back next to the spine and the flesh is flaky and white. Remove fish to the large warmed platter.

Pour off all but 3 tablespoons oil from the pan. (Remove thermometer if you are using one.) Turn up heat under the pan or wok. When the oil begins to sizzle, add the garlic, ginger root and scallions. Stir-fry 1 minute. Add the bamboo shoots; stir-fry 30 seconds. Add the drained peas and carrots and stir-fry-toss 1 minute. Add the drained mushrooms. Stir-fry 1 minute. Now add the shrimp and stir-fry-toss 3 minutes. Stir in the soy sauce mixture. Stir to blend. Combine the 1 tablespoon cornstarch with the stock and stir into the vegetable-shrimp mixture. Blend 1 to 2 minutes until sauce thickens and becomes clear. Pour over fish on the platter and bring to the table at once. What skin there is on the fish will be crisp; the flesh will be tender and flaky. The sauce will be a rich dark brown with a piquant flavor. This is a Honan banquet specialty, less sweet than the Cantonese versions of sweet-and-sour foods. Ingredients such as pineapples, sweet pickles, tomatoes and peppers are not used here. Artificial red coloring is never used.

SERVINGS: Enough for 6 as a single course with rice or for 10 to 12 in a full menu.

BATTER-COATED PORK BALLS

Cooking Time: 15 minutes for each batch

Utensils
12-inch skillet, wok or electric frypan
Slotted spatula

Ingredients

Double recipe Basic Thick Batter
Mixture (page 250)

1 recipe Classic Steamed Minced
Pork Balls (page 207)

4 cups peanut oil or corn oil

Before Cooking
Prepare a double recipe of Basic Thick Batter Mixture at least 30 minutes ahead of time. If refrigerated, remove from refrigerator 30 minutes before using to allow to come to room temperature. Prepare pork ball mixture. Shape into balls and dip into batter.

Cooking Instructions
Heat oil in skillet or wok until it foams around a cube of fresh bread (360° F. on electric frypan). Fry the golfball-size batter-coated balls a few at a time 15 minutes or until they are golden brown on the outside and show no pink when tested with a fork. (Cocktail-size balls will take less time.) Drain the balls on paper towels, arrange on a serving dish and serve with saucers of Chinese-Style Mustard, "Chekiang" Vinegar, Garlic-Soy Dip or Ginger-Soy Dip (pages 351–352). The larger-size balls may be topped with any of the Pouring Sauces (pages 352–359).

SERVINGS: This amount will make about 75 cocktail balls or about 24 golfball-size balls; the larger size is enough for 6 as a single course with rice or for 8 to 12 in a full menu.

BATTER-COATED BEEF BALLS: Substitute the beef ball mixture for Classic Steamed Minced Beef Balls (page 209) for the pork mixture. Fry a few at a time at 380° F. 10 minutes. (The beef mixture will make about 75 cocktail balls or 24 golfball-size balls; the larger size is enough for 6 as a single course with rice or for 8 to 12 in a full menu.)

BATTER-COATED CHICKEN BALLS: Substitute chicken ball mixture for Classic Steamed Minced Chicken Balls (page 214) for the pork mixture. Fry a few at a time at 380° F. 10 minutes or until golden brown on the outside and white on the inside. (The chicken mixture will make about 40 cocktail balls or 16 golfball-size balls; the larger size is enough for 3 to 4 as a single course with rice or for 6 in a full menu.)

BATTER-COATED SHRIMP BALLS: Substitute shrimp ball mixture for Classic Steamed Minced Shrimp Balls (page 220) for the pork mixture. Fry a few at a time at 380° F. 8 to 10 minutes or until crusty golden brown on the outside and pink inside. (The shrimp mixture will make about 40 cocktail balls or 16 golfball-size balls; the larger size is enough for 3 to 4 as a single course with rice or for 6 in a full menu.)

BATTER-COATED DICED PORK

Cooking Time: 8 minutes for each batch

Utensils
Chinese cutting knife
Flat dish or pie plate
12-inch skillet, wok or electric frypan
Slotted spoon or spatula

Ingredients

1 recipe Basic Thick Batter (page 250)	1 pound pork tenderloin
	4 cups peanut oil or corn oil

Before Cooking
Prepare Basic Thick Batter ahead of time. Refrigerate at least 30 minutes--but allow batter to come to room temperature before beginning to cook. If you are using a cut of pork that is less lean than tenderloin, remove all excess fat. Cut pork into ¾-inch dice. Dry diced pork on paper towels. Place in the flat dish or pie plate and pour batter over pork. Toss to make sure the cubes are well coated. Have oil ready to go.

Cooking Instructions

Heat oil in skillet or wok over medium-high heat until it foams around a cube of fresh bread (360° F. on electric frypan). Add a third of the diced pork. Deep-fry 8 minutes or until the outsides are a crusty golden brown and the insides show no pink when tested with a fork. Remove the pork with the slotted spoon to a heated dish. Continue frying the remaining pork, in thirds. Serve with small bowls of "Chekiang" Vinegar, Chinese-Style Mustard, and Cantonese or Spiced Salt.

SERVINGS: Enough for 2 as a single course with rice or for 3 to 4 in a full menu.

SWEET-AND-SOUR BATTER-COATED DICED PORK

Prepare any one of the Sweet-and-Sour Sauces (pages 353–356) ahead of time. Follow the recipe for Batter-Coated Diced Pork but before frying the pork cubes, gently reheat the sauce. When the pork has all been fried, combine with the sauce and simmer 2 to 3 minutes until the pork is thoroughly heated. Serve with rice.

SERVINGS: Enough for 2 as a single course with rice or for 3 to 4 in a full menu.

NOTE: For Southern-style sweet-and-sour pork, use the Cantonese recipe or its variations. For Northern-style, use the Mandarin recipe.

BASIC THICK BATTER

1	large egg	¾	teaspoon salt
¾	cup flour	½	cup cold water

Break egg into a quart bowl and beat, gradually adding the flour and salt. Add water by the tablespoonful; beat until thick and smooth. Cover and let stand or refrigerate at least 30 minutes. Before using, let batter come to room temperature. Use for coating meat, chicken and fish balls and diced pork for sweet-and-sour recipes.

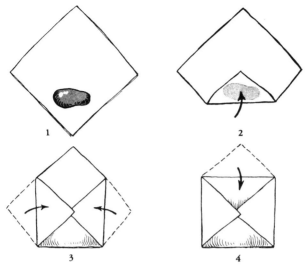

Gift-Wrapped Chicken Packages
1. Place chicken on paper square.   2. Fold bottom flap over chicken.   3. Fold over sides.
4. Tuck top flap in to close package securely.

GIFT-WRAPPED CHICKEN,

Szechuan Style

Cooking Time: 3 minutes for each batch

Utensils
Chinese cutting knife
Bowl for chicken slices
Wax paper (12x32 inches) or parchment
     paper (15x32 inches)
12-inch skillet or electric frypan
Tongs
Colander

Ingredients

1	whole fryer (3 pounds) or 2 chicken breasts	½	teaspoon salt
2	tablespoons soy sauce	1	teaspoon brown sugar
2	teaspoons vodka, gin or sherry	⅛	teaspoon red pepper flakes (optional)
2	teaspoons Hoisin sauce	2	scallions
1	teaspoon peanut oil	4	cups peanut oil or corn oil
½	teaspoon sesame oil		

Before Cooking

Skin and bone the chicken. Remove all gristle. Flatten the chicken meat with the side of the Chinese cutting knife. Cut into thin 1-inch squares. You should have about 40 squares. Set aside. Combine the soy sauce, liquor, Hoisin sauce, 1/2 teaspoon peanut oil, sesame oil, salt, sugar and pepper flakes in the bowl. Blend well. Add the chicken squares and let stand 30 minutes. Trim the scallions and cut each into 10 pieces. Cut wax or parchment paper into twenty 4-inch squares (see note). Drain the chicken on paper towels. Place 1 square of chicken in the center of a square of paper, put a piece of scallion on the chicken and cover with another square of chicken. The scallion is thus sandwiched between 2 chicken slices. Fold the wax paper or parchment envelope-fashion. Set aside. Have 4 cups oil ready to go.

Cooking Instructions

Put oil in skillet over medium-high heat until it foams around a cube of fresh bread (375° F. on electric frypan). Add wrapped chicken packages, four or five at a time. Fry 3 minutes. Remove with tongs to a colander to drain while frying the rest of the packages. Serve on a heated dish. The chicken is served in its paper wrapping and opened by the guests. The chicken meat will be tender and just cooked with a savory flavor imparted by the marinade.

SERVINGS: Enough for 10 as an appetizer or for 4 as a main course.

NOTE: To make wax-paper or parchment squares, fold a 12x32-inch strip lengthwise in thirds; fold the resulting long strip in half 3 times. You will have creases for twenty-four 4-inch squares. Cut the squares, discarding four. (Baking parchment is usually 15 inches wide. Tear off a 32-inch strip and cut off 3 inches from the width.)

GIFT-WRAPPED SHRIMP: Substitute 20 small to medium shrimp, peeled, washed and drained, for the chicken. Cut each shrimp in half lengthwise and pound slightly to flatten. Proceed as directed above, sandwiching a piece of scallion between 2 pieces of flattened shrimp.

GIFT-WRAPPED GOLD COIN CHICKEN: Use the 2 chicken breasts and cut 40 thin rounds of meat. Cut 20 paper-thin rounds of smoked ham and sandwich between chicken. Omit scallions. Proceed as directed above.

CLASSIC DEEP-FRIED WHOLE SHRIMP

Cooking Time: 2 minutes for each batch

Utensils
Soup plate
Chopsticks
12-inch skillet, wok or electric frypan
Slotted spoon or spatula
Wire strainer

Ingredients

1	pound shrimp (36 to 40 small, 24 to 26 medium)	$\frac{1}{8}$	teaspoon white pepper
$1\frac{1}{2}$	teaspoons sherry, gin or vodka	1	medium scallion
$1\frac{1}{2}$	teaspoons salt	2	slices ginger root (2x1x$\frac{1}{8}$ inch)
		3	cups peanut oil or corn oil

Before Cooking
Wash and shell shrimp, removing feelers and tails. Slash down the back of each shrimp and devein. Place in soup plate; toss with liquor and sprinkle with salt and pepper. Stir to blend. Trim scallion, leaving about 2 inches of green; cut into $1\frac{1}{2}$-inch lengths. Top shrimp mixture with scallion and ginger root. Have oil ready to go.

Cooking Instructions
Heat oil in skillet or wok over medium-high heat until it foams around a cube of fresh bread (375° F. on electric frypan). Add half the shrimp with the scallion and ginger root. Toss and stir with chopsticks to separate shrimp. Fry 2 minutes. The shrimp should be a bright pink. Scoop up with slotted spoon or spatula and put into strainer to drain off oil. Remove scallion and ginger root. Fry the remaining half of the shrimp 2 minutes and add them to the first lot in the strainer. Serve with small dishes of Cantonese Salt, "Chekiang" Vinegar; Ginger-Soy Dip or Garlic-Soy Dip (pages 351–352).

SERVINGS: Enough for 3 as a single course with rice or for 4 to 6 in a full menu.

OPTIONAL SAUCES: Ahead of time, prepare any one of the following sauces: Brown Sauce (page 357), Pouring Oyster Sauce (page 356), Curry Sauce (page 358) or any of the Sweet-and-Sour Sauces (pages 353–356). Combine with the deep-fried shrimp.

DEEP-FRIED WHOLE SHRIMP WITH VEGETABLES

Follow the recipe for Classic Deep-Fried Whole Shrimp. (Use a skillet or wok.) After draining the shrimp, pour off all but 2 tablespoons oil from the pan. Combine 1 teaspoon cornstarch with 2 tablespoons water; set aside. Turn the heat under the pan to high. Before the oil begins to smoke, add 1 cup (mixed or unmixed) of any of the following vegetables:

1	can (8 ounces) water chestnuts, drained and sliced in thin rounds		3 minutes and drained thoroughly, or slightly more than $\frac{1}{2}$ package (10-ounce size) frozen asparagus, thawed and drained
$\frac{1}{2}$	hairy melon, peeled and cut in $\frac{1}{2}$-inch dice		
$\frac{1}{2}$	large cucumber, seeded and cut into $\frac{1}{2}$-inch dice	1	pound green peas, parboiled 3 minutes and drained, or $\frac{1}{2}$ package (10-ounce size) frozen peas, thawed and drained
6	ounces fresh asparagus, cut in $1\frac{1}{2}$-inch diagonal slices, parboiled		

Fry the vegetables 1 to 3 minutes, depending on the time required to cook through. Stir in the cornstarch-water mixture and allow to thicken. Return drained shrimp to pan. Mix carefully with vegetables and serve at once.

SERVINGS: Enough for 3 to 4 as a single course with rice or for 6 to 8 in a full menu.

NOTE: The oil that has been poured off should be strained and refrigerated. Use again—but only for frying fish.

DEEP-FRIED WHOLE SHRIMP WITH VEGETABLES AND SAUCES

Ahead of time prepare any of the Sweet-and-Sour Sauces, Brown Sauce, Pouring Oyster Sauce or the Curry Sauce (see pages 353–358). Gently reheat the sauce while you prepare and fry Classic Deep-Fried Whole Shrimp. Pour off all but 2 tablespoons oil from the pan. To the oil remaining in the pan, add 1 cup of any of the vegetables listed in the recipe for Deep-Fried Whole Shrimp with Vegetables and fry vegetables as directed. Omit the cornstarch-water step. Return drained fried shrimp to the pan. Stir to blend shrimp and vegetables. Add heated sauce and serve at once.

SERVINGS: Enough for 3 to 4 as a single course with rice or for 6 to 8 in a full menu.

BATTER-COATED FISH FILETS

Cooking Time: 3 minutes for each batch

Utensils
Medium bowl for egg whites
Small bowl for cornstarch mixture
12-inch skillet, wok or electric frypan
Slotted spatula
Pyrex pie plate or heated dish

Ingredients

1½ pounds fish filets (sea bass, hali-
    but or cod)
2   egg whites
1   tablespoon cornstarch

1   tablespoon cold water
½   teaspoon salt
4   cups peanut oil or corn oil

Before Cooking
Rinse fish filets, split lengthwise and cut across into 2-inch sections. Blot dry with paper towels. Beat egg whites until frothy. Combine cornstarch with cold water and salt until mixture is a thin, smooth paste. Add to egg whites and beat until well blended. Have oil ready to go.

Cooking Instructions
Heat oil in skillet or wok over high heat until it foams around a cube of fresh bread (375° F. on electric frypan). Dip the pieces of fish in the egg white–cornstarch mixture. Fry the pieces, one-fourth at a time, 3 minutes. The fish should have a pale gold exterior. Remove with slotted spatula to a heated dish and continue frying remaining pieces until all are done. Serve with wedges of lemon and Ginger-Soy Dip (page 352) or Garlic-Soy Dip (page 351).

SERVINGS: Enough for 3 as a main course with rice or for 6 to 8 in a full menu.

OPTIONAL SAUCES: Prepare one of the Sweet-and-Sour Sauces (pages 353–356) ahead of time. Pour over the deep-fried filets.

BATTER-COATED FISH FILETS WITH VEGETABLES

Follow the recipe for Batter-Coated Fish Filets, using a skillet or wok. Place the fried fish on a heat-proof dish and keep it warm. Pour off all but ¼ cup oil from pan. Be sure to remove all bits of broken batter from the oil. Maintain high heat. When the oil is hot, add 2 slices peeled ginger root. Stir-fry 2 minutes. Add 2 cups snipped, threaded snow peas and 1 cup water chestnuts, halved and drained. Stir-fry 2 minutes. Add 6 sliced dried mushrooms (rinsed, soaked in warm water 15 minutes and drained). Stir-fry 2 minutes longer. Quickly combine 1 tablespoon cornstarch, ¼ teaspoon salt, 2 teaspoons sugar, 1 tablespoon soy sauce, ⅓ cup dry sherry and ¼ cup chicken stock. Blend well and add to vegetables in the pan. Cook and stir only until sauce has become thick and clear. Turn heat to medium-low. Return fish filets to pan and heat through 2 minutes, with sauce and vegetables. The vegetables should be bright in color and the fish still quite crisp.

SERVINGS: Enough for 4 as a single course with rice or for 6 to 8 in a full menu.

OVEN BARBECUING (ROASTING), OUTDOOR BARBECUING AND SMOKE-COOKING-TECHNIQUE 7

⊑⊒⊑⊒⊑⊒⊑⊒⊑⊒⊑⊒⊑⊒⊑⊒⊑⊒⊑⊒⊑⊒⊑⊒⊑⊒⊑⊒⊑⊒⊑⊒

The arts of barbecuing and smoke-cooking are almost as ancient as China itself, yet surprisingly little attention is given to these methods in most Chinese cookbooks. The beautifully roasted foods sold in most cities with a Chinatown of any size may be one reason for this. Even in China, few homes boasted the luxury of special smoke ovens and roasted foods were generally purchased.

While barbecuing in the Chinese manner may sound like a complex business, it is not—it is simply a matter of knowing what to do and how to do it. For this type of cooking, whether it be oven-barbecuing or outdoor barbecuing, determines whether the food is fast-cooking or slow-cooking. For example—fish filets, shellfish and liver should be cooked rapidly to prevent their drying out. Spareribs, pork strips and poultry require longer cooking.

Foods to be barbecued are usually marinated before cooking, marination periods differing for each cut or type of meat, poultry or fish. Spareribs and pork roasts should be marinated for no longer than 12 hours as they tend to toughen after that. Chicken parts and fish require considerably less marinating. The correct time is specified in each recipe. All ingredients can be barbecued in the oven as well as barbecued or smoke-cooked in outdoor units. Lacking expensive Chinese barbecue ovens, it is wisest to cook a complex dish such as Peking Duck in the oven.

OVEN BARBECUING

If you want foods with a true barbecued flavor, crisp exteriors and moist insides, do not broil in the oven. Heat from above tends to cook too rapidly, scorching the outer surface of food and leaving the interior raw. Any but the shortest cooking time causes the meat to dry out. Oven-broiling may be fine for Western-style steaks, when rare meat and charred exteriors are desirable; but for meats such as spareribs or pork strips, which require long, slow cooking in order to melt and drain fat and cook thoroughly, broiling is disastrous.

The Chinese method of barbecuing involves hanging the meat or poultry and cooking it over indirect heat from below. Food cooked in this manner is assured of even roasting. There are three satisfactory methods of oven barbecuing. The first and most effective means is to hang whatever is being barbecued wired from the top rack of the oven. The second is to use a rotisserie. The final method, using a roasting rack and pan, is the one most likely to be used because of its ease and familiarity. These methods are described in detail in the recipes themselves and are only outlined here.

NOTE: If you have an oven, the top rack of which is high enough to use the hanging method, the meat is hung in the following manner. Insert the tip of a 6-inch skewer 2 inches from the top of the meat and bend to form a hook. Pry open the curved top of the skewer and hang it from oven rack.

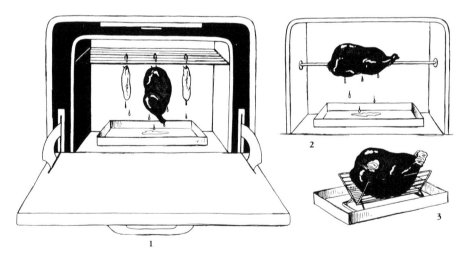

Oven Barbecuing
1. Hanging method.   2. Rotisserie method.   3. Rack method.

OUTDOOR BARBECUING

Barbecuing on cooking units outdoors is more a matter of skill than of equipment. Any of the wide range of available barbecue ovens, from the least expensive table-top units and hibachis to the high-priced double grill types with electric rotisseries, can serve your purpose. If this is a new area of cooking for you, and you plan to buy a cooking unit, may I suggest you consider versatility rather than deluxe features which you may never use? For heat control, look for an adjustable grill, firebed or vent. For roasting large cuts, you will need a unit with a motorized rotisserie.

While I have shown an illustration or two of barbecue and smoke-cooking stoves, I am going to explain this technique assuming that you have only the simplest of units, say a brazier or a hibachi.

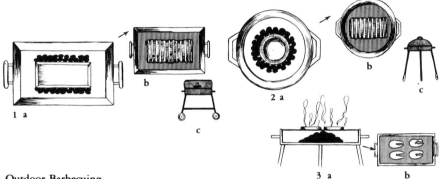

Outdoor Barbecuing
1. Slow cooking on rectangular grill. a. For large pieces, such as spareribs or a split chicken, arrange briquets along sides of foil broiler pan. b. Grill is set in place and ingredients arranged on grill. c. Unit is covered for smoke-cooking.   2. Slow cooking on round grill. a. For large pieces, arrange briquets around foil pie pan. b. Grill is set in place and ingredients arranged on grill. c. Unit is covered for smoke cooking.   3. Fast cooking. a. For small pieces requiring intense heat, such as fish steaks and chicken parts, briquets are set close together in a mound. b. Grill is set in place and ingredients arranged on grill.

Materials needed for building a fire
Any kind of barbecue unit.

ALUMINUM FOIL: Line the unit with foil shiny-side-up to intensify the heat. The foil also helps to keep the base of the unit clean. (The use of foil is optional.)

FIREBASE: This is a type of light gravel which is used to line the unit and form a base for the firebed. It allows the coals to breathe, conserves heat and, by absorbing the fat drippings, helps to prevent flare-ups. Firebase is available in 2½-pound bags.

Or use sand instead. Depending on how often you use your barbecue, the foil and firebase can be discarded in two weeks to a month—or whenever you decide it's time to clean out the barbecue.

CHARCOAL BRIQUETS: These are by far the most effective fuel for barbecuing. They are generally made of hardwood; their uniform size gives off even heat and makes it simple to arrange an efficient firebed; available in 5- and 10-pound bags. Other fuels which may be used, but which are less satisfactory, are hardwoods, coal briquets and lump charcoal. Soft or resinous woods, such as pine, are unsatisfactory for a firebed. They burn too quickly and fail to develop adequate coals.

FIRE-STARTERS: The most convenient of these is the liquid type sold in pint- and quart-size cans. It is an odorless, smokeless petroleum product made specifically for barbecuing. Odorless paint thinner or jellied alcohol sold in cans may also be used. Electric starters are inexpensive and safer to use than the liquid- or jellied fire starter but they require an electric outlet. They are shaped somewhat like a horseshoe and come in at least two sizes.

LONG TONGS, ASBESTOS GLOVES, WATER SPRAYER, AND PASTRY BRUSH: The tongs are necessary for turning coals and adjusting the distance of food from the heat. Asbestos gloves enable one to remove food at relatively close distance from the heat without the danger of scorching the hands. A water sprayer is great for dealing with flare-ups; a dime-store water pistol or a plastic hair-rinse bottle with a nozzle also works well. A pastry brush or long-handled brush for barbecuing comes in handy for basting food as it is cooking.

Where to Set Up Your Barbecue
Small units, such as table-top braziers or portable grills, should face into the wind. This placement provides the best draft for the fire and should carry the smoke away from the guests and the person doing the cooking. If you are barbecuing in a wooded area, make sure that the wind does not blow embers about. An excellent precaution is to thoroughly dampen the area surrounding the barbecue with a hose. And a fire bucket is a good item to have under any circumstances.

To Begin Barbecuing
Marinate the food to be cooked according to recipe directions; arrange it near the barbecue unit. If you have an elaborate barbecue unit (with a work shelf), you can place the food and the necessary adjuncts to cooking (tongs, gloves, etc.) on it. Line the firebed with foil and cover with 1½ inches of firebase or sand. Squirt

starter fluid over the firebase (enough to saturate), then arrange briquets over it. Let briquets stand for a minute to absorb fluid. Then light with a match. When the fire has burned down, allow the coals to become gray all over before placing food on the grill. It will take from 30 to 40 minutes for the coals to turn gray. This is important. Coals which are still flaming and have black areas produce uneven heat. Barbecued foods are properly cooked only by direct infrared radiation—and this is given off from thoroughly heated coals, not by flame.

The size of your unit and how open it is will determine the amount of briquets required. On the average, 25 briquets will provide enough heat for food that requires relatively short-term barbecuing—for example, thin strips of meat, fish filets, chicken parts. For this rapid grilling, the coals should be placed directly under the grill, leaving little space between each coal.

For barbecuing thicker cuts of meat or whole poultry, you will need a longer cooking time and consequently more fuel. To prevent the outside of the food from charring while the inside is still raw, first arrange the briquets in a ring at the outer edges of the food; add briquets as needed to this outer ring of coals and push the already gray ones to the center. This is to prevent the newly flaming coals from making the food sooty. When you use this ring arrangement of briquets, it is necessary to place a foil pie pan or broiler pan directly under the grill to catch the drippings. The distance of the grill from the heat is adjusted according to the directions in the recipe. The food is placed on the grill and barbecued according to the time specified in each recipe.

Cooking Temperatures

A thermometer is of course the best way to check the cooking temperature of food. Most of the large units have built-in thermometers. With a small unit an accurate temperature reading can be achieved by placing a grill thermometer directly on the grill. If you have no thermometer and wish to gauge the approximate temperature of your firebed, this is how to do it. Place your hand, palm down, near the grill and begin counting. If you can feel the heat by the time you have counted to three, the temperature is between 350° and 400° F. If you cannot keep your hand close to the grill for even 3 seconds, it is probably even too hot for quick-cooking foods such as steaks or fish. Using the long tongs, separate the coals to reduce the heat; then test the heat again. If you find that you can keep the palm of your hand close to the grill for 6 to 8 seconds, the temperature is about 200° to 250° F. To increase the heat, bring the coals closer together; or add fresh coals to the outer edges of the firebed.

The general rule is this: for a hot fire and short cooking, you use more coals and arrange them close together; for a cooler fire and longer cooking, the coals should be spread apart or arranged around a foil drip pan. The more open your unit, the more coals you will require since heat naturally escapes when it is not closed in. Remember, too, that heat can be controlled by raising or lowering the level of your adjustable grill.

Fish filets, fish steaks and skewered foods should be barbecued at 350° to 375° F. Steaks and chops require a temperature of 350° to 400° F. Poultry parts and pork spareribs and strips need less intense heat—325° F.—and longer cooking. For large items, such as whole chicken or duck, shoulders or legs of lamb and pork, the barbecuing temperature should be 300° F.

Firebed Temperatures
200° to 250° F. Low
250° to 350° F. Medium
350° to 400° F. Hot
400° to 500° F. Very Hot

Barbecuing Times
The cooking time is given in the individual recipes. Bear in mind that, aside from the equipment and flavor, barbecuing is much like roasting in your oven. Both methods take approximately the same amount of time. Follow the same testing devices for doneness that you would in your kitchen—ideally by using a meat thermometer. Failing that, test a chicken leg by piercing the drumstick to see if the juices run clear, or twist the leg to see if it moves freely. Cut a sliver of pork to determine that it is no longer pink. A little experimenting both with temperatures and cooking times will reward you with superbly flavored food.

SMOKE-COOKING

Smoke-cooking should not be confused with the smoking process, which causes chemical changes in the food and takes days. Smoke-cooking refers to food which is cooked by heat and flavored by smoke. There are two methods by which to smoke-cook Chinese style—the closed barbecue method (Outdoor Smoke-Cooking) and the use of brown sugar over direct heat (Indoor Smoke-Cooking).

OUTDOOR SMOKE-COOKING
The traditional Chinese smoke-cooking pit was made of clay or bricks and relied on indirect heat from a wood fire. Food was suspended in the pit and smoke-

cooked. Until a few years ago, this was the only outdoor smoke-cooking method known—home smoke-cooking units were unheard of. Happily, there are many barbecue stoves today which feature either installable smoking units or simple units which serve as smoke cookers with the addition of a hood. You can smoke-cook on any barbecue unit with a hood or cover. Even those with partial hoods may be sealed with foil. If you have a small brazier, use a high-domed pot cover, such as the lid of a wok, over the food. An inverted roasting pan with vents works very well over the top of a hibachi.

The beginning steps of outdoor smoke-cooking are identical to those of barbecuing. We will again assume that you are using the simplest of small units, such as a hibachi. Prepare the firebed as directed for outdoor-barbecuing. When the coals have turned gray, it is time to add the smoking agents. For this you will need either prepared hardwood chips (such as hickory), or any fresh-cut hardwood (such as oak or myrtle), any nutwood or fruitwood (such as lemon or orange) or wood shavings or sawdust which have been soaked in water. An unusual flavor, characteristically Chinese, can be achieved by sprinkling used tea leaves over the coals. Stay away from resinous types of wood, such as pine, cedar, fir or eucalyptus. They result in food with a tarry surface and a flavor suggestive of turpentine.

Once the smoke gets going, adjust the distance of the grill from the firebed as directed in the recipe. Place the food to be smoke-cooked on the grill. Place a cover over the unit and smoke for the time given in the recipe.

Cooking time is about the same in smoke-cooking as in open barbecuing. The smoke flavor can be controlled. To accentuate the smokiness, add wood, twigs or tea leaves throughout the cooking process. For less smoke flavor, add the smoking agents 15 minutes before the food is done.

For roasts, whole birds, legs of ham or lamb, you naturally require a large cooking unit, with a larger cover than a pot lid. Start your fire in exactly the same manner as described, but once your coals are hot, use tongs to place them on either side of the firebed. This provides indirect heat in the same manner as the Chinese smoke-roast. Whether the meat is resting on the grill or is attached to a rotisserie spit, place a foil pan directly under it to catch the drippings. Food smoke-cooked in this manner develops a beautiful russet glaze, and the flavor is quite unlike that achieved through any other roasting method.

INDOOR SMOKE-COOKING

Indoor smoke-cooking, or sugar-smoking, can be done on your own stove. For equipment, you will need an 11-inch iron skillet, 2 sheets of heavy-duty aluminum foil (22x18 inches), a 10-inch cake rack and a wooden spoon. The fish or poultry (meat is not generally sugar-smoked) should be marinated ahead of time. Fold a

Indoor Smoke-Cooking
1. Line skillet and lid with a double thickness of foil.   2. Turn heat under skillet to medium-high, add liquor and ignite. When flames have died down, add brown sugar.
3. When sugar has melted, fit cake rack into skillet. As sugar begins to smoke, place ingredients on rack.   4. Cover skillet and smoke-cook for time specified in recipe.

sheet of the foil in half and shape it into a lining for the skillet, bending the excess foil over the top rim. Then fold the remaining sheet of foil in half and shape it into a lining for the cover of the skillet. This is to protect your pan from the charring caused by burnt sugar. Turn the heat to medium-high. Next add the liquor to the skillet, light it with a match and, when the flames have died, add the brown sugar. When the sugar has melted, place a lightly oiled rack in the pan. A 10-inch cake rack will fit snugly in an 11-inch skillet lined with foil. When the sugar gets bubbly and begins to smoke, place the drained ingredients on the rack. Put the cover on the skillet and open all the windows. Fish filets and fish steaks cook very quickly. Do not attempt to turn them, as the fish breaks easily. Use a spatula to remove food from the rack. For poultry, proceed in the same manner—except that the food should be turned several times during the smoking.

As soon as the food is smoked, remove to a warm platter or tray. Wearing asbestos gloves, lift out the aluminum foil (the rack will come with it). Drop the rack in hot sudsy water and use a cleaning pad to scrub off any food particles that may have stuck to it. Your skillet should be as clean as it was when you started. If you prefer a plain smoke taste to your food, try omitting the marinade; season with salt and brush with a light coat of oil instead. Sugar-smoked salmon steaks cooked in this manner are delectable.

Although this procedure should be followed with as much ventilation as possible—an overhead fan, if your stove has one, and doors and windows open to prevent the smoke odor from permeating the house—it is an easy indoor technique. Food smoked over brown sugar is moist and uniquely tangy in flavor, while food smoked over wood is generally crisper and has a richer, more full-bodied flavor. For the sugar technique, allow approximately 15 minutes per pound of fish and 20 minutes per pound of chicken.

BARBECUED PORK STRIPS

Char Siu

Oven Time: 1 hour, 10 minutes
Outdoor-Barbecuing Time: 45 to 60 minutes
Smoke-Cooking Time: 45 to 60 minutes

Equipment for Oven Method
Pan for marinating pork
Foil-covered shallow pan
6 metal skewers (6 inches long)

Equipment for Outdoor Methods
Any barbecuing unit
Materials and utensils for building and
    tending fire (pages 259–260)
Barbecue hood or cover (for smoking)
Foil broiling pan or round cake pan (for
    smoking)
Dampened hickory chips or fruitwood
    prunings (for smoking)

Ingredients

Marinade I or II (page 268)

2   pounds pork tenderloin, shoulder or butt, boned and trimmed

Before Cooking
Prepare marinade; pour into the pan. Cut pork into 6 strips, each approximately 6x2x2 inches. (It is unlikely that you will get evenly sized strips.) Pierce pork

strips all over with a fork and brush them with the marinade. Refrigerate pork in the marinade 2 hours, turning the strips several times. Bring to room temperature before barbecuing.

Cooking Instructions for Oven Method

Do not preheat oven. Place foil-covered shallow pan on the bottom of the oven to catch drippings. Skewer the meat strips and hang from the top rack of the oven. Reserve the marinade remaining in the pan for basting. Turn oven to 425° F. and roast 10 minutes. Reduce heat to 325° F. Roast 1 hour, or until the strips are a russet brown on the outside and almost white on the inside. (Watch out for scorching.) Strips thicker than 2 inches will require longer roasting. For thinner strips, reduce cooking time.

Outdoor-Barbecuing Instructions

During the last hour of marinating, prepare a low to medium firebed (250° F.). The coals must be gray all over (30 to 40 minutes). Lay the pork strips on the lightly greased grill 4 inches from the firebed. Barbecue 45 to 60 minutes, turning strips with long tongs during the cooking. Baste with additional marinade from time to time unless the marinade is thick or contains quantities of sugar or honey. Then baste only during the last 15 minutes to prevent a scorched exterior. Should the meat appear to be turning too dark, place a sheet of foil under the meat. Douse flare-ups with a water pistol or bulb baster.

Smoke-Cooking Instructions

During the last hour of marinating, start the fire. Place a foil pan directly below the grill on the firebed or if your unit is too small to accommodate either, make a small pan of double-thickness foil. Arrange the briquets in a circle or two rows, depending upon the shape of the grill. Light and allow 30 to 40 minutes for the coals to turn gray all over. For a strong smoke flavor, begin scattering the coals with the dampened hickory chips or fruitwood prunings. Place the pork strips over the lightly greased grill about 4 inches from the firebed. Close the barbecuing unit with its own hood or cover the grill with a high-domed lid of any sort. Be sure that there is some ventilation between the fire and the grill. Smoke the meat 30 minutes, turning the strips, basting with marinade and adding more twigs or chips as needed to create smoke. For less smoky flavor, add the smoking agents only during the last 15 minutes of cooking. With a sharp knife, cut each strip into $\frac{1}{8}$-inch diagonal slices. Arrange on a platter in rows, with the slices overlapping. For an appetizer plate, arrange in overlapping slices, alternating with slices of tissue-thin Virginia ham, White-Cut Chicken (page 194) or cold Red-Stewed Spiced Beef (page 160). Garnish with Chinese pickles. Thin slices of barbecued pork are often used to garnish soups, eggs and noodle dishes. Minced, it forms the basis of pastry stuffings.

SERVINGS: Enough for 6 as a single course or for 12 as an appetizer.

BARBECUED SPARERIBS

Oven Time: 30 minutes for bony sections, 1 hour for thicker sections
Outdoor-Barbecuing Time: 30 minutes for bony sections, 1 hour for thicker sections

Equipment for Oven Method
Pan for marinating pork
Foil-covered shallow pan
6 metal skewers (6 inches long)

Equipment for Outdoor Method
Any barbecuing unit
Materials and utensils for building and
    tending fire (pages 259–260)

Ingredients
Marinade I or II (page 268)   3   pounds lean meaty spareribs

Before Cooking
Prepare Marinade I or II; pour into the pan. Try to find short back ribs, which are smaller, meatier and have less fat. Have butcher split the ribs down the middle and crack them for easier serving. Trim away excess fat. Pierce through the meaty sections of the ribs with a fork and brush them with the marinade. Let them marinate in the pan at least 2 hours. They may be refrigerated during this time but should be brought back to room temperature before cooking.

Cooking Instructions for Oven Method
Do not preheat oven. Pierce the ribs with metal skewers and hang them from the top rack of your oven over the foil-covered shallow pan. Turn oven to 325° F. and

roast bony sections of ribs 30 minutes, brushing occasionally with marinade remaining in the pan. Roast thicker portions 1 hour. Roast only until the meat no longer shows pink. The ribs will crisp nicely in the even low heat. Cut into serving pieces, allowing 2 rib sections per person.

Outdoor-Barbecuing Instructions
During the last hour of marinating, prepare a low firebed (200° to 250° F.). The coals must be gray all over (30 to 40 minutes). Lay the ribs on a lightly oiled grill 4 inches from the firebed. Barbecue the bony sections 30 minutes and allow 1 hour for the meatier portions. Turn the ribs often and baste with remaining marinade. Cut into serving pieces, allowing 2 rib sections per person.

SERVINGS: Enough for 3 as a single course or for 6 as an appetizer.

MARINADES FOR BARBECUED PORK STRIPS OR SPARERIBS

MARINADE I

¼ cup sugar
3 tablespoons sherry
2 teaspoons soy sauce
⅓ cup Hoisin sauce
1 teaspoon minced ginger root

¼ teaspoon five-spice seasoning
1½ teaspoons salt
⅛ teaspoon red food coloring (optional)

Dissolve the sugar in the sherry and soy sauce. Add Hoisin sauce, ginger root, five-spice seasoning and salt. Tint with red food coloring, adding more if you prefer a deeper red. This recipe will produce a rich glaze without a predominantly soy sauce flavor.

AMOUNT: Enough for 2 to 3 pounds pork strips or 3 pounds spareribs.

MARINADE II

3 tablespoons soy sauce
⅓ cup Hoisin sauce
2 tablespoons sherry
2 tablespoons honey

⅛ teaspoon salt
1 teaspoon minced ginger root
⅛ teaspoon red food coloring

Combine the ingredients. This marinade will produce a deep brown glaze with a distinct soy sauce flavor.

AMOUNT: Enough for 2 to 3 pounds pork strips or 3 pounds spareribs.

OUTDOOR-BARBECUED BEEF SHORT RIBS

Barbecuing Time: 15 to 25 minutes

Equipment
Pan for marinating short ribs
Bowl
Any barbecuing unit
Materials and utensils for building and
    tending fire (pages 259–260)
Chinese cutting knife

Ingredients

4	pounds short ribs	$\frac{1}{4}$	cup sherry
1	teaspoon finely minced ginger root	$\frac{1}{4}$	cup water
		1	tablespoon sesame oil
2	cloves garlic, finely minced	$\frac{1}{2}$	teaspoon star anise
3	scallions with some of green, cut in $\frac{1}{2}$-inch rounds	$\frac{1}{4}$	teaspoon Szechuan pepper
$\frac{1}{2}$	cup soy sauce	2	tablespoons brown sugar

Before Cooking
Have short ribs cracked at 2-inch intervals. Pierce well with a fork and place in the pan. Add ginger root, garlic and scallions to the meat in the pan. Combine the soy sauce, sherry, water, sesame oil, star anise, Szechuan pepper and brown sugar in the bowl. Stir well to blend and pour over meat. Marinate in the refrigerator 3 to 4 hours. Bring to room temperature before barbecuing.

Barbecuing Instructions

Prepare a medium to hot firebed (300° to 350° F.). The coals must be gray all over (30 to 40 minutes). Place short ribs bone-side-down on grill 4 inches from firebed. Turn every few minutes until the meat is crisply browned on all sides. Allow 15 minutes for rare, 17 for medium rare, 20 for medium and 25 for well done. Chop into 2-inch serving pieces.

SERVINGS: Enough for 4 as a single course or for 6 to 8 in a full menu.

PRECOOKED BARBECUED BEEF SHORT RIBS

If you like your meat well done, very tender, but still with a barbecued flavor, try this procedure. Have the butcher crack 4 pounds of short ribs at 2-inch intervals. Place the short ribs in a saucepan with 1 onion and enough water to cover. Bring to a boil and let simmer 2 to $2\frac{1}{2}$ hours, or until the meat is very tender. Turn the ribs during the simmering for even cooking. Drain and reserve the rich beef stock for soup. Place the drained short ribs in the marinade and let stand 1 hour. Prepare a medium to hot firebed (325° to 350° F.). The coals must be gray all over. Drain the short ribs and place on the barbecue grill 4 inches from the firebed. Barbecue 10 minutes, turning the ribs from time to time. Short ribs precooked in this manner are less resilient than the non-precooked; the fibers are more gelatinous and the flavor of the marinade is deeply absorbed. It is obviously not a dish for those who like their meat rare.

SERVINGS: Enough for 4 as a single course or for 6 to 8 in a full menu.

OUTDOOR-BARBECUED BEEF OR LAMB ON SKEWERS,
Peking Style

Barbecuing Time: 6 to 8 minutes for beef
              12 to 16 minutes for lamb

Equipment
Chinese cutting knife
Pan for marinating meat
Bowl
Any barbecuing unit
Materials and utensils for building and
    tending fire
Skewers

Ingredients

2	pounds filet of beef or boned leg of lamb	$\frac{1}{8}$	teaspoon salt
2	tablespoons soy sauce	1	small leek, white part only, chopped semi-fine
1	tablespoon sherry, gin or vodka	2	large cloves garlic, minced
1	teaspoon brown sugar	1	slice ginger root (2x1x$\frac{1}{8}$ inch)

Before Cooking

Trim the gristle and fat from the meat. Cut meat into $1\frac{1}{2}$-inch dice. Combine the soy sauce, liquor, brown sugar and salt in the bowl. Add the leek, garlic and ginger root. Pierce the meat cubes with a fork and add to the soy-leek mixture. Let meat marinate while you prepare the firebed.

Barbecuing Instructions

Prepare a hot firebed (375° F.). The coals must be gray all over (30 to 40 minutes). Drain the meat cubes and skewer them. Place on grill 3 inches from firebed. Barbecue 3 to 4 minutes on each side for rare beef, 6 to 8 minutes on each side for medium-rare lamb. Both the beef and lamb may be barbecued longer if you prefer the meat well done. Serve as is or with steamed rice.

SERVINGS: Enough for 4 to 6 as a single course or for 8 as an appetizer.

NOTE: The type and size of skewers that you use is unimportant. If you are serving this dish as an appetizer you may want to cut the meat into $\frac{3}{4}$-inch dice and thread them onto bamboo skewers.

OVEN-BARBECUED CHICKEN OR DUCK,

Cantonese Style

Cooking Time: 1 to $1\frac{1}{4}$ hours for chicken
$1\frac{3}{4}$ to 2 hours for duck

Utensils
Roasting pan
Rack for roasting pan
6-inch metal skewer
Foil-covered shallow pan for drippings
4 squares of aluminum foil (4x4 inches)

Ingredients

1	whole fryer (3½ pounds) or duckling (4 to 6 pounds)	1	teaspoon fennel seeds, crushed
1	teaspoon salt	¼	teaspoon five-spice seasoning
4	cloves garlic, minced	1	cup soy sauce
2	teaspoons minced ginger root	1	tablespoon sherry, gin or vodka
2	teaspoons minced Chinese parsley	2	tablespoons honey
4	scallions with some of green, cut in ½-inch rounds		Chinese parsley for decorating

Before Cooking

Rinse the bird thoroughly. Blot dry with paper towels. Rub inside and out with 1 teaspoon salt. Set aside to dry while you prepare marinade. Place the garlic, ginger root, parsley, scallions, fennel seeds and five-spice seasoning in the roasting pan. Add the soy sauce, liquor and honey. Blend well. There are two ways of marinating the bird. The first and simplest method is to place the bird in the marinade and let it stand 1 hour, turning it several times and making sure that the cavity is filled with the sauce. The second method is slightly more painstaking, but it is also more authentic. Rub the surface of the bird with the marinade and sew up the neck cavity. Pour the marinade into the body cavity and sew shut so that the liquid cannot leak out. The roasted chickens and ducks seen in Chinatown grocery stores are cooked with their heads and necks intact, which makes the business of hanging a filled bird much easier. If you choose to fill the bird with marinade, use the roasting-rack method of cooking or buy a fresh bird with head and neck intact (see Classic Peking Duck, pages 273–276).

Cooking Instructions for Roasting-Rack Method (For bird filled with marinade)

FOR CHICKEN: Turn oven to 350° F. (do not preheat). Rest chicken, breast side up on a rack in the roasting pan. Place on the middle rack of the oven. Roast 15 minutes; turn chicken and roast breast side down 15 minutes. Reduce heat to 325° F. Turn chicken breast side up again and continue cooking 30 to 45 minutes or until done. When pulled, the chicken leg should move easily.

FOR DUCK: Turn oven to 325° F. (do not preheat). Rest duck breast side up on rack in the roasting pan. Place on the middle rack of the oven. Roast 15 minutes; turn duck and roast breast side down 15 minutes. Cover wings and legs with foil. Siphon off accumulated fat in pan with a bulb baster. Reduce heat to 250° F. and roast breast side up 30 minutes, then breast side down another 30 minutes. Turn heat up again to 350° F. and roast breast side up 15 to 30 minutes. Do not prick or baste duck during roasting.

When the chicken or duck has been roasted, remove from the oven and let stand 15 minutes. Remove threads. Drain bird in a colander. The drained sauce may be served as an accompaniment to the bird. Cut into Chinese-style serving pieces and decorate with sprigs of Chinese parsley.

Cooking Instructions for Rotisserie Method (For marinated but not filled bird)
Use the same timing and temperatures for chicken and duck as for the Roasting-Rack Method. Cover wings and legs of duck with foil after 30 minutes. Collect drippings in foil-covered pan at the bottom of the oven and siphon off fat periodically.

Cooking Instructions for Hanging Method (For marinated but not filled bird)
With a skewer, hang the bird by its neck from the top rack of the oven. Place a foil-covered pan in the bottom of the oven to collect drippings. Use the same timing and temperatures for chicken and duck as for the Roasting-Rack Method. Cover wings and legs of duck with foil after 30 minutes if they appear to be browning too quickly.

SERVINGS: Enough for 4 as a single course or for 6 in a full menu.

BARBECUED CHICKEN OR DUCK WITH SWEET-AND-SOUR SAUCE
OR LICHEE SAUCE
Before roasting the bird, prepare any of the Sweet-and-Sour Sauces (pages 353–356) or the Lichee Sauce (page 358). Set aside. When the bird has been barbecued, reheat sauce gently and pour over. Or cut bird into Chinese-style serving pieces and combine with the sauce.

SERVINGS: Enough for 4 as a single course or for 6 in a full menu.

CLASSIC PEKING DUCK

Cooking Time: 1¾ to 2 hours

Utensils
Small sharp knife
Plastic or glass straw
Twine

Continued on next page

Large colander
Roasting pan
Saucer for glaze
Pastry brush
6-inch metal skewer
Roasting rack
Foil-covered shallow pan
4 squares of aluminium foil (4x4 inches)

Ingredients

1	dressed fresh duck (5 pounds), with head	2	tablespoons soy sauce
2	tablespoons honey	1	tablespoon light corn syrup (optional)
4	cups boiling water	1	teaspoon soy sauce (optional)
2	cups sherry		Mandarin Pancakes (page 325)

Before Cooking

The night before roasting, wash the duck inside and out. Pull away the threadlike particles in the cavity and remove excess fat which clings to skin at the opening. Remove oil sacs directly above tail. Reserve the duck feet, gizzard and heart to make a stock with the duck carcass later.

Authentic Peking Duck depends entirely on the treatment of the skin, which must be crackly yet succulent. To achieve this, the skin must be separated from the flesh by means of air, which is blown underneath it. The air acts as insulation between the flesh and the skin. With the small sharp knife, pierce the duck's neck in the front below the head. The cut should be $\frac{1}{8}$-inch deep and $\frac{1}{2}$-inch long. Grasp the duck's head with one hand and insert the straw into the hole. Blow air into the space between the skin and the neck until the duck has puffed up to its maximum. Tie the twine several times around the neck below the incision to prevent the air from escaping. Don't worry about the cavity. Correctly blown into the duck's skin and secured by twine, the air will remain there. At this point, however, you can dispose of the head by cutting it off above the incision. You will need this hole to hang the duck for drying and, if the construction of your oven permits, for roasting as well.

Hold the inflated bird in a colander over the roasting pan. Combine the honey with the boiling water. Pour the honey-water mixture in a slow trickle over the bird. Siphon back the water and repeat the pouring or, after one pouring, remove the colander and dip the duck on each side in the hot honey-water about 5 times or until the duck is almost white. This blanching process has an astringent effect on the skin and allows for a crisply roasted surface. Drain the bird and blot outside and in the cavity with paper towels. Rinse out the roasting pan and combine the sherry and soy sauce in it. Place the duck in the marinade and let stand 3 hours, turning the bird 4 times.

Drain the duck. Blot with paper towels inside and out. Combine the corn syrup and soy sauce in the saucer and, using the pastry brush, "glaze" the duck all over. Glazing makes the duck darker in color when done and is optional.

Bend the length of the metal skewer into a hook. Force the hooked tip of the skewer into the hole in the duck's neck. Hang the duck by the skewer from a clothes line or a nail on the molding of your kitchen door. Place a pan under the bird to catch the drainage. Let the duck hang 8 to 12 hours, preferably in a draft. At this point the duck will be a creamy golden color with the skin parchment-dry. There will be surprisingly little drainage in the pan. Do not attempt to blot the insides. Moisture contained within the bird's body is desirable. Only the exterior must be dry.

While the duck is hanging, make the Mandarin Pancakes (page 325) and refrigerate until 10 to 15 minutes before serving time. The Scallion Flowers and sauces at the end of recipe to be served with the duck may be prepared just before roasting.

If you are ready to roast right after the hanging and drying process, proceed at once with Cooking Instructions. If you have several hours before roasting, refrigerate the bird on a rack and cover with plastic wrap until 30 minutes before cooking. Remove from refrigerator and let come to room temperature.

Cooking Instructions
There are three methods of roasting:

HANGING METHOD: Turn oven to 325° F. (do not preheat). Using the skewer, suspend the bird from the top rack of the oven and place a foil-covered pan beneath it to collect the drippings. Roast 30 minutes, watching for areas which brown too rapidly. If the wings and legs are getting too brown, cover them with the squares of foil. Remove the accumulated fat in the pan. Reduce heat to 250° F. Roast 1 hour. Remove fat again. Turn up heat to 350° F. and roast 15 to 30 minutes. Do not prick or baste the duck during the roasting.

ROTISSERIE METHOD: Follow the Hanging Method, except use the rotisserie.

RACK-ROASTING METHOD: Turn oven to 325° F. (do not preheat). Place the duck on the rack in the roasting pan. Place on the middle rack of the oven. Roast the bird breast side up 15 minutes. Then turn the duck breast side down and roast 15 minutes. Remove accumulated fat from the pan with bulb baster. Cover wings and legs with foil. Reduce heat to 250° F. Roast breast side up 30 minutes, then breast side down 30 minutes. Siphon off accumulated fat in the pan. Turn heat up to 350° F. Roast breast side up 15 to 30 minutes. Do not prick or baste the duck during the roasting. It is absolutely essential that a rack be used to elevate the duck from the roasting pan. If it were to lie flat, the resulting steam would cause the skin to become soggy and the portions resting in its own fat would tend to scorch and stick to the pan.

When done, the duck will have a dark russet-brown skin, crisp to the point of being crackly. The cavity will contain juices like a broth and the meat will be tender and succulent. Allow the duck to stand uncovered in a warm place 20 minutes before carving.

TO SERVE: Traditionally, the skin alone is served. The duck meat is used for another occasion. But the idea of a banquet of duck skin is just too removed for most Westerners to appreciate, and since the duck meat roasted in this manner is delectable, I suggest that you serve the meat along with the skin. Traditionally also, no salt is used in the cooking of Peking Duck, since the bland richness of the duck skin is meant to be accentuated by the condiment sauces. The small amount of soy sauce incorporated into the marinade and glaze is just enough to enliven the duck flavor.

Each person should be given a pair of chopsticks and a plate (bowls are not used with this specialty). The Scallion Flowers and condiment sauces should be on the table. The duck is brought on a platter at the same time that the Mandarin Pancakes are served. These must be piping hot and should come to the table in a closed container. Each guest takes one of the folded pancakes and opens it on his plate. Working fast, the host begins to carve. First the wings are removed. The skin and meat from the breast, thighs, legs and back are sliced into 2-inch squares. A square of duck is placed on the Mandarin Pancake of each guest, who then dips a scallion in one of the sauces, places it on top of the duck and folds the pancake up and over and begins to eat. This process is repeated until all the duck has been eaten.

SERVINGS: Enough for 4 as a single course with Mandarin Pancakes or for 6 in a full menu.

SAUCE TO SERVE WITH PEKING DUCK

¼ cup canned Hoisin sauce   ½ teaspoon sesame oil
1 tablespoon light soy sauce

Combine ingredients and spoon into 3 Chinese condiment saucers or ordinary saucers. Allow 1 saucer of condiment for 2 people.

PLUM SAUCE TO SERVE WITH PEKING DUCK

Spoon from can into 3 Chinese condiment saucers or ordinary saucers. Allow 1 saucer of condiment for 2 people.

SCALLION FLOWERS TO SERVE WITH PEKING DUCK

12 scallions   Ice water

Wash scallions and trim ½ inch from root end. Cut away the green tops, leaving 3 to 4 inches of the white tubular portion. Make sharp notches ½ inch deep all around at both ends of each scallion piece. Place in a bowl of ice water 1 to 2 hours. The scallion ends will curl into petals. Drain and serve in a bowl.

OUTDOOR-BARBECUED OR
SMOKE-COOKED CHICKEN OR DUCK

Cooking Time: 1 to 1½ hours for chicken
1 to 2 hours for duck

Equipment
Large bowl for marinating bird
Any barbecuing unit and materials for
   building fire
Barbecue hood or cover (for smoking)
Dampened hickory chips or fruitwood
   prunings (for smoking)

Ingredients

1   fryer (3 pounds) or duckling (4
    to 6 pounds), split
¾   cup soy sauce
¼   cup sherry
2   teaspoons brown sugar
1   tablespoon finely minced ginger
    root

1   teaspoon crushed fennel seeds
4   scallions, cut in ½-inch rounds
    (for duck only)
1   piece dried tangerine peel, 2
    inches in diameter (for duck
    only)

Before Cooking
Rinse the bird in cold water; drain and blot dry with paper towels. Combine the
soy sauce, sherry and brown sugar in the large bowl. Add the ginger root and fennel to the soy-sherry-sugar mixture. If the marinade is for duck, also add scallions
and tangerine peel. Place the bird in the marinade and refrigerate 2 hours. Let the
bird come to room temperature before barbecuing. Drain well, reserving marinade
for basting.

Barbecuing Instructions
During the last hour of marinating, prepare a medium-hot firebed (300° to
350° F.) for the chicken and a low-medium firebed (275° F.) for the duck with
the briquets arranged around a drip pan. The coals must be gray all over (30 to 40
minutes). Lay the bird skin-side-up on the lightly greased grill 5 inches from the
firebed for chicken and 6 inches for duck. Barbecue the chicken 1 hour, turning
after 30 minutes. Barbecue a 4-pound duck 1 to 1½ hours and a 6-pound duck 1½
to 2 hours. Turn frequently during the barbecuing. Baste either bird with reserved
marinade. The chicken is done when the fleshiest part of the drumstick is fork-tender. The duck's legbone will twist easily from its joint when the bird is cooked.

The duck will be a crusty dark brown with a crackly skin and moist insides. Cut chicken or duck into Chinese-style serving pieces and mound on a platter.

Smoke-Cooking Instructions

Follow the Barbecuing Instructions. When the coals turn gray, scatter with dampened hickory chips or fruitwood prunings. Lay the bird skin-side-up on lightly greased grill 5 inches from the firebed for chicken and 6 inches for duck. Close hood or cover grill. Make sure that there is space between the fire and the covered grill. Smoke-cook chicken 35 to 45 minutes on each side. Smoke-cook 4-pound duck 1 to 1½ hours and 6-pound duck 1½ to 2 hours, turning the halves frequently. Baste chicken or duck with reserved marinade and add chips or prunings to the firebed as needed. Chicken and duck cooked in this manner will be glazed a deep brown. The duck will be crisp on the outside and succulent inside.

Tea-Smoked Chicken or Duck

Follow the Smoke-Cooking Instructions but scatter the coals with 1 or 2 tablespoons of damp used tea leaves, adding more as needed. The timing and other instructions remain the same. Tea leaves with flower buds, such as jasmine, add an exotic flavor. Whole cloves of garlic or star anise sprinkled on the coals enhance the aroma and gently season the bird while it smoke-cooks.

SERVINGS: Enough for 4 as a single course or for 6 in a full menu.

INDOOR SMOKE-COOKED SQUAB, CHICKEN OR DUCK

Steaming Time: 30 to 45 minutes for squab
　　　　　　　45 to 60 minutes for chicken
　　　　　　　1½ to 2 hours for duck
Smoking Time: Same lengths as Steaming Times

Utensils
Large bowl for marinating bird
Steaming unit (See Steaming Instructions,
　　pages 205–207)
11-inch skillet with cover
2 sheets 18-inch aluminum foil (24 inches
　　long)
10-inch cake rack
Wooden spoon

Ingredients

3 squab (1 pound each), 1 fryer (3 pounds) or 1 duckling (4 pounds)	1 tablespoon minced ginger root
¾ cup soy sauce	1 teaspoon crushed fennel seed
¼ cup sherry	1 piece dried tangerine peel (2 inches in diameter)
2 teaspoons sugar	2 tablespoons gin
1 medium onion, cut in wedges	3 tablespoons brown sugar
	Mandarin Pancakes (page 325)

Before Cooking

Split the bird or birds in half. Combine the soy sauce, sherry and sugar in the large bowl. Add the onion, ginger root, fennel seed and dried tangerine peel. Place the birds or bird in the bowl and marinate 2 hours, turning every 30 minutes. While the bird is marinating, assemble your steaming unit. The skillet, wok or electric frypan method may be used for the squab. The chicken or duck requires larger steaming equipment—a soup kettle or roasting pan. When the poultry has marinated, drain the halves well and steam them. The squab will require 30 to 45 minutes, the chicken 45 to 60 minutes and the duck 1½ to 2 hours. While the poultry is steaming, line the skillet and its cover with folded sheets of foil. Grease the rack lightly and set aside. Have gin and brown sugar ready to go. Ventilate the kitchen as much as possible.

Cooking Instructions

Turn heat under foil-lined skillet to medium-high. Add the gin and when warm, light it. When the flames go out, add the brown sugar. Stir with wooden spoon. When the sugar has melted, fit the cake rack in the skillet. When the sugar begins to get dark and bubbly and smokes, place the well-drained steamed poultry halves on the rack. Cover with the foil-lined lid. Smoke the squab 30 to 45 minutes, the chicken 45 to 60 minutes and the duck 1½ to 2 hours. Turn the poultry halves several times during the process. These birds will have a rich brown glaze on their skins. As soon as the birds are done, remove to a chopping board and cut into 1½-inch serving pieces. Assemble on a heat-proof dish and keep warm in 170° F. oven until serving time. Poultry cooked by this indoor-smoking method is juicier and has a tangier flavor than poultry cooked by the outdoor smoke-cooking method.

SERVINGS: Enough for 4 as a single course with rice or Mandarin Pancakes or for 6 in a full menu.

TEA-SMOKED SQUAB, CHICKEN OR DUCK: Substitute used tea leaves for the brown sugar. The tea leaves impart a subtle and unusual smoked flavor to the poultry.

OUTDOOR-BARBECUED OR
SMOKE-COOKED FISH STEAKS

Cooking Time: 16 to 20 minutes

Equipment
Pan for marinating fish
Small bowl for marinade
Any barbecuing unit
Materials and utensils for building and
    tending fire
Barbecue hood or cover (for smoking)
Dampened hickory chips or fruitwood
    prunings (for smoking)

Ingredients

2	pounds fish filets or steaks (¾-inch thick), with skin	½	teaspoon sesame oil
2	tablespoons soy sauce	½	teaspoon salt
2	teaspoons sherry	1	slice ginger root (2x1x⅛ inch)

Before Cooking
Place fish in the pan. Combine soy sauce, sherry, sesame oil, salt and ginger root in the small bowl; sprinkle over fish. Cover with plastic wrap and refrigerate 4 hours. Before starting fire, remove fish from refrigerator. Drain well on paper towels and reserve marinade for basting.

Barbecuing Instructions

Prepare a medium-hot firebed (325° F.). The coals must be gray all over (30 to 40 minutes). Place grill 3 inches from firebed and brush lightly with oil. Place the fish on the grill. Barbecue 8 to 10 minutes on each side, brushing the top side with reserved marinade. Turn fish carefully with a spatula. Test with a fork. If the fish flakes easily, it is done. Do not overcook or the fish will dry out.

Smoke-Cooking Instructions

Follow the Barbecuing Instructions. When the coals turn gray, scatter with dampened hickory chips or fruitwood prunings. Place fish on lightly oiled grill 3 inches from firebed. Close hood or cover grill with a lid that fits over it. Make sure there is space between the fire and covered grill. Smoke fish 8 to 10 minutes on each side. It will have a dark brown glaze.

SERVINGS: Enough for 4 as a single course or for 6 in a full menu.

NOTE: Instead of the marinade, you may simply brush the fish with a mixture of 2 tablespoons lemon juice, 1 tablespoon oil, 1 teaspoon salt and ½ teaspoon minced ginger root.

OUTDOOR-BARBECUED OR
SMOKE-COOKED WHOLE FISH

Cooking Time: 50 minutes

Equipment
Large pan for marinating fish
Baking parchment
Aluminum foil
Expanded aluminum mesh (available in
    hardware stores)
Narrow wire
Pastry brush
Any barbecue unit
Materials and utensils for building and
    tending fire
Barbecue hood or cover (for smoking)
Dampened hickory chips or fruitwood
    prunings (for smoking)

Ingredients

1	whole bass, carp or salmon (2½ to 3 pounds)	⅛	teaspoon salt
½	cup soy sauce	3	scallions with some of green, cut into ¼-inch rounds
¼	cup sherry	2	slices ginger root (2x1x⅛ inch)
1	teaspoon sesame oil	1	tablespoon peanut oil or corn oil
½	teaspoon brown sugar		

Before Cooking

Have the fish cleaned and scaled but leave the head and tail intact. Rinse fish in cold water and blot dry with paper towels. Combine the soy sauce, sherry, sesame oil, brown sugar, salt, scallions and ginger root in the large pan. Place fish in the marinade and refrigerate 1 hour, turning once. While the coals are burning down in the firebed, remove fish from the refrigerator and blot dry with paper towels. Wrap the head and tail first in baking parchment and then in foil. Measure a strip of expanded aluminum slightly longer than the length of the fish and about 2½ times its width. The casing must be loose enough to permit the fish to expand during cooking. Thus, it can be turned without breaking. Bend the expanded aluminum mesh so that it makes a jacket or casing into which you can now slip the fish. Secure the sides of the casing with narrow wire. Using a pastry brush, paint both sides of the encased fish with a thin coat of oil.

Barbecuing Instructions

Prepare a low to medium firebed (about 275° F.). The coals must be gray all over (30 to 40 minutes). Place the fish in its mesh casing on the grill 4 inches from the firebed. Barbecue approximately 25 minutes on each side or until the thickest part of the fish flakes easily with a fork when tested. Remove the fish from the grill. Snip the wire which has secured the casing and fold the top layer back. Remove foil and parchment from head and tail and slide fish with back of casing intact onto a heated platter. Removing the fish from the casing entirely at this point might cause it to break.

Smoke-Cooking Instructions

Follow the Barbecuing Instructions. When the coals turn gray, scatter with dampened hickory chips or fruitwood prunings. If your unit has a hood, close it or cover your grill with a lid that fits over it. Make sure there is ventilation between the fire and grill. Smoke fish approximately 25 minutes on each side. Whole fish lends itself perfectly to smoke-cooking and is even more succulent than when open-barbecued.

SERVINGS: Enough for 6 as a single course or for 8 to 10 in a full menu.

INDOOR SMOKE-COOKED FISH SLICES

Prefrying Time: 8 minutes
Smoking Time: 5 minutes

Utensils
Pan for marinating fish
11-inch skillet with cover
Two sheets 18-inch aluminum foil (24 inches long)
9-inch foil pie plate
10-inch cake rack
Wooden spoon
Spatula

Ingredients

2 pounds carp or scup filets or steaks (¾ inch thick), with skin	½ teaspoon five-spice seasoning
2 teaspoons salt	1 slice ginger root (2x1x⅛ inch)
1 tablespoon soy sauce	2 tablespoons gin
1 teaspoon sherry	3 tablespoons brown sugar
	2 tablespoons peanut oil or corn oil

Before Cooking
Rub fish with salt and wrap loosely with plastic wrap. Refrigerate 12 hours or overnight. Rinse in cold water to remove salt. Place in the pan and sprinkle with the soy sauce, sherry and five-spice seasoning. Marinate at room temperature 30 minutes. Drain well and blot dry before frying. Prepare ginger root. Measure gin and brown sugar. Have oil ready to go.

Prefrying Instructions
Turn heat under skillet to medium-high. Add oil. When oil begins to sizzle, add ginger root and fish. Fry 4 minutes on each side, turning with spatula. Drain fried fish on paper towels. Discard ginger slice.

Smoke-Cooking Instructions
Wash out skillet in which fish slices were fried. Line the skillet and its cover with folded sheets of foil. Pierce the base of a lightly oiled 9-inch foil pie plate all over with a pick and lay fish on it. Have cake rack ready. Ventilate the kitchen as much as possible. Turn heat under foil-lined skillet to medium-high. Add the gin and

when warm, light it. When the flames go out, add the brown sugar. Stir with wooden spoon. When the sugar has melted, fit the cake rack into the skillet and put the perforated pie plate on top of it; cover with the foil-lined lid. Smoke, without turning the fish, 5 minutes. Remove fish with a spatula to a heated dish. The fish will have a brown glaze and tangy flavor.

SERVINGS: Enough for 4 as a single course or for 6 in a full menu.

PLAIN SMOKE-COOKED FISH SLICES: Prefry as directed but omit soy sauce, sherry and five-spice seasoning when smoke-cooking. This will produce golden-brown fish slices with a subtle smoky flavor.

HOT POT COOKING-TECHNIQUE 8

己己己己己己己己己己己己己己

Hot Pot Cooking is a uniquely Oriental type of cooking and quite unlike any Western method, almost too simple a procedure to be labeled a technique.

The basic idea of the hot pot originated with the nomadic Mongolians, who speared thin slivers of lamb or mutton and plunged them into large cauldrons filled with boiling liquid. The household fire pot began as a method of heating rooms by burning charcoal in a small pot. With typical thriftiness, the Chinese made the fuel serve two purposes; thus the chafing pot, which could warm a room and serve as a cooking utensil at the same time, evolved.

Chafing pots are made of copper, brass or pewter. The most popular and readily available are the brass ones. They have a tapered chimney 5 to 7 inches tall with a bowl, or moat, 9 to 15 inches in diameter. The bowl is filled with liquid (usually stock) and the chimney half-filled with coals which have already been ignited and are at the glowing stage. There is a cover which fits over the chimney and bowl. Oriental chafing pots are available in Chinese hardware stores and at import outlets. They come in several sizes and range from under $5 to about $25. Make sure that the one you buy is intended for cooking and not solely for decorative purposes. (Ornamental pots may have metal lining that is unsuitable for cooking.)

If you own an Oriental chafing pot, pour the liquid into the bowl, or moat, before adding the coals to the chimney. If you don't happen to have one, try the following recipes in any covered casserole or pot on a hot plate set at simmer or in a large electric frypan set at 250° F. An ordinary chafing dish is not practical because the heat is difficult to control.

In Hot Pot Cooking, the bowl is filled with broth and the food to be cooked is finely sliced and presented on little plates. The guests select their portions and place them in a small bowl. Each guest uses chopsticks to dip the meat, fish or fowl for just a minute or two in the steaming broth. (Pork strips cook longer. They should be dropped in the pot for about 5 minutes.) Then the food is eaten. When all the meats have been consumed, the greens are added and cooked with the lid of the pot on. They are then served with the broth. Sometimes the host cooks and serves his guests, but cooking one's own tidbits is much more fun. If the idea of each person dipping his chopsticks into the bowl seems unhygienic to you, get some long-handled mesh spoons (available at Chinese hardware stores). Those serve perfectly to transport the food from the pot to the individual bowls.

There are many variations of Chinese Hot Pot Cooking, as well as adaptations by the Koreans (who use ground pork and nuts in their most popular version, called *Sin-Su-Low*). The Japanese, too, borrowed the basic idea—the resultant country dish, which they call *Mizutaki,* is enormously enhanced by the addition of a crushed sesame seed sauce. The recipes given here are for the Chinese versions, including a Fukienese Hot Pot recipe which consists entirely of fish. The Fukienese Hot Pot resembles to a slight degree the French *bouillabaise* or some of the Japanese *suimonos,* but because it relies on a base of chicken stock rather than a fish stock, it is much more delicate. The Cantonese generally treat their Hot Pot Cooking as a kitchen affair. The recipe for Cantonese Hot Pot may be cooked in the kitchen if you prefer, but it is a little more festive if the food is cooked at the table. Also given here is the more ceremonial Chrysanthemum Pot, which entails the use of that flower's petals.

USING AN ORIENTAL CHAFING POT

Put 3 or 4 charcoal briquets on a foil broiling pan. You may have to cut the briquets in half, depending on the size of the chimney. Sprinkle briquets with liquid fire starter and ignite. Be sure to light the briquets away from curtains and other

Oriental Chafing Pot
Pot, filled with broth heated by briquets in center funnel, is surrounded by dishes of food to be cooked.

flammable materials. Do it outdoors, if you can. Let the briquets burn down until they are gray. Pour 6 cups of the boiling stock into the bowl, or moat, of the hot pot. Using tongs, place the coals on the grill of the cooker. Cover the pot and ask your guests to sit down.

POINTS TO REMEMBER IN HOT POT COOKING

This is a single-course dinner. The guests need a plate for the food, a bowl for the broth, a small saucer for dipping sauce, a small bowl for tea, chopsticks and long-handled mesh spoons. These are the only utensils needed except for an Oriental chafing pot, a 2½-quart casserole on a hot plate set at simmer or an electric frypan set at 250° F. Since these are so basic, they are not repeated with each recipe.

All the ingredients, except a few which are dried or canned, must be raw and finely sliced or shredded. They should be very fresh and of the best quality.

Let your imagination go when it comes to ingredients—baby abalone, squid, slivers of eel. Also use imagination in choosing the dipping sauces. And remember, the food must be held in the boiling stock only until it is just cooked. The Chinese call this "rinsing" the food.

Pass scented hot towels after the broth has been drunk. Fresh fruit or canned mandarin oranges, lichees or loquats are appropriate for dessert.

Hot Pot Cooking
1. Cut all ingredients in wafer-thin strips.   2. Strips are dipped into boiling broth by each guest until just cooked.   3. When the variety of meat, poultry or fish has been eaten, vegetables are added and simmered in covered pot. Broth and vegetables are then served in bowls.

PEKING TEN PRECIOUS POT

Cooking Time: 1 to 2 minutes for meats, poultry and fish
                 3 to 4 minutes for vegetables

Ingredients

16	small shrimp	½	cup squid
1	raw chicken breast, skinned and boned	½	pound spinach
		½	pound celery cabbage
⅛	pound Virginia ham	8	cups seasoned chicken stock
½	pound pork tenderloin	2	slices ginger root (3x1½x⅛ inch)
1	cup chicken livers		Dipping Sauces (pages 351–352)
½	pound boned carp		

Before Cooking

Wash, peel and devein shrimp. Cut chicken breast, ham and pork into strips, 2x½x⅛ inch. Wash chicken livers and remove connective tissue; slice thinly. Cut the carp and squid into thin 1½-inch squares. Choosing only the youngest stalks of spinach, rinse in warm water to remove grit. Scrub the roots and retain them. Pluck into small clusters. Slice the celery cabbage into thin shreds. All this may be done the night before or several hours ahead of time. Arrange the foods attractively on plates and cover with plastic wrap. Thirty minutes before cooking, remove food from the refrigerator. Add the ginger slices to the stock and bring to a boil in the kitchen. Fill the cooking utensil with 6 cups of boiling stock.

Cooking Instructions

Place the covered hot pot, casserole on a hot plate or electric frypan on the table. Have the guests help themselves. When all the meats have been eaten, add the extra 2 cups of stock if necessary and cook the vegetables 3 to 4 minutes with the cover on. The vegetables and soup are ladled into each bowl as the last step in the meal. Each guest should be supplied with a small dish of dipping sauce; for instance, Ginger-Soy Dip, Garlic-Soy Dip, "Chekiang" Vinegar or all three if you wish.

SERVINGS: Enough for 6 to 8.

INGREDIENT VARIATIONS: Raw crab meat, pork kidneys, precooked chicken gizzards, bass, eel, duck meat, pork balls, Chinese sausage, flank steak, dandelion greens, watercress, mustard greens, fresh or fried bean curd, bean thread noodles, rice noodles, egg noodles, dried soaked mushrooms—these are but a few of the wide assortment of Chinese ingredients which may be used in Hot Pot Cooking. Only the freshest of raw ingredients should be considered.

MONGOLIAN HOT POT

Cooking Time: 1 hour to presimmer stock
2 to 3 minutes for lamb and liver

Ingredients

3	pounds boned leg of lamb	2	tablespoons sherry, gin or vodka
3	lamb livers (optional)	2	whole leeks, cut in ¼-inch rounds
8	cups seasoned chicken stock	3	cloves garlic, minced
	Lamb bone, cracked		Dipping Sauces (pages 351–352)

Procedure

Trim all fat from the lamb and cut into sheer strips (2x½x⅛ inch). Rinse livers. Cut away connective tissue and slice into matching strips. Arrange liver and lamb on separate plates, allowing one plate of each per guest. Combine the stock with the cracked lamb bone and sherry and bring to a boil in the kitchen. Simmer 1 hour. Add the leeks and garlic. Meanwhile, set the table. Arrange dishes of "Chekiang" Vinegar, Chinese-Style Mustard and a small bottle of Red Pepper Oil for the guests to dip their food into. Use only 6 cups of broth, reserving 2 to be added as needed.

SERVINGS: Enough for 6 to 8.

NOTE: Additional vegetables and cooked wheat noodles may be added at the end of the meat cooking, but the traditional Mongolian Hot Pot is starkly simple, principally the lamb strips and liver barely cooked in the hot stock and eaten with strong condiment sauces. Steamed Chinese wheat buns may be served to eat with the lamb sandwich-fashion.

器 CANTONESE HOT POT

Cooking Time: 1 to 2 minutes for meat and fish
3 to 4 minutes for vegetables

Ingredients

8	cups unsalted chicken stock	½	pound raw crab
1	tablespoon soy sauce	1	cup canned button mushrooms
1	tablespoon sherry, gin or vodka	3	squares bean curd
2	teaspoons sesame oil	½	pound Chinese chard
2	slices ginger root (3x1½x⅛ inch)	½	pound spinach
½	pound flank steak, partially frozen	3	scallions
¼	pound Virginia ham		Dipping Sauces (pages 351–352)
½	pound sea bass, boned and skinned		

Procedure

Combine the stock, soy sauce, liquor, sesame oil and ginger root in a saucepan. Thaw flank steak about 15 minutes and cut into diagonal slices (2x½x⅛ inch). Cut ham into slices similar to the beef. Cut the sea bass into thin 1½-inch squares. Pick over the crab for shells and cartilage and shred coarsely. Arrange beef, ham, sea bass and crab on individual plates. Slice button mushrooms in half. Cut each square of bean curd into 4 cubes. Wash the Chinese chard, pick away yellow flow-erets and cut diagonally into ½-inch slices. Soak spinach in warm water to loosen grit and rinse in cold water. Retain roots. Separate into small clusters. Trim the scallions, retaining about 1 inch of the green, and cut into ¼-inch rounds. Arrange mushrooms, bean curd, chard, spinach and scallions on separate plates. Set the table. Arrange dishes of condiment sauces, such as Ginger-Soy Dip or Garlic-Soy Dip, "Chekiang" Vinegar and/or Chinese-Style Mustard for dipping. Bring the stock mixture to a boil in the kitchen. Pour 6 cups of the stock into the cooking pot on the table; reserve the other 2 cups for adding to the pot as needed. When the meat and fish are eaten, cook the vegetables adding the scallions last.

SERVINGS: Enough for 6.

FUKIENESE HOT POT

Cooking Time: 1 to 2 minutes for fish slices
              3 to 4 minutes for vegetables and noodles

Ingredients

8	cups unsalted chicken stock	1	pound canned abalone
1½	tablespoons soy sauce	½	pound squid
1	tablespoon sherry, gin or vodka	1	pound sea bass, boned and skinned
2	teaspoons sesame oil		
2	slices giner root (3x1½x⅛ inch)	1	large bamboo shoot
3	scallions with some of green, cut in ¼-inch rounds	1	bunch watercress
		¼	pound rice stick noodles
½	pound small shrimp	2	cups boiling water
¾	pound scallops		Few sprigs Chinese parsley
½	pound oysters, shucked		Dipping Sauces (pages 351–352)

Before Cooking

Combine the stock, soy sauce, liquor, sesame oil, ginger root and scallions in a saucepan. Wash, peel and devein shrimp. Drain well. Cut scallops in half, rinse and dry on paper towels. Drain oysters. Drain abalone and cut into wafer-thin squares. Clean and peel squid; cut into wafer-thin squares. Cut bass into 1½-inch squares. Arrange fish slices on individual plates. Cut bamboo shoot into thin strips. Soak watercress; drain well and pluck into flowerets. Arrange bamboo shoots and watercress on separate plates. Soak rice stick noodles in 2 cups boiling water 20 minutes; drain well. You should have about 2 cups. Place rice noodles on a separate plate. Rinse Chinese parsley, chop semi-finely and place on a small dish. Set table with cooking pot in the center; surround with plates of the food. Provide each guest with a dish of dipping sauce. Bring the stock to a boil in the kitchen. Pour 6 cups of stock into the cooking pot on the table, reserving the other 2 cups of stock to add as needed.

Cooking Instructions

Cook the slivers of fish briefly, allowing just enough time for the color to change from transparent to opaque. The canned abalone, which has been precooked, should be dipped into the stock just long enough to heat it. Longer cooking will cause toughness. When the fish has been eaten, add the bamboo shoots, watercress and drained rice noodles. Sprinkle with Chinese parsley. Cover and let simmer 3 to 4 minutes. Serve the vegetables and noodles; follow with bowls of broth. The different types of fish impart a very delicate flavor to this soup. Do not add the liquid from the abalone or oysters to the stock. It would destroy the subtle flavor.

SERVINGS: Enough for 6.

NOTE: An authentic dip for this specialty is Chinese shrimp sauce, which is intensely fishy in flavor—so much so that it is used only as a condiment. More acceptable to Western tastes might be dishes of oyster or Hoisin sauce, mustard and Ginger-Soy.

CHRYSANTHEMUM POT

Cooking Time: 1 hour to presimmer stock
2 to 3 minutes for meats, poultry and fish
3 to 4 minutes for vegetables

Ingredients

1	tablespoon dried shrimp	¼	pound chicken livers, connective tissue removed
3	Chinese red dates		
1	piece dried tangerine peel	½	pound flank steak
8	cups seasoned chicken stock	½	pound halibut, boned and skinned
1	tablespoon sherry, gin or vodka	½	pound Chinese cabbage
2	slices ginger root (3x1½x⅛ inch)	1	bunch watercress
1	Chinese sausage, cut in thin diagonal slice	¼	pound bean thread noodles
		2	large chrysanthemum blossoms
1	large chicken breast, skinned and boned	4 to 6	eggs
			Dipping Sauces (pages 351–352)

Before Cooking

An hour ahead of time, soak the dried shrimp, red dates and tangerine peel separately. Combine the stock, liquor and ginger root. Drain the shrimp, dates and tangerine peel. Shred the dates and add all 3 ingredients to the stock with the Chinese sausage. Simmer 1 hour. Cut the chicken breast and livers into thin slices. Cut flank steak into strips, $2\frac{1}{2}$x1x$\frac{1}{16}$ inch. Slice the halibut into thin $1\frac{1}{2}$-inch squares. Slice the Chinese cabbage finely. Soak the watercress and pick into small clusters. Soak bean threads in boiling water 20 minutes; drain. Wash the chrysanthemum blossoms thoroughly and pick off the petals. Arrange the chicken breast and livers, steak and halibut separately on small plates. Arrange the cabbage, watercress, bean threads and chrysanthemum blossoms on other plates. Set the eggs (in their shells) in a bowl.

Cooking Instructions
Put 6 cups stock with the ginger root, dried shrimp, red dates and Chinese sausage into the cooking unit on the table. The guests help themselves to the plates of chicken, beef and liver, and halibut, which have been placed around the cooking pot. The food is steeped in the hot broth for a minute or two and then dipped into the dishes of Ginger-Soy, Garlic-Soy or Chinese-Style Mustard. When the meats have been eaten, the cabbage, watercress, bean threads and chrysanthemum petals are added to the pot with the additional 2 cups stock if needed. The lid is closed while the vegetables cook 3 to 4 minutes. At this point the eggs may be cracked and slid from a shallow soup plate into the pot to poach with the vegetables, or each guest may break an egg into his own bowl and beat it with his chopsticks. The cooked vegetables, bean threads and poached egg are eaten next, with the broth served finally. The chrysanthemum petals provide a delicate fragrance and a pleasantly tart flavor to the broth.

SERVINGS: Enough for 4 to 6.

HAPPY FAMILY

Cooking Time: 20 to 25 minutes

Ingredients

6	dried scallops	$\frac{1}{2}$	recipe Classic Steamed Minced
$\frac{1}{4}$	recipe Classic Steamed Minced		Shrimp Balls (page 220)
	Pork Balls (page 207)	1	ounce fish maw, sliced*
$\frac{1}{2}$	recipe Classic Steamed Minced	$\frac{1}{4}$	cup grass mushrooms
	Chicken Balls (page 214)	$\frac{1}{4}$	cup canned button mushrooms

* Deep-fried dried fish maw is available at Chinese grocers. Store refrigerated.

½ cup sliced canned abalone

½ medium bamboo shoot

½ cooked chicken breast (¾ pound)

⅛ pound Virginia ham

2 cooked chicken gizzards

⅛ pound snow peas

½ cup canned gingko nuts

6 cups seasoned chicken stock

2 slices ginger root (2x1x⅛ inch)

1 tablespoon sherry, gin or vodka

1 tablespoon cornstarch

2 tablespoons cold water

Before Cooking

The night before, soak the dried scallops in warm water to cover. Two hours before serving, simmer in 1 cup water. Drain and reserve. The morning of the day on which you plan to serve the meal, prepare the minced pork, chicken and shrimp mixtures. Shape them into balls the size of marbles and either steam or shallow-fry them. You should have about 20 balls of each. Set aside. Soak the fish maw in hot water 10 minutes. Then soak again, gently squeezing with fingers to remove excess fat. Slice into 1-inch squares; set aside. Rinse the grass mushrooms and soak 20 minutes in warm water; drain and set aside. Leave the button mushrooms whole. Cut the abalone into thin slices. Cut the bamboo shoot into fine shreds. Slice the cooked chicken breast into thin strips. Cut the ham into fine shreds. Slice the cooked gizzards paper thin. Snap off ends of the snow peas and thread them but leave whole. Set the gingko nuts aside. Combine the chicken stock, ginger root and liquor. Combine the cornstarch and cold water.

Cooking Instructions

Here the procedure differs somewhat from the usual Hot Pot cooking that takes place at the table. In this recipe, the precooked dried foods and vegetables are simmered in the kitchen and then brought to the table and served to the guests. Put the stock, ginger root and liquor mixture into a 4-quart pot and bring to a boil. Reduce heat to simmer. Add the pork, chicken and shrimp balls. Then add the fish maw, scallops, grass mushrooms, button mushrooms and bamboo shoots. Simmer 5 minutes. Add the ham, chicken strips and sliced cooked gizzards. Cook about 2 minutes, only enough to heat through. Add the gingko nuts and snow peas. Simmer 5 minutes. Turn heat up, give the cornstarch-water mixture a quick stir and add to the pot. Remove from heat as soon as the mixture thickens.

This dish may be served as is, on a hot plate on the dining table, in an Oriental chafing pot or in an electric frypan set at 250° F. When the utensil is on the table, add the abalone slices. Wait only to heat the abalone through and ladle the ingredients and stock into the guests' bowls. Because of its many ingredients, Happy Family can be served as a one-course meal. Additional side dishes of Deep-Fried Rice Sticks (page 315), soaked bean thread noodles or rice might be served. If you choose bean thread noodles, soak them first in boiling water 20 minutes. Drain and add to the cooking pot.

SERVINGS: Enough for 6 as a single course with Deep-Fried Rice Sticks (page 315), bean thread noodles or rice.

VARIED TECHNIQUES

ᔭᔭᔭᔭᔭᔭᔭᔭᔭᔭᔭᔭᔭᔭᔭᔭᔭ

Now we come to a few recipes which employ a unique procedure or which require more than one technique. In Beggar's Chicken, the ingredients are fried and stuffed in a chicken which is then wrapped in foil and baked in clay. In Peking Pressed Duck, the bird is marinated, steamed, boned, coated with water chestnut flour, pressed flat, steamed again and then deep-fried. In each case, some of the techniques involved apply only to that particular recipe. Thrice-Cooked Pork, on the other hand, includes three common techniques—boiling, deep-frying and steaming—none of which is subordinate to the others. Raw Fish Feast is in a class by itself. It does not involve cooking at all; rather, it depends on cutting and presentation.

While few in number, each of these recipes is a famous Chinese specialty.

THRICE-COOKED PORK

Cooking Time: 1 hour to simmer pork
5 minutes to deep-fry pork
5 minutes to deep-fry taro
2 hours to steam pork

Utensils
Chinese cutting knife
Small bowl for seasonings
2½-quart saucepan
Bowl of cold water
12-inch skillet
Colander
Enameled or Pyrex baking dish
2-quart heat-proof bowl
½-pound coffee can (with 6 holes punched in
    the bottom)
6- to 8-quart pot with cover

Ingredients

1	clove garlic, minced	4	cups water
⅓	cup soy sauce	¼	cup honey
⅓	cup red bean cheese (optional)	3	cups peanut oil or corn oil
3	tablespoons sherry, gin or vodka	½	cup rice vinegar or cider vinegar
3	tablespoons brown sugar	1	large taro root
2	pounds unsalted pork belly		

Before Cooking
Mash the garlic with the soy sauce, red bean cheese, liquor and brown sugar in the small bowl. Place the pork and water in the 2½-quart saucepan. Measure the honey, oil and vinegar and set aside. Peel the taro root and cut into strips, 2½x1x¼ inch. Place in the bowl of cold water until ready to use.

Cooking Instructions
Bring the pork and water to a boil over medium heat. Reduce heat and simmer 1 hour. Drain the pork. While still warm, prick all over with a fork and brush with honey. Let stand until pork has cooled. Cut the pork in half so that it will fit into the skillet. Pour the oil into the skillet and turn heat to medium. Heat oil until it foams around a cube of fresh bread. Deep-fry the pork about 5 minutes or until the skin becomes golden brown. Drain in a colander, reserving the oil. Pour the vinegar into the baking dish. Place the still-warm pork in the dish and prick again with a fork. Marinate in the vinegar 10 minutes. Put the pork in the 2-quart bowl and cover with cold water. Let stand 30 minutes. Heat the oil in the skillet again until it foams around a cube of fresh bread. Drain the taro slices well and deep-fry about 5 minutes or until crisp. Drain. Pour the cold water off the pork and blot dry with

paper towels. Cut into strips matching the size of the taro. Arrange a layer of meat in the 2-quart heat-proof bowl. Top with a layer of taro strips. Spoon some of the soy-liquor-cheese mixture over the layers. Repeat until all the pork, taro and seasonings have been used. Invert the coffee can (holes side up) and place in the large pot. Add boiling water up to ⅔ the height of the can. Place the bowl containing the pork and taro on the coffee can. Cover the outer pot and steam 2 hours, at which time the pork should be translucent and gelatinous. Add boiling water to the pot during the steaming to replenish the water which has evaporated.

SERVINGS: Enough for 4 as a single course with rice or for 6 in a full menu.

CHICKEN VELVET

Cooking Time: 2 to 3 minutes to poach each dumpling

Utensils
Electric blender or meat grinder
Bowl for chicken mixture
10½-inch electric frypan
Slotted spoon
Colander

Ingredients

½	recipe Brown Sauce (page 357)	½	teaspoon salt
1	chicken breast, skinned and boned	¼	teaspoon sugar
		1	tablespoon cornstarch
1	cup unsalted chicken stock*	3	egg whites (medium eggs)
½	teaspoon vodka or gin	2	cups peanut oil or corn oil

Before Cooking
Prepare Brown Sauce ahead of time; set aside. Cut chicken breast into coarse dice. Make a paste out of the chicken by blending at low speed a little at a time with 1

* If you are using canned chicken broth, either decrease salt to ¼ teaspoon or omit it entirely.

or 2 teaspoons of stock or by putting it through the medium blade of the meat grinder twice and then through the finest blade once. Place the smoothly ground chicken in the bowl. Add the remainder of the stock to the chicken paste. Add the liquor, salt, sugar and cornstarch. Stir until smooth. Beat the egg whites until they are just frothy but not stiff. Fold into the seasoned chicken paste and blend well. The mixture will be thin. Have oil ready to go.

Cooking Instructions

Pour oil into electric frypan; set at 300° F. When the required temperature has been reached, pour a dessert-spoonful of the chicken paste in a layer into the oil. The layer of chicken paste will sink into the oil at once. Repeat with another layer of chicken paste over the first, then another over the second. Fry gently without stirring 2 to 3 minutes or until the layered chicken paste turns opaque and seems to hold its shape. Do not let it brown. Remove with slotted spoon to the colander to drain. Repeat until all of the chicken paste has been used. Allow to drain in the colander while you gently reheat the Brown Sauce. Place the Chicken Velvet in a heated dish, cover with sauce and serve at once. These delicate dumplings resemble the French *quenelles* in texture and flavor. It is most important to remember that Chicken Velvet is literally poached in oil. To do this correctly, the oil must be hot but not too hot. (For this reason, an electric frypan works best with this recipe.) It is not semi–deep-fried, and must not become crusted or even slightly browned.

SERVINGS: Enough for 3 as a single course with rice or for 4 to 6 in a full menu.

NOTE: This extremely elegant dish is a specialty of Shantung Province, in the North. Because of the skill and time required to produce the feathery dumplings, it is rarely served in restaurants here. On the few occasions I have had Chicken Velvet in this country, it has been gilded with button mushrooms, snow peas and other garnitures. This is not an authentic presentation, though you may experiment if you choose.

BEGGAR'S CHICKEN

Cooking Time: 6 to 7 minutes to stir-fry-toss
          2 hours to bake

Utensils

Chinese cutting knife
12-inch skillet or wok
Slotted spoon or spatula
Chopsticks for stir-frying
Lotus, *ti* or palm leaves or aluminum foil
Foil-covered cookie sheet
5-pound bag moist ceramic clay*
Mallet

Ingredients

¼	pound lean pork	2	teaspoons sesame oil
½	medium onion	1	teaspoon salt
½	medium bamboo shoot	1	teaspoon cornstarch
6	dried mushrooms	¼	teaspoon five-spice seasoning
1	tablespoon dried cloud ears	1	tablespoon soy sauce
⅛	pound bean thread noodles	3	tablespoons peanut oil or corn oil
1	whole fryer (3 pounds)		

Before Cooking

Cut the pork into shreds. Slice the onion finely. Cut the bamboo shoot into thin strips. Soak the mushrooms and cloud ears separately in warm water 15 minutes. Drain the mushrooms and cut into thin strips, discarding the hard centers. Leave the cloud ears whole. Soak the bean threads in boiling water 20 minutes; drain. You should have slightly more than a cup of soaked noodles. Wash and drain the fryer; blot dry with paper towels. When the bird is thoroughly dry, rub all over and in the cavity with the sesame oil, salt, cornstarch and five-spice seasoning. If you cannot find large leaves in which to wrap the bird, use a double thickness of foil. Have the soy sauce and oil ready to go.

Stir-Fry-Toss Instructions

Turn heat under skillet or wok to high. When the pan is hot, add the oil. It should sizzle at once. Before the oil begins to smoke, add the pork shreds and stir-fry 2 minutes. Remove with slotted spoon or spatula to a plate. Add the onion to

*   Moist ceramic clay is available in art-supply stores. A 5-pound bag will be just enough to coat a 3-pound bird. If you are unable to find ceramic clay, you may use powdered clay, combining it with just enough water to make a spreading consistency. But look for the moist type—it's easier to use and less messy.

the oil remaining in the pan; stir-fry-toss 2 minutes. Add the bamboo shoots and drained mushroom strips and cloud ears. Stir-fry-toss another 2 minutes. Return the pork to the pan and stir to blend. Add the bean threads. Mix well with pork and vegetables and add soy sauce. Set the pan aside for the mixture to cool.

Baking Instructions
Fill the bird's cavity with the cooled pork mixture and either skewer or sew the cavity. Wrap the stuffed bird in the large leaves, making sure that it is thoroughly covered. If you are using foil, make sure that it is double thickness and large enough to make a butcher's wrap (folded over on top). Place the wrapped chicken on the foil-covered cookie sheet. Cover the entire package with moist ceramic clay, spreading it about ½-inch thick. Bake the clay-covered bird at 400° F. for 1 hour. Reduce heat to 200° F. and bake 1 hour longer. Bring the bird baked in clay to the table; crack the clay covering with a mallet and remove foil or leaf undercovering. Since the hardened clay tends to fly when cracked, you may prefer to bring the bird in the clay to the table to show your guests and then return to the kitchen to crack it open. This "sealed-in" cooking process makes the pork-stuffed chicken particularly delectable.

SERVINGS: Enough for 4 as a single course with rice or for 6 in a full menu.

NOTE: This dish did indeed originate with the beggars in China. They would bury a chicken—head, entrails, feathers and all—in hot clay. The gourmets of Peking refined the recipe to include a savory stuffing.

SALT-SMOTHERED CHICKEN

Cooking Time: 1½ hours

Utensils
Bowl for marinade
6- to 8-quart enameled casserole with cover
Strainer
1-pint saucepan

Ingredients

1	whole fryer (3½ pounds)	2	teaspoons Chinese orange wine or Cointreau
1	teaspoon minced ginger root		
1	scallion with 1 inch of green, cut in ¼-inch rounds	1	cup warm water
		2	teaspoons cornstarch
1	teaspoon minced Chinese parsley	2	tablespoons cold chicken stock or cold water
1	piece dried tangerine peel (1 inch in diameter)		
		5	pounds rock salt
1½	teaspoons salt		Chinese parsley for decorating
⅛	teaspoon ground Szechuan or black pepper		

Before Cooking

Wash bird and blot dry with paper towels. Hang 1 to 2 hours in a cool, dry place. Combine the ginger root, scallion, parsley, dried tangerine peel, salt, pepper, orange wine and water in the bowl. Tie or sew the bird's neck opening. Pour the marinade into the body cavity. Sew cavity shut to prevent marinade from leaking. Combine cornstarch and stock or water. Have rock salt ready to go.

Cooking Instructions

Put the rock salt in the casserole. Turn heat to high and stir salt crystals until they become red-hot, about 30 minutes. Scoop out enough salt to make a well in which you can place the chicken, leaving a bed of salt about 2 inches thick. Place the filled bird breast-side-down in the salt and pack it all around with the scooped-out salt. Cover casserole and reduce heat to medium-low. Cook 45 to 60 minutes. Remove bird and cut away threads. Pour marinade from the cavity into a strainer over the pint saucepan. Chop chicken into Chinese-style serving pieces and arrange on a platter. Heat the marinade over medium heat until boiling. Give the cornstarch-stock mixture a quick stir to dissolve any lumps; add to marinade. Stir 1 to 2 minutes or until the mixture becomes clear. Pour over bird. Decorate with sprigs of Chinese parsley and serve. The chicken will be tender and moist without being overly salty. It will have a subtle fragrance.

SERVINGS: Enough for 4 as a single course or for 6 to 8 in a full menu.

PEKING PRESSED DUCK

Cooking Time: 2 to 2½ hours to steam unboned duck
                 30 minutes to steam boned duck
                 20 minutes to deep-fry

Utensils
Chinese cutting knife
Small bowl for seasonings
Pan for marinating bird
8- to 10-quart pot or 12-inch or larger wok
   —with cover
½-pound coffee can (with 6 holes punched in
   the bottom)
Shallow heat-proof dish or 10-inch Pyrex
   pie plate
Electric deep-fry cooker or 6-quart pot
   with frying thermometer

Ingredients

½ recipe Pouring Oyster Sauce (page 356) or any of the Sweet-and-Sour Sauces (pages 353–356)	½ teaspoon five-spice seasoning
1 duckling (5 pounds), split in half	3 scallions, trimmed but left whole
½ cup soy sauce	½ cup water chestnut flour*
1 tablespoon sherry, gin or vodka	½ cup cornstarch
½ teaspoon salt	8 cups peanut oil or corn oil
1 teaspoon brown sugar	½ head lettuce, shredded
	½ cup semi-finely chopped toasted almonds or cashews

Before Cooking
Prepare the Pouring Oyster Sauce or the Sweet-and-Sour Sauce ahead of time.
Wash and drain duck. Combine the soy sauce, liquor, salt, brown sugar and five-

* Water chestnut flour is available at Chinese grocery stores. If you cannot find
it, use all cornstarch.

spice seasoning in the small bowl. Place the split bird in the pan and sprinkle with the soy sauce mixture. Top with scallions and let stand 30 minutes. Turn the duck during the marinating and rub soy mixture in the cavities. Drain the duck. It is now ready for the first steaming. Toward the end of the steaming, combine the water chestnut flour and cornstarch; sift and set aside. Prepare nuts and lettuce; set aside. Have oil ready to go.

Steaming Instructions

Invert the coffee can (holes-side-up) in the center of the pot or wok. Pour boiling water up to ⅔ the height of the can. Turn heat to medium-high and bring water to a boil. Place the duck on the heat-proof dish or pie plate and put on the coffee can. Cover pot or wok. Keep heat just high enough to keep the water actively boiling. Steam the bird 2 to 2½ hours, adding more boiling water to the pot or wok as needed. The duck is ready when the meat is very tender and the bones can be literally slipped out. Carefully remove the bird and allow it to cool. When the duck can be handled comfortably, bone it. Take care not to pull it apart or shred the meat. Keep the shape of the duck as intact as possible and do not remove any of the skin. Place the boned duck halves on a cutting board. Using your palms, press them flat so that they are ½ to ¾ inch thick all over. Sprinkle the water chestnut-cornstarch mixture all over the flattened boned duck, coating it on both sides thoroughly. Return the coated duck to the shallow dish and steam it again 30 minutes. Let it cool.

Deep-Frying Instructions

Pour the oil into the deep-fry cooker or pot and bring to 375° F. Fry the steamed coated duck halves, one at a time, until golden brown (about 10 minutes each). Place on paper towels to drain. When cool enough to handle, cut into 1½-inch squares, with skin on. Gently reheat the Pouring Oyster Sauce or the Sweet-and-Sour Sauce. Arrange the shredded lettuce on a platter. Reassemble the duck squares over the shredded lettuce. Pour the sauce on top and sprinkle with chopped nuts. The deep-frying enhances the crispness of the coated skin in contrast to the delicacy of the meat.

SERVINGS: Enough for 4 as a single course with Mandarin Pancakes (page 325) or rice or for 6 in a full menu.

"SMOKED" FISH SLICES

Cooking Time: 6 to 8 minutes to deep-fry
10 seconds to simmer in marinade

Utensils
Baking pan for marinating fish slices
12-inch skillet, wok or electric frypan
Slotted spatula

Ingredients

4	tablespoons soy sauce	1	clove garlic, minced
3	tablespoons sherry, gin or vodka	1	pound carp, cod or halibut, cut in
1	tablespoon brown sugar		½-inch slices
2	teaspoons sesame oil	1½	teaspoons five-spice seasoning
2	scallions, cut in 1-inch lengths	4	cups peanut oil or corn oil
3	teaspoons minced ginger root		

Before Cooking
Combine the soy sauce, liquor, brown sugar and sesame oil in the baking pan. Add the scallions, ginger root and garlic. Place fish slices in marinade, cover with plastic wrap and refrigerate 12 to 24 hours. Before frying, remove fish from marinade; drain well and blot dry with paper towels. Reserve marinade remaining in the baking pan. Have five-spice seasoning and oil ready to go.

Cooking Instructions
Place the baking pan with the marinade over low heat. Keep at a simmer. Heat oil in skillet or wok over high heat until it foams around a cube of fresh bread (375° F. on electric frypan). Add half the fish slices. Deep-fry 3 to 4 minutes. Remove fish from oil with slotted spatula and drain well on a double thickness of paper towels. Dip the fried fish slices in the simmering marinade 10 seconds. Remove to a heated platter covered with paper towels. Repeat the frying and dipping with the remaining fish. Add to the platter. Sprinkle with half of the five-spice seasoning. Turn slices and sprinkle with the remaining seasoning. The finished slices will be very dark brown in color and dry on the surface but moist inside. The general appearance will be that of slow-smoked fish.

SERVINGS: Enough for 3 as a single course with rice or for 4 to 6 in a full menu.

RAW FISH FEAST

Yee Sang Jook

Cooking Time: None

Utensils
Long thin knife
Grater or vegetable slicer
Platters, plates, assorted small dishes
Bowls for Congee Rice
Chopsticks

Ingredients

3	pounds pike or sea bass, skinned and boned	4	long white Chinese turnips, finely shredded
2	tablespoons lemon juice	2	teaspoons salt
3	tablespoons minced pickled ginger root*	1	recipe Congee Rice (page 314)
6	scallions, chopped semi-finely		Small dishes of soy sauce, mustard, Cantonese Salt and Spiced Salt (page 352)
½	bunch Chinese parsley, in small clusters		Cruet of peanut oil
4	carrots, finely shredded		Cruet of sesame oil

Procedure
Cut fish into tissue-thin layers. Slice into 1-inch squares. If you are on friendly terms with your fish dealer, try to get him to do the slicing. Sprinkle the fish slices with lemon juice and arrange on a platter. Cover with plastic wrap and refrigerate until serving time. Place the ginger root, scallions, parsley and carrots on separate plates and refrigerate. Put the shredded turnips in a bowl, sprinkle with salt and refrigerate 1 hour. Drain and place in a clean kitchen towel. Roll the towel and wring out any excess liquid from the turnips. Place the turnips on a cookie sheet lined with paper towels and refrigerate. Prepare the Congee Rice.

---

* Pickled ginger root is peeled ginger root preserved in sweet wine. It is sold at Chinese grocery stores. If you are unable to find it, use peeled fresh ginger root, finely chopped.

To Serve

Set the table, giving each person a small plate, a bowl for the rice and a pair of chopsticks. Place the platter of raw fish slices in the center of the table. Arrange the plates of shredded turnips, carrots, minced ginger, scallions and parsley around it. Place the dishes of condiments and the bottles of oil in a circle around the vegetables. The guests help themselves, taking some of the fish onto their plates with chopsticks. Then a little of both oils is sprinkled on the fish and it is rapidly stirred. Next the ginger, scallions and parsley are added, then dashes of the condiment sauces to taste. The turnips and carrots are sprinkled generously over the fish and it is ready to eat. Repeat the procedure until all the fish has been eaten. The Congee Rice (gruel) may be served afterward or along with the fish. If served with the fish, it can be used as a hot dip into which the fish and vegetables may be plunged for an instant.

This is a simplified recipe for a very popular repast, usually served during the Moon Festival Season, in autumn. In the more elaborate feasts, many additional ingredients are served as toppings to the raw fish—nuts, pickles, sesame seeds, additional vegetables and deep-fried rice sticks. Much is made of the business of stirring up the fish with the oils. The mixing is begun on order of the host and symbolizes the stirring up of good fortune. Even more simplified versions of this feast than the one provided here are served at a number of small Chinese restaurants. A point of authenticity to remember is that after the fish has been mixed with the oils and condiments and is topped with the crisp shredded turnips, it is no longer stirred. The contrast of crisp vegetables and raw fish must be preserved. The food is lifted with the chopsticks from the bottom of the plate to the top. Since it is eaten raw, the fish must be of the highest quality and absolutely fresh.

SERVINGS: Enough for 6 as the entire meal with bowls of Congee Rice.

RICE

Much has been made of the correct technique for cooking rice—so much that it has become a mystique. It needn't be so. Yes, it is true that every Chinese housewife gauges the amount of water to use by touching the rice with the index finger and bringing the water up to the first joint. How many varying sizes of index fingers there are in China I'll never know. But the fact remains that the Chinese all seem to cook perfect rice using this method.

Since the purpose of this book is to rely as much as possible on exact measurements rather than colorful, but perhaps not entirely dependable, folk methods, I have based these recipes for rice on standard and workable measures. The best rice to serve with Chinese food is Texas or Carolina long-grain rice. The shorter (or round) rice from California or Japan, does not produce as firm, individually cooked grains; it is best suited for making congee rice, the gruel so popular with the Chinese. Glutinous rice is used most often for desserts, stuffings, or to coat steamed foods.

A matter worthy of consideration is the business of washing rice. Distributors of the highest grades of packaged rice caution against washing, presumably with the sanction of the National Rice Council. They claim that the standard light milling leaves the rice with a flourlike covering which gives it more food value than fully milled rice has. Washing removes these elements from the already fully sterilized rice. On the other hand, Chinese chefs disagree to a man. They insist that washing the rice rids it of excess starch and creates fluffier grains.

I have tested rice both ways. In truth, raw rice which has been washed in several changes of cold water does produce fluffier, brighter-looking grains of cooked rice. However, unwashed raw rice produces highly satisfactory cooked grains and, since I dislike the idea of pouring essential vitamins and minerals down the drain, my tendency is not to wash. The choice is yours. For the short, or round, rice, follow the distributor's suggestions. Glutinous rice should always be washed before cooking.

STEAMED RICE

Cooking Time: 16 to 18 minutes

Utensils
1½-quart straight-sided enameled saucepan
    with tight-fitting cover
Chopsticks

Ingredients

1 cup long-grain rice	½ teaspoon peanut oil or corn oil
1¾ cups cold water	(optional)

Before Cooking
Measure rice into the saucepan. Measure cold water and pour into rice. Measure oil and add to the pan. The small amount of oil decreases the chances of the rice boiling over. Shake pan to level the rice.

Cooking Instructions
Turn heat under saucepan to medium-high. Let rice and water come to a boil. Bubbling foam will rise. Stir with a fork to distribute rice grains and prevent lumping. Reduce heat to very low. Cover and slow-simmer 16 minutes. Rice is done if the grains are dry and separate and if there are narrow holes through the rice as though the surface had been pierced with a chopstick. If the rice appears too moist, cover and let it cook for another minute or two. Remove from heat. If you plan to serve the rice within minutes, let it stand covered on the stove. This will serve to firm the grains by steaming away any excess moisture. If there is to be a delay of an hour before serving the rice, keep it warm, covered, in a 170° F. oven. Should the wait be longer than an hour, sprinkle 1 or 2 tablespoons of water around the edges of the rice where it tends to become encrusted. While doing this, lift the rice

gently from top to bottom with chopsticks to permit the water to go to the bottom of the pan. Do not mix or stir the rice at any time after it has been cooked—this causes the grains to break and become pasty. Rice cooked in this manner will be fluffy, with the grains separate and slightly firm to the bite—what Italians call *al dente*. For softer rice, increase the water for cooking to 2 to $2\frac{1}{4}$ cups.

SERVINGS: Enough for 2 to 3; about 3 cups of cooked rice.

TO REHEAT LEFTOVER RICE: Leftover rice should always be stored covered in the refrigerator. The simplest means of reheating rice is to spread it with chopsticks in an even layer over the surface of freshly simmering rice. The new rice must be just about done, with the surface almost dry (after about 15 minutes of cooking). Do not mix the old rice with the new. Just cover and let it steam until the fresh rice is done. The leftover rice will be heated through perfectly. If you are not making fresh rice and want to reheat rice, you can use a double boiler. Cover and heat over medium-low heat. To reheat rice in the oven, stir the rice in a saucepan with 1 tablespoon cold water to every 1 cup rice. Cover the pan and place in a 300° F. oven 15 to 20 minutes.

TO SAVE BURNED RICE: Rice will scorch if the heat is not reduced after the rice and water come to a boil. If this should happen, immediately remove the pan from the stove and place it in about 2 inches of cold water in your sink. This stops the cooking process. Remove the cover and scoop the unscorched portions of rice into another pan. Avoid scooping out any of the brown sides and bottom of the rice. The amount of water to be added depends on how cooked the rice was at the time it became scorched. If it was nearly done, sprinkle it with 1 to 2 tablespoons cold water. If it was still fairly grainy, add $\frac{1}{2}$ to 1 cup. Stir and cover. For nearly cooked rice, reduce heat to very low and steam until the grains are separate and fluffy. For rice requiring $\frac{1}{2}$ to 1 cup of water, turn heat to medium. When the rice begins to steam again, reduce heat to low and cook until there is no more water in the pan and the grains are fluffy and separate.

RICE CRUSTS I

Double ingredients in recipe for Steamed Rice, using a $2\frac{1}{2}$-quart pan with cover. Prepare rice as directed. Allow the covered pan to remain over very low heat for an additional 5 minutes. This creates a crust on the bottom of the pan. Scoop out the fluffy cooked portions of rice into a bowl and reserve. When the crust in the pan has cooled, break it into chunks. Bring 3 cups of peanut oil or corn oil to 360° F. in an electric frypan. Deep-fry the rice-crust chunks 3 to 5 minutes or only until they are pale golden brown. Drain quickly in a sieve or colander. If the fried crusts are to be used for soup (see Sizzling Rice Soup, page 179), bring them to the table at once. Deep-fried Rice Crusts may be used as a base for stir-fried prawns, pork, beef or chicken.

RICE CRUSTS II

Sprinkle ½ cup long-grain rice in a 10-inch Pyrex pie plate. Add 1 cup cold water. Place over medium heat. When the water boils, reduce the heat to low. Simmer 10 minutes. Flatten the surface of the rice with the back of a soup spoon dipped in cold water. This is to even the rice and make it firm. At this point the rice will be a flat layer of semi-hard grains. Let it stand overnight to dry. Shortly before using, break off bits of the crust and deep-fry in 2 cups peanut oil or corn oil (360° F. on electric skillet). Deep-fry the pieces of rice crust only until they are golden brown, 3 to 5 minutes. Drain and bring to the table at once if they are to be used for Sizzling Rice Soup (page 179).

FRIED RICE

This is another of those tasty dishes so popular with Americans that evolved from the Chinese abhorrence of waste. The basis is leftover rice, to which any number of leftover ingredients may be added. Fried rice may be as simple as you like or festooned with the choicest ingredients. When it becomes elaborate, the Chinese award the dish complimentary titles: Eight Precious Fried Rice or Young Jewel Fried Rice. Call it what you will, in the final analysis it is simply rice, a day or two old, stir-fried with vegetables and meat and eggs scrambled into it. Below is a basic recipe and some suggested embellishments.

Cooking Time: 8 to 10 minutes

Utensils
Chinese cutting knife
Small bowl for eggs
12-inch skillet or wok
Chopsticks or spatula

Ingredients

3 scallions with most of green, cut in ¼-inch rounds	¼ teaspoon black pepper
	1½ tablespoons soy sauce
1½ cups shredded or diced cooked pork, ham, chicken breast or shrimp	1 teaspoon sherry
	2 eggs
2 teaspoons minced ginger root	4 cups day-old cooked rice
1 teaspoon salt	3 tablespoons peanut oil or corn oil

Before Cooking
Prepare scallions and meat. If the shrimp are tiny, leave them whole; otherwise, dice them. Peel and mince ginger root. Combine the salt, pepper, soy sauce and sherry. Lightly beat the eggs in the small bowl. Have rice and oil ready to go.

Cooking Instructions
Turn heat under skillet or wok to medium-high. When the pan is hot, add the oil. Before the oil begins to smoke, add the rice and stir 2 minutes, breaking up lumps. Add scallion rounds and ginger root. Toss with rice 1 minute. Add the meat or shrimp and pour in the seasonings. Stir-fry-toss 2 minutes, blending the ingredients without mashing the rice. With chopsticks or spatula, shape the rice into a ring, leaving a well in the center. Pour the lightly beaten eggs into the well. Let stand without stirring 1½ minutes to permit the egg to set partially. Toss the rice mixture with the eggs 1 to 2 minutes or until the eggs become threads laced throughout the rice and meat. Remove from heat.

SERVINGS: Enough for 4.

FRIED RICE EMBELLISHMENTS
For more elaborate fried rice in the Jewel or Precious category, add ½ cup of one or more of any of the following ingredients:

VEGETABLES: Shredded bamboo shoots; sliced water chestnuts; drained button mushrooms; soaked, drained and sliced dried mushrooms; pea sprouts; sliced celery, cabbage hearts; parboiled fresh green peas or thawed frozen peas; thinly sliced green peppers; celery shreds, sliced Chinese chard hearts; whole threaded snow peas with ends snipped.

MEATS: Shredded or diced barbecued pork, shredded roast duck, thinly sliced cooked chicken gizzards, thinly sliced Chinese sausage.

FISH: Diced cooked lobster, shredded cooked crab, cooked fish filets, canned sliced abalone. (Add only a minute before removing from heat, just long enough to heat through.)

MISCELLANEOUS: 2 tablespoons almonds, cashews or peanuts.

NOTE: If you plan to add more than ½ cup of any ingredient, increase the oil to ¼ cup. Adjust seasonings to allow for the extra ingredients and increase the eggs to three. Cooking time and amounts depend on the quantity of additional foods.

CONGEE RICE

This is a type of gruel extremely popular with the Chinese. It is eaten in bowls as a breakfast food or as a mid-day or evening snack. As a snack, it is eaten either as is or with ingredients added to it or cooked with it. While Congee Rice is a Chinese national standby, the pasty texture and tasteless flavor is an acquired taste for most Westerners. Once you have learned to appreciate the blandness of this dish in contrast to pickled and salted greens or salt fish, you may become a convert. Boiling Congee is sometimes served over raw fish (see Raw Fish Feast, page 307) or over finely slivered marinated raw meat.

Cooking Time: 1¾ to 2¼ hours

Utensils
2-quart saucepan with cover

Ingredients
½	cup round California or Japanese rice	6	cups cold water

Before Cooking
Wash rice in cold water until the water runs clear; drain. Combine rice and 6 cups cold water in the saucepan.

Cooking Instructions
Place pan with rice and water over medium-high heat. Allow mixture to boil 15 minutes. Reduce heat to low; cover and simmer 1½ to 2 hours, stirring occasionally, until the rice loses its shape and the mixture resembles porridge. The thickness of the Congee can be adjusted to suit your taste by adding more boiling water.

SERVINGS: Enough for 3 to 4.

NOTE: Unsalted chicken stock may be substituted for the water.

RICE STICKS

Cooking Time: 1 to 2 minutes

Utensils
2-quart saucepan or electric frypan
Chopsticks
Slotted spoon

Ingredients

2   cups peanut oil or corn oil   ¼   pound rice stick noodles (do not presoak)

Procedure
Heat the oil in the saucepan until it foams around a cube of fresh bread (365° F. on electric frypan). Add rice sticks and stir with chopsticks 1 to 2 minutes or until the noodles become a pale honey color. Remove with slotted spoon to drain on paper towels. Crumble coarsely and use to decorate dishes or as the base for fried meat, poultry or fish.

AMOUNT: About 4 cups.

NOODLES

No one who has ever sampled the delicate texture of fresh egg noodles or enjoyed the perfect contrast of crisply fried and soft noodles will need my recommendation on the quality of Chinese dough-making. Nor will you need to be reminded that it was China, presumably by courtesy of the enterprising Marco Polo, from whom the Western world borrowed the fine art of making noodle dough and translated it into glories of its own. In the North of China, where wheat is abundant, noodles are the mainstay of everyday eating, as is rice in other regions. So bread is in Western civilizations. As with any other technique of cooking, the art of dough-making depends on practice and on learning the knacks involved. To make a fine egg noodle dough in the Chinese manner is admittedly considerable bother and not the easiest thing in the world. Nor is it the most difficult. It is far more exasperating, for example, to go through the lifting and pulling process associated with strudel dough, which needs to be considerably sheerer. The recipes given in this section relate almost exclusively to noodles. There is a single recipe for Mandarin Pancakes, which falls into a category of its own, but is best included here. Look for the pastries associated with *deem sum* (such as Egg Rolls, Spring Rolls and *Won Ton*) immediately after this section, with Appetizers.

TO PREPARE FOR MAKING NOODLE PASTRY

It is essential to have a few things in order before you start. Enough space for rolling out the dough is of primary importance—a large table or counter is ideal. You will need a pastry board on which to mix your dough, but not to roll it. To mini-

316

mize the chore of repeated rollings, I use what is called an oven cloth in England. This is a 23x33-inch rectangle of heavy twill-like cloth used to remove hot dishes from the oven. Oven cloths can be bought at specialty utensil stores. If you are unable to find one, go to a sports supply house and buy a piece of canvas duck of the same dimensions. The standard foot-long rolling pin is not an entirely satisfactory piece of equipment. Instead, use a wooden dowel. Buy one 36 inches long and 1 inch in diameter; available at any hardware store. Have the hardware man saw the dowel in half and you will have two 18-inch Chinese-style rolling pins. You will also need a cheesecloth bag containing 1 to 1½ cups of cornstarch. This is for dusting the oven cloth and rolling the pastry. You can tie the cornstarch in any makeshift bag (an old clean handkerchief, for example), or you may use a fine sieve. With these items in hand, you are ready to start.

BASIC EGG NOODLE PASTRY

Equipment
Pastry board
Oven cloth or piece of canvas duck (23x33 inches)
Cheesecloth bag or sifter for cornstarch
Dowel or rolling pin
Long thin knife

Ingredients

2	cups sifted all-purpose flour	3	medium eggs
½	teaspoon salt	1½	tablespoons cold water

Procedure
Sift the flour with the salt onto a pastry board. Form a well in the center of the flour. Crack the eggs and drop them into the well. Mix the eggs and flour. The mixture will resemble coarse meal and will be partly dry and partly moist. Sprinkle with 1 tablespoon of the water, knead together and add the remaining ½ tablespoon. You may require more or less water, depending on the moistness of the flour and the weather conditions. (Under no circumstances should you use too much water.) At this point the dough will be sticky. Shape the dough into a ball or mound and begin kneading it, using the balls of your palms to push it away.

Gather back with the fingers and push away again, repeating the kneading until the dough is smooth and pliable. This should take from 5 to 8 minutes. Shape the dough into a flattened ball, about 5 inches in diameter, and cover with a damp cloth. Let the dough stand covered 30 to 45 minutes.

Then roll out the dough. Lightly moisten the table or counter with a damp sponge and place the oven cloth or canvas duck on the table. Dust the entire cloth with a sprinkling of cornstarch from the cheesecloth bag. Divide the ball of dough in 2 equal parts. Place one part in the center of the cloth and pat it with the palm of your hand into a flat disc, rather like a thick pancake. Sprinkle the top of the dough with cornstarch and sprinkle the dowel or roller as well. Roll the dough out hard but evenly from top to bottom and left to right, turning the cloth as needed. Keep rolling the dough until it is very thin, almost transparent. You should have a rectangle of pastry about 22x24 inches. If the dough is not too moist and if you are using enough cornstarch on your cloth and roller, you should have no problem with the dough sticking or tearing. Remove the rolled-out sheet of pastry to an area covered with paper towels that have been sprinkled with cornstarch. Let it stand until it no longer feels moist. It should be slightly dry but not brittle. Allow 45 minutes to 1 hour for this. While the pastry is drying, repeat the procedure with the remaining dough. When the pastry sheets have stood the necessary time, transfer one sheet back to the oven cloth. Sprinkle front and back with cornstarch, smoothing it on with the palms of the hand. Roll up jelly-roll fashion. Using a long sharp knife, cut the roll into ⅛-inch slices. When the whole roll has been sliced, use fingers to toss lightly and separate the slices. There you have your noodles. Repeat with the remaining pastry sheet. To store, sprinkle with 2 tablespoons cornstarch to prevent sticking and put in a tightly closed jar. (They disappear so quickly that you don't have to worry about how long they will keep.) These will be true egg noodles, bright with the natural color of eggs.

AMOUNT: About 1 pound.

BOILED NOODLES

These are simply noodles boiled in water. Once cooked, they may be used as the basis for many other dishes. When boiling noodles, always allow at least 3 quarts of water to every ½ pound of noodles. Because of the highly seasoned nature of the Chinese foods that are served on or with noodles, no salt is added to the water.

Cooking Time: 4 minutes

Utensils
6-quart pot
Wire strainer or colander

Ingredients

3	quarts water	½	pound fresh egg noodles

Procedure
Bring the water to a rolling boil in the 6-quart pot. Add the noodles, stirring with a fork to prevent them from sticking together. The uncooked noodles will decrease the rate of boiling temporarily. Boil 4 minutes, including the time it takes for the water to come back to a rolling boil. (Dried noodles require a somewhat longer boiling time. Check the package for instructions, but taste-test anyway.) Drain noodles in a strainer or colander. If you are not using the noodles at once, rinse with cold water to prevent them from massing together. Drain thoroughly and use in chicken- or pork-based soups or top with cooked slivered beef, pork, ham, chicken or shrimp. Vegetables might include thinly sliced celery, celery cabbage, Chinese chard, mustard greens or snow peas. For a more elaborate noodle in broth recipe, see the following recipe for *Woh Mein.*

AMOUNT: 2½ cups cooked noodles or 4 to 5 soup servings.

NOTE: When doubling this recipe, you will need 6 quarts of water for the pound of noodles and an 8- to 10-quart pot.

WOH MEIN
Noodles, Meats and Vegetables in Broth

Cooking Time: 12 to 15 minutes, including boiling time for noodles

Utensils
Chinese cutting knife
8- to 10-quart pot for boiling noodles
Colander
6-quart serving casserole

Ingredients

½ cooked fryer's breast, thinly sliced

2 cooked chicken gizzards, thinly sliced
   Double recipe Boiled Noodles (page 318)

8 cups seasoned chicken stock

2 chicken livers, blanched

¼ pound shrimp, peeled and de-veined

¼ pound barbecued pork, diagonally sliced

1 can (2 ounces) button mush-rooms, drained

1 cup snow peas, threaded, with ends snipped off

½ cup water chestnuts, cut in half

1 cup thinly sliced canned abalone

3 scallions, each with 1½ inches of green, semi-finely chopped

1 teaspoon sesame oil

Before Cooking

Beforehand, prepare the chicken breast, gizzards, noodles and stock. Prepare the re-maining ingredients and have ready to go. Measure the sesame oil; set aside.

Cooking Instructions

Bring the stock in the casserole to a boil over medium heat. Add the snow peas, water chestnuts and button mushrooms. Reduce heat and simmer 2 minutes. Add the chicken breast and gizzards. Simmer 2 minutes. Add the drained noodles, liv-ers, shrimp and barbecued pork. Simmer about 2 minutes to heat through. Add the abalone slices. Turn heat up and remove from heat just before mixture comes to a boil. Top with sesame oil and chopped scallions. Here you have double-simmered noodles—first in water and then in stock. This dish is more a meal than a soup be-cause the amount of stock is small in proportion to the amount of noodles, meats and vegetables. *Woh Mein* may be served as a combination soup and main course or simply as a one-course meal. It can be brought to table in the cooking casserole; guests should be provided with bowls, chopsticks and/or Chinese soup spoons.

SERVINGS: Enough for 6 as a single course or for 8 in a full menu.

CHOW MEIN

Shallow-Fried Noodles

Cooking Time: 22 to 25 minutes, including boiling noodles

Utensils
Chinese cutting knife
8- to 10-quart pot for boiling noodles
Colander
Soup plate
12-inch skillet
Slotted spatula

Ingredients

Double recipe Boiled Noodles (page 318)	2 cups pea sprouts
	1 small bamboo shoot, shredded
½ pound pork or 1 fryer's breast, shredded	1 tender stalk celery, shredded
	1 teaspoon minced ginger root
2 teaspoons soy sauce	1½ tablespoons cornstarch
1 teaspoon sherry	½ cup cold chicken stock
½ teaspoon salt	⅓ cup peanut oil or corn oil
2 teaspoons cornstarch	2 tablespoons peanut oil or corn oil

Before Cooking
Cook noodles. Combine the pork or chicken shreds, soy sauce, sherry, salt and 2 teaspoons cornstarch in the soup plate. Toss to blend and let stand. Wash the pea sprouts and pick out green hoods. Drain well. Prepare bamboo shoot, celery stalk and ginger root. Combine the 1½ tablespoons cornstarch and the stock. Pour ⅓ cup oil into the skillet. Have 2 tablespoons oil ready for later use.

Cooking Instructions
Turn heat under skillet containing oil to medium. When the oil is hot, add the drained noodles, pressing them into a large flat cake. Fry 5 minutes. (When lifted with a spatula, the bottom of the noodles should be crisp and golden.) Turn and brown on the other side 5 minutes. Remove to a platter and keep warm in 170° F. oven. Add the 2 tablespoons oil to the skillet and heat until the oil sizzles. Add dredged pork or chicken. Stir-fry-toss 4 minutes for pork, 2 minutes for chicken. Remove with spatula to a warm dish. Add the pea sprouts, bamboo shoot, celery and ginger root to the oil remaining in the skillet. Stir-fry-toss 3 minutes. Return pork or chicken to the skillet. Blend together with vegetables 1 minute. Give the cornstarch and chicken stock a quick stir to blend; pour into skillet. Blend 1 to 2 minutes or until sauce thickens and is clear. Pour over crisply fried noodles and serve at once. Here you have the contrast of noodles crisped on the exterior and tender in the middle with delicate slivers of meat and vegetables in a smooth sauce.

SERVINGS: Enough for 4 as a single course and for 6 in a full menu.

TEN PRECIOUS CHOW MEIN

Cooking Time: 25 to 30 minutes, including boiling noodles

Utensils
Chinese cutting knife
8- to 10-quart pot for boiling noodles
Colander
12-inch skillet
Small bowl for seasonings
Slotted spatula

Ingredients

	Double recipe Boiled Noodles (page 318)	$\frac{1}{2}$	pound celery cabbage
1	recipe Egg Threads (page 235)	2	scallions
$\frac{1}{4}$	pound pork, shredded	1	teaspoon minced ginger root
$\frac{1}{8}$	pound Virginia ham, shredded	$1\frac{1}{2}$	tablespoons soy sauce
$\frac{1}{2}$	chicken breast, boned, skinned and shredded	2	teaspoons sherry
$\frac{1}{4}$	pound small shrimp (if medium, cut in half lengthwise)	1	teaspoon sugar
		$\frac{1}{2}$	teaspoon salt
6	medium dried mushrooms	2	tablespoons cornstarch
$\frac{1}{2}$	cup snow peas	$\frac{2}{3}$	cup cold chicken stock
$\frac{1}{2}$	cup water chestnuts	$\frac{1}{3}$	cup peanut oil or corn oil
		3	tablespoons peanut oil or corn oil

Before Cooking
Prepare noodles, Egg Threads, pork, ham, chicken breast and shrimp. Set aside. Soak the dried mushrooms in warm water 20 minutes. Drain and cut into strips, discarding hard centers. Thread snow peas; snip off ends but leave whole. Cut each water chestnut into 2 coins. Cut celery cabbage into $\frac{1}{2}$-inch slices. Trim scallions, leaving about an inch of green; cut into $\frac{1}{2}$-inch rounds. Mince ginger root. Combine soy sauce, sherry, sugar and salt in the small bowl. Combine cornstarch and chicken stock. Pour the $\frac{1}{3}$ cup oil into the skillet. Have the 3 tablespoons oil ready for later use.

Cooking Instructions
Turn heat under skillet containing oil to medium. When the oil is hot, add the drained noodles, pressing them into a large flat cake. Fry 5 minutes (when lifted

with a spatula, the bottom of the noodles should be crisp and golden). Turn noodles and brown on the other side 5 minutes. Remove to a platter and keep warm in 170° F. oven. Turn heat to high. Add the 3 tablespoons oil to the skillet. Heat until the oil sizzles. Add pork shreds. Stir-fry-toss 2 minutes. Add ham and chicken shreds. Stir-fry 1 minute. Add shrimp and stir-fry-toss 2 minutes or just until shrimp turns pink. Remove to a heated dish. To the oil remaining in the pan (add 1 tablespoon if too much oil has been absorbed), add the snow peas, water chestnuts and mushrooms. Stir-fry 2 minutes. Add the celery cabbage, scallions and ginger. Stir-fry-toss 2 to 3 minutes or until the hearts of cabbage become slightly transparent. Return the pork, ham, chicken and shrimp to the pan. Toss just to blend. Add the soy sauce mixture. Blend quickly. Give the cornstarch-stock mixture a quick stir to blend; pour into the pan. Stir only until sauce thickens, about 1 minute. Pour over fried noodles, decorate with egg-thread garnish and serve at once.

SERVINGS: Enough for 4 as a single course or for 6 to 8 in a full menu.

NOTE: Any combination of meats, such as pork, beef and lamb, and any variety of fish and vegetables may be used in this recipe.

TSO MI
Soft-fried Noodles, Shanghai Style

Cooking Time: 12 to 15 minutes, including boiling noodles

Utensils
8- to 10-quart pot for boiling noodles
Colander
Soup plate for meat
Slotted spatula

Ingredients

	Double recipe Boiled Noodles (page 318)	6	medium dried mushrooms
1	tablespoon dried shrimp	½	pound pork or flank steak, shredded or cut in thin strips

Continued on next page

1	teaspoon cornstarch	1	medium bamboo shoot, cut in thin strips
1	teaspoon sugar		
½	teaspoon salt	½	pound Chinese chard or celery cabbage, cut in ½-inch diagonal slices
3	tablespoons soy sauce		
2	scallions, each with 1 inch of green, cut in ¼-inch rounds		
1	clove garlic, minced	2 to 3	tablespoons peanut oil or corn oil
		2	tablespoons peanut oil or corn oil

Before Cooking

Prepare noodles; rinse with cold water and set aside. Soak the dried shrimp in warm water 1 hour before beginning to cook. Soak the dried mushrooms in warm water 20 minutes. Place the shredded pork or flank steak in the soup plate and dredge with cornstarch, sugar and salt. Sprinkle with soy sauce. Mix well and set aside. Prepare the scallions, garlic, bamboo shoot and chard. Drain the soaked shrimp and mushrooms. Cut mushrooms into thin strips, discarding the hard centers. Have all portions of oil ready to go.

Cooking Instructions

Turn heat under skillet to high. When the pan is hot, add the 2 tablespoons oil. It should sizzle at once. Before the oil begins to smoke, add the seasoned dredged meat and stir-fry-toss rapidly—2 minutes for beef, 4 minutes for pork. Remove to a warm plate. If there is almost no oil left in the pan, add 1 tablespoon. When the oil is hot, add the scallions and garlic. Stir once and add the bamboo shoot. Stir-fry 1 minute. Add the chard or celery cabbage, putting the stalky pieces in before the leaf sections. Stir-fry 2 minutes. Add the drained shrimp and the mushroom shreds and toss 1 minute to blend. Remove vegetables to a warm dish. Reduce heat to medium. Add the remaining 2 tablespoons oil to the pan. When the oil is hot, add the drained cooked noodles. Stir to coat the noodles with oil but do not allow to become crisp. Stir constantly 2 minutes, making sure that the heat is not too high. Return the meat and vegetables to the pan. Mix quickly to blend ingredients with noodles and serve at once. This is a method in which the noodles are twice-cooked, once boiled and once fried. They should be fairly soft in texture but not mushy.

SERVINGS: Enough for 4 as a single course or for 6 in a full menu.

NOTE: In contrast to the chow mein recipes, soft-fried noodles are not crisped by the oil and the ingredients are mixed into the noodles rather than resting on top.

Also absent is the cornstarch-stock sauce. Characteristic of Shanghai cooking, soy sauce is used more liberally. Cantonese soft-fried noodles, which are similar but cooked with less soy, are called *lo mein*.

MANDARIN PANCAKES
Pao-Ping

Cooking Time: 4 to 6 minutes for each pancake
 35 to 50 minutes for the whole batch

Utensils
Equipment for making pastry (pages 316–317)
Bowl for pastry
Large wooden spoon
Plate for extra flour
Saucer for oil
Pastry brush
9-inch skillet
Spatula
8-inch foil pie plate
Lined rubber gloves

Ingredients

2 cups sifted all-purpose flour	Sifted extra flour for kneading
1 cup boiling water	and rolling
	1 tablespoon sesame oil

Before Cooking
Sift 2 cups flour into bowl. Gradually add boiling water, stirring continually with wooden spoon. The mixture will form coarse large flakes, more like dumplings than like peas. Stir 1 to 2 minutes or until the mixture forms a ball. Dust hands with the extra flour and bounce the ball of dough lightly from one hand to the other, kneading it in the process. Knead 5 minutes, dusting the hands with flour periodically, as the dough becomes quite sticky. Replace the dough in the bowl and cover with a damp cloth so the surface will not harden. Let dough stand 30 minutes. Lightly flour pastry board or oven cloth. Using palms of the hands, roll

the dough into a 16-inch roll. Cut the roll crosswise at 1-inch intervals into sixteen 1-inch slices. Using the base of your palm, flatten each slice into a pancake 4 inches in diameter and ¼ inch thick. Put the sesame oil in a saucer; with the pastry brush, lightly paint the top of each pancake with oil. Place one pancake on another, oiled surfaces together, so that you have 8 double pancakes. Gently press each double pancake with the ball of your palm to make it as even as possible. Lightly flour the board or cloth and rolling pin. This is tricky. If you use too little flour, the pastry will stick to the board and rolling pin. If you use too much, the pancake will be floury. Roll out each double pancake into an 8-inch circle. To insure even thickness, turn each pastry circle between rollings, making sure that it is not too thick at the edges. Place the 8-inch foil pie plate by the stove.

Cooking Instructions
Turn heat to medium under the ungreased 9-inch skillet. (The skillet may be larger, but not smaller. The pastry circle must lie flat or it will buckle and cook unevenly. The edges of the top circle will stick to the lower, making it difficult to separate them later without tearing.) Fry 2 to 3 minutes or until tan spots appear on the lower side when you lift the pancake with a spatula. Turn pancake over and fry 2 to 3 minutes on other side or until tan spots appear. Pull on the lined rubber gloves and with your fingers quickly lift one pastry circle off the other. Place each pancake browned side up on the pie plate. Continue until you have fried all 8 circles and have a total of 16 Mandarin Pancakes. During the frying process, cover the cooked pancakes with the damp cloth to prevent them from becoming brittle. When all the pancakes are fried, fold each one into quarters (like a fan), place them in a closed serving dish and bring to the table at once.

Mandarin Pancakes may be made the day before and refrigerated or even earlier and frozen. Leave the cooked, unfolded pancakes in the foil pie plate and wrap in a layer of foil for freezing or refrigeration.

TO REHEAT: Put 1½ inches cold water in a 4-quart pot with a cover. Place a trivet or a ½-pound coffee can with top and bottom removed in the water. Bring to a boil and turn heat to medium-low. Remove foil wrapping from pie plate containing pancakes and place on top of the trivet or can. Cover pot and steam—30 minutes for frozen pancakes, 10 minutes for refrigerated. Be careful not to have the heat too high—the water should simmer and not touch the pancakes. Remove from pot, fold and serve. Mandarin Pancakes are eaten with a number of Northern specialties, mainly minced or scrambled foods, and always with Peking Duck (page 273).

SERVINGS: Enough for 5 to 8.

APPETIZERS

The spectrum of *deem sum* includes salted, preserved and pickled meats, fruit, vegetables and nuts, all kinds of steamed, boiled or fried pastries and of course the delectable barbecued meats and shellfish specialties which enjoy the flexibility of being main course dishes as well. (Sweet *deem sum* are in the Desserts chapter.)

The best-known among the wide variety of *deem sum* pastry marvels is the *won ton*. In spite of Western adaptations such as ravioli, the Mongol-inspired *pelmeni* of the Russians and the *kreplach* of Yiddish cooking, Chinese pastry-making remains an unrivaled art. Its forms and fillings are so varied that it was not unusual to find over a hundred kinds of boiled, steamed or fried pastries served on the *deem sum* platters at banquets in Old China.

Chinese immigrants brought their love of pastries to this country. For a long time, while Americans were content with more commonplace interpretations of Chinese food, the pastry shops were patronized by Chinese clientele and a few lucky initiates. Today the appetizer pastry has come into its own, and shops exclusively devoted to the making of these delicious snacks are to be found in every Chinatown.

Better than that, fresh *Won Ton* and spring-roll wrapping are available at most Chinese grocers and even at a number of supermarkets. Round pastry wrappings especially created for the Northern-style dumplings, *chiao tsu* or *kuo teh*, are also for sale by the pound at some Chinese grocers. For those of you not so blessed as to have a conveniently located Chinese grocer, I have included recipes. I have also given the recipe for Thousand-Layer Rolls in this section, for the sake of convenience.

The following appetizers can be found in the technique chapters:

APPETIZERS

Red-Stewed Spiced Beef
White-Sliced Pork
White-Sliced Beef
White-Sliced Lamb
Drunken Pork
Drunken Chicken
Drunken Duck
Drunken Squab
White-Cut Chicken
White-Cut Duck
White-Cut Squab
Clear-Simmered Shrimp
Drunken Shrimp
Classic Steamed Minced Pork Balls and Variations
Classic Steamed Minced Beef Balls and Variations
Classic Steamed Minced Lamb Balls and Variations
Classic Steamed Minced Chicken Balls and Variations
Steamed Chinese Mushrooms Stuffed with Minced Pork
Classic Steamed Minced Shrimp Balls
Barbecued Pork Strips *(Char Siu)*
Barbecued Spareribs
Outdoor-Barbecued Beef or Lamb on Skewers, Peking Style
Semi-Deep-Fried Pork Balls and Variations
Semi-Deep-Fried Beef Balls and Variations
Semi-Deep-Fried Lamb Balls and Variations
Semi-Deep-Fried Chicken Balls and Variations
Semi-Deep-Fried Shrimp Balls and Variations
Deep-Fried Gift-Wrapped Shrimp
Deep-Fried Gift-Wrapped Gold Coin Chicken
Deep-Fried Gift-Wrapped Chicken, Szechuan Style
Deep-Fried Batter-Coated Pork Balls
Deep-Fried Batter-Coated Beef Balls
Deep-Fried Batter-Coated Chicken Balls
Deep-Fried Batter-Coated Shrimp Balls

TEA PORCELAIN EGGS

Cooking Time: Approximately 1½ hours

Utensils
2½-quart sturdy pot

Ingredients

12	small eggs	2	tablespoons soy sauce
4	cups cold water	1	tablespoon salt
4	cups cold water	1	teaspoon star anise (optional)
4	tea bags or 4 teaspoons black tea in a metal tea bag		

Procedure

Place eggs in the pot with 4 cups cold water. Turn heat to medium-high and bring to a boil. This will take about 15 minutes. Then reduce heat to low and simmer 10 minutes. Place the hard-boiled eggs under running cold water 2 to 3 minutes to set them. When the eggs are cool, drain them and tap briskly on the surface of a counter so that the shells will crackle. Do not allow the shells to break off. You can tap the eggs two at a time, one in each hand. Return the crackled eggs to the pot and add another 4 cups cold water. Add the tea bags, soy sauce, salt and star anise; bring to a boil. Reduce heat and simmer 1 hour. Let the eggs cool in the tea-soy water (in the refrigerator if you like) and shell them just before serving. (They may be kept unshelled and stored in the liquid for a couple of days before using.) The combination of tea and soy sauce seeping through the crackled shells makes a handsome aged-porcelain design. Use the smallest eggs possible, since these are most attractive served whole.

SERVINGS: Enough for 6 to 12, depending on the variety of other appetizers being served.

NOTE: These eggs can be made without soy sauce, but they are somewhat pallid in comparison.

SHRIMP TOASTS

Cooking Time: 10 minutes for each batch

Utensils
12-inch skillet, wok or electric frypan
Slotted spatula

Ingredients

1	recipe Classic Steamed Minced Shrimp Balls (page 220)		6 to 7 slices day-old bread
6	water chestnuts, finely diced		Salt
2	teaspoons finely minced parsley		White pepper
		3	cups peanut oil or corn oil

Before Cooking
Prepare mixture for Classic Steamed Minced Shrimp Balls. Add the diced water chestnuts and minced parsley to the raw shrimp paste. Trim the crusts from bread and cut each slice into 4 triangles. Spread the shrimp mixture generously on each triangle, mounding it to a peak. You should have between 24 and 28 Shrimp Toasts. Have salt and pepper shakers handy. Have oil ready to go.

Cooking Instructions
Heat oil in skillet or wok over medium-high heat until it foams around a cube of fresh bread (375° F. on electric frypan). Fry the Shrimp Toasts six at a time, 5 minutes shrimp-side-up and 5 minutes shrimp-side-down. The Shrimp Toasts should be golden brown all over. Remove to paper towels to drain. Sprinkle lightly with salt and pepper. Repeat frying and draining until all the Shrimp Toasts have been fried. They should be delectably pink and firm on the inside with crisp and golden exteriors.

SERVINGS: Enough for 6 as an appetizer.

BUTTERFLY SHRIMP

Cooking Time: About 4 to 6 minutes for each batch

Utensils
Sharp knife
12-inch skillet, electric frypan or 3-quart
    Dutch oven with frying thermometer
Slotted spoon

Ingredients

1	recipe Basic Thin Batter (page 333)	6	paper-thin slices Virginia ham
24	large shrimp	4	cups peanut oil or corn oil

Before Cooking
Prepare Basic Thin Batter ahead of time and refrigerate at least 30 minutes. Remove from refrigerator 30 minutes before using to allow batter to come to room temperature. Wash and shell shrimp. Remove feelers but retain tail. With the point of a sharp knife, split each shrimp along the inside curve (not the back), cutting almost but not all the way through to the back. Spread the split shrimp wide and rinse away the black back vein under cold water. Blot the shrimp very dry with paper towels. Spread each shrimp cut-side-up to form the shape of butterfly wings. Score wings with the back of a knife to help keep their shape. Cut each slice of Virginia ham into 4 squares. Press 1 square of ham gently on the split shrimp. Place the bowl containing the Basic Thin Batter near the shrimp. Have oil ready to go.

Cooking Instructions
Heat oil in skillet or Dutch oven over medium-high heat until it foams around a cube of fresh bread (375° F. on electric frypan). Holding the shrimp by the tail, dip it into the batter but do not coat the tail. Then gently lay the butterfly shrimp, ham-side-up, in the hot oil. Fry no more than 2 or 3 shrimp at one time. Fry 3 to 4 minutes or until bottoms are golden. Turn shrimp and fry on the other side 2 to 3 minutes. Remove with slotted spoon and drain on paper towels. The shrimp should be crusty and golden; the tails, which double as handles, should be bright red. Serve as an appetizer with Chinese-Style Mustard, Hoisin sauce or a soy sauce dip (page 22). Or cover with any of the Pouring Sauces (pages 351–359) and serve as a main course.

SERVINGS: Enough for 12 as an appetizer or for 6 as a main course.

SESAME SEED CHICKEN WINGS OR LEGS

Cooking Time: 10 to 12 minutes for each batch

Utensils
Colander
Pie plate
12-inch skillet, wok or electric frypan
Slotted spatula

Ingredients

1 recipe Basic Thin Batter (page 333)

4 cups peanut oil or corn oil

2 pounds fryer wings (12 to 14) or

3 pounds small fryer legs (about 12)

$\frac{1}{3}$ cup sesame seeds

Before Cooking
Prepare Basic Thin Batter ahead of time and refrigerate at least 30 minutes. Remove from refrigerator 30 minutes before using. Wash chicken wings or legs; cut off bony wing tips and discard. Place in colander to drain. Blot dry and arrange in rows on paper towel to dry thoroughly before frying. Put sesame seeds in pie plate. Have oil ready to go. Heat oil in skillet or wok over medium-high heat until it foams around a cube of fresh bread (375° F. on electric frypan). Dip each chicken wing or leg in batter. Sprinkle with sesame seeds and deep-fry, no more than four at one time, 10 to 12 minutes, turning the pieces 2 or 3 times during the frying. Remove with slotted spatula and drain on paper towels. Repeat until all chicken pieces have been fried. Place fried chicken on fresh paper towels while you are frying the remainder. The chicken will have crusty, golden brown exteriors and will be moist and tender inside.

SERVINGS: Enough for 6 to 12 as an appetizer, for 3 to 4 as a single course or for 6 in a full menu.

NOTE: A 3-pound frying chicken, cut in Chinese-style serving pieces, may be used in place of the wings and drumsticks.

SWEET-AND-SOUR SESAME SEED CHICKEN WINGS OR LEGS: Prepare any of the sweet-and-sour Pouring Sauces (pages 353–356) ahead of time. Heat gently while the chicken is frying. Put fried chicken on a serving platter and pour sauce over.

BASIC THIN BATTER

2 medium eggs	3/4 teaspoon salt
3/4 cup flour	3/4 cup cold water

Break eggs into a quart bowl and beat, gradually adding the flour and salt. Add water by the tablespoonful and beat until smooth. The batter should be thin. Cover and let stand or refrigerate at least 30 minutes. Before using, let batter come to room temperature. Use for coating shrimp and chicken parts.

CANTONESE EGG ROLLS

Cooking Time: 1 minute to shallow-fry each skin
8 minutes to shallow-fry filling
5 to 8 minutes to deep-fry rolls

Utensils
Medium bowl for egg mixture
Small bowl for sealing mixture
8-inch skillet
Cooking spoon
Pancake turner
12-inch skillet or electric frypan
Pastry brush

Ingredients

1 recipe Pork Filling for Egg Rolls (page 335)	2/3 cup water
4 eggs	4 tablespoons peanut oil or corn oil
1/2 cup flour	2 tablespoons flour
1/2 teaspoon salt	3 tablespoons water
	3 cups peanut oil or corn oil

Procedure
Prepare the filling ahead of time. Then prepare the "skins." Place the eggs in a medium-size bowl. Beat until light, gradually adding the 1/2 cup flour and salt. When the mixture is smooth, add the 2/3 cup water. Beat until blended.

COOKING THE SKINS: Place the 8-inch skillet over medium heat. When it is hot enough for a drop of water to bubble into steam, add ½ tablespoon oil. When the oil is hot, pour just enough batter into the pan to coat its surface thinly when the pan is tilted. Fry less than 1 minute. Remove, unfried-side-up, to a clean towel or flat plate. Continue frying until all the batter is used up. You should have 8 skins.

TO FILL THE ROLLS: Blend the 2 tablespoons flour and 3 tablespoons water for a sealing mixture. Place a circle of the egg roll in front of you. Spoon about ¼ cup of the filling horizontally along the lower third of the circle. With the fingers, roll up the edge of the circle over the filling. Continue rolling away from you, tucking in the sides of the circle as you roll. This forms a packet. Now brush the "sealer" along the outer edge of circle and fold over to make a flap. Press lightly with fingers to seal roll. Place each filled roll on a clean towel or cookie sheet until ready to deep-fry. At this point the cooled, filled rolls may be wrapped in aluminum foil and frozen for later use.

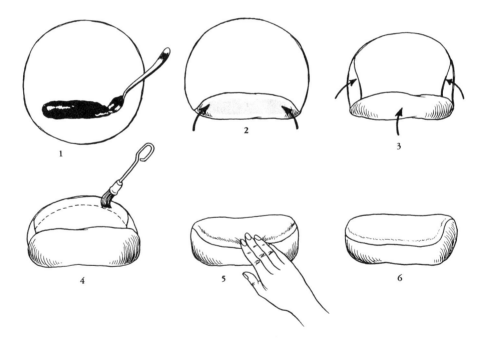

Filling Egg Roll "Skins"
1. Circle of egg roll in front of you, with ¼ cup filling spooned along length of lower third of circle.   2. Fold bottom of circle over filling.   3. Continue rolling away from you, tucking in sides of circle as you roll.   4. Brush outer edge of circle with sealer.   5. Fold over to make a flap. Press gently with fingers to seal roll.   6. Correctly folded egg roll ready for deep-frying.

TO DEEP-FRY EGG ROLLS: Heat oil in 12-inch skillet over medium heat until it sizzles around a cube of fresh bread (380° F. on electric frypan). Fry the egg rolls, two at a time, until they are golden brown all over. Drain singly on paper towels. Do not stack or the steam from the rolls will cause sogginess. For easier handling with chopsticks, cut each roll diagonally into 2-inch slices. Arrange on a platter in the original roll shape and serve with small dishes of mustard or oyster or plum sauce.

SERVINGS: Enough for 8 to 10 as an appetizer or for 4 as a course in a full menu.

NOTE: These are Cantonese Egg Rolls, quite different in taste and texture from the Peking Spring Rolls, which are made with wheat pastry skins.

PORK FILLING FOR EGG ROLLS

Cooking Time: 8 minutes to stir-fry-toss

Utensils
Chinese cutting knife
12-inch skillet or wok
Slotted spatula
Wire strainer

Ingredients

½ pound (1 cup) lean pork, shredded

1 scallion with 2 inches of green, cut in ⅛-inch rounds

10 water chestnuts, cut into ⅛-inch dice

½ bamboo shoot (6 to 8 ounces), shredded

1 large stalk celery, shredded, or 1 cup pea sprouts

6 medium dried mushrooms

½ teaspoon salt

½ teaspoon sugar

2 teaspoons soy sauce

2 teaspoons cornstarch

½ teaspoon sesame oil

2 tablespoons peanut oil or corn oil

Before Cooking

Prepare the pork, scallion, water chestnuts, bamboo shoot and celery. If you are using pea sprouts, rinse and drain. Soak the dried mushrooms in warm water 20 minutes. Drain well and slice into thin shreds, discarding the hard centers. Measure salt, sugar, soy sauce, cornstarch and sesame oil. Have the peanut oil or corn oil ready to go.

Cooking Instructions

Turn heat under skillet or wok to medium-high. When the pan is hot, add the oil. It should sizzle at once. Before the oil begins to smoke, stir in the pork shreds and stir-fry 3 minutes. Remove pork with slotted spatula to a warm plate. To the oil in the pan, add the scallion, water chestnuts, bamboo shoot and celery or pea sprouts. Stir-fry-toss 2 minutes. Add mushroom shreds and stir-fry 1 minute. Return the pork to the skillet. Stir 1 minute to blend. Add the salt, sugar, soy sauce, cornstarch and sesame oil. Stir, blending ingredients, 1 minute. Remove from heat and pour into wire strainer to drain off oil. Cool thoroughly before filling egg roll skins. The filling should be as dry as possible before rolling. Moisture can cause the ingredients to leak into the deep-frying oil.

CHICKEN FILLING: Substitute 1 cup shredded chicken breast for the pork; dredge with the cornstarch. Stir-fry vegetables first. Add dredged chicken strips and stir-fry 2 minutes or until the chicken turns white. Add seasonings and blend 1 minute. Drain and cool before using.

SHRIMP FILLING: Substitute 1 cup diced raw shrimp for the pork; dredge with the cornstarch. Stir-fry vegetables first. Add shrimp and stir-fry only until the shrimp turns pink. Add seasonings and blend 1 minute. Drain and cool before using.

PORK AND SHRIMP OR CHICKEN FILLING: Reduce pork shreds to $\frac{1}{2}$ cup. Stir-fry 3 minutes as directed. Remove from pan. Stir-fry vegetables as directed. Add $\frac{1}{2}$ cup dredged diced shrimp or dredged chicken shreds. Return pork to the pan and add seasonings. Blend 1 minute. Drain and cool before using.

FILLINGS USING COOKED INGREDIENTS: One cup of any of the following ingredients, cooked and shredded, may be substituted for the raw pork: pork, Virginia ham, barbecued pork, chicken or duck breast, shrimp (diced), crab, lobster meat or any other leftover meat. Follow the directions for Pork Filling, but do not add the cooked ingredients until the seasonings are added. Stir about 1 minute or just long enough to heat through and blend the flavors. Drain and cool before using.

PEKING SPRING ROLLS

Cooking Time: 7 minutes to prefry filling
                    5 to 8 minutes to deep-fry each batch of filled rolls

Utensils
Equipment for making pastry (pages 316–317)
12-inch skillet, wok or electric frypan
Wire strainer
Small bowl for sealer
Pastry brush
Large colander

Ingredients

1	recipe Basic Egg Noodle Pastry (page 317)	1	medium bamboo shoot, shredded
$\frac{1}{4}$	pound pork butt, shredded or cut in thin strips	8	medium dried mushrooms
$\frac{1}{4}$	pound barbecued pork or Virginia ham, shredded or cut in thin strips	1	cup pea sprouts
		$1\frac{1}{2}$	teaspoons soy sauce
		$\frac{1}{2}$	teaspoon salt
$\frac{1}{2}$	cooked fryer's breast, skinned and boned, cut in strips	$\frac{1}{2}$	teaspoon sugar
		$1\frac{1}{2}$	teaspoons cornstarch
1	small leek, white part only, cut in strips	1	egg
		2	tablespoons cold water
		4	cups peanut oil or corn oil
		2	tablespoons peanut oil or corn oil

Procedure

Prepare Basic Egg Noodle Pastry. After it has been covered with a damp cloth 30 minutes, divide dough in half. Refrigerate half the pastry for future use. Divide the remaining half into 2 equal lumps. Flatten one lump and roll out as thinly as possible to a rectangle about 17x20 inches. Trim away the ragged edges and cut into 6-inch squares. You will have 4 Spring Roll "skins" with about two 3-inch squares left over. Save the leftover squares for making *won tons* or *sieu mai*. Lightly sprinkle the Spring Roll squares with cornstarch and put them aside. Repeat with the remaining lump of pastry. You will now have 8 Spring Roll "skins."

PREPARING THE FILLING: Prepare the meats, chicken, leek and bamboo shoot. Soak the dried mushrooms in warm water 20 minutes. Drain and cut the mushrooms into thin strips, discarding the hard centers. Wash and pick over the pea sprouts;

drain well. Measure the soy sauce, salt, sugar and cornstarch and set aside. Make the sealer by beating the egg with the cold water and set aside. Have both portions of oil ready to go.

PREFRYING FILLINGS: Turn heat under skillet or wok to medium-high. When the pan is hot, add the 2 tablespoons oil. It should sizzle at once. Before the oil begins to smoke, add the raw pork shreds and stir-fry-toss 3 minutes. Add the pork or ham and the chicken; stir-fry 2 minutes. Add the leek, bamboo shoot, mushroom strips and pea sprouts. Stir and toss 2 minutes. Add the soy sauce, salt, sugar and cornstarch. Blend well and remove from heat. Let mixture drain and cool in a wire strainer. Fill the Spring Rolls following the illustrated instructions.

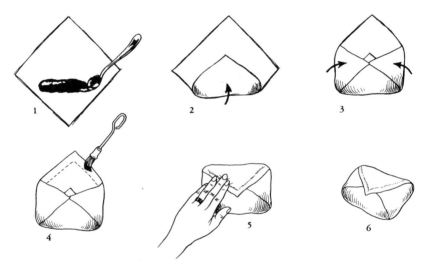

Filling Square Spring Roll "Skins"
1. Place square of Spring Roll "skin" in front of you with one corner pointing toward you. Put ¼ cup filling horizontally about 1 inch below the center of "skin." 2. Fold the corner nearest you over the filling. 3. Bring the left corner over and fold. Then bring right corner over and fold. Press the filling in securely to prevent leakage. 4. You now have the shape of a filled envelope with an outer corner remaining. Using a pastry brush or fingers, spread sealer on the edges of the outer corner. 5. Fold over like an envelope flap and press gently with fingers to seal. 6. The finished roll will resemble a sealed package.

DEEP-FRYING SPRING ROLLS: Heat the 4 cups oil in the skillet or wok over medium-high heat until it foams around a cube of fresh bread (375° F. on electric frypan). Fry 4 rolls at a time 5 to 8 minutes or only until the pastry is golden (remember the filling has been precooked). Place the fried rolls on end in the colander to drain off the oil as you fry the remaining four. Do not stack the rolls once they are fried or the pastry will steam and become soggy. Cut each roll diagonally into 3 pieces and arrange on a warm platter. Serve with small dishes of mustard, plum sauce, red pepper oil or "Chekiang" vinegar. Although slightly larger in size than the original Spring Rolls, these are the authentic Northern-style rolls, with crisp pastry wrappings rather than the egg-batter skins of the Cantonese versions.

SERVINGS: Enough for 8 to 10 as an appetizer or savory *deem sum* or for 4 as a single course.

WON TON

Cooking Time: 5 to 8 minutes to boil each batch
5 to 8 minutes to fry each batch

Utensils
Equipment for making pastry (pages 316–
    317)
Long, sharp knife
Meat grinder
Bowl for filling
6-quart pot for boiling
Electric frypan or 2½-quart pot with fat ther-
    mometer

Ingredients

1	recipe Basic Egg Noodle Pastry (page 317) or 36 *Won Ton* squares (3x3 inches)	½	cup water chestnuts, finely diced
½	pound pork butt or 1 cup ground pork	2	scallions with 1 inch of green, minced
12	medium shrimp, peeled and deveined	1	teaspoon soy sauce
		½	teaspoon salt
		1	teaspoon cornstarch

Procedure
Prepare Basic Egg Noodle Pastry. After it has stood covered with the damp cloth, divide the pastry in half. Cover one half with plastic wrap and refrigerate to use

later for making noodles, Spring Rolls or another batch of *Won Tons,* if you prefer. Divide the remaining pastry into 2 small lumps. Take one lump, flatten into a patty and begin rolling from the center out until you have formed as thin a sheet of pastry as possible, about 12x20 inches. The pastry should be almost transparent and the edges will be papery. Trim the ragged edges of the pastry, making as neat a rectangle as possible. This will give you more usable squares. Discard the trimmings. With a long, sharp knife, cut lines all the way down and across the pastry at 3-inch intervals. You should now have about 18 three-inch *Won Ton* squares. Take the second lump of pastry and repeat the rolling out and cutting. You will have a total of 36 *Won Ton* "skins" to work with. Stack the "skins," making sure that they have enough cornstarch on them so that they will not stick together.

PREPARING THE FILLING: Put the pork through the medium blade of your meat grinder twice. Mince the shrimp until they are a fine paste. Combine the ground pork and shrimp in a bowl. Add water chestnuts, scallions, soy sauce, salt and cornstarch to the pork-shrimp mixture. Mix thoroughly, blending all ingredients well.

FILLING THE "SKINS": Place the bowl of filling on your right. Put a square of pastry on the palm of your left hand in a diamond shape. Put a scant teaspoonful of filling about ½ inch from the point of the square facing you. Fold this bottom corner over the filling, then fold it again away from you to ⅔ the height of the square. Put a tiny dab of filling on the tip of the right hand corner, bring the tip of the left corner over and pinch together firmly to seal. You will now have what looks like a nurse's cap with a peaked front. The *Won Tons* are now ready to boil or fry. If you do not plan to use them at once, they can be frozen on a cookie sheet until they are solid and then stored in plastic bags with twist seals. When you are ready to use them, add directly to boiling water. *Won Tons* freeze well and will taste as good as the fresh ones when they are cooked.

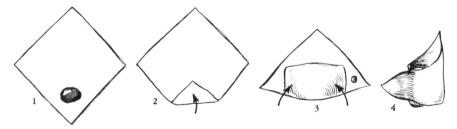

Wrapping *Won Tons*
1. Place filling ½ inch from point of pastry square. 2. Fold point over filling. 3. Fold pastry and filling up ⅔ the height of the square. Put a tiny dab of filling on the right tip, bring left tip over to meet it and seal. 4. Finished *Won Ton* resembles a peaked cap.

DEEP-FRYING WON TONS (AS A COURSE OR APPETIZER): Pour 3 to 4 cups oil in an electric skillet set at 350° F. or into a 2½-quart saucepan with a frying thermometer attached. When the oil has reached the required temperature, fry the *Won Tons,* twelve at a time, until they are golden brown (about 5 to 8 minutes). Drain the fried *Won Tons* on paper towels and serve covered with any of the Sweet-and-Sour Sauces (pages 353–356) or with little dishes of Plum Sauce or Ginger-Soy Dip.

SERVINGS: Enough for 4 as a single course or 6 to 8 as an appetizer or savory *deem sum.*

BOILING WON TONS (FOR SOUP): Bring 4 quarts of water to a rolling boil in a 6-quart pot. Add 18 *Won Tons.* When the *Won Tons* rise to the surface, add 1 cup cold water and bring to a boil again. The second boiling is to guarantee that the raw ingredients in the filling are thoroughly cooked. Transfer the cooked *Won Tons* to 2 quarts simmering chicken stock and keep them warm while you boil the remainder. Serve in soup bowls topped with chopped scallions.

SERVINGS: Allowing 6 to 9 *Won Tons* per person, you will have enough for 4 to 6 people.

SIEU MAI
Pastry-Wrapped Pork Balls

Cooking Time: 20 minutes for steaming

Utensils
Equipment for making pastry (pages 316–317)
1-pint saucepan
Meat grinder
Bowl for filling
Steaming unit
11-inch skillet or electric frypan
Circle of aluminum foil (11 inches in diameter), pierced all over
10-inch cake rack

Ingredients

1	recipe for Basic Egg Noodle Pastry (page 317) or 18 *Won Ton* squares (3x3 inches)	6	medium shrimp, peeled and deveined
2	ounces salt pork	1/2	medium bamboo shoot, diced finely
1	cup water	1/4	teaspoon salt
1/4	pound pork butt or 1/2 cup ground pork	1/8	teaspoon white pepper

Procedure

Prepare Basic Egg Noodle Pastry. After it has stood covered with a damp cloth 30 minutes, divide into fourths. Store three fourths of the pastry in plastic wrap and make 18 *Won Ton* squares (page 339) with the remaining fourth.

PREPARING THE FILLING: Put the piece of salt pork in the saucepan with 1 cup water. Bring to a boil and simmer 10 minutes. Drain and dice the pork finely. Put the pork butt through the medium blade of your meat grinder twice or, if you are using ground pork, place it in a bowl with the salt pork. Mince the shrimp until they are a paste. Add the shrimp paste, diced bamboo shoot, salt and pepper to the bowl containing the minced salt pork and the ground raw pork. Mix until thoroughly blended. Pinch off enough of the mixture to roll into a ball the size of a marble. Make 18 balls, using up all the filling.

WRAPPING THE FILLING: Place each ball in the center of a pastry square and draw up the sides of the pastry to form a cup with crimped edges. Leave the top of the meatball exposed.

STEAMING THE PASTRY: Brush the circle of foil lightly with oil. Put the cake rack in the skillet or electric frypan. Pour 2 cups boiling water into the pan and turn heat to medium (300° F. on frypan). When the water in the pan begins to boil actively, place the foil on the rack and put the pastry-wrapped pork balls on the foil. Cover the pan and steam 20 minutes, adding more boiling water as needed.

SERVINGS: Enough for 4 to 6 as an appetizer or savory *deem sum.*

HAR GOW
Steamed Shrimp Dumplings

Cooking Time: 15 to 20 minutes for each batch

Utensils
Chinese cutting knife
Equipment for making pastry (pages 316–317)
1-pint saucepan
Bowl for filling
Pastry brush
11-inch skillet with cover
10-inch cake rack
Aluminum foil (11 inches in diameter),
    pierced all over

Ingredients

2	cups flour	24	canned water chestnuts, minced
1	cup boiling water	1	teaspoon minced ginger root
	Cornstarch for rolling	1	teaspoon minced Chinese parsley
2	ounces salt pork	¾	teaspoon salt
2	pounds shrimp, peeled and deveined	2	tablespoons peanut oil or corn oil

Before Cooking

Pour flour in a bowl. Stir the boiling water into it and blend with a fork. Shape dough into a ball. Dust an oven cloth lightly with cornstarch. Begin kneading the hot dough on it. Press dough with the palm of the hand, gather back and fold over. Do this for about 10 minutes. The dough should be smooth and velvety. Cover with a damp cloth and let stand 20 minutes. Shape the dough into a log and roll with the fingers of both hands until it is about 15 inches long and 1 inch in diameter. Cut into 1-inch sections, then cut each section in half to make 30 pieces. Flatten the pieces with the palm of the hand. They will look like buttons. Using the dowel or a rolling pin, roll each piece out to a round of dough 4 inches in diameter. Dust lightly with cornstarch and stack. Cover with plastic wrap to keep them from drying out while you prepare the filling.

PREPARING THE FILLING: Put the salt pork and 1 cup water into the saucepan. Bring to a boil and simmer 10 minutes. Drain and mince finely. Put in the bowl. Mince the shrimp until they are a sticky paste. Add to the minced salt pork. Add the water chestnuts, ginger, parsley and salt to the bowl containing the shrimp and pork. Mix well with chopsticks or a fork.

FILLING THE DUMPLINGS: Place a generous teaspoon of filling in the center of a pastry round. Fold like a turnover and crimp edges, making sure that they are sealed. Continue until all the pastry rounds have been filled and crimped. Using a pastry brush, lightly coat the filled pastries with the 2 tablespoons oil. Cover the filled pastries with plastic wrap as you work to prevent them from drying out.

STEAMING THE DUMPLINGS: Place the cake rack in the skillet. Pour 2 cups boiling water into the skillet. Lightly brush the circle of foil with oil and place on the rack. Turn heat to medium. When the water boils actively, place the dumplings ½ inch apart on the oiled foil. You will be able to steam 8 to 10 at a time. Cover and steam 15 to 20 minutes. The pastry will be translucent when done. Repeat the steamings until all the dumplings have been cooked. Serve as an appetizer with small bowls of mustard or condiment sauces or steam and then simmer in 3 quarts seasoned chicken stock to serve as soup.

SERVINGS: Enough for 8 to 10 as an appetizer or savory *deem sum* or for 6 as a main-course soup.

CHIAO TSU AND KUO TEH
Lamb- or Pork-Filled Dumplings

Cooking Time: 4 to 5 minutes to boil each batch
3 to 5 minutes to shallow-fry each batch

Utensils
Equipment for making pastry (pages 316–317)
Bowl for filling
6-quart pot
11-inch flared skillet with cover
Slotted spoon
Large colander

Ingredients

2	cups flour	6	scallions, white parts only, minced
1	cup boiling water		
	Cornstarch for rolling	1	teaspoon finely minced ginger root
¾	pound ground lamb or pork		
¼	pound celery cabbage, chopped or shredded	1½	tablespoons soy sauce
		2	teaspoons sherry

3/4 teaspoon salt
1   tablespoon sesame oil
4   quarts water

1/2 cup peanut oil or corn oil (for shallow-frying)

Procedure

Pour flour in a bowl. Stir the boiling water into it and blend with a fork. Shape dough into a ball. Dust a pastry board or oven cloth lightly with cornstarch. Begin kneading the hot dough on it. Press dough with the palm of the hand, gather back and fold over. Do this for about 10 minutes. The dough should be smooth and velvety. Cover with a damp cloth and let stand 20 minutes. Shape the dough into a log and roll with the fingers of both hands until it is 18 inches long and 1 inch in diameter. Cut into 1-inch sections, then cut each section in half to make 36 pieces. Flatten the pieces with the palm of the hand. They will look like buttons. Using the dowel or a rolling pin, roll each piece out to a round of pastry 3 inches in diameter. They should not be larger or the pastry will be too thin. As you become proficient, you may be able to roll two pieces of pastry at a time. Dust lightly with cornstarch and stack. Cover with plastic wrap to prevent from drying out while you prepare the filling.

PREPARING THE FILLING: Put the ground lamb or pork in a bowl. Add the celery cabbage, scallions and ginger to the meat in the bowl. Add the soy sauce, sherry, salt and sesame oil. Blend the ingredients with chopsticks or a fork.

FILLING THE DUMPLINGS: Place a generous teaspoon of filling in the center of a pastry round. Fold like a turnover and crimp the edges together securely. If the skins have become too floured with cornstarch and you have trouble sealing the edges, moisten fingers with a little cold water. You will have 36 dumplings ready to cook. Put 4 quarts water in the 6-quart pot. If you are going to shallow-fry the dumplings after boiling, set aside 1/2 cup peanut or corn oil.

BOILING THE DUMPLINGS: Put the pot containing water over high heat and bring to a rolling boil. Carefully drop 12 dumplings into the boiling water. They will sink to the bottom. When they rise in 1 to 2 minutes, add 1 cup of cold water to the pot. When the water boils actively again, the dumplings are cooked. Remove with a slotted spoon to a colander, arranging the dumplings so that they are not stacked. Repeat until all the dumplings are cooked. Room can be made in the colander by putting the already boiled and drained dumplings on paper towels to absorb any excess moisture. Served with condiment sauces, these boiled dumplings are called *Chiao Tsu*. But they are infinitely more delicious served shallow-fried, at which point they become *Kuo Teh*.

SHALLOW-FRYING DUMPLINGS: Turn heat under skillet to medium. When it is hot enough for a drop of water to bubble into steam, add 2 tablespoons of the oil. When the oil begins to sizzle, arrange 10 dumplings close together in 2 rows. This will leave enough room to pry up the dumplings and remove them from the pan. Fry 2 to 3 minutes, lifting with a spatula from time to time to make sure that the bottoms do not become stuck to the pan. (If the dumplings stick to one another, it is all right.) When the bottoms are golden brown, slip the dumplings from the skillet onto a platter (a skillet with flared sides makes this easier) and keep them warm in 170° F. oven. Add 2 tablespoons oil to the pan and repeat until all the dumplings are fried, adding oil to the pan each time. Between each frying, scrape up any particles of pastry which may have stuck to the pan, washing it out if necessary. Serve the *Kuo Teb* with small dishes of Garlic-Soy Dip (page 351), vinegar and a bottle of red pepper oil. These dumplings, translucent on top and tender crisp on the bottom, are a Northern specialty. They were sold, however, by mobile vendors in most large cities in Eastern and Central China. They are not too well known among the Cantonese.

SERVINGS: Enough for 6 as a course or for 12 as an appetizer or savory *deem sum*.

BAO
Steamed-Filled Buns

Cooking Time: 10 minutes for each batch

Utensils
Equipment for making pastry (pages 316–317)
Large bowl
Wooden spoon
12 to 15 four-inch squares wax paper
11-inch skillet with cover
10-inch cake rack
Aluminum foil (11 inches in diameter),
    pierced all over

Ingredients

1	package dry yeast	1	tablespoon peanut oil or corn oil
1	cup lukewarm water	2	cups flour

1	tablespoon sugar	1	recipe Lamb Filling or Barbecued
⅛	teaspoon salt		Pork Filling (below)

Procedure

Sprinkle the dry yeast over the lukewarm water in the large bowl; stir until completely dissolved. Add oil. Put flour, sugar and salt in a sifter and gradually sift into yeast mixture, beating well with the wooden spoon after each addition. The dough will be quite rubbery at this point. Beat with the spoon 5 minutes, lifting, folding and mixing the dough. The dough will now be smoother in texture but still springy. Form into a ball and cover with a damp dishcloth. Let dough rise in a warm place away from drafts—an unlit oven without a pilot light is fine. When the dough has doubled in volume (about 2 hours), place it on a pastry board or oven cloth which has been well sprinkled with cornstarch; knead lightly 1 minute. Pinch off 12 to 15 pieces of dough, equal in size. Roll each piece into a 4-inch round about ¼ inch thick. Make sure that the rolled rounds of dough are not too thin. The filling should not show through when the buns are steamed.

FILLING THE BUNS: Spoon a generous tablespoon of filling in the center of each round. Bring the edges of the pastry up and over the filling like a pouch. Twist the edges with thumb and forefinger to seal. Put each bun, twist-side-down, on a square of wax paper on a tray or cookie sheet. Place in a warm spot and let the buns rise 15 to 30 minutes.

STEAMING THE BUNS: Put the 10-inch cake rack in the 11-inch skillet. Pour 2 cups boiling water into the skillet. Turn heat to medium high. When the water boils, place the circle of foil over the cake rack and put the buns with the wax paper squares on the foil. Leave room between the buns for expansion. You will be able to steam 4 to 5 buns at a time. Cover and steam about 10 minutes or until the tops of the buns are glossy. Do not steam longer than 15 minutes or the pastry will begin to wrinkle. Keep the steamed buns warm in a 170° F. oven while you steam the remainder. Remove the waxed paper before serving with dishes of Chinese-Style Mustard, Garlic-Soy Dip, "Chekiang" Vinegar (page 351) and Red Pepper Oil (page 352).

SERVINGS: Enough for 4 or 5 as an appetizer or savory *deem sum*.

NOTE: Steamed *Bao* may be wrapped and frozen after cooling. To reheat, place frozen buns on squares of wax paper and steam until heated through. Cold *Bao* can also be reheated in this manner.

LAMB FILLING FOR STEAMED BUNS,
Peking Style

Cooking Time: 5 to 6 minutes for stir-frying

Utensils
Meat grinder
Chinese cutting knife
Small bowl for seasonings
12-inch skillet or wok
Tongs or chopsticks

Ingredients

½ pound lean lamb, boned and trimmed

6 scallions, white part only, minced

1 teaspoon minced ginger root

1 medium bamboo shoot, diced finely

¼ pound celery cabbage, chopped or shredded

2 large dried mushrooms

1½ tablespoons soy sauce

2 teaspoons sherry

1 teaspoon sesame oil

¼ teaspoon salt

⅛ teaspoon pepper

½ teaspoon sugar

¼ teaspoon five-spice seasoning

2 tablespoons peanut oil or corn oil

Before Cooking
Put the lamb through medium blade of meat grinder twice. Prepare the vegetables. Soak the mushrooms in warm water 20 minutes. Drain and dice finely, discarding the hard centers. Combine the soy sauce, sherry, sesame oil, salt, pepper, sugar and five-spice powder in the small bowl. Have peanut oil or corn oil ready to go.

Cooking Instructions
Turn heat under skillet or wok to medium-high. When the pan is hot, add the 2 tablespoons oil. It should sizzle at once. Before the oil begins to smoke, add the scallions and ginger. Stir-fry 30 seconds. Add ground lamb; stir-fry-toss 2 minutes. Add diced mushrooms and stir-fry 1 minute. Add bamboo shoots and celery cabbage. Stir and toss 2 minutes. Pour in soy sauce mixture and blend well. Remove from heat. Cool before filling buns.

AMOUNT: Enough to fill 12 to 15 buns.

CHAR SIU BAO
Barbecued Pork Filling for Steamed Buns

Cooking Time: 4 to 5 minutes

Utensils
Small bowl for seasonings
12-inch skillet or wok
Tongs or chopsticks

Ingredients

½	pound barbecued pork,* chopped finely	1	tablespoon sherry
6	scallions, each with 1 inch of green, chopped semi-finely	1	teaspoon sesame oil
½	medium bamboo shoot, diced finely	¼	teaspoon salt
		⅛	teaspoon pepper
2	large dried mushrooms	½	teaspoon sugar
1½	tablespoons soy sauce	1	tablespoon cornstarch
		½	cup cold chicken stock or water
		2	tablespoons peanut oil or corn oil

Before Cooking
Prepare the pork, scallions and bamboo shoot. Soak the dried mushrooms in warm water 20 minutes. Drain and squeeze out excess moisture with fingers. Discard hard centers and mince. Combine the soy sauce, sherry, sesame oil, salt, pepper and sugar in the small bowl. Combine cornstarch and chicken stock or water. Have oil ready to go.

Cooking Instructions
Turn heat under skillet or wok to high. When pan is hot, add the 2 tablespoons oil. It should sizzle at once. Before the oil begins to smoke, add the pork and scallions. Stir-fry 1 minute. Add the bamboo shoot and minced mushrooms and stir-fry-toss 2 minutes. Add the seasoning mixture and stir well 30 seconds to blend. Give the cornstarch-stock mixture a quick stir to blend and add it to the pan. Stir 1 minute or just until sauce thickens. Remove from heat and cool before using.

AMOUNT: Enough to fill 12 to 15 buns.

* Barbecued pork can be bought ready-cooked at Chinese grocery stores or see recipe for *Char Siu* (page 265).

SWEET FILLED BAO

Prepare Sweet Red Bean Paste (page 362) or buy it canned from your Chinese grocer. Use 1 to 1½ tablespoons filling for each bun. This sweet filling is quite popular with the Chinese but is an acquired taste for most Americans.

THOUSAND-LAYER ROLLS

Chinese-Style Bread

Prepare dough as directed in recipe for *Bao* (page 346). After the dough has risen, place it on a board or cloth well sprinkled with cornstarch. Knead lightly for a minute and then pinch off 30 pieces of dough, equal in size. With a well-floured dowel, roll out 20 of the pieces to 2½-inch rounds. The dough will spring back about ½ inch. You will now have 20 rounds of dough 2 inches in diameter. Next roll the remaining 10 pieces of dough into rounds of 3½ to 4 inches in diameter. These will also shrink back about ½ inch. Take three of the 2-inch rounds and brush the tops of each lightly with sesame oil. Then stack the three together and cover them with one of the larger rounds. Bring the ends of the larger round over the stack and tuck the edges under. Brush the tops of the covered layered buns with sesame oil and set each one on a square of wax paper. Steam about 10 minutes as directed for *Bao* or until the dough has a translucent look.

DIPS AND POURING SAUCES

DIPPING SAUCES

The followir g dips should be prepared as needed and served in small saucers or in the 3-inch round Chinese dishes especially made for this purpose. When used as dips, bottled or canned condiment sauces (oyster sauce, Hoisin sauce, brown bean sauce and plum sauce) are served in the same manner. For more information about the condiment sauces, see page 22.

CHINESE-STYLE MUSTARD: Mix $\frac{1}{4}$ cup dry mustard powder with $1\frac{1}{2}$ tablespoons cold water. Make a creamy, lump-free paste. (If you like, add $\frac{1}{8}$ teaspoon sesame oil; blend well and let stand 10 minutes before using.) Leftover mustard should be refrigerated in a tightly covered small jar or bottle. Do not add fresh mustard to old. Make small amounts as needed. Serve with simmered, steamed or batter-fried dishes.

"CHEKIANG" VINEGAR: The original vinegar from Chekiang Province is very dark in color and pungent in fragrance. A reasonably acceptable substitute can be made by combining $\frac{1}{3}$ cup malt vinegar and 1 tablespoon soy sauce. (If you like, add 2 teaspoons minced ginger root or scallions.) Serve with simmered or steamed dishes.

GARLIC-SOY DIP: Add 2 cloves garlic, minced, to $\frac{1}{4}$ cup soy sauce; let stand 30 minutes. Serve with simmered, steamed, fried or roasted foods.

SESAME-SOY DIP: Add 1 tablespoon peanut oil and 1 teaspoon sesame oil to $\frac{1}{4}$ cup soy sauce. (If you like, stir in $\frac{1}{2}$ teaspoon brown sugar.) Serve with simmered or steamed foods.

SHERRY-SOY DIP: Combine 2 tablespoons sherry with 3 tablespoons light or dark soy sauce and 1 teaspoon brown sugar. (If you like, add $\frac{1}{4}$ teaspoon red pepper oil.) Serve with simmered, steamed or fried foods.

GINGER-SOY DIP: Combine ¼ cup light or dark soy sauce with 2 teaspoons finely minced ginger root. Serve with steamed, simmered or fried foods.

SOY-MUSTARD-VINEGAR DIP: Combine ¼ cup dark soy sauce with 1 tablespoon prepared mustard, 1 teaspoon brown sugar and 1 teaspoon rice vinegar or cider vinegar. Add 1 teaspoon finely minced scallions. Serve with steamed foods (especially pastries) or deep-fried batter dishes.

CANTONESE SALT: Heat ¼ cup salt in an ungreased skillet over medium heat. Stir constantly about 5 minutes or until the salt becomes brown. Remove from heat and add 1½ teaspoons ground Szechuan pepper. Blend well, cool and store in a tightly closed jar. Serve with roasted or barbecued foods.

SPICED SALT: Heat ½ cup salt in an ungreased skillet over medium heat. Stir constantly until the salt becomes very light brown. Remove from heat and add ¼ teaspoon brown sugar and ¾ teaspoon five-spice seasoning. Serve with roasted or barbecued foods.

RED PEPPER OIL: In a 6-inch round skillet, combine ½ cup peanut oil or corn oil, 1 tablespoon sesame oil and 2 tablespoons crushed dried red pepper flakes. Heat over medium heat 3 to 5 minutes or until the oil begins to sizzle. Don't let the pepper flakes darken. Remove from heat. Cool and strain through cheesecloth. The oil will be a deep orange. Use a few drops at a time to spike bland foods, steamed or fried pastries or whenever intense pepperiness is desired.

POURING SAUCES

These are basic sauces, and you will find them used in a vast range of recipes. Some of them appear with slight variations as part of a recipe; for example, in Sweet-and-Sour Fish, Mandarin Style. To repeat the same sauces with every recipe would require many more pages in an already long book. Pouring sauces must not be confused with bottled or canned condiment sauces, which are used as either ingredients or dips.

Most of these sauces call for the use of wine and/or vinegar. Therefore, avoid using aluminum saucepans or skillets, which will discolor. Enameled or Pyroceram (Corning Ware) utensils resist discoloration.

SWEET-AND-SOUR SAUCE,

Cantonese Style

Cooking Time: Approximately 8 minutes

Utensils
1-quart bowl
12-inch enameled skillet

Ingredients

1	tablespoon finely minced ginger root	2	tablespoons cornstarch
½	large onion, thinly sliced	½	cup rice vinegar or cider vinegar
1	medium green pepper, cut in thin strips	2	teaspoons soy sauce
1	medium sweet red pepper, cut in thin strips	1	tablespoon tomato paste or 2 tablespoons tomato puree
1	teaspoon salt	2	cups chicken stock
4	tablespoons brown sugar	1 to 2	drops red food coloring (optional)
		2	tablespoons peanut oil or corn oil

Before Cooking

Prepare ginger root, onion and both peppers. Combine the salt, brown sugar and cornstarch in the bowl. Stir to blend. Add the vinegar, soy sauce and tomato paste or puree. Blend well and stir in the stock. Measure oil and have ready to go.

Cooking Instructions

Turn heat under skillet to high. When the skillet is hot, add the oil. It should sizzle at once. Before the oil begins to smoke, add the minced ginger. Stir-fry 30 seconds. Add the onion slices and stir-fry 1 minute. Add the pepper slices and fry together 2 to 3 minutes. Turn heat to medium. Add the seasonings-cornstarch-stock mixture and stir to blend. Allow the mixture to come to a boil. Add 1 to 2 drops red food coloring and remove from heat. The sauce will be thick, clear and pungent.

AMOUNT: About 3 cups sauce.

PINEAPPLE SWEET-AND-SOUR SAUCE

Follow recipe for Sweet-and-Sour Sauce, Cantonese Style, but decrease chicken stock to 1¼ cups. Drain 1 can (14 ounces) pineapple chunks. Reserve fruit and measure ¾ cup syrup, adding it to the stock. Add the drained pineapple chunks after the peppers have cooked. Stir to blend well and add seasonings, cornstarch, syrup-stock mixture. Allow to come to a boil. Add optional red coloring and remove from heat.

AMOUNT: About 4 cups sauce.

SWEET-AND-SOUR SAUCE WITH PICKLES

Follow recipe for Sweet-and-Sour Sauce, Cantonese Style, but add ½ cup well-drained Chinese sweet pickles or ½ cup well-drained bottled American sweet pickles after the peppers have cooked. Add seasonings-cornstarch-stock mixture. Allow to come to a boil. Add optional red food coloring and remove from heat at once.

AMOUNT: About 4 cups sauce.

MANDARIN SWEET-AND-SOUR SAUCE

Cooking Time: 6 to 8 minutes

Utensils
Chinese cutting knife
Bowl for seasonings, cornstarch and stock
12-inch enameled skillet
Slotted spatula for stirring

Ingredients

⅓	cup small dried mushrooms	⅓	cup soy sauce
2	cloves garlic, finely minced	⅓	cup rice vinegar or malt vinegar
1	teaspoon minced ginger root	4	teaspoons sherry
3	scallions, each with 1½ inches of green, cut in ¼-inch rounds	¼	teaspoon salt
		⅓	cup brown sugar
½	medium (6 ounces) bamboo shoot, cut in ½-inch dice	2	tablespoons cornstarch
		⅔	cup chicken stock
½	cup peas	2	tablespoons peanut oil or corn oil
½	cup carrots in ½-inch dice		

Before Cooking
Soak the mushrooms in warm water 20 minutes. Drain and set aside. Prepare the garlic, ginger root, scallions and bamboo shoot. If you are using fresh peas and car-

rots, parboil in ⅓ cup boiling water 3 minutes; drain well. If you are using frozen peas and carrots, simply thaw, drain and measure. Combine the soy sauce, vinegar, sherry, salt, brown sugar and cornstarch in a bowl. Blend well and add stock. Have oil ready to go.

Cooking Instructions

Turn heat under skillet to high. When the skillet is hot, add the oil. It should sizzle at once. Before the oil begins to smoke, add the garlic, ginger root and scallions. Stir-fry-toss 30 seconds. Add the bamboo shoot and stir-fry 1 minute. Add the drained peas and carrots and toss with other vegetables 1 minute. Add mushrooms and stir-fry 1 minute. Give the seasonings-cornstarch-stock mixture a quick stir; pour into the vegetables in the pan. Stir and blend 2 to 3 minutes, until the mixture comes to a boil and is thick and clear. This makes a rich, dark-brown sauce that is slightly more tart than the Cantonese variety. It is never made with fruit or sweet pickles.

AMOUNT: About 2½ cups sauce.

MANDARIN SWEET-AND-SOUR SAUCE WITH SHRIMP

Follow recipe for Mandarin Sweet-and-Sour Sauce but before cooking, shell, wash and devein 9 to 10 small raw shrimp. Cut each shrimp into 3 pieces. (You should have about ½ cup diced shrimp.) After the mushrooms have been stir-fried 1 minute, add the diced shrimp. Stir and toss together 2 to 3 minutes. Pour in seasonings-cornstarch-stock mixture. Cook 2 to 3 minutes, stirring until the mixture thickens and is clear. This makes an excellent topping for any kind of steamed or fried fish.

AMOUNT: About 3 cups sauce.

NOTE: If you prefer, substitute raw frozen lobster tail for the shrimp.

PLUM SWEET-AND-SOUR SAUCE

Cooking Time: 6 to 10 minutes

Utensils
Bowl for seasonings-stock mixture
Small bowl for cornstarch-water mixture
1½-quart enameled saucepan
Wooden spoon

Ingredients

2	scallions, each with about 1 inch of green, cut in ¼-inch rounds	1	package (1 ounce) pressed plum candy*
1	teaspoon finely minced ginger root	2	tablespoons cornstarch
½	cup rice vinegar or cider vinegar	½	cup cold water
½	teaspoon salt	1 to 2	drops red food coloring (optional)
4	tablespoons brown sugar	1	tablespoon peanut oil or corn oil
1	cup chicken stock		

Before Cooking

Prepare scallions and ginger root. Combine vinegar, salt, brown sugar, stock and pressed plum candy in the bowl. Combine cornstarch and cold water. Have oil ready to go.

Cooking Instructions

Place saucepan over medium heat. When a drop of water on its surface bubbles into steam, add the oil. When the oil is very hot add the scallions and ginger root. Stir with wooden spoon 30 seconds. Pour in the seasonings-stock mixture. Stir over medium-low heat 3 to 5 minutes or until the plum candy has melted completely. Give the cornstarch-water mixture a quick stir and add to saucepan. Turn the heat to medium-high and stir 2 to 3 minutes or until the sauce comes to a boil and is thick and clear. Remove from heat and add 1 or 2 drops of red food coloring to enhance the plum shade.

AMOUNT: About 2 cups.

NOTE: This sauce has a distinct plum flavor and is used as a pouring sauce over steamed or fried meat, poultry or fish. It should not be confused with canned plum sauce, which is used as a condiment or dip.

*   Pressed plum candy is not listed among the Chinese Ingredients since its use is largely as a confection. It comes in rolls of ½- to 1-ounce packages. The plum discs are slightly larger than a quarter in size and are coppery red in color.

POURING OYSTER SAUCE

Cooking Time: 3 to 5 minutes

Utensils
1-quart enameled saucepan
Wooden spoon

Ingredients

½ cup bottled oyster sauce

1 tablespoon cornstarch

¾ teaspoon brown sugar

1 teaspoon soy sauce

2 teaspoons sherry

1½ cups chicken stock

Before Cooking

Combine the oyster sauce, cornstarch, brown sugar, soy sauce and sherry in the saucepan. Pour in the stock, stirring to dissolve solids.

Cooking Instructions

Place the saucepan over medium heat and cook 3 to 5 minutes, stirring until the sauce has thickened. Use over egg, fish or chicken dishes.

AMOUNT: About 2 cups.

NOTE: This is a delicate oyster-flavored sauce used for pouring over foods. For dipping, use bottled oyster sauce.

BROWN SAUCE

Cooking Time: Approximately 5 minutes

Utensils

1-quart enameled saucepan
Wooden spoon

Ingredients

2 tablespoons cornstarch

½ teaspoon salt

½ teaspoon brown sugar

½ teaspoon monosodium glutamate

2 tablespoons soy sauce

1 tablespoon sherry, gin or vodka

2 cups unsalted chicken stock or canned chicken stock

Before Cooking

Combine the cornstarch, salt, sugar and monosodium glutamate in the saucepan. Blend with soy sauce and liquor. Add stock gradually, stirring to dissolve solids.

Cooking Instructions

Place the saucepan over medium heat. Cook about 5 minutes, stirring constantly, until the sauce comes to a boil and is thick and a clear golden brown.

AMOUNT: About 2¼ cups sauce.

NOTE: If you are using canned chicken broth, one 14-ounce can and ¼ cup water will make up the necessary 2 cups. Omit both the salt and monosodium glutamate.

LICHEE SAUCE

Cooking Time: About 5 minutes

Utensils
1-quart enameled saucepan
Wooden spoon

Ingredients

1	can (1 pound) lichees	2	teaspoons sherry
1	tablespoon sesame oil	1	tablespoon brown sugar
½	cup chicken stock	1	tablespoon cornstarch
1½	tablespoons soy sauce		

Before Cooking
Drain lichees and measure ¾ cup syrup. Reserve lichees. Pour lichee syrup into the saucepan. Add sesame oil, stock, soy sauce, sherry, brown sugar and cornstarch. Blend with wooden spoon until smooth.

Cooking Instructions
Place the saucepan over medium heat about 5 minutes, stirring until the mixture comes to a boil, thickens and is clear. If you plan to use the sauce at once, stir in the lichees and simmer just to heat through. If you intend to use the sauce later, cool and refrigerate; bring to a boil just before serving and add the lichees then. Serve over steamed or deep-fried chicken balls or deep-fried whole chicken or duck.

AMOUNT: 2 to 2½ cups sauce, with lichees.

CURRY SAUCE

Cooking Time: 9 to 10 minutes

Utensils
Small bowls
Mortar and pestle or blender
12-inch skillet
Slotted spatula or spoon for stirring

Ingredients

1	large onion, diced semi-finely	3	tablespoons cornstarch
2	cloves garlic, finely minced	1	tablespoon brown sugar
1	tablespoon crushed cumin seeds (optional)	½	teaspoon salt
		2	cups chicken stock
2	tablespoons curry paste or 3 tablespoons curry powder	1	cup heavy cream
		3	tablespoons peanut oil or corn oil
2	tablespoons tomato puree		

Before Cooking
Prepare the onion and garlic. Crush the cumin seeds in a mortar with a pestle or whirl them for a second in the blender. Measure the rest of the ingredients and set aside separately.

Cooking Instructions
Turn heat under skillet to high. When the pan is hot, add the oil. It should sizzle at once. Before oil begins to smoke, add the diced onion. Reduce heat to medium and stir-fry 2 minutes. Add minced garlic and stir-fry 1 minute. The onion should now be transparent and soft. Stir in the curry paste or powder and blend well, allowing the curry to cook 2 minutes. Add the tomato puree and blend well. Add the cornstarch, sugar, salt and crushed cumin seeds. Gradually pour in the chicken stock, stirring as you pour to smooth out lumps. Allow the sauce to simmer gently 3 minutes. Add heavy cream and simmer 2 to 3 minutes or until the sauce has thickened. The finished sauce will be a creamy golden brown and may be used for any stir-fried or deep-fried foods. It is particularly good with Deep-Fried Lamb Balls (page 236). Curry is a spice borrowed by the Chinese from the Indians. The Chinese interpretations are less stewlike in consistency than the Indian. The use of cream is not at all Chinese in character and reflects both Western and Indian influences.

AMOUNT: About 3 cups.

DESSERTS

‎‗‗‗‗‗‗‗‗‗

Unlike Westerners, the Chinese do not believe in featuring desserts as the finale of a meal. At that point, no Chinese host expects his guests to have any appetite left. Instead, desserts are used as relishes, savories or pacers between the courses of a large meal. The Chinese term for dessert is *deem sum,* which literally means "to dot the heart." These "heart touchers" are not confined merely to confections. The scope of flavors ranges from salted, pickled, sweet-and-sour and peppery-hot to bland.

Because the Chinese are great nibblers, *deem sum* are served at various times of the day or night and may take the form of pastries, with or without fillings. Or they may simply be sugared or spiced nuts, fruits or even vegetables. A variety of infusions, such as almond or ginger tea, is usually served with salty or spiced dishes.

Of course there are elaborate sweet dishes too, the kind we would serve at the end of a meal as dessert. But the Chinese reserve these dishes for banquets. Those recipes which are most acceptable to our tastes are of Northern origin: Almond Jelly with Fruit, Peking Dust or Glazed Apples, Bananas or Yams.

To most Westerners, who envision desserts as sweet and creamy concoctions, a pastry made of strained pork suet and filled with beans or barley or a jelly made of sweetened green peas is a distinct shock. The recipes in this section are for dishes which might well be adapted to Western tastes—that is, they satisfy the need for something sweet at the end of the meal. A number of the boiled, steamed and fried pastry *deem sum* appear in the chapter on Appetizers.

EIGHT PRECIOUS PUDDING

Cooking Time: 55 to 60 minutes

Utensils
1½-quart Pyrex bowl, lightly oiled
2-quart saucepan with cover
Wooden spoon
Trivet, vegetable steamer or ½-pound coffee
    can with 6 holes punched in the bot-
    tom
6- to 8-quart pot with cover
1-pint saucepan
10-inch round platter

Ingredients

1 cup red bean paste (below) or 1 can (8¾ ounces) candied chestnut paste*	2 cups glutinous rice
	4 cups water
½ pound Chinese sugared plums, dates, lotus seeds, gingko nuts, kumquats, glacé chestnuts, raisins, almonds or ½ pound mixed glacé fruit and nuts	½ cup sugar
	1½ tablespoons lard, softened
	¼ cup sugar
	1 tablespoon cornstarch
	1½ cups cold water

Before Cooking
Prepare the red bean paste or open can of candied chestnut paste; set aside. Arrange the mixed fruit and nuts in the bottom of the Pyrex bowl, working outward from the center in a circular design and allowing the fruit to come slightly up the side of the bowl. Set aside. Measure the rest of the ingredients and set aside.

Cooking Instructions
Wash the rice. Combine the rice and 4 cups water in the 2-quart saucepan. Bring to a boil over medium-high heat. Cover and reduce heat. Simmer covered 25 to 30 minutes. The grains of rice should be translucent and sticky. Blend the rice with the ½ cup sugar and softened lard, stirring gently so the sugar dissolves. Do not

* Candied chestnut paste is available in cans of various sizes. They can be found in specialty food stores and in the gourmet sections of supermarkets.

mash the rice. Divide the rice in half. Spread one half over the fruit pattern, using the wooden spoon to shape it with the curve of the bowl. Do not disturb the fruit pattern. Spoon the red bean paste or the candied chestnut paste into the hollow left by the rice. Press down with the wooden spoon and cover with the remaining rice, making sure that all the bean or chestnut paste is well covered. Set the trivet, vegetable steamer or coffee can in the 6- to 8-quart pot. (If you are using the coffee can, invert it so the holes are on top.) Pour in boiling water up to ⅔ the height of the trivet or vegetable steamer or ⅔ the height of the coffee can. Bring to boiling over medium-high heat. Put the bowl of rice and fruit on top of the support. Cover the outer pot and steam 30 minutes. During the steaming, add boiling water to the large pot as needed. While the pudding steams, make the sauce. Combine the ¼ cup sugar and cornstarch in the pint sauce pan, add the 1½ cups cold water and stir to dissolve solids. Bring to a boil over medium heat, stirring constantly until the sauce thickens. Remove from heat. When the pudding is done, carefully remove the bowl from the large pot. Place the round platter over the top of the bowl. With a quick movement, invert the bowl and platter so that the pudding rests on the platter with the fruit design on top. Pour the sauce over and serve at once.

SERVINGS: Enough for 6 to 8.

NOTE: This recipe gives you the option of substituting candied chestnut paste for the red bean paste and glacé fruit, such as that used in making fruitcakes, for the Chinese sugared fruit. The red bean filling and Chinese fruits are the authentic ingredients, but most Westerners are likely to find the chestnut filling and the familiar candied fruit more appetizing.

SWEET RED BEAN PASTE

Cooking Time: 1½ to 2 hours

Utensils
2-quart saucepan
Sieve
1½-quart bowl
Wooden spoon

Ingredients

½ pound dried red beans (*azuki*)	1½ tablespoons oil
4 cups cold water	½ tablespoon oil
½ cup sugar	

Procedure

Wash the beans and place them in the 2-quart saucepan with the cold water. Turn heat under the pan to medium-high and bring to a boil. Simmer covered at medium-low heat 1½ to 2 hours or until the beans are soft and shed their jackets. You may have to add boiling water to the pan from time to time. Push the beans through a sieve into a bowl. Add the sugar and 1½ tablespoons oil to the mixture; mash together to blend and dissolve sugar. Wash out the saucepan and put the ½ tablespoon oil in it. Put the bean mixture into the saucepan and stir rapidly 5 minutes over low heat. Red bean paste is used as filling for cakes, steamed buns and puddings. It has a bland and mealy taste, somewhat like chestnuts.

AMOUNT: 3 cups.

NOTE: Sweet red bean paste is sold in cans at both Chinese and Japanese grocery stores. Ask for *dow sa* in Chinese markets and for *an* in the Japanese stores. Do not confuse it with red bean curd "cheese," *naam yu,* which is entirely different.

PEKING DUST

Cooking Time: 30 to 40 minutes

Utensils
Sharp knife
3-quart pot
Bowl
Food mill or meat grinder
Round platter

Ingredients

2 pounds fresh chestnuts or 1 can (1 pound, 14 ounces) French whole chestnuts*	1 cup sugar
	½ teaspoon salt
	1 teaspoon vanilla extract

Continued on next page

* French chestnuts are available in cans in specialty food stores or gourmet sections of supermarkets. Buy unsweetened (*au nature*) whole chestnuts.

1 teaspoon sherry
1 cup whipping cream (optional)
1 tablespoon powdered sugar (optional)

Chinese sugared plums, sugared lotus seeds, preserved kumquats, glacé cherries

Before Cooking

Score the tops of the fresh chestnuts with the sharp knife. Place in the pot, cover with cold water and begin cooking. (Simply drain the canned chestnuts.) While the chestnuts are simmering, measure the sugar, salt, vanilla, sherry, whipping cream and powdered sugar and set aside separately. Slice the sugared plums in half; set aside with sugared lotus seeds, preserved kumquats and glacé cherries.

Cooking Instructions

Place the pot with the chestnuts and water over medium heat and bring to a boil. Simmer 30 to 40 minutes or until the jackets have burst and the chestnuts are tender. Drain and peel. Remove the inner skins. Place the cooked or the canned drained chestnuts in the bowl and mash with sugar, salt, vanilla and sherry. When the ingredients are well mixed, put them through a food mill or meat grinder. There should be no lumps. Mound in a pyramid in the center of the platter. Whip the cream with the powdered sugar until stiff; put in a pastry tube and decorate the chestnut mound. Garnish with plums, lotus seeds, kumquats and cherries. Peking Dust is a classic Northern sweet. The addition of vanilla and the whipped cream topping is a Western touch which vastly improves this dessert.

SERVINGS: Enough for 6 to 8.

PEKING GLAZED APPLES, BANANAS OR YAMS

Cooking Time: 15 minutes for syrup
5 to 8 minutes for apples or yams
5 minutes for bananas

Utensils
1½-pint saucepan
Small bowl for egg
2½-quart saucepan or electric frypan
Slotted spoon
Large bowl of water with crushed ice
Chopsticks for each guest

Ingredients

2   tablespoons peanut oil or corn oil
1½ cups sugar
2   medium pippin apples, 4 just-ripe bananas or 1 pound yams
1   egg

3   tablespoons cornstarch or water chestnut flour
2   tablespoons toasted sesame seeds
3   cups peanut oil or corn oil

Before Cooking
Ahead of time, combine the 2 tablespoons oil with the sugar in the 1½-pint saucepan. Gently bring to a boil, reduce heat and simmer 4 minutes. Keep hot. Peel and core apples; cut each into 6 wedges. Or peel bananas, scrape away stringy material and cut each banana into 3 fingers. Or peel the yams and cut into 2½-inch lengths. Beat the egg in the small bowl. Spread the cornstarch or water chestnut flour in a pie plate. Dip the sections of apples, bananas or yams into the beaten egg. Drizzle lightly with the flour. Place on paper towels. Measure the sesame seeds and the 3 cups oil and have ready to go.

Cooking Instructions
Pour the 3 cups oil into the 2½-quart saucepan or electric frypan. Heat until the oil foams around a cube of fresh bread (375° F. on frypan). Add the coated apples, bananas or yams, a few at a time. When they have become golden brown (5 to 8 minutes for apples or yams, less for bananas), remove with slotted spoon to a warm serving dish. Pour the hot syrup over the fruit, coating the sections entirely. Sprinkle with sesame seeds. Place the bowl of water with crushed ice in the center of the table. Bring in the candied ingredients at once. Then either the host dips the wedges into the ice water and holds them there a minute or the guests do so themselves. The syrup dipped in ice water forms a hard crackly glaze over the deep-fried fruit or yams, providing an unusual contrast of flavor and textures.

SERVINGS: Enough for 6.

STEAMED SPONGE CAKE

Cooking Time: 20 to 25 minutes

Utensils
2 large mixing bowls
Electric beater
Spatula
Wooden spoon
½-pound coffee can, with 6 holes punched in
    the bottom
8- to 10-quart pot with cover
9-inch springform or square cake pan
Baking parchment or waxed paper
10-inch cake rack or platter

Ingredients

6	eggs, separated	6	tablespoons cold water
1½	cups sugar	¼	teaspoon baking powder
1	teaspoon vanilla, almond or lemon extract	2	cups sifted flour

Before Cooking
Place the egg whites and yolks in separate mixing bowls. Beat the whites at high speed until stiff. Add sugar, ¼ cup at a time, and continue beating 2 to 3 minutes or until peaks form. Rinse the beaters in cold water. Add the flavoring and cold water to the egg yolks. Beat at high speed 2 to 3 minutes or until thick. Add the baking powder to the sifted flour. Sift into the egg yolk mixture and beat at low to medium speed until thoroughly blended, scraping the sides of bowl with the spatula. Carefully fold in the egg white mixture with a wooden spoon until the whites are just incorporated. Do not overmix or the whites will lose volume. If you are using baking parchment, line the bottom and sides of the pan with it. If you are using wax paper, grease it lightly on both sides with corn oil before lining the pan.

Cooking Instructions
Place the coffee can, holes side up, in the center of the 8- to 10-quart pot. Add boiling water up to ⅔ the height of the can. Turn heat to medium-high. When the water is actively boiling, set the cake pan on top of the coffee can. Line the cover of the outer pot with a damp kitchen cloth to collect the moisture created by the

steaming. Cover the pot and steam 20 to 25 minutes. Test the cake for doneness by inserting a toothpick in the center. If it comes out clean, the cake is done. Remove cake pan from steamer and invert on the 10-inch cake rack or large platter. Remove paper and set cake right-side-up. This may be served hot or cold.

SERVINGS: Enough for 6 to 9.

GINGER TEA

Cooking Time: Approximately 25 minutes

Utensils
Chinese cutting knife
2½-quart saucepan with cover

Ingredients
2   ounces ginger root   8   cups water
2   cups brown sugar

Procedure
Peel the ginger root and cut into slivers. Combine with the sugar and water in the saucepan. Stir over medium heat until boiling. Reduce heat, cover and simmer 20 minutes. Strain and serve in bowls.

SERVINGS: Enough for 8.

ALMOND TEA OR SOUP

Cooking Time: Approximately 10 minutes

Utensils
Electric blender
2½-quart saucepan

Ingredients

¼ pound blanched almonds or 4 ounces almond paste*	2 cups water
¾ cup cooked rice	1½ cups rich milk
½ cup rose water**	¼ cup sugar
	¼ teaspoon almond extract

Before Cooking

Grind the almonds in the blender until they are powdery. Add the cooked rice and the rose water. Blend at medium speed until smooth. Follow the same procedure if you are using the canned almond paste. Add the 2 cups water, ½ cup at a time, blending between additions. Pour into the saucepan. Add milk. Measure sugar and almond extract and set aside.

Cooking Instructions

Place the saucepan over medium heat. Bring the mixture just to the boiling point, stirring constantly to prevent scorching. Add sugar and stir to dissolve. Remove from heat, add almond extract and serve warm in small bowls. Almond "tea" or "soup" is made by straining the mixture through a sieve lined with a double layer of damp cheesecloth. It is traditionally served as a pacer between the many courses of a large banquet. In China, this dessert was made by grinding the kernels of peaches or apricots and combining them with ground uncooked rice and water.

SERVINGS: Enough for 4.

*   Canned almond paste is available in specialty shops or in the gourmet sections of supermarkets. If you are using it, either omit or decrease the sugar in the recipe.
**   Rose water can be bought at any drugstore. Its use in this recipe is optional. Dah Su felt that it gave the almond paste a more delicate flavor.

ALMOND JELLY WITH FRUIT

Cooking Time: 15 to 20 minutes

Utensils
Small bowl
1-quart saucepan
8x8-inch cake pan, lightly oiled
1-pint saucepan
Flat bowl

Ingredients

1	envelope plain gelatin	1	cup evaporated milk
¼	cup cold water	¾	teaspoon almond extract
1	can (1 pound) mixed Chinese		Few drops green food coloring
	fruit (longans, lichees, loquats	⅓	cup sugar
	and mandarin oranges)	1½	cups water
1	tablespoon sugar	¼	teaspoon almond extract

Procedure

In the small bowl, sprinkle the gelatin over the ¼ cup cold water to soften. Drain the canned Chinese fruit, reserving ¾ cup syrup. Refrigerate the remaining syrup and fruit. Pour the reserved ¾ cup syrup into the 1-quart saucepan and add the 1 tablespoon sugar and the evaporated milk. Place over medium heat until boiling. Pour about ¼ cup of the hot liquid into the bowl containing the gelatin. Stir well to blend and return the gelatin mixture to the liquid in the pan. Stir over low heat until the gelatin is completely dissolved. Remove from heat and add the ¾ teaspoon of almond extract and a few drops of green food coloring. Pour into the cake pan and chill until set. While the jelly is setting, heat the ⅓ cup sugar and 1½ cups water in the pint saucepan until it comes to a boil. Simmer 10 minutes. Remove from heat and add the ¼ teaspoon almond extract. Cool the syrup. When the jelly has set, cut it into 1-inch squares or diamond shapes. Arrange the jelly shapes in a flat bowl. Sprinkle with drained mixed Chinese fruits and pour cooled syrup over fruits.

SERVINGS: Enough for 6.

NOTE: This was originally a Northern dessert. As prepared in Peking, it was composed of *agar-agar* and ground peach or apricot kernels. Most Chinese restaurants that serve this dessert have Westernized it to the point of serving it with fruit cocktail and maraschino cherries. However, since canned Chinese fruits are now available, I feel they are much closer to the Oriental scheme of flavors.

EMPRESS FRUIT BOWL

Cooking Time: None

Utensils
Long, pointed knife
Serving or cooking spoon
Melon-ball scoop

Ingredients

1   melon (Persian, Cranshaw, casaba or watermelon), 5 to 10 pounds
Canned lichees stuffed with pineapple*
Canned mixed Chinese fruits*
Fresh or canned mangos

Fresh or canned papayas
Bananas
Chinese rose wine or orange wine** or kirsch
Crystallized ginger

Procedure

Scrub the surface of the melon. Slice off a piece of the bottom so that the melon can stand. Using the long, pointed knife, make zigzag cuts, like pinking, one sixth of the way down from the top of the melon. Make the cuts deep and all the way around to create a lid that can be removed easily. With a serving spoon, scoop out the seeds and discard. Scoop out the pulp in large pieces. (Do not break up the pulp.) Leave about 1 inch of pulp in the walls of the melon. Do not drain the liquid from the melon. With a melon-ball scoop, make balls from the pulp. Put the balls back in the melon shell. Drain the canned lichees with pineapple, the canned mixed Chinese fruit and the canned mangos and papayas. Peel fresh mangos and papayas, discard seeds and cut into slices or fingers. The amount of canned fruit will depend on the size and type of melon you use. Peel bananas and cut each into 2-inch lengths. Add the wine or liqueur to taste. Blend carefully with fruit and

* Canned lichees stuffed with pineapple and canned longans, loquats and mandarin oranges are now sold either separately or mixed. If you cannot find lichees stuffed with pineapple, stuff drained canned lichees with glacé (not maraschino) cherries.

** Chinese rose wine is sold under the name of *Mooi Gway Lo* and Chinese orange wine is called *Chahng Fah Lo.* Obtainable only at Chinese grocery stores.

chill with the lid on. Before serving, place on a large platter and top with about 1 tablespoon chopped crystallized ginger.

SERVINGS: From 8 to 16, depending on the size of the melon.

CHINESE DELICACIES WHICH MAY BE SERVED AS SAVORIES OR DESSERTS

Crystallized Ginger: A confection of ginger preserved in sugar.
Pickled Ginger: Ginger root preserved in wine.
Preserved Ginger: Ginger root preserved in syrup.
Red Ginger: Dried, salty, sweet and fiery-hot.
Dried Olives: Salty, sweet and pungent.
Dried Plums: Sweet-and-sour, flavored with cloves.
Sugared Plums: Sweet, like candied plums.
Sugared Lotus Seeds: Sweet, with a smoky flavor.
Dried Lichee Nuts: Chocolate-brown shells with soft datelike fruit.
Preserved Kumquats: In syrup, sweet with a slightly bitter aftertaste.
Melon Seeds, Black or Red: Black often flavored with anise; salted or unsalted.
Pumpkin Seeds: White, with salted skins.
Sunflower Seeds: Striped gray and white.
Mixed Chinese Pickled Fruit: Sweet-and-sour, in heavy syrup.
Tea Melon: Sweet and crunchy, in syrup.

A variety of these should be arranged separately in little round dishes. They are never served in a communal bowl. These savories are considered mouth-waterers and are often served during the meal to enliven the taste buds.

HOW TO COMBINE THE RECIPES INTO A MEAL

᠊᠊᠊᠊᠊᠊᠊᠊᠊᠊᠊᠊᠊᠊᠊᠊᠊᠊᠊᠊᠊᠊᠊᠊᠊᠊᠊᠊᠊᠊᠊᠊᠊᠊᠊᠊᠊᠊᠊

I had planned to present a series of recipes culled from the book under the title of Suggested Menus. Most Chinese cookbooks have just this sort of dispassionate listing of recipes, and when I look at them, I find the menus suggested often contain recipes which I haven't the least interest in trying.

Planning a meal is an emotional adventure, based primarily on individual tastes and hopefully tempered with logic. I must concede, however, that some sort of guideline is necessary, if only to clarify the overworked, and possibly misleading, business about immortal flavors, fragrances and mysteries which have served as the focal point in a number of books on Chinese cooking. What this mystique boils down to is the simple application of a common-sense culinary factor: variety.

The Chinese achieve variety by dividing a meal into five or more distinct flavors. These usually are: salty, sweet, sour, hot and bitter. The more glorified categories such as fragrant and golden are somewhat elusive in that they are based on olfactory or aesthetic responses. Is this, then, so unlike our own approach to cooking? In planning any menu I'm sure that it would never enter your mind to compile one which included a cream soup, an entrée blanketed in *Béchamel,* salad with a *Mousseline* sauce, artichoke bottoms au gratin and *crème brulée.* Cream from beginning to end would create a disaster. So it is within the framework of any Chinese meal. There must be variety in the foods as well as in the textures and flavors.

With these familiar culinary signposts in mind, you should not find it too difficult to assemble a Chinese menu. Obviously, differences exist between what is served at a family, or home-style, dinner and what is offered on a formal occasion. Chinese banquets are resplendent affairs, consisting of a minimum of sixteen courses, served one at a time. They include two or three soups, cold dishes, light dishes, heavy dishes and finally, almost as an afterthought, rice or noodles. Salty, sweet, sweet-and-sour and hot relishes are served throughout the meal to whet flagging appetites. This is quite necessary when you consider that a formal Chinese banquet may take up the entire night. Wine is served before eating and during the meal until the serving of rice or noodles. Tea may be poured at the end of the meal but is never served during the actual dining.

A family-style menu is another matter entirely. Naturally the same sensible rules of contrast and variety apply, but the number of dishes served is generally limited to one per person, beginning with a soup. And rice is served with the meal. At this type of dinner, all the courses may be brought to table at one time, after the soup has been served. The matter of wine is optional and tea is served at any time. Desserts are usually limited to fruit or savory *deem sum;* elaborate sweet dishes are seldom included.

I have outlined two sample menus. The first is for a family-style dinner for 6 to 8. It is followed by a formal, or banquet, menu to serve 12 to 18.

FAMILY-STYLE MENU

Choose one dish from each of the following categories:

BOILED OR SIMMERED: Egg Flower, Easy Winter Melon or Sizzling Rice Soup

SIMMERED OR SHALLOW-FRIED: Steamed Rice, Fried Rice, Soft-Fried Noodles

STIR-FRY-TOSSED: Celery Cabbage, Mixed Fresh Vegetables, Mixed Dried Chinese Vegetables

STEAMED: Mushrooms Stuffed with Minced Shrimp, Ginger Chicken with Black Beans, Pork Pearl Balls

BRAISED: Diced Ginger Pork, Pork with Bean Curd, Yangchow Lion's Head, Chicken with Dried Chestnuts, Spiced Honey Chicken, Duck with Leafy Vegetables, Whole Fish, Szechuan Style

SHALLOW-FRIED: Egg Foo Yung, Surprise Packets, Cantonese Egg Rolls

SEMI–DEEP-FRIED: Spiced Beef Shreds, Chicken Shreds with Almonds, Batter-Coated Chicken Balls, Classic Whole Shrimp

DESSERT: Fresh or canned Chinese fruit, melon, sugared lotus seeds

NOTE: You may add to any of these categories or delete an entire grouping to suit yourself. These suggestions are merely offered to illustrate the use of practically every technique in a single meal.

FORMAL DINNER OR BANQUET

APPETIZERS: Choose four of the following (meats thinly cut) and serve on separate plates: Drunken Chicken, White-Cut Chicken, Red-Stewed Spiced Beef, Barbecued Pork, Preserved Eggs, Tea Porcelain Eggs

FIRST SOUP: Shark's Fin

FOUR STIR-FRY-TOSS HOT DISHES: Fresh Scallops with Vegetables, Classic Sliced Pork, Diced Chicken with Black and White Mushrooms, Sliced Lamb and Leeks

SAVORIES: Melon seeds, dried olives, preserved ginger, dried lichee nuts, sugared lotus seeds, green plums—passed in small dishes

SECOND SOUP: Squab and Hairy Melon

FOUR VARIOUS DISHES: "Smoked" Fish, Sesame Seed Chicken Wings and Legs, Batter-Coated Pork with Pouring Oyster Sauce, Braised Spiced Lamb

FOUR MAJOR COURSES: Hidden Treasure Chicken; Red-Stewed Pork, Shanghai Style; Steamed Stuffed Whole Fish; Tea Smoked Duck or Classic Peking Duck with Mandarin Pancakes

TEN PRECIOUS NOODLES

STEAMED RICE

THIRD SOUP: Almond Tea

DESSERT: Eight Precious Pudding, Peking Glazed Apples, Bananas or Yams, Almond Jelly with Fruit, Empress Fruit Bowl

A dinner such as this would represent a Herculean effort and would be impossible to present without assistance. By using the process of elimination or by substituting, you can arrive at the formal dinner best suited to your own needs and manner of entertaining. Again you will notice that this menu embraces practically every technique and is composed of contrasts in textures and flavors from beginning to end.

CHINESE GROCERS AND HARDWARE STORES

〓〓〓〓〓〓〓〓〓〓〓〓〓〓〓〓〓〓〓〓〓〓

(Mail Orders Accepted)

Gim Fat Company
953 Grant Avenue
San Francisco, California

Wo Kee & Company
949 Grant Avenue
San Francisco, California
(Write to or ask for Bruce Jang.)

Ginn Wall Hardware Company*
1016 Grant Avenue
San Francisco, California
(Write for free brochure.)

See Sun Company
36 Harrison Avenue
Boston, Massachusetts

Sun Sun Company
34a Oxford Street
Boston, Massachusetts

Wing Fat Company, Inc.
35 Mott Street
New York, N.Y.

Sam Wah Yick Kee
2146 Rockwell Avenue
Cleveland, Ohio

Adler's Fine Foods
2014 Broadway
San Antonio, Texas

Wah Young Company
717 South King
Seattle, Washington

Mee Wah Lung Company
608 H Street N.W.
Washington, D.C.

*   With the exception of the Ginn Wall Hardware Company in San Francisco, which carries hardware exclusively, most of these stores are primarily grocers. Some carry hardware as well.

INDEX

Italic figures indicate illustrations.